D0485421

Turn Out the Lights

SOUTHWESTERN WRITERS COLLECTION SERIES

CONNIE TODD, EDITOR

*The Southwestern Writers Collection Series originates from the
Southwestern Writers Collection, an archive and literary center
established at Southwest Texas State University to celebrate the
region's writers and literary heritage.*

Turn Out

the Lights

CHRONICLES
OF TEXAS
DURING THE
80S AND 90S

Gary Cartwright

FOREWORD BY ROBERT DRAPER

UNIVERSITY OF TEXAS PRESS
Austin

Most of the essays in this book were originally published in a slightly different form in *Texas Monthly* and appear here with the magazine's permission.
Copyright © 2000 by the University of Texas Press

All rights reserved
Printed in the United States of America

First edition, 2000

Requests for permission to reproduce material from this work should be sent to Permissions, University of Texas Press, Box 7819, Austin, TX 78713-7819.

♾ The paper used in this book meets the minimum requirements of ANSI/NISO z39.48-1992 (R1997) (Permanence of Paper).

Library of Congress Cataloging-in-Publication Data
Cartwright, Gary, 1934–
Turn out the lights : chronicles of Texas in the 80s and 90s / Gary Cartwright ; foreword by Robert Draper.— 1st ed.
    p.   cm. — (Southwestern Writers Collection series)
ISBN 0-292-71199-9 (cloth : alk. paper) —
ISBN 0-292-71226-X (pbk. : alk. paper)
    1. Texas—Social life and customs—20th century—Anecdotes.
2. Texas—Social conditions—20th century—Anecdotes.
3. Texas—Biography—Anecdotes.   4. Cartwright, Gary, 1934—Anecdotes.   I. Title.   II. Series.
F391.2 .C35   2000
976.4'063—dc21   00-039297

In memory of—

MARK CARTWRIGHT

1957–1997 . . . until I see you again.

Contents

Foreword | ROBERT DRAPER

If there is a tear left, shed it for Jack Ruby.
He didn't make history; he only stepped in front of it.

Not many words can pierce a 17-year-old male's skull. But those did, like heat-seeking missiles, and I was never the same after reading them. At the time—and this was 1975—I had never given much thought to magazine journalism, which to me suggested *Time, Life, U.S. News & World Report*, and other temples of banality. But the terse romanticism of Gary Cartwright's words in the November 1975 issue of *Texas Monthly* blasted open a whole new world for me. As when my father had sat me down in the basement a decade earlier and explained to me how babies were made, for days thereafter I found myself pacing, skipping meals, talking to myself: "If there is a tear left . . ."

Though those two sentences became the Pied Piper I would follow into the abyss of magazine journalism, I never attempted to mimic Cartwright's prose, preferring instead to quote it like scripture. Such writing cannot possibly be easy to craft; but the seamlessness of his style gulls one into the belief that Gary Cartwright can unspool a classic while drinking a glass of wine in his bathtub. On one level, he remains the archetypal Texas sportswriter, with all the attendant raw wit and masculine sentimentality. But to stop there would be to miss everything that great writing is about, and for the past quarter century Gary Cartwright has been one of America's greatest storytellers of any genre. That which in his writing has always inspired me can be seen in the above passage from "Who Was Jack Ruby?"—namely, the omnipresence of a tough-ass intellect, a free spirit, and a deeply empathetic heart. To read Cartwright's work was, for this boy, to recognize that journalism could be affecting, lastingly so . . . not to mention as much fun as one could possibly have with one's clothes on.

By the time he and I first met, it was 1991 and *Texas Monthly* was readying to hire me as a staff writer—meaning we would be colleagues. The editors assigned me to write a story on Cartwright's friend Willie Nelson, and on the set of a Willie movie Cartwright had coscripted with Bud Shrake (*Another Pair of Aces*), we ate lunch together. I could not have been more unctuous. After effusing over a recent story he'd published, I was surprised to see him shrug and say, "I hated it." The article in question hadn't met his high standards, and now I was left to fret over his evaluation of my impending Willie Nelson story. Was it too late to consider law school?

Thankfully, he was generous in his praise of my article—which, I would learn, was vintage Gary Cartwright: if you weren't a total nitwit, he would always dispense support to young writers in need. I have never met a veteran journalist so appreciative of newness and so fearless of change. Though it always brought me joy to hear Cartwright employ antediluvian terms like "sider" (for sidebar, a short accompaniment to a longer story) or growl pugnaciously, "Nothing's off the record!", or to watch him coerce the administrative assistants into helping him comprehend the new office voice-mail system, he is otherwise thoroughly engaged by the here and now. During the seven years that he and I were comrades at *Texas Monthly*, I waited in vain for any sign that Cartwright was content to rest on his laurels. Instead of relying on his personal archive of bygone yarns— which, when he cared to offer them up (see "Turn Out the Lights," the title story in this collection, for example), smoldered with vitality in a way that made your own life experience seem pitiably malnourished—Cartwright was always rooting around for a story that the rest of us were missing. He gives the lie to the assertion that journalism is a young person's profession: over forty years into it, Gary Cartwright remains attuned to the latest twisted felony, to the cultural oddity du jour, to Viagra.

This collection is testament to that. All of the stories gathered herein were published well after "Who Was Jack Ruby?"—a point at which many a journalist would've declared victory and gotten out. Every writer should read these. Stories such as "The Innocent and the Damned" and "The Sting" offer proof that a "straight reporting" piece need not be bereft of panache. For that matter, Cartwright's depiction of the old Black Power crowd in Dallas ("The Bad Brother") reveals a social outrage that is as appropriate as it is authentic. Few writers are blessed with his range: Cartwright strides confidently, if ironically, among both gangsters and psychic gurus, through the King William District and the Gila Wilderness, within the mythic landscape of the cattle ranch or the football field, and in the all-too-real world of his own son's death. The key, of course, is that while illuminating places and people hitherto unseen by us, Gary Cartwright has never been afraid to reveal himself, right down to the marrow.

It is this humanness that suffuses his work and makes it soar. Few writers in America are as hilarious as Cartwright, but his jokes are poignant, playful, usually self-deprecating, and never at the expense of the less fortunate. Like many reporters, his affinity for the down-and-out is matched by a basic loathing of bureaucrats and bullies; unlike others in his profession, Cartwright has never mistook his typewriter for a pulpit. It happens that this collection consists of stories he has written for *Texas Monthly*. But calling Gary Cartwright a regional writer is like calling Joe DiMaggio a regional hitter. His insights are germane anywhere human breath is drawn. I have little doubt that Cartwright would excel in Lapland or Tonga, provided an able wine steward is nearby and the Cowboys' games can be retrieved via satellite.

Today, as my luck would have it, Gary Cartwright is no longer just a mentor to me; he is my good friend. It's been my privilege to discuss sundry truths and inanities with him on barstools stretching from Mexico City to Venice. Yet there are some things I would never be moved to ask him. Among these is, Which writers have influenced you the most? The question does not seem relevant to anything. Gary Cartwright is wholly original.

Nor have I asked him why he has entitled this collection *Turn Out the Lights*. But I confess I don't like the sound of it. When he hangs it up, there will be another tear left to shed.

Acknowledgments

With the exception of the opening chapter, which I wrote especially for this book, all of the stories in this collection were originally published in *Texas Monthly*. It is not immodest to claim that fact alone assures a certain quality of excellence.

Texas Monthly isn't merely the best regional magazine in the country; it is one of the five or six best magazines of any category or description. Starting with publisher Mike Levy, who founded *TM* against my good advice ("A monthly magazine will never fly in this state, Mike!"), the staff of *TM* is talented, thoroughly professional, and doggedly dedicated to quality. Levy and I have enjoyed a love-hate relationship since that first prophetic meeting in 1972. Mike has the personality of a stick of dynamite, but he grows on you until you reluctantly concede that he is indispensable. In the idiom of our trade, *Texas Monthly* is "a writer's magazine," meaning that it hires the best writers and gives them their head. But at its heart *TM* is a publisher's magazine. Mike is the one element that can never be replaced. He made it happen, made it work, made it endure. He is the only publisher I know who keeps his nose (well, at least his hands) out of the editorial department. I'll admit that he's a man of very strong opinions—which is like saying Nolan Ryan throws fast—but they never show up in the pages of the magazine. Mike never stops attending to the business of *Texas Monthly*. On two occasions when I was rushed to the hospital to atone for my lifelong bad habits, Mike was there almost ahead of the doctors. He has been there for me all the way, as he has for everyone at the magazine. I wouldn't want this to get back to him, but the hate part of our relationship went south long ago. As for the love part . . . what do you want me to say, that I love the miserable jerk?

My name decorates the cover of *Turn Out the Lights*, but the names of dozens of others properly belong there, too—the editors, writers, copy editors, fact checkers, artists, accountants, administrators, technical experts, and people in advertising, circulation, marketing, production, and sales who encouraged, assisted, supported, corrected, and put up with me.

It was my pleasure to write in the first issue of the magazine back in 1973, and my great luck to join the staff in 1981, after my hiatus in Taos. In the second story of this collection, "Back Home," home refers to *Texas Monthly* as much as it does the state of Texas. Joining the staff of *Texas Monthly* was more than merely coming home; it was coming in from the cold. I'll always be grateful to Editor Greg Curtis for hiring me, giving me direction, and finally allowing me to pursue a career in whatever way I read the tea leaves. Greg is a great editor, an outstanding writer, and a good friend.

The list of editors, writers, and support players I've worked with and alongside is too long for a single volume. But among those to whom I owe a large debt are: Paul Burka, Evan Smith, Stephen Harrigan, Larry Wright, Jan Reid, Joe Nick Patoski, Mimi Swartz, Robert Draper, Jan Jarboe, Pat Sharpe, and Anne Dingus. Copy editors such as Jan McInroy and Jane Dure nursed me through incomprehensible sentences and dangling participles, and fact checkers such as Pat Booker, David Moorman, and Chester Rossan saved my bacon too many times for comfort. Nor will I ever find words to thank our very gifted team of attorneys, David Anderson, Jim George, and Julie Ford. Among their many other contributions, they saved me from a $400 million judgment that would have certainly ruined my sunny disposition.

Finally, I'm enormously grateful to my friends Bill Wittliff and Connie Todd for offering to include this book in the prestigious Southwestern Writers Collection, and to the editors and staff of the University of Texas Press for publishing it.

Turn Out the Lights

1963
My Most
Unforgettable Year

Why, you may ask, does this collection of essays begin with a remembrance of 1963 when its purpose is to chronicle things I saw and people I met during the decades of the eighties and the nineties? There is a perfectly good answer to this question, though I'm not sure I can articulate it. For reasons I'm still trying to grasp, the subtext of these stories—indeed, of everything I've written over the past thirty-something years—can not escape the gravity of the sixties, specifically the unparalleled weirdness that a lot of us experienced when John F. Kennedy was assassinated in what was essentially our neighborhood. I think of the event as the great power outage—my own as well as the city's. In a flickering of our collective strobe light, the best of times transformed into the worst of times. Or was it the other way around? All I know is that until the assassination, everything in my world seemed clean, transparent, and orderly. Nothing has seemed clean, clear, or orderly since.

One of my last unambiguous memories is those minutes leading up to the assassination. It was a crisp, bright, surreal afternoon in November. Bud Shrake and I had walked from the apartment we shared on Cole Avenue to the corner of Lemmon and Turtle Creek Boulevard to watch the presidential motorcade. We were young sportswriters for the *Dallas Morning News* back then, longtime friends between marriages, and our apartment had become a late-night hangout for musicians, strippers, and other nocturnal creatures. One of our regular drop-bys was George Owen, manager of the University Club, a former SMU basketball player who had dated the fabulous Candy Barr before the Dallas power structure sent her away on a phony marijuana charge. Two other regular visitors were Jack

Ruby, the cheesy little hood who owned the Carousel Club, and Jada, an exotic stripper who was the club's headliner that year. Shrake was having an affair with Jada, which caused Ruby great distress and occasionally complicated things around our apartment.

We had talked all week about Kennedy's trip to Dallas. For most of us, his election was a landmark event. He wasn't just the first president I'd ever voted for—in fact, the first *politician*—JFK connected me with the system. He made me feel good about the country and about myself. He had emerged as our national cheerleader, hero, and role model. Not long after his election the president urged the nation to become more physically active, suggesting that anyone under the age of 40 should be able to walk fifty miles at a stretch. Our entire sports staff did the walk, or at least attempted it.

As the motorcade turned onto Turtle Creek for its final leg into downtown, Kennedy looked directly at us, his famous grin flashing like a polished diamond, his hand flicking a sort of salute of recognition, as though to say *I've heard all about you two Cole Avenue rogues!* Ten minutes later, as we drank coffee in the drugstore across from the SMU campus, a radio whose existence we hadn't previously noticed stopped us cold with an urgent bulletin. The president had been shot! It happened as the motorcade approached the triple underpass on the eastern edge of downtown, a landmark that we could have seen from our desks at the *News*, if we'd been at our desks. The motorcade was at the moment racing for the emergency room at Parkland Hospital. Shrake and I traded small, silly smiles, the way people do when they suspect someone is putting them on. The announcement was so off-the-wall, so intrinsically unbelievable, that we at first assumed it was a joke. Some moronic disk jockey begging for attention. For a long time nobody in the drugstore moved or spoke above a whisper. As journalists, our impulse was to rush to the scene of this breaking story, but rush where? There was no scene; there was only chaos. This was before the days of CNN, before television's ability to crank up instant news coverage, so each of us created his own images from the series of radio updates that fell like black snow. After a while the terrible truth enveloped us. The president was dead! The clock had stopped. The end of the world might well be at hand.

When the clock started again—how many minutes or weeks later?—it was one of those Dali clocks, a metaphysical meltdown in which perceptions of reality were grotesquely warped, where common objects that you saw every day during your lunch break became Rorschach tests for the severely paranoid. Dapples of sunlight transposed themselves into snipers.

A rainbow viewed through the spray of a fountain gradually refocused as an exploding skull. Daily affairs and routines, once predictable and comfortable, threatened to become nightmare excursions into the unknowable. It was as if we had dropped through a rabbit hole into a void where lies were truth and truth a dark deception. The entire cultural upheaval of the sixties—the drugs, the music, the free love, Vietnam, the ghetto riots, the rejection of traditional values—was a reaction to the murder of John Kennedy, and the subsequent murders of Robert Kennedy and Martin Luther King Jr. And to a perceived Armageddon. The forces of evil had conspired to ethnically cleanse or at least neutralize those who would deny them absolute power. Or so it seemed. Of course the threat of cultural genocide was mostly in our minds, and yet the shock waves of that upheaval were real. They defined us politically and culturally in the sixties, and they define us today.

Since that seminal autumn in the summer of my youth I've spent hundreds of hours reviewing the assassination, only to return again to the beginning, older but never wiser. I've read most of the twelve-volume Warren Commission Report and all the other official documents I could find, interviewed countless people who claimed to have inside information, rethought, wrote, and rewrote the events of November 1963. Every time I believe I've put it behind me, another report or source surfaces to stir up old memories and muddy the picture.

A lot of bizarre things were happening in Dallas in the fall of 1963. Madame Nhu, wife of the president of South Vietnam, bought a dozen shower caps at Neiman Marcus and tried to drum up support for the Diem regime in Saigon—even while the CIA, with Kennedy's approval, laid plans to assassinate her husband. Members of the American Nazi Party danced around a man in an ape suit in front of the Dallas Times Herald Building. Dallas congressman Bruce Alger, who had accused Lyndon Johnson of being a traitor, went on TV to denounce the Peace Corps as "welfare socialism and godless materialism, all at the expense of capitalism and basic U.S. spiritual and moral values." Zealots from the National Indignation Committee picketed a UN Day speech at the Adolphus Hotel by Ambassador Adlai Stevenson; they called him Addle-Eye, booed and spat on him, and hit him on the head with a picket sign. When a hundred Dallas civic leaders wired apologies to Ambassador Stevenson, General Edwin Walker, who had been cashiered by the Pentagon for force-feeding his troops right-wing propaganda, flew the American flag upside down in front of his military gray mansion on Turtle Creek. Someone took a potshot at General Walker about that same time. We know now the shooter was Lee Harvey Oswald. The piety of the Dallas business climate was perfect cover for all brands of extremism—pro-Castro cabals and anti-Castro cabals with overlapping membership, international arms smugglers, con men who lived under assumed identities in the near North Dallas apartment complexes, airline flight attendants who smuggled sugarcoated cookies of black Turkish hash.

Ruby was having one of his customary feuds with the Carousel Club's star attraction, Jada. The exotic stripper feared for her life and placed Ruby under a peace bond. Newspaper ads for the Carousel Club during the historic week of November 22 featured a comic ventriloquist, Bill Demar, hardly Ruby's style but the best he could manage at the moment. Shrake and I spent a lot of time at the Carousel that fall. Ruby loved cops and newspaper guys, and neither ever paid for a drink at his club. The Carousel was a dingy, cramped walkup in the 1300 block of Commerce. In those days that stretch of downtown Dallas was a lively strip of bars and restaurants where conventioneers mingled with cops, reporters, gamblers, and hustlers. Unlike Abe Weinstein's Colony Club where Candy Barr had made her mark a few years earlier, the Carousel was a clip joint. Ruby's girls hustled $1.98 bottles of champagne for anywhere from $15 to $75, and made their own private arrangements. Ruby did not knowingly hire prostitutes. He was an overly sentimental sexual prude who could cry at the drop of a hat, or just as suddenly go mental and wreck the place. A friend had watched him break a bottle of whiskey over the head of a customer who tried to smuggle a bottle into the club.

The other strippers and champagne girls hated Jada. She was a star and acted the part. The bus-station girls from Tyler and Odessa came and went—Ruby fired any girl who agreed to have sex with him—but Jada treated Ruby like a dog and he always came back for more. She called him a pansy and worse, and spread word among the customers that the hamburgers served in the club's tiny kitchen were contaminated with dog shit. One of Jada's great pleasures was driving around Dallas in her gold Cadillac with the letters JADA embossed on the door, her orange hair piled high on her head, wearing high heels and a mink coat and nothing else. A few weeks before the assassination she drove the car across the Mexican border with a hundred two-pound Girl Scout cookie tins of high-grade marijuana in the trunk. Her companion, who knew nothing about the contraband, was a state politician. The first thing she did at customs was fall out of the Cadillac with her mink flaring open, revealing to startled customs officers far more than any customer at the Carousel ever saw.

Ruby planted a story that Jada was trained in ballet, had a college degree in psychology, was a descendant of John Quincy Adams, and a granddaughter of Pavlova. Jada's name was Adams, Janet Adams Conforto, but she hadn't been inside a classroom since she ran away from a Catholic girls school in New York at age 15, and she couldn't dance her way out of a dishrag. Her act consisted mainly of hunching a tiger skin rug while making wildly orgasmic sounds with her throat. This pushed Ruby to the limits of his sexual comfort zone. Her grand climax—Jada would spread her legs and pop her G-string—frequently drove him over the edge. At such moments Ruby was likely to turn out the lights and wrestle her off the stage. One night while we were watching Jada ravaging her tiger skin, a tourist stepped up and popped a flashbulb in her face. Ruby threw the startled customer down the stairs. Jada popped her G-string about a foot and Ruby threw her off the stage. All this took but a few seconds, but during those seconds Ruby was an absolute madman. Then he walked over to our table and said in this weary, ultracalm voice: "How's it going boys? Need anything?" I don't think he remembered what had just happened.

In the days leading up to the assassination we saw Ruby several times. He was always hurrying to a meeting with some very important person—the mayor, the police chief, some judge, Stanley Marcus, Clint Murchison Jr.—or so he would have us believe. We wrote it off as typical Ruby bullshit. Ruby was always looking for the big score, whether it was a new line of pizza ovens, a Hoola Hoop franchise, or marshland in Florida. A day after the assassination he telephoned Pappy Dolsen, another old-time club owner, and told him: "I'm going places in show business and when I do you're going with me." Ruby always carried a big roll of cash, and he usually had a gun, though I couldn't imagine him actually using it. He had an expression that dated from his street-fighting days in Chicago: "Take the play away"—meaning to strike first. You never knew what was on his mind, though Jada was obviously in his thoughts that week. The morning of the assassination he called our apartment looking for her. Shrake said he hadn't seen her, which, as I recall, was true. "I'm warning you for your own good," Ruby said in a threatening tone, "stay away from that woman. She's evil."

Two days later we found ourselves in Cleveland, covering a game between the Cowboys and the Browns, a game that nobody wanted to play. As far as I know we were the first group clearly identifiable with Dallas to travel outside the city after the assassination. The trip was ugly and unreal. People spat in our direction or turned away as though we carried the plague. Sunday morning, as I walked across the parking lot in the direction of Cleveland's Municipal Stadium, Shrake came running toward me, out of breath and excited. "Someone just shot Oswald in the basement of the Dallas police station!" he shouted. "Guess who?"

"Jack Ruby," I said. To this day I don't know why I said what I did. I was stretching for an absurd reply to an absurd revelation. Ruby's name just popped into my mind, or rather onto my lips, bypassing the normal thought process entirely. Shrake looked stunned. When I realized that Ruby was the correct answer, that this two-bit punk who had sat sulking on the couch of our apartment just a few nights earlier had just eliminated the chief suspect in the murder of our president, I couldn't do anything except shake my head. It was all too bizarre.

Jada left town a short time later, fearing for her life. Before leaving she told us that she had met Oswald at the Carousel a few weeks before the assassination. Ruby introduced him as his CIA contact. While they were having drinks Beverly Oliver, a singer at the Colony Club, stopped by the Carousel and was also introduced to Oswald. In the flood of facts, factoids, and rumors that swamped us, Jada's story did not seem exceptional. Over the years I heard hundreds of stories, bits and pieces of information that suggested a wide but highly confusing conspiracy, but they tended to bump together. Gradually, I compartmentalized them, afraid that my brain might otherwise explode.

In 1975 I wrote a cover story for *Texas Monthly* in which I assured readers Ruby acted alone, that one lone nut killed another lone nut. For some reason I chose to forget what Jada had told me. I know now that my conclusions about Ruby were not correct. Ruby was more than the violence-prone punk I portrayed; he was at minimum a messenger boy for the Mafia. He ran guns to Cuba and other hot spots, and he may have been Plan B in a conspiracy involving the Mob and CIA—the sacrificial hit man assigned to eliminate Oswald when Plan A went haywire. There is uncontested documentation that when the Mob needed to spring Santos Trafficante from a Cuban jail they dispatched Ruby to Havana with the bag of money. Trafficante was a key figure in the CIA-Mafia plot to assassinate Castro. Who would have guessed back in 1975—much less in 1963—that there existed such a plot, or that JFK had approved it?

In the decade after the assassination I saw Jada a couple of times. She lived on and off in San Francisco, under a variety of names. Once I located her by looking up *A. Lincoln* in the phone book. She also used *G. Wash-*

ington as an alias. She became a drug courier for the Mafia and later organized a gang of hijackers who traveled around the country robbing banks. She was strung out on drugs the last time I saw her, aged and shrunken as beef jerky. She introduced us to several members of her gang, including a shriveled-up little junkie who turned out to be Chet Baker, one of the great jazz artists of the fifties. Chet Baker—I still can't believe it! From the vacant look in his eyes, I assumed that it had been a long time since he had sung "My Funny Valentine." Meeting Chet Baker at Jada's apartment in San Francisco was just another episode in the moment-to-moment reality that became commonplace after the assassination. My friendship with Jada, and with Chastity Fox, who played Jada in a Dallas Theater Center production, led indirectly to a meeting some months later with Candy Barr. Candy had refused dozens of requests for interviews but granted mine because Chastity vouched for me, and because she'd liked my Ruby story in *Texas Monthly*. After much negotiation we arranged to meet at her cottage on Lake Brownwood, where she kept me waiting on the living room couch for three hours while she primped. When she finally appeared from her bedroom Candy hit the room like one of Sergeant Snorkle's Ping-Pong smashes. Her blond hair was in curlers. She had scrubbed her face until it was blank and bleached as driftwood. Her famous green eyes collapsed like seedless grapes too long on the shelf. She wore a poor-white-trash housedress that ended just below the crotch, and no panties. "Don't think I dressed up just for you," she told me. At that moment I fell instantly and eternally in love with Candy Barr.

Jada was dead by the time I wrote "I Was Mandarin . . . ," one of the pieces in this collection. She was killed in a car wreck near New Orleans, one more witness dead under mysterious circumstances. I managed to track down Beverly Oliver, however. She was a gospel singer, living in California. I asked if she remembered meeting Oswald at the Carousel as Jada told us. "Sure do!" she said bluntly. "Ruby introduced him as 'my friend Lee from the CIA.'"

"I Was Mandarin . . ." is a suitably bizarre tale from the grave. It's the story of a mysterious journal, supposedly written by an ex-Dallas cop, confessing that he was the hit man who assassinated JFK. The ex-cop's wife just happened to work at Ruby's Carousel Club at the time of the assassination, and he just happened to serve in the First Marine Air Wing with Oswald. Up to a point, the story checked out. It makes good reading but like nearly all the postassassination accounts it doesn't advance the ball. These days, when someone offers to supply new information on the assassination, I pretend to be late for an important appointment with the premier of China. In the spring of 1999, as I was putting the final touches on this book, yet another source cornered me with a story that he claimed to have directly from the CIA. In this version Kennedy was killed because he violated the Monroe Doctrine. Say what? This guy was actually convinced that "the Wise Men who run this country"—meaning, I suppose, the military-industrial complex—gave Kennedy the choice of resigning or being killed because the president allowed Soviet troops into Cuba. In this scenario, the Wise Men, the CIA, and the Mafia collaborated in Kennedy's murder. See what I mean? The crazier it gets, the more reasonable it sounds.

A few years ago Shrake gave me a picture that he had painted, inspired I think by the madness wrought in the autumn of 1963. The painting depicts a naked couple seated on a park bench, next to a beach. Mysterious footprints lead from the water's edge. The man appears to have a bullet hole in the center of his forehead. He clutches a trumpet and the woman dangles a fishing pole. The caption reads: "All things are bound by their own chain of fate."

My chain of fate is Dallas, 1963. Like Diogenes, who lived in a tub and wasted his days looking for an honest man, I seem condemned to revisit the same dark streets, seeking the same lost souls, hoping that when the time comes I've got enough left to pay the tab. But I'm not complaining. Diogenes never met Jack Ruby or Jada or Don Meredith or Willie Nelson or the peerless Candy Barr, or any of the other characters I've known and written about. Maybe that's why none of his writings survive.

Back Home
Why I Had to Leave Texas, and Why I Had to Come Back

APRIL 1982

TUESDAY, JANUARY 6, 1982: LEAVING TAOS

Long before dawn I am awake with the ghosts. I can feel the chill in the adobe walls and in my bones. I'm going home and I don't know why. I don't even know why I came to this strange, very distant place, but I do know that it's time to go home. Let's just say that in both cases I was drawn by forces beyond the level of my consciousness and control.

In the predawn darkness I can hear dry voices, rehearsing. They can tell from the packing crates and disarray that we are moving. "You've picked the perfect day," the old dry voices call from their secret places. "As usual!" The movers were supposed to be here this morning, but I called yesterday and cancelled, figuring to save seven or eight hundred bucks by doing it myself. I was sucked in by a U-Haul commercial touting "Adventures in Moving." I draw the blanket over my head and count the reasons to never move again. I mean from this *bed*. I can hear my wife's light breathing and the rustling of the Airedales as they sense it is about to begin. The U-Haul truck that I rented last night is stuck halfway up the icy, rutty slope that masquerades as a driveway here on the Llano Quemado.

I haven't had a cold in two years, but I'm catching one now. A monstrous one. Without looking, I know it's snowing again. Until I moved to Taos eighteen months ago, I'd seldom seen snow, but now I hear it in my dreams. We may not find the truck until spring. I know, too, that the last piece of firewood is now cold ash. The utilities will be shut off in a few hours, if they don't go off by themselves, which they frequently do during a snowstorm.

Moving is nothing more than a test of character, but I don't know if

I have any character left. Once I had a future full of money, love, and dreams: now all I have is a past. But the ghosts know all about it. In the last twenty-five years we've moved no less than a dozen times, the ghosts and I—until now mostly in Austin or in Texas—looking for something better, something we can't define. I don't sleep as well as I used to, and the ghosts don't sleep at all. I listen to Phyllis's steady breathing and wonder what will become of us.

I told people that I moved here to work on my book, *Dirty Dealing*— to get a fresh perspective. But that's only part of it. I had felt burned out in Texas. The newness of discovery had lost its zest. Texas had lost its flavor. I could barely recall writing about Jack Ruby and Candy Barr and all the others, the newsmakers and explorers of the sixties and the seventies. Knowing them was like knowing the shadowy figures of a dream. Did I really spend that incredible evening at Candy's lakeside cottage in Brownwood, snorting speed, eating fried chicken, and listening to her stories about dirty Dallas cops, porno flicks, and Mickey Cohen? She had kept me waiting for hours, and when she finally came out of the bedroom it was like a scene in a surreal film noir.

Part of my move to Taos was a fear that I had lost—or was losing—the ability to write and feel as I had in the days of Jack Ruby and Candy Barr, that the edge was gone. But there was something else. Living in Taos was an old dream, dating back ten years to a time when I first saw the place. It was October after an interminably long and blistering Texas summer, and Taos came over me like a narcotic. The maples were scarlet and the aspens shimmering gold. Fields of yellow and rust-colored chamisa rolled over the valley, and the sweet scent of piñon curled from adobe chimneys. It was like discovering a new season. I knew then that I had to come back, not just to visit but to stay. I don't mean stay in the sense that a stump stays in a field until it rots. I've seen people do that, and I tell you frankly I'd rather be a heroin addict. I'm more afraid of withering than dying.

That feeling, that phobia, probably explains better than anything why I moved to Taos. Someone described Austin as "a fur-lined trap." A friend who left Austin nine years ago used the word "flee"—she didn't just leave, she fled. That's the way I felt. I was sitting around a bar one night when it came to me. We'd ordered one more round and I was telling or listening to one more story. Same story, same drink, same friends, same faces, same memories. I began to feel myself fading into the walls. In another five years I'd be a piece of furniture, covered with favorite recipes and cartoons clipped out of the *New Yorker*.

I couldn't feel, I couldn't write, I couldn't think. I would drive across the Capitol grounds at night and look up at the massive walls of pink granite and try to recall what it all meant. The Alamo was just a motel on South Congress. San Jacinto was the street where you parked your car in preparation for a night of beer-swilling at Scholz Garden. Sam Houston was a softball team. I'd walk along Barton Creek and see nothing except the streams of sweat that poured down my forehead and streaked my glasses. Crazy notions leaked into my brain: I began to wonder if mockingbirds make good chili? . . . would Texas advance itself if we paved over the Hill Country and painted it with bluebonnets? . . . are we doomed by cultural inbreeding? Friends called but I seldom answered. I would sit for hours in dark rooms, listening to the wisdom of the air-conditioning motor, and fall asleep staring at *National Geographic* photographs of Norwegian fishermen. When Phyllis and I made the decision to move to Taos, everyone predicted we'd be back. Maybe. Maybe not. At that moment, all I knew was that I had to get over that wall before I suffocated. Now I've got to get back for many of those same reasons.

By midmorning I've made two extra trips across town to the U-Haul station, first to replace the truck's muffler, then to seek assistance in attaching the tow bar by which I intend to tow my Bronco to Texas. Nothing in Taos ever gets done the first time: it's like Mexico except most people speak English and you can drink the water. A thousand miles to go and I've already used half of the thirty-gallon tank of gas.

The truck won't make it up the icy driveway. I remove a section of a neighbor's fence and bring the truck in from the back, carefully avoiding goats and stacks of firewood. It is snowing harder. I can barely see the tracks from this morning.

I stand under the portal, drying my hair with a blanket, looking out over the pastoral valley of Ranchos de Taos, thinking of the months, the work, the love, the heartbreak. A lot of things happened here, some of them bad—our prize Airedale, Dashiell, was killed last Labor Day weekend, then Phyllis broke her jaw, then we ran out of money. Taos wore thin as we felt ourselves eaten alive with its quaintness. We got tired of women with hair under their arms. Tired of seeing them breast-feed sour-faced babies while waiting in the checkout lines at the Safeway. Tired of jumpsuits and goggles. Tired of trust-fund hippies pretending to be artists and writers. Tired of New Mexico Mexican food that can burn off the roof of your mouth but not satisfy like the Tex-Mex of Austin can.

Most of all, we tired of the mystique of the "three cultures" and its phony claim of harmonic convergence, which we now realize is something that only gringos think about. The Spanish don't speak to the Indians, and the Indians don't speak to either the Spanish or the gringos, except to cadge loose change. There is an endemic snobbery among the gringos. Most of them hate Texans. Most of them *are* Texans, those who didn't come from New York or California. None of them have a good word to say about the place they came from. They like to talk about chain saws, old trucks, herb gardens, solar houses, and natural childbirth. The grandson of Amon Carter, founder of the *Fort Worth Star-Telegram*, lives in a tepee. We made a lot of friends here, but we never grasped their gospel of cold showers and outdoor plumbing. The magic didn't exactly wear off, but we eventually came to the realization that we would always be outsiders. Some gringos stay for thirty years but never understand that they can't truly belong. One gringo artist who came here from Dallas complained to me of burnout. From his studio he had a magnificent view of the majestic Taos Mountains and Wheeler Peak, but I couldn't help noticing that the model for his painting was a photograph of Wheeler on a 10¢ postcard.

By the time the truck is loaded and we've hooked the Bronco to the tow bar, the storm has whipped itself into a small blizzard. Phyllis has coaxed our two Airedales, Abigail and Bucky, into the back seat of her Lincoln, and we stand under the portal looking out over the llano one last time—at the orchards in their winter nakedness, at the village that always appears abandoned, at the old church that countless artists have painted but never captured. The frozen white face of Wheeler stares through us as though we were already gone, and the valley is absolute silence.

"I think it's time to go," I say. Only now I'm not so sure. The storm is getting worse. There are seventy miles of icy mountain road between here and Santa Fe, and God knows what beyond that. My cough sounds like feeding time in the zoo of hell. Only about three hours of daylight remain. Normally, we could make Albuquerque in three hours, but not today, not driving a loaded van and towing a Bronco. Maybe we should wait until morning. Maybe we should forget the whole thing.

"Call the highway department," Phyllis suggests. Good idea. We need an omen.

"How's the weather?" I ask a man at the highway department.

"Weather?" he replies in a heavy Spanish accent. "We don't know nothing about no weather." I hear him talking to someone else in the room, then he says, "Oh, you mean the big snowstorm. That will be here tonight, maybe tomorrow." I wash down some cold pills with a slug of whiskey. For a moment my head clears and I feel better.

"What did they say?" Phyllis asks.

"They said it was a good day to travel. Lead the way."

I walk along the side of the truck. From tip to tail the rig is about the length of an 18-wheeler. In the warm cab I close my eyes. I hope somebody knows how to drive this son of a bitch. Phyllis is inching the Lincoln down the slope toward the highway. There is a prayer on my lips as I slam the truck into granny and steer a wide path around the goats.

WEDNESDAY: REMEMBERING 40

Made it as far as Santa Fe, using the remaining half-tank of gas, most of the daylight, and all my nerve. Physically and mentally exhausted, we dine in the motel room in the company of our Airedales, on whiskey and Colonel Sanders' fried chicken, me remembering the chicken Candy Barr cooked that night so long ago. The memory surprises me, not just the unfocused image of the famous Dallas stripper standing at the stove examing a breaded thigh for doneness, but the visceral intensity of the experience— I can almost smell and taste it. Overdosed on cold pills, I dream that I am trying to crawl inside the carcass of a frozen wolf. Wake with echoes of Jack Ruby and gunfire ringing in my ears, coughing and gasping.

Luck seems to be with us as we wind out of Santa Fe and across a series of narrow bridges to Albuquerque, where we begin the slow grind east, over the mountain pass. A sign warns that the speed limit is enforced by aerial radar, and the governor on the truck assures that I need not be concerned. Even downhill, this turkey won't break fifty. The blizzard is still behind us, to the north and west. Sleet peppers our windshields as we fight the crosswinds, but the highway is sanded and reasonably safe. I slip a Jerry Jeff Walker cassette into the recorder on the seat beside me, glancing in the rearview mirror to make sure my loved ones in the Lincoln are well. Watching the country drift by, I feel at peace.

I'm remembering another move seven years ago. It was the week of my fortieth birthday, and though I didn't know it yet, I was about to be divorced for the second time. Jerry Jeff, Bud Shrake, and I were sitting on a neighbor's steps drinking beer when my wife came home from a very hard day at nursing school. We'd had an argument about something that morning, I don't remember what. Without speaking or looking my direction she raced upstairs to our apartment and reappeared a few minutes later, carrying everything that I owned. She dumped it unceremoniously at my feet, turned, and still without speaking, vanished more or less from my life. I remember thinking: Is that *all?* After eleven years of marriage, and before that another seven years of marriage to yet another woman, my life's possessions were a pitifully small pile of shirts, shorts, broken clocks, and old manuscripts. The really traumatic part about moving is deciding when. Divorce is one answer. The next day I was on a plane to New York, my life indeterminately altered.

My mind is still rummaging dim alleys when I become aware of an increasingly shrill noise from the engine. The Lincoln has taken the lead by this time. I'm making faces at my Airedales as they study me from the foggy rear window when I realize there is smoke pouring from the hood of the truck! The shrill noise becomes a beat, then a violent pounding as though some madman is trying to break out. Easing the rig over to the shoulder, I calculate that we're a hundred miles east of Albuquerque.

From Bowlin's Flying C Ranch and Curio Shop, which carries possibly the world's largest collection of knives, plastic longhorns, and pueblo-shaped ashtrays, I telephone the U-Haul representative in the next town, Santa Rosa. A friendly man named Sanchez says he'll be there in less than an hour. "I'd say you blew an engine," Mr. Sanchez observes as soon as he has opened the hood. He doesn't appear worried, which makes me feel better immediately. Blowing an engine seems less sinister than the usual bullshit I expect from a person of the mechanical persuasion: *Just offhand, you ignorant swine, I'd say you terminated the camshaft fusion simulator, and it's gonna cost you both kidneys and your cervical cortex.* Instead, the mild-mannered Sanchez assures me: "These things happen. We'll take care of everything. We'll tow you back to Albuquerque, slap a new engine in her, and have you back on the road by morning."

I walk back to the Lincoln, mentally calculating the nonlinear progression of our lives to date. We may think we know where we're going, but we don't have the faintest idea how or when or if we're going to get there. The unflappable Phyllis opens a bottle of wine and unwraps pieces of cold chicken. "Is this what they meant by adventures in moving?" she asks sweetly.

One of the things we missed most in Taos was Chinese food, so in Albuquerque we buy $29 worth and devour it while watching *Becket* on cable TV. Long time since these old eyes feasted on cable television. I fall asleep making a mental list of things I will not miss about Taos.

THURSDAY: ANOTHER STATE OF MIND

True to their promise, the U-Haul people have us back on the road before noon. Weather bulletins warn that highways west of Albuquerque are mostly closed, but it's smooth trucking to the east. The new engine is even slower than the one that blew, but by now I've got the routine. Cold pills, coffee, and whiskey: life reduced to essentials. The cab of the truck is so warm and pleasant I can't imagine ever being anywhere else.

We reach Santa Rosa by lunch. While Sanchez hooks the Bronco to the truck, we dine at the Sun 'n' Sand, on grilled liver and onions. While dining, we watch a curious sight out the window. Two burros are pulling a man in a psychedelic VW bus along the highway, at a rate of about two miles an hour. The omen doesn't immediately register.

The next town is Fort Sumner, forty-something miles, and I'm cruising along trying to recall where I've heard that name before. "Shot heard round the world"? No, that's not it. Then without warning, the engine sputters and dies. I can't believe it but I'm out of gas. I had three-quarters of a tank when we left Santa Rosa. I had calculated that the new engine was getting about two miles to the gallon, but I was overly optimistic—figuring in burro power rather than horsepower. Meanwhile, the Lincoln has disappeared over a distant rise. Phyllis is so far in front that it's more than half an hour before she realizes I'm not following.

Anticipating the problem, she returns with a five-gallon can of gas, which takes me six miles closer to Fort Sumner before the tank goes dry a second time. This time the truck stops near a sign inviting us to visit Billy the Kid's grave: only three miles! After Phyllis has returned with a second can of gasoline, I spill much of it down my pants leg and over my gloves.

By the time we make it to the service station in Fort Sumner my fingers are numb from the cold and I stink with fumes. Listening to the banal chatter of some teenagers who are excited about the approaching snowstorm, I try to contain the darkening rage descending over my Gypsy heart. The kid who fills the tanks of our two vehicles (total: 58 gallons) notices the license plate of the Bronco and asks about skiing conditions in Taos. I tell him it hasn't snowed in months, and that all the hotels are buried under mudslides. And another thing, I say, my voice grown shrill, I know for damn certain that Billy the Kid was seen as recently as last year, selling shoes in South Dallas! I can tell from his long-gone expression that the kid is stoned and hasn't heard a word I said.

It's dark by the time we reach Clovis. I hate arriving in a strange town after dark. It's like blind dating. Clovis looks and smells like the bad side of Lubbock. My mood improves slightly when we discover a vintage Holiday Inn with enough space to park the rig, and next to the parking lot a vacant lot for our dogs' immediate requirements. Bucky is still a puppy—we bought him after Dash was killed—and has no inhibitions concerning certain delicate matters. But Abby is more set in her ways, very ladylike, and has been patiently holding it since Taos. She's beginning to look like a bagpipe.

We've been on the road for most of three days and haven't reached the Texas state line. And yet New Mexico already seems far away.

FRIDAY: ON THE ROAD AGAIN

There it is, the skyline of Texas! It has taken me years to fully appreciate its eccentricities, its uniqueness, its *Texasness!* The cosmic city of refineries south of Houston, for example, or the soaring sentinel of naked palms as you settle into the Rio Grande Valley. These are unmistakable Texas landmarks, and they validate the native and confirm his existence. What I'm seeing now are cotton gins and grain elevators projected like skyscrapers above the empirical vastness of the Staked Plains. Frozen blocks of compressed cotton as large as the adobes of Taos squat on fields of dark red earth, sleeping in its winter coat. Tufts of cotton waste swirl in eddies of wind, then settle in unbroken ribbons that stretch along both sides of the highway to the horizon and beyond for a hundred miles.

Willie is singing "On the road again . . . ," and I'm singing with him as we brush by places with warmly familiar names: Muleshoe, Littlefield, Lubbock, First Baptist Church, Big Spring, Ace's Barbeque, Smitty's Hickery Hut, Mutt's Auto Repair. I can feel it in my mouth and in my bones, feel it coming to life. A billboard provided by the West Texas Chamber of Commerce proclaims: "Free Enterprise!" I can dig it.

Presently, the cotton fields are spotted by oil rigs until there is no cotton at all. The land gradually surrenders to the rawhide beauty of mesquite, cactus, cattle, rolling hills, and subterranean springs as cold, clear, and sweet as creation's first morning.

San Angelo, its river sparkling with freshwater pearls, its collective memory bustling with recollections of Buffalo Soldiers and cowboy saloons. One more Holiday Inn and tomorrow we'll be home.

SATURDAY: HOMECOMING

"This is it!" I tell Bucky, the puppy. "Texas! You may have been born in Albuquerque, but this is where you belong." The blizzard conditions continue to hurtle in our direction—the storm is right behind us—but for the moment it's one of those pluperfect Hill Country days when the sun feels like warm fingers on your back and the sky is a relentless, lazy, lacy blue.

We stop for a picnic on the banks of the San Saba, outside the Hill Country town of Brady. I suddenly realize that Brady is one of dozens of Texas towns I've never visited. Never mind. I'm back for another look— longer, deeper, less about me, more about the place. We're inseparable, me and Texas; I see that now. A billboard beside the highway touts the boy-hood home of Lyndon Baines Johnson, as though it were just over the next hill. When you read the small print, however, you learn that his boyhood home is nearly a hundred miles away in Johnson City. That's the kind of mindless Texas boosterism that helped drive me to New Mexico. Back in the mid-1970s, during Vietnam, I hated LBJ, or at least I thought I hated him. Things look different now. Johnson's legacy wasn't just Vietnam; it was civil rights, the Great Society, a vision of a better America. His em-pathy with the poor and downtrodden was genuine. He wasn't a bad man, just a man with flaws, caught up in the time warp with the rest of us. His time and mine don't just parallel, they intersect. Looking at Brady's en-chanting old Baron Frankenstein courthouse, I try to picture the future president of the United States scrambling up its steps, pursued by his am-bitions and private ghosts, knowing even at that early age that if he ever stops running he's a goner.

In town I bought enough German sausage, longhorn cheese, fried okra, and bottles of Iron Brew to feed a high school basketball team, and I spread the homecoming feast on the hood of the Lincoln. This is the kind of day when you fall in love. I look at Phyllis and see it in her eyes, too. The dogs bounce among the cedars and winter vines, and we take our time with lunch. The peace is overwhelming, not disturbed but energized by the occasional far-off sizzle of pickup tires and the rumble of an oil tanker highballing along some lonely stretch. I write in my notebook: "A different kind of peace."

I stand on the bank, watching contentedly as Bucky and Abby drink from the clear, bottle green river, the tangy smell of cedar invading my senses. Then it strikes me, something else I missed about Texas: the color *green*. The color of new life. New Mexico is earth-colored and shadows. Old life.

Crossing the bridge, I read a historical marker identifying this as the site of the Voca Waterwheel Mill, built in 1876. The old church across the llano from our hacienda in Taos was built more than a hundred years be-fore this mill, and some of the adobes date to the early 1600s. Things like age and historical seniority used to seem important. But either way, it's just a tick of time.

We follow the chain of Highland Lakes, reaching Austin by late afternoon. Maybe it's just me, but the city seems greatly changed. New condos on the bluffs along Bee Caves Road, new roofs protruding through tree lines, new shopping centers. Barton Creek is a stagnant trickle. Some of the new bank towers were under construction when we left, but it's still a shock to see how they pollute the skyline. Having worked as a journalist for a quarter century, I can't stop the questions, but at least I'm more comfortable with the answers. In a few weeks the changes will seem as though they've been here forever.

The blizzard is catching up with us. So is my cold, which I thought I'd lost a couple hundred miles back. Time to give thanks, time to pay dues. We find a room at the Villa Capri, across from the LBJ Library. After a hot shower and a few shots of whiskey, we venture out to look for real Austin Tex-Mex. We decide on Jaime's Spanish Village, mostly because it's not crowded. It was a good place twenty years ago, but it's better now. It changed, then changed again.

SUNDAY: FINDING AUSTIN

This is the coldest day in thirty-one years! By tomorrow night Austin and much of Texas will be covered by snow. I knock off half a bottle of codeine cough medicine and watch the Cowboys lose to the Forty-Niners.

Later, we bundle up and take the dogs across the street to the manicured lawn of the LBJ Library, that they may at long last divest themselves of a little Texas hospitality. I think of the "fur-lined trap," but for now I feel so sane, so alert and welcome and needed that I start to laugh. I can't wait to look up old friends.

For the first time in many weeks, I feel that I have a future. I don't know what it is, but I know it's here. A lot of things haven't happened yet, things I can't imagine, and I'll be here to write about them.

The Snootiest Neighborhood in Texas

There are those who believe that the King William neighborhood just downriver from the Alamo began to lose its character when it was no longer tolerable for a wino to relieve himself on the sidewalk. They set the date at 1967, the year King William was declared the state's first national historic district. Not coincidentally, 1967 was also the year that an aristocratic investment broker named Walter Mathis moved there.

The neighborhood was on the verge of becoming an inner-city slum when Mathis purchased and began restoring the Italianate mansion at 401 King William Street. His grand design was to rehabilitate the entire neighborhood, or at least enough of it to protect his investment. In all, he bought and restored fourteen old homes. He persuaded friends to buy and restore other homes, and he made loans from his own pocket at a time when banks wouldn't touch property in that part of San Antonio. Today King William is a wondrous mixture of middle-class and wealthy Hispanics and whites—gays, artists, poets, prosperous lawyers, out-of-work layabouts, and plain old eccentrics. I'm not sure that the neighborhood has succumbed to gentrification, as some critics assert, but it is practically reeling with eccentrification—about a century's worth, I'd judge.

I would also call it iconoclastic, opinionated, stubborn, cranky, volatile, and especially, fractured. It is fractured the way French society is fractured, which is to say that the only thing everyone agrees on is their mutual distaste for outsiders. King William residents party together, picnic together, and sponsor an annual street fair during which certain of the gentry permit the rabble to tour their homes, while others expressly do not. There is even a King William Yacht Club. The yachts—canoes, actually—race from the Nueva Street Dam to the Johnson Street Bridge each Fourth of July. It's "all for one and one for all" in King William, until someone does something tacky—painting a porch the wrong color, for example—at which time a holy war is likely to erupt. The man most responsible for this healthy but habitual factionalism is the same man whose bucks saved the neighborhood: Walter Mathis, the neighborhood's self-appointed viceroy and arbiter of taste.

Mathis is one of those authentic period pieces endemic to San Antonio, so prim and formal you want to rub him with tung oil. Here is a man born and bred to rule. Descended from the original Canary Island oligarchy that was dispatched by the Spanish Crown in 1731 to settle the presidio that became San Antonio—and from John William Smith, the last messenger from the Alamo and San Antonio's first mayor—Mathis has been the president or a charter member of nearly every order and club ordained by the city's ruling class. But lofty social position didn't keep him from being driven out of his former home on Mulberry Street by the construction of the North Expressway. That's why, shortly after moving to King William in 1967, Mathis got himself elected chairman of the city's Board of Review for Historic Sites and the San Antonio Riverwalk Commission, two groups with primary influence over almost everything that happens in his neighborhood. If history repeats itself, Mathis wants it to be on his terms.

In the manner of an inspector general, Mathis regularly cruises the shaded streets of his domain, ever alert for the tiniest deviation or impurity. King Williamites cannot repair their roofs, repaint their porches, or make any other exterior changes on their homes without approval from the review board, which in the past has meant approval from Walter Mathis. Neighbors say that Mathis is not above approaching a property owner and demanding that the grass be cut. Before Prince Charles visited the district last February, word went around for people to tidy up their yards, or else the future king of England—and, worse, Mathis—might be offended. Many people believe that if matters were entirely up to Walter Mathis, electricity and internal combustion engines wouldn't be allowed on the streets of King William, and women would be required to wear bustles.

The late O'Neil Ford, an old family friend, was the one who convinced Mathis that he should invest his money and time in this neighborhood. Ford, whose architectural firm used to have offices at the foot of King William Street, saw the thirty-seven-block district as "a museum of homes." Along these streets was every style of nineteenth- and twentieth-century architecture known to Texas. By preserving the homes, Ford believed, an irreplaceable part of Texas' heritage would be preserved. He didn't mean just the limestone, gingerbread, and balustrade balconies; what needed saving, too, was the diversity of spirit that made these streets —and San Antonio—unique in Texas. Ford wanted to maintain the composite of cultures, the once-in-a-millennium mix of Mexican, Irish, English, French, and German (especially German).

There is a theory, first advanced by Kenneth Wheeler in a book called *To Wear a City's Crown*, that the personalities of Houston, Galveston, Austin, and San Antonio were formed in the critical years just before the Civil War. Look at how things were back then and you'll see pretty much how they are today. That is certainly true of San Antonio in general and King William in particular.

Other neighborhoods have struck compromises and sacrificed the longings of the individual for the larger good, but King William is special precisely because it preserved its differences. "This place is like a small town," Julian Trevino, a school administrator who lives at 332 King William Street, tells me. I hear this same sentiment over and over. Like the residents of a small town, torn between the need to be left alone and the greater need to be recognized, homeowners have their own perceptions of style, their own tickets to immortality: The images are linked inseparably to the past, as though only with the approval of ghosts is there salvation. King William is a microcosm of San Antonio's love affair with the past and its passion for strife. That these different kinds of people have created a place of undisputed, almost magical beauty has always made the residents of King William a little different, a little (get used to it!) superior. In King William, smugness is a virtue. Mike Casey, a past president of the King William Association, says, "People who ask a lot of questions— Where will the kids go to school? Where can I buy groceries? Is it safe?— probably don't belong here anyway."

The one person who unequivocally does belong is Mathis, of course. Something of a mystery man, he is a World War II hero and a lifelong bachelor who periodically emerges from the isolation of his mansion to host extravagant parties. He can intimidate with a glance, and his nose is so far in the air that friends fear a spring shower may drown him. One housewife told me that the high point of her decade in King William came when Mathis reviewed her restoration plans and remarked that she had done "a good job." Mathis is shy and anxious during interviews, but like most people in King William, he can't help but reveal himself in his surroundings. His house speaks for him.

At first glance his mansion resembles the Cathedral of the Anointed Shepherd. Its baby white limestone tower looms above a formal garden with a lacy gazebo. A pair of lead-molded red lions flank the front walk, perched regally to digest the passing scene. Like all the old houses on the street, this one was built in stages and has endured many transitions and indignities. Over the past 113 years it has been home to a hardware merchant, a stockman, a trail boss, a colonel, and numerous others. When Mathis purchased it, the house was divided into nine low-rent apartments. Obsessed with his mandate to restore it as closely as possible to the original—whatever that was—Mathis oversaw every tiny detail, including the scraping, repairing, and repainting of each hand-stamped shingle.

Inside, the house is as hushed as a museum. I have seen museums that were not as pristine or as meticulously furnished. No period of Texas history has been overlooked. As I follow Mathis from room to room (each crammed with one collection or another, from old canes to mugs to Russian icons to framed photographs of Texas ancestors), I find it hard to believe that someone really lives in this place. A journalist friend had told me of a rare but telling glimpse of the lord of this magnificent manor, one night as she walked along King William Street: she described "a man alone in his kitchen, cooking his lonely pork chop under a single light."

After a while I work up the nerve and ask to see his private quarters. He has no objection. He leads me to the southwest corner of the second floor and shows me two rooms that are magnificently furnished but otherwise indistinguishable from what I have already seen. His canopied bed is unmade (maid's day off), but I detect no other sign that anyone lives on the premises, or has ever lived here. No cigarette butt or toothpaste tube or magazine folded back against its spine. No comb or brush. No half-eaten lonely pork chop.

At the beginning of my tour, as is his habit, Mathis put a paper roll on his Bechstein Welte player piano, instantly filling a triple room with the sounds of Paderewski playing Wagner. The room brims with his Napoleonic collection: paintings, sketches, replicas, swords, daggers, toy soldiers, toy cannons—even an original death mask, one of the few known to exist. "I've been fascinated with Napoleon since I was twelve," he tells me. Somehow I am not surprised.

When you approach King William Street from almost any direction, what you see first is the flour mill elevator that rises like a national monument at the southwest foot of the street. This is such a local landmark that old-timers in King William still check the weather by observing which direction the flag atop the mill is flapping.

The mill was the progenitor of the serendipity that has always worked its magic on this street. When Ernst Altgelt, who had previously founded the utopian community of Comfort, named this street Kaiser Wilhelm Strasse for his beloved king of Prussia, Wilhelm I, he had in mind a broad, tree-lined avenue that would stretch for miles—maybe all the way to Corpus Christi. In fact, the street got only as far as the bend in the river, five blocks by today's reckoning. What stopped him was the project of another German visionary, Carl Hilmar Guenther, who put his first flour mill smack in the middle of Altgelt's plan. Guenther's original mill, called Pioneer Flour Mills, is still controlled by his heirs.

The mill has always been an integral part of the neighborhood: until the late fifties, anyone who happened along could get a free biscuit breakfast there. Another integral part of the neighborhood is the old United States Army Arsenal directly across the river from the ruins of Guenther's second mill. Charles Butt funded a massive restoration of the old military complex, which today serves as corporate headquarters for the H.E.B. chain.

At the head of King William Street, the end nearest downtown, is the Anton Wulff house, built around 1870. Wulff, a merchant and the city's first park commissioner, was the man who laid out Alamo Plaza. When anti-German paranoia swept the city during World War I (the street was temporarily renamed Pershing Avenue), rumor had it that the tower of the Wulff house was used for spying on the arsenal. Some of that paranoia may have been well founded: discovered in a house on Madison, the street paralleling King William to the east, was a stack of sheet music for the German national anthem inscribed "To our suffering brothers in the homeland, 1916."

Long before the Germans arrived, the peculiar pattern of the streets had been determined by the contours of the San Antonio River, the course of the Spanish irrigation ditches (*acequias*), and the outlines of the original land grants. In the late 1700s the land that makes up the King William Historic District was used to grow food to support the Alamo and other missions. The Alamo *acequia* ran down the side of what is now South Alamo Street, which divides the district east and west.

The Germans who created the neighborhood were the struggling visionaries of the great Austwanderung ("emigration") of the 1840s. The homes that they built were personal expressions of satisfaction and point of view, monuments to their aesthetic sensibilities as well as their vanities.

Those immigrants were a lively mix of petite bourgeoisie and utopians, a mix not unlike the eccentric composite you find today. The freethinkers among them saw Texas as an alternative fatherland, while the bankers, builders, and merchants saw it as a land of economic opportunity. Disagreement was a natural part of life: Joseph and John Ball planned matching cottages in the 100 block of King William Street, but the brothers' wives had a falling-out, and so John's house was built without windows on the side facing Joseph's house. The curse of their hostility was so powerful that today, 114 years later, the cottages bear no resemblance to each other.

Most of the immigrants had fled Germany because of the prevailing oppressions; they valued freedom so highly that the Fourth of July became an instant holiday for the newcomers. More cultured and educated than their Anglo and Hispanic neighbors, they took pro-Union and anti-slavery stands that put a strain on their relations with the community. Anglo settlers were absolutely aghast to discover how the Germans observed the Sabbath—by reading poetry, playacting, dancing, and competing in sports, all while consuming massive quantities of beer. In the freethinking community of Comfort, it was said, few homes had family Bibles, and when ministers at funerals asked German mourners to join in the Lord's Prayer, most of the congregation didn't know the words.

Because San Antonio was strategically located on the Mexican trade route, along which all Civil War supplies moved, the Germans of San Antonio made huge fortunes. At the war's end, control of San Antonio's politics and economy was firmly in the hands of German businessmen. For at least the next half century—while San Antonio was becoming the largest and most interesting city in Texas—it was more or less governed from Casino Hall, the private playpen of the German elite, which was just across the river from King William.

The late nineteenth and early twentieth centuries must have been idyllic times in King William. An English-speaking boarding school opened, and Johanna Steves built the city's first indoor swimming pool behind her gingerbread mansion at 509 King William. The homes were shaded by enormous pecan and cypress trees, and many houses had ballrooms on the top floor, formal gardens, and boat docks along the river. A streetcar line ran down South Alamo between rows of saloons. At twilight the residents of Washington Street, which ran by the ford and past Guenther's second mill, could hear taps being played across the river, on the quadrangle of the arsenal. From their sleeping porches, awaiting the evening breeze that always blew in just after eight o'clock from the Gulf, they could hear the creak of the mill wheel.

Today, King William gives you the feeling that you have stumbled onto a Hollywood back lot and are the only one here without a guild card. A kid with a punk haircut flashes by on a skateboard, and a group of young Chicanos cluster around a Trans Am, smoking and speaking of sexual conquests. One white house with roof terraces seems to have blown in from Miami Beach: it's the home of Armando Morales, a retired factory manager born in Sabinas, Mexico. He built it in 1948 from an architectural design he ordered out of a catalog. "It is, what you say, a modernistic home," Morales tells me. Neighbors call it "the Love Boat."

King William has an eerie time-warp quality that tugs you back to the King William of a hundred years ago. A horse and carriage clops along. A tourist snaps photographs of a gardener behind a wrought-iron fence, trimming gumdrop-shaped hedges. The exemplary Victorian mansion at 335 King William, designed by famed local architect Alfred Giles, once celebrated the greatness of banker Carl Wilhelm August Groos, maker of money. Today, after a tenure as Girl Scout headquarters, the house is elegantly restored and celebrates the greatness of Charles Butt, the H.E.B. scion. The carriage house that once stood behind the old Bergstrom home was used as the meeting place for a fraternity called the Merry Knights of King William (the fraternity wore robes copied after the Ku Klux Klan's, but while the Knights may have been prigs, there is no evidence that they were racists). It is befitting of the neighborhood that the man who preserves the fraternity's memory is the flamboyant and nationally known criminal attorney and constitutional expert, Gerry Goldstein. Gerry and his wife, Chris, have owned the house since 1975.

A man carrying an armload of groceries pauses at the worn granite curb in front of the Joske mansion to watch workers hoist new lumber to the roof. A stray chicken appears from a patch of cane. Chickens are not uncommon in King William. The barn behind Mike Casey's house on South Alamo was there when he moved in, but he had to get approval from the review board to add a fence to make a chicken coop. Down the street an old woman who speaks no English sits on the steps of her small cinderblock bungalow beneath a tall palm, a picture of dejection and sorrow.

Dorothy Schuchard and Caroline Elmendorf don't look like radicals. Both are small, genteel, good-humored women with snow-white hair and

bright, friendly eyes, grandmotherly types of almost Disneyesque proportions. They are widows of men whose families settled the neighborhood—
Ernst Schuchard, Carl Guenther's grandson, who took a turn as president
of the mill, and Hugo Elmendorf, whose family was active in commerce
and politics. Though Dorothy is in her late seventies, she still swims a
mile each day at the San Antonio Country Club. Caroline, 85, oversees
the preparation of chicken and shrimp salads for the Lenten lunches at St.
Mark's Episcopal Church. The women may not look like radicals, but they
are among the last survivors of the formidable brigade of little old ladies
in tennis shoes (golf shoes would be more accurate) who, in the years just
after World War II, fought to save the good life in King William.

Their activity hardly seemed militant at the time. As Dorothy recalls,
"Miss Carrie Steves would ring her tea bell, and we would take our sew-
ing baskets over to her parlor and spend an hour or so chatting about this
and that, women's talk mostly." One day in the late forties, word reached
them that a mortician planned to set up a business in the Wulff house at
the head of the street. "My goodness, it would have been so depressing
watching all those funerals pass by," Dorothy says. "Ernst said we would
just have to move unless we could stop it." Margaret Gething, who had
acted on the New York stage and been a member of the Park Avenue Association, suggested that the neighborhood get organized. That's how the
current King William Area Conservation Association (not to be confused
with the current King William Association) was founded.

All it took to bury the undertaker was a few letters and well-placed
phone calls—the women were not without influence in high places, particularly Margaret Gething, who was on a first-name basis with more than
one congressman. In the years that followed, the association tangled with
and almost always prevailed against much stronger opposition. In 1953 the
group stopped a freeway that would have crossed King William at Sheri-
dan, thereby destroying the Groos, Steves, Guenther, and Altgelt ances-
tral homes. A decade after that, the women persuaded the Army Corps of
Engineers to reroute the river someplace other than through their back-
yards. They deluged the city council and the San Antonio River Authority
with petitions, kept the phone lines busy to Washington and Austin, and—
who knows?—maybe even used their considerable wiles to win favor.

When they weren't saving the neighborhood from outsiders, they
wrote newsletters to each other, suggesting ways to hide sagging walls and
fire escapes with flowering vines. In one publication, association president
Nellie Pancoast broached the subject of garbage cans. "Even in our most
spiritual and artistic moments, not one of us can find beauty or dignity in

the humble garbage can," Nellie wrote, suggesting that they camouflage the cans by painting them a uniform olive green.

There are several versions of what exactly tore the group apart. Originally membership was by invitation only and limited to women of the "fine old families." Eventually men were allowed to join, and later the meetings were opened to all homeowners, and scheduled for evenings rather than afternoons. But the association effectively ceased functioning, Caroline Elmendorf remembers, when a dentist took control by rigging the election. "His wife was very flamboyant and loud, definitely not one of us," Caroline says. "I think I had been president for two terms but I was persuaded to run again. Her husband voted twice, and I lost by a single vote. That's when we stopped attending."

Another version is that the association dissolved because of a long-smoldering debate on whether to open the members' homes to the public on special occasions, such as during Fiesta Week. When the association voted against the plan in 1954, for example, minutes of the meeting gave as one reason the belief that the association "can't afford a flop" — as though the association were talking about a Broadway play. The organization was so obsessed with preserving what had been that it ceased to be. In 1974 there was an attempted merger between the King William Area Conservation Association and the King William Association. The merger failed in the face of unyielding opposition by Margaret Gething, who insisted to the bitter end that the word "historic" be added to the group's name.

A t the corner of South Alamo and Beauregard, in the heart of the district, is the A&E Food Market, and on its south exterior wall a colorful mural depicting a glorious moment in Mexico's history—Father Hidalgo leading the Diez y Seis de Septiembre revolt. The mural is not to everyone's taste—though what is in King William? They say that Walter Mathis turned the color of plum jelly when he saw it. The beer drinkers across the street at the Friendly Spot icehouse loved it, of course. Ah, Father Hidalgo, scourge of tyrants, reader of forbidden books, raiser of forbidden grapes, presser of forbidden wine. The Friendly isn't there anymore, but the mural is: Gentry 1, Rabble 1.

The story of how the battle went down says something about the way cantankerousness serves the neighborhood. It's like gravity: once you accommodate it, everything works quite well. The mural was painted about four years ago as the backdrop for a poster advertising Budweiser. The poster, now a collector's item, shows several generations of Hispanics, smiling and paint-splattered, posing in front of the mural with a tub of beer. The wall bears no hint of a commercial message, but as an expression of ethnic pride, the painting is pretty good.

Nevertheless, Walter Mathis and his faction protested: it seems that nobody had bothered to get a permit from the historic review board. "That's okay," the owner of the market replied. "We're going to white-wash the wall anyhow." From that point on, the absurdity escalated in a peculiarly King William way until it threatened to take on genuine racial overtones and erupt at the city council. Old friend turned against old friend, husband against wife. Walter Mathis wouldn't discuss the incident with me—in fact, he forbade me to write about it. Finally a compromise was worked out with the help of Maria Watson-White, great-granddaughter of Carl Wilhelm August Groos. The market wall mural could become a permanent objet d'art, provided that the subject matter was changed periodically and approved by the review board. Four years later Father Hidalgo is still there, looking as fierce and menacing as ever. "The funny part is, there's an RC Cola mural on the north wall of the market," Mike Casey points out. "Nobody has ever complained about that."

The Friendly Spot met with a crueler fate. In the late seventies the legendary icehouse (in San Antonio "icehouse" means "beer joint") was a quiet, peaceful hangout, locally owned and frequented almost exclusively by people from the neighborhood. The trouble started about 1981, when owners Gerry Goldstein and Jay Monday introduced a neighborhood rock band called the No. 2 Dinners, whose music was said to be capable of rattling the wastebaskets across the river. There were complaints, but serious opposition didn't get rolling until the fall of 1983, when the city bulldozed an old slum apartment that had been torched some months earlier. The building had acted as a buffer between the Friendly Spot and much of the neighborhood—in particular, the home of Rusty and Madeline Guyer. Rusty was president of the King William Association and tried to remain neutral, but Madeline rallied a small group of dissidents, many of them senior citizens whose complaints had gone unheeded.

"At first the music wasn't a regular event," Madeline Guyer says. "But by February of '84 some band was there almost every night. People were coming from all over town, dancing in the streets, urinating on the lawns, blocking traffic. I began to watch the clock every night, dreading for nine o'clock to roll around. That's when the music started."

The strain was made worse because the opposing factions were long-time friends. Madeline Guyer had known Jay and Susie McAtee Monday since their college days at Trinity University, and Rusty Guyer and Gerry Goldstein were colleagues in the legal profession. The Guyers were even fans of the No. 2 Dinners. "One of the Dinners is my dentist," Madeline told me. "His daughter plays with my daughter. Before this situation got completely out of hand, we even took a friend from Denton to hear the Dinners. The music was so loud he put peanuts in his ears and had to go to the doctor the next day to have them removed."

Despite meetings and efforts at compromise, the music continued. Only now, Goldstein and Monday had moved their concerts next door to an outdoor beer garden at the Beauregard Café, which they also happened to be leasing. They erected a "soundproof" stage and booked the Dinners to test it, but neighbors reported hearing something resembling a sonic boom that lasted five hours. Physical violence almost broke out when a manager at the Beauregard suggested that if Madeline didn't like the music, she should move. By coincidence, the Guyers were about to move to the John Ball house at 120 King William, several blocks farther north. "But by then it had become a battle of wills," Madeline admits.

In the summer of 1985 the dissidents filed a formal complaint with the Texas Alcoholic Beverage Commission. Goldstein and Monday had already decided against renewing their lease on the Friendly. The icehouse that had once been a service station became a place that sold bottled water. Rather than face legal charges, Goldstein and Monday moved the music inside the Beauregard. When I was there in February, you could hear the No. 2 Dinners on weekends. Clearly.

Not surprisingly, the most-inspired King William fights center on restoration. Though the motives behind historic preservation are presumably noble and aesthetic, there are financial advantages as well. Federal and local tax breaks can be had, but only if owners play according to rules. San Antonio's historic review board uses the tax credit guidelines established by the U.S. Department of the Interior. Local approval is necessary to win city tax abatements, but the review board has little real power—except to recommend denial of building permits. What the review board does have is the power to interpret the guidelines, which is how things can get interesting. "Frankly, a lot of our rulings are very subjective, very personal," a member of the board says. "Who happens to be sitting on the board that day can change the entire complexion of a decision."

Consider the case of Julia Cauthorn's bay window. Julia, a widow and real estate broker, looks a little like Gloria Swanson and is sometimes called the Duchess of King William. Newcomers to the neighborhood say that they know they've been accepted when she invites them to her front porch for lemonade and mint juleps. Naturally, as a broker of historic homes, she is a realist on the subject of restoration. Julia's pragmatic philosophy is diametrically opposed to the make-it-like-it-was worldview of Walter Mathis—and that's a recipe for trouble.

Julia sold some jewelry and gold coins in 1973 to buy a Gothic revival cottage known as the Sartor house. She bought it against her trust officers' wishes because, like most King William homeowners, she had a passion for the house that far exceeded the bounds of logic. She had been in love with the house since one afternoon in the twenties when her godmother took her there for a musicale. "It was the first time I ever heard live music outside of church," she tells me. "I couldn't have been more than five, but it changed my life." Julia became an accomplished pianist, and though she doesn't play much anymore, she has a standing offer to every child in the neighborhood: master five classical pieces and Julia will host a musicale in your honor.

Anyway, about ten years ago Julia decided to add a third bay window to the cottage, something on the scale of the original bay window built in 1882, and another added in the twenties. She was about to make an application to the review board when Walter Mathis and O'Neil Ford passed on some information at an informal meeting. Her plan for a third bay window was "inappropriate," they told her, because the new window wouldn't look like the existing two—which, of course, didn't look like each other to begin with. That interpretation struck Julia as curious because the review board guidelines state that external additions to historic properties should reflect the form and style of the original architecture but not mimic it; changes must be clearly identifiable as additions. In their interpretation, Ford and Mathis had come up with a peculiar twist on the guidelines that they helped to write. Politics had its way, and to this day Julia Cauthorn's cottage has only two bay windows.

"There is more than one philosophical approach to restoration," Julia insists. "Some of the oldest houses on the street—including the Norton-Polk home that Walter himself restored—were updated several times before they were restored. Who is to say what the original builder had in mind? Who is to say it wouldn't have been done differently if the original builder had had the materials and the good sense? If you carry Walter's philosophy to its logical conclusion, we ought to all be living in Indian tepees."

Nobody ever warns the people on City Street that Prince Charles is coming, so please mow the grass. City Street is west of the river, and though it is in the National Register of Historic Places, it isn't part of the designated King William Historic District. When the petition to join the district circulated in 1967, the residents of City Street said: *no, gracias.*

To get to City Street from King William, you cross the Johnson Street pedestrian bridge. A traffic bridge that was called the O. Henry Bridge because it was mentioned in one of O. Henry's stories was here until the sixties, when the city took it down while improving the river channel. Accidentally cut up into scrap metal, only one of the original four spires remains. From this spot at night you can see the emerald dome of the Tower Life Building downtown, reflected in the shimmering water.

City Street is a beguiling little ghetto of Victorian bungalows, each unique. Some of the houses are in poor repair, but every year you see a few more redos, the telltale clue being a King William Association plaque (you don't have to live in the district to belong to the association). The houses are painted in Mexican pastels. Yellow concrete ducks and fake tree stumps made into planter boxes decorate the yards, and some of the tree stumps support painted coffee cans. Behind an ornate column bleached the color of cold ashes is an old refrigerator for sale, and on another porch the family wash has been strung out to dry. "This is the poor Mexicano side of the river, the side where the people with eight or ten kids live, the side where the yards look like . . . well, like there are eight or ten kids in the family," Alma Hernandez tells me.

Alma's mother, Carolina S. Garza, is the main reason that City Street isn't part of the King William Historic District. A widow of 83 who supported her children by working in the Bexar County tax office, Carolina kept an eagle eye on properties that were about to be auctioned for back taxes. "At one time she owned eighty-six pieces of property, this little Mexicano gal with a sixth-grade education," Alma says proudly. "When a district goes hysterical"—like some others I spoke with, Alma sarcastically mispronounced the word *historical*—"it is subject to the review board, to this, to that. My mother doesn't play that game. A rent house is a rent house to Mother. If the plumbing breaks, she'll have it fixed. If rats come in, she'll buy you some poison and cover up the hole. But this is her business, and she doesn't want anyone telling her how to run it."

Alma, an educational diagnostician, and her husband, Ernesto, a plumber, live across the street from her mother, in a handsome two-story frame and brick home. Surrounding the house is an eight-foot chain-link fence, inside of which prowl three snow-white German shepherds. The place has been a halfway house, a rooming house, even a nunnery; the nuns erected the fence, destroying in the process the original stone wall that circled the property. The Hernandezes have lost track of how much money they have spent on restoration—none of it tax exempt, incidentally. "It is my impression that our aluminum siding and chain-link fence are the reasons we wouldn't qualify for the tax break," Alma tells me. "The fence is a no-no. But I love my dogs, and so I keep the fence and lose the tax break."

Alma and Ernesto socialize with some of their King William neighbors—they are active members of the King William Yacht Club, for example—but they enjoy the freedom to pick and choose their friends. "To be frank about it, I joined the King William Association because I finally figured out that it was the people on that side of the river who pulled all the strings," she says. "If there were plans to change a bend in the river, you knew which side was going to get rooked."

In a passion for the past that resembles that of die-hard New Englanders, longtime residents of King William calculate social status by how long one has lived in the neighborhood. Still, the irascible ghosts keep watch, and when the neighborhood gets too high and mighty, the inextricable forces of time are called to smite it. In the fifties the neighborhood almost slipped away entirely. By the time O'Neil Ford and his hot-lick group of young architects moved to King William in the mid-fifties, the neighborhood population was predominantly Hispanic, with a generous mixture of what one old-time resident described as "carnival people, cheap girls, and dope peddlers." The rambling Joske mansion was a halfway house for mental patients, and the Sartor house was a family services center. The Raised Bavarian cottage at the corner of Madison and Turner, the one that looks like something out of Hans Christian Andersen, was a bordello, at least until 1952, when Opal Smith got religion. After that, the sign out front read: "Meditation, Consultation, and Colonic Irrigation." Fred Cecere, who lives there now, told me he still gets Frederick's of Hollywood catalogs addressed to the fabulous Opal.

Over lunch one day at El Mirador, where almost everyone in King William goes to eat the peppery caldos—and to watch and be watched—I heard that "401" used to be a bordello too. The house at 401 King William belongs to Walter Mathis. Certified King Williamites always refer to individual homes by just the street number, and the woman who told me that 401 had been a bordello is as certified as they come. Her name is Maria Watson-White (the name is pronounced "mah-RYE-ah"; longtime friends call her Ann Maria). As director of the San Antonio Conservation Society and as one of the few aborigines around, Maria is generally called on to arbitrate historical and aesthetic disputes—the mural of Father Hidalgo, for example.

"Are you sure about 401 being a bordello?" I ask. "When I interviewed Walter, he failed to mention it."

"Walter does not talk about it," she says.

With such a checkered history, one might think that King William would have welcomed O'Neil Ford's architectural firm with open arms, but true to form, a few mossbacks seriously suggested that the business wasn't appropriate for the neighborhood—even though crime was rampant and bums used sidewalks as comfort stations.

"There was an element not willing to admit that the neighborhood had blown away," says Lewis Tarver, a lawyer who in the late fifties rented a carriage house there. Tarver and his wife, Tinka, were newly married back then, and they chose King William because it was cheap and close enough to downtown that they could walk to work.

"King William was so hard-core that most artists wouldn't even live down here," Lewis tells me. In those days the Tarvers' bedroom window faced Madison Street, which was inhabited mostly by poor Mexican Americans. The Tarvers went to sleep listening to the boys talking about whose mother was the biggest whore, and they got used to waking up and finding that something else had been stolen from under their car hood. "The real difference," Lewis says, "is we were down here BWM—before Walter Mathis."

The couple moved out of the neighborhood when they decided to have a family—the area back then was no place to raise children—but a quarter century later the children are grown. Tinka, a sculptress, recently rented a studio in the neighborhood. What drew her back was not the manicured, official history of local guidebooks but the crankier, livelier past that she remembered.

The Tarvers missed the BWM eccentricities: the four giant doors of the carriage house, and the wrench that was inexplicably embedded in the concrete floor; the woman across the street who welcomed her sister to town with a bottle of Christmas wine across the skull; the elderly and dignified man next door who put on his Boy Scout uniform every morning and raised the American flag; and the mildly retarded woman whose need to serve was so strong that on garbage collection day she went from house to house returning empty cans to the porches.

Most of all, they missed the sense of community. The neighbors in King William may be crazy bastards, all agree, but at least they are our crazy bastards.

Meet the Binions

Benny Binion might not recognize his old joint. His name still flashes in gold lights above Fremont Street in downtown Las Vegas, but the atmosphere at Binion's Horseshoe Hotel and Casino is distinctly sanitized, as if someone has given a bubble bath to a wild boar. A pedestrian mall stretches in front of the Horseshoe, the Golden Nugget, and the remaining gambling houses of Glitter Gulch, and a roof with laser lights blocks the sun and stars. Potted palms rigged to spray a mist on passersby have been positioned between kiosks that sell T-shirts and cheap souvenirs. You won't find fountains, topless chorus girls, roller coasters, pyramids, or cheesy replicas of New York, Paris, or Venice downtown, as you do along the far more fashionable Strip—and forget about a string quartet in tuxedos playing Bach, like the one in a lobby bar at the Bellagio—but an acoustic guitar player named Buzz Evans entertains the lucky souls who venture there after dark, mostly Asian tourists with cameras and young couples who look like they've just jumped off a boxcar. All this refinement is part of what the chamber of commerce calls the "Fremont Street Experience," a misguided attempt to make Glitter Gulch seem hip to the times. It misses the point. In the words of Oscar Goodman, the former Mob lawyer who was elected mayor of Las Vegas earlier this year: "People don't come here looking for Disneyland; they come looking for Bugsy Siegel."

When Benny, a gambler and racketeer with few peers in Texas or anyplace else, left Dallas in 1946 for the more forgiving atmosphere of Sin City, he couldn't have envisioned the multimillion-dollar legacy he would one day leave his children. And he couldn't have imagined what a mess they'd make of it. Two of Benny's five kids have died of a drug overdose—one an apparent suicide, the other a victim of foul play. In his day mobsters didn't use drugs; they just sold them. Greed, betrayal, and cold-blooded murder are traditions in this company town, but the current generation seems to have forgotten that it's only business. Following the death of Benny in 1989 and of his wife, Teddy Jane, in 1994, an all-out war erupted among the Binion siblings for control of the Horseshoe. Jack Binion squared off against his sisters, Brenda Michael and Becky Behnen, while little brother Lonnie "Ted" Binion was forced to watch from the sidelines. Ted's gambling license had been suspended . . . for hanging out with mobsters! Who was he supposed to hang with, the Moral Majority? Ted's suspension was merely another symbol of change in the nature of families, crime and otherwise. He carried a pistol, just like his daddy, only to him it was an ornament. The battle of the Binions was fought with court pleadings and depositions instead of machine guns, but in some respects it was dirtier and less honorable than the bloodlettings of yore. You don't have to be Tony Soprano's shrink to understand what happened here: The Binions had met the enemy, and it was them.

The battle concluded, at least temporarily, in the summer of 1998, when an out-of-court settlement was reached. It followed, and was no doubt hastened by, an order from the Nevada Gaming Commission that forced Ted to sell his 20 percent interest in the casino. Nearly all of it was bought by Becky, the youngest of Benny's kids. A month later, Ted was found dead of an overdose of heroin, a drug he had used since high school. At first police officers thought the 55-year-old had either killed himself or accidentally overdosed, but the evidence now suggests that he was the victim of a bizarre, almost comically inept plot by the paramour of his live-in girl-friend to murder him and steal his fortune. Ted's demise was a final crushing blow to the Binions. He'd been Benny's favorite—his carbon copy, only without the edge and tempering that made the old man a natural survivor. In the wake of Ted's death, one of Las Vegas' last family-owned casinos is a shadow of its former self. So is the family.

Before there was a Strip, and long before gaming mogul Steve Wynn began replicating the Seven Wonders of the World and installing slot machines in their every nook, Binion's Horseshoe was a haven for hard-eyed, no-nonsense gamblers. It was the cornerstone of Glitter Gulch—the noisiest, rowdiest, most wide-open casino in downtown Las Vegas. The doors never closed and the action never stopped. Benny boasted that he offered the world's best odds, and he never flinched from covering a bet. Texas high rollers, in particular, were attracted by his steadfast policy of no limits and no frills. "The size of your limit is the size of your first bet," Benny pledged. The story of the man who walked into the Horseshoe with $1 million in a satchel and lost it on the pass line at the craps table is now part of Vegas folklore. Binion's Horseshoe didn't merely win a million dollars that night, it won a permanent reputation as the only pure gambling joint in town.

There was no health spa at the Horseshoe, no Swedish masseuse, no barbershop, no entertainment. "I don't want to see my money blown out the end of some guy's trumpet," Benny explained. The drinks were generous—Benny pioneered the tradition that players drink free—and the food was cheap and utilitarian. His late-night $2 steak became a classic casino come-on. There was no fancy dining room or French chef, just a man in a stained apron who stirred up pots of greasy, fiery chili using an old Dallas jailhouse recipe. For years the Horseshoe didn't even include a hotel. When Steve Wynn told Benny about his plan to build an extravagant two-thousand-room hotel and casino called the Golden Nugget across the street, Benny wrapped a fatherly arm around his shoulder and said, "Great, they can sleep in your place and gamble in mine."

Benny learned the business in the twenties from Warren Diamond, an old-time Dallas racketeer who operated a no-limits craps game in the St. George Hotel, near the Dallas County Courthouse. Though he claimed never to have set foot in a schoolroom, Benny knew about numbers. In the idiom of the trade, he was a "square craps fader"—"square" meaning honest, and "fader" being the one who covers the bet. The margin favoring a craps fader is small, like 1.4 percent, but over the years it made Benny enormously wealthy. By the early thirties he was the king of the Dallas rackets, a title he had to defend periodically with a weapon. His motto was, Do your enemies before they can do you. He earned his nickname, Cowboy, for reasons that had to do with shooting, not riding; he gunned down at least two business rivals and scared away many more. Long after he left Dallas, he continued to control the rackets there and in Fort Worth—and the bodies of rival gangsters continued to pile up.

When Benny hit town, Las Vegas was a woeful cluster of dives on an empty highway to Los Angeles, undiscovered except by Bugsy Siegel and his mobster friends. It was a milieu in which he was very much at home. As he had in Dallas, Benny cultivated friends in high places: judges, politicians, police chiefs. They were essential in this climate. Enforcers like Chicago Mob boss Tony "the Ant" Spilotro enjoyed squeezing their enemies' heads in vices until their eyeballs popped out, and the desert brimmed with freshly dug graves and spent cartridges. "Benny never had to fight a turf war in this town," recalls Harry Claiborne, who was his attorney for more than forty years and is an unofficial godfather to all of his children. "I never knew anybody who didn't like him." Before they were friends, Claiborne was the chief deputy district attorney of Clark County, and he had personally prosecuted and sent away for life Benny's old Texas sidekick, Cliff Helms. "Just after I started in private practice," Claiborne told me, "Benny came up to me one day and asked if I wanted to be his lawyer. I told him that I knew he didn't feel kindly about what I'd done to Helms, but Benny stared at me with those cold blue eyes and said, 'There's no goddamn law you gotta be in love with your lawyer.'" Later, Claiborne earned the distinction of being one of a handful of federal judges impeached and convicted in this century, which made him an icon in Vegas.

The Binion children grew up knowing that they were heirs to a dangerous business. The home that Benny bought for his family on Bonanza Road was a forty-five-hundred-square-foot fortress on six acres, and it was equipped with elaborate security refinements. There were no hidden corridors, which he feared kidnappers would use for their own purposes, but there was a barn out back, and he told his kids to hide there in the event of an air attack. The threat was real: In 1951 police officers arrested Herbert "the Cat" Noble, Benny's longtime Dallas rival, as he prepared to take off for Las Vegas in his stagger-wing Beechcraft with two bombs mounted in the bomb rack. Not long after, the Cat was blown to pieces by a bomb planted in his mailbox. Everyone assumed Benny was responsible, but nobody ever proved it.

The wise guys of Las Vegas always thought that Ted would end up running the Horseshoe when Benny's string ran out—that sober, serious Jack was a great accountant but lacked the panache to run such a flamboyant place. Benny's eldest daughter, Barbara, had died of a drug overdose in 1983, and the other two didn't seem suitable for the job. Brenda, the middle girl, lived in Amarillo, far from the action. Becky, the youngest, had operated the Silver Star Casino in the late seventies, but only because the Nevada Gaming Commission balked at issuing a license to her husband, Nick Behnen. Behnen was barred from even entering the Silver Star, but everyone figured that he was the real boss.

Ted was a younger version of Benny, or he tried to be. He dressed like him, in boots and cowboy hat, tucked a pistol in his jeans, and drove a pickup truck with his dog, Princess, riding shotgun. In the summer he worked on the family's more-than-100,000-acre ranch in Montana. (When Brenda used her power as executrix of their mother's estate to sell the ranch in 1997, Ted was nearly inconsolable.) Wild and fearless and always ready for fun, he was instantly likable. He was also generous and loyal to a fault. "Ted had a lot of strange friends with bad reputations, but Benny was the same way," says Claiborne. "If you were his friend, you were his friend." Ted didn't care for formal education but read American and Western history with a passion and could recite Civil War battles in minute detail. "He was a Renaissance man," recalls attorney David Chesnoff, another friend. "A cowboy, but probably the most worldly guy I ever met." From the time he was a teenager Ted collected antique and limited-edition guns, rare and mint coins, and old casino chips; later, he purchased bars of silver and inherited his mother's coin collection. Eventually his own collection of coins and silver grew to twenty-four tons and had to be stored in two vaults at the Horseshoe.

Benny's kids were aristocrats by Vegas standards, young royals who grew up in a home where luxuries were commonplace and in a town where doors opened on command. Ted practically grew up in the casino, learning the trade as a preteen from his father and from some of the shrewdest players in the country. By the time he was eighteen, he was an old hand. "Benny told me that Ted was the best in the business," Claiborne recalls. He was also a junkie, having moved from pot to opium and LSD and, finally, to his drug of choice: black tar heroin. "Benny was devastated," Claiborne says. "He hated drugs more than anything in the world, but there was nothing he could do." Because Ted hated needles, he didn't inject the drug; he smoked it. "Chasing the dragon," he called it. Even zonked out, Ted had more brains and moxie than the others. That made him the obvious candidate to assume command of the Horseshoe—someday.

Benny's string ran out prematurely, however. His good ol' boy network was no match for two crusading district attorneys from Dallas. First Will Wilson and then Henry Wade had been after him since the mid-forties. In 1953 Wade finally nailed Benny on income tax evasion and gambling charges dating from his Mob days in Dallas and sent him away for forty-two months. Benny got out in 1957 but never again held a gaming license. Until he died, he watched the action from a corner table in the Horseshoe coffee shop while Teddy Jane worked the cashier's cage and Jack ran the business.

To the surprise of some, Jack was more than up to the task. He retained the policy that a gambler's first bet was his limit and used as a marketing tool the catch phrase "a fair game and fair odds." Though Jack's personality was tamer and far more subdued than Benny's, he had his father's eye for an advantage. In 1988 he more than quadrupled the size of the hotel by purchasing the Mint Casino and Hotel next door for $27 million. He also shared Benny's appreciation for characters and scoundrels: As ever, all customers were to be treated as guests. When he learned that an infamous nickel-and-dime player named Goldie had talked a Horseshoe supervisor into sending a limo to her house to deliver a dozen doughnuts and a pack of cigarettes, Jack asked himself, "What would Benny do?" and decided to forget it. For nearly thirty years he put the Horseshoe ahead of almost everything else in his life. "He is an ungodly hard worker," says Tom Stephenson, a Dallas writer who ghosted *Jack Binion's Little Black Book on Gambling*. "He's usually in his office by six, and he's still there that night at ten. I don't think he ever took a break in his life."

T ed first got his gambling license in 1964. Despite his heroin habit, he began working the casino floor, much as Benny had done—greeting big shots, dealing with troublemakers, endeavoring to keep everyone happy. The slippery slope that eventually took him to his death began in 1987, when he was convicted of drug possession and his license was suspended.

At that time Ted was married and lived with his wife, Doris, and their daughter, Bonnie, in a fine home on Palomino Lane. He also owned a sixty-acre ranch in Pahrump, a small town fifty-three miles west of Las Vegas. Ted kept large amounts of cash and other valuables at his home and ranch, and he sometimes buried his treasure—the only sure way to protect it, he believed. Heroin wasn't his only demon: He also had weaknesses for booze, big-breasted showgirls, and underworld types. Maybe because of Benny's reputation, Ted felt he had to show he was a tough guy. In 1990 the FBI charged him and seven other Horseshoe employees with beating and robbing players suspected of cheating at blackjack. The charges exposed an ugly side of the family business: Each of the supposed cheats was black. Federal prosecutors mishandled the case, so it never went to trial, but Ted again lost his license temporarily.

He got it back in 1993 but lost it again the following year. This second suspension was for eighteen months, but the Nevada Gaming Commission later continued it indefinitely. The problem was no longer merely drugs, it was Ted's continued association with mafiosi: The commission uncovered evidence that he had made $100,000 loans to reputed Kansas City mobster Peter Ribaste and to an old Chicago thug named Herbert

"Fat Herb" Blitzstein, who had once been the top lieutenant of Tony "the Ant" Spilotro. Blitzstein ran a lucrative segment of Vegas's street rackets, including loan-sharking and an insurance scam run out of an auto repair shop. On one occasion, even though the gaming commission prohibited Ted from setting foot in the Horseshoe, he cashed $11,000 in auto insurance checks for Fat Herb there. Ted seemed fond of Herb and enjoyed hanging out with the hefty hood at topless bars, where much of his business was conducted. Ted must have known that agents were monitoring his moves, but either he was too reckless to care or he believed the friendship was helping, not hurting, his efforts to regain his license. On the list of public officials that Fat Herb claimed to have bribed was Steve Du-Charme, a member of the Gaming Control Board who was formerly a Vegas police sergeant. What neither Fat Herb nor Ted knew was that Du-Charme was working undercover at the time he took the bribe. Ted parted ways with Fat Herb in December 1996, when the board added the mobster to its infamous Black Book of undesirables, but the damage was done.

A few weeks later, Fat Herb was assassinated in his home by a hit man hired by L.A. Mob bosses as part of their move to take over the rackets. Word on the street was that Ted was also targeted, and sure enough, within a few days someone sprayed his home with bullets. Vegas police officers advised Claiborne to get Ted out of town, but there was a problem: A condition of Ted's suspension required him to submit to three urine tests a week and be available for other random tests. "This was a very vulnerable period in his life," Claiborne recalls. "He was practically a prisoner in his own home. The gaming authorities were threatening to take away his license permanently. Plus he and his wife had separated. Doris had lived so many years with his addiction that she was worn out. He was no longer a husband, a lover, or even a companion."

Not to her, at least. By then Ted had a new companion, a topless dancer half his age named Sandy Murphy, aka the Irish Venus. The daughter of a repo man, Sandy had been a teen pageant princess in the small Los Angeles suburb of Bellflower but had dropped out of high school when she discovered the lucrative possibilities of a career in adult entertainment and fast talk. Ted met her in 1995 at a Vegas topless joint called Cheetah's Lounge. At the end of the evening he slipped her a couple thousand bucks, but she threw it back in his face. "She's not like the others," he cooed to his friends. He was right, though not in the way he supposed. Shortly after Doris moved out of the Palomino Lane house, Sandy moved in—and into a lifestyle of high-limit credit cards (her monthly bill averaged $5,100), expensive jewelry, and European vacations, all paid for by Ted. Sandy had so much cosmetic surgery done that Becky once cracked, "She must be getting made over for her next boyfriend." Sandy and Ted both loved to party all night and sleep all day. Before long, she was taking over his life. First she remodeled his house, replacing Doris's bedroom furniture with a handmade set she ordered from Italy and ripping out the carpet and replacing it with marble; then she began handling his banking transactions, monitoring his phone calls, and nagging him to put her in his will. Sandy was famous for her big mouth: She called Ted "old" and "ugly" and openly admitted that she was just sticking around for the money. Ted slapped her around regularly, which she appeared to accept as part of the deal—she referred to the beatings as "my punishment"—but he always made it up to her. For one particularly expensive reconciliation, he bought her a $97,000 Mercedes.

As Ted was to discover, Sandy "chipped around" often with Rick Tabish, a 33-year-old hustler who had come to Vegas in 1997 looking for some easy money, leaving a wife, two children, and some large debts back home in Missoula, Montana. Though his father was a wealthy businessman, Tabish was a blue-collar loser who had failed at every legitimate venture he'd ever attempted. His assets were his good looks and his smooth line, which he used to work his way into Ted's inner circle. He soon was confiding to friends that he was "laying the pipe to Binion's girlfriend" and using her to advance his plan to steal the bulk of Ted's fortune, including the tons of silver and rare coins stored in the vaults at the Horseshoe.

According to an arrest warrant affidavit issued by the office of the Clark County district attorney, Rick had a lot of big ideas. With a $200,000 loan from a Nevada bank, he set up a corporation, MRT Transportation of Nevada, and muscled his way into a lucrative sandpit operation by torturing and threatening to kill one of the partners. By the spring of 1998, the affidavit says, the blue-collar loser had hired his own airplane and pilot and was talking to a broker in Beverly Hills about selling Ted's treasure. At Rick's urging, the broker flew to Las Vegas to inventory and appraise the silver while he and Sandy watched. The broker estimated its value at between $5 million and $7 million.

A showdown was clearly coming—one involving not just Ted's messy romantic life but the entire Binion family business. Flare-ups had escalated on the Horseshoe's board of directors, which at the time consisted of Jack, Brenda, and Becky (because of his suspension, Ted couldn't serve on the board or vote his 20 percent ownership stake). The issue that initially divided the siblings was Jack's proposal that they expand their casino holdings to other states. Becky and Brenda felt cut out of the decision making and said no. Though Jack owned 42.2 percent of the stock versus his sisters' combined 9.6 percent, Brenda controlled another 27.5 percent as executrix of their mother's estate. Jack found his own investors, however, and opened casinos in Mississippi and Louisiana, using the Binion's Horseshoe logo. As court documents make clear, Becky and Brenda became convinced that Jack was skimming assets from the Horseshoe to finance his other casinos. They also suspected that he was plotting to stack the board with "more-compliant" outsiders and feared that he was recklessly endangering the business by continuing the casino's no-limits policy.

Claiborne contacted all of Benny's children, offering to mediate the dispute. "I warned them," he says, "that if they took this to the courthouse, it would be the ruin not only of the Binion family but of Binion's Horseshoe as well." Claiborne says that Jack and Brenda agreed to meet with him but Becky never responded. In January 1996 Becky filed suit against Jack, asking the court to remove him as president. A judge ruled that Becky and Jack should act as temporary copresidents and ordered that major decisions be unanimous, effectively deadlocking the operation. For the next year and a half the bitterness escalated and became public. In papers filed with the court, Becky alleged that Horseshoe profits had slipped dramatically since her brother began focusing his attention on his other casinos and that for the fiscal year ending in June 1997 the Horseshoe suffered "unprecedented" losses of $20 million. Jack responded that the reason for the losses was the deadlock that Becky had created. Becky also charged that Jack was flouting gaming regulations, mismanaging baccarat and slot machine operations, and concealing crucial financial information. She said he had posted a $2 million bond for a Mexican high roller jailed on tax evasion charges, then loaned him another $4 million to gamble at other casinos—a loan that was never repaid. She also said he got a high-interest, $2.5 million personal loan from Indonesian high rollers while permitting them to gamble large sums at the Horseshoe.

In April 1998 the Nevada Gaming Commission permanently revoked Ted's license, ordering him to sell his 20 percent stake in the Horseshoe. Becky had said that the Horseshoe didn't even have enough cash on hand to buy Ted's interest, but the order forced a quick resolution of the lawsuit. In a flurry of transactions Jack bought out Brenda and Ted, then sold their interests and his own to Becky, who got complete control of the Horseshoe for the bargain price of $20 million, to be paid over two years. By some estimates, the Horseshoe's true worth was $80 million.

His ties to the casino forever severed, Ted had to move his collection of coins and ingots from the casino vaults. Sandy, Rick, and some drivers from MRT volunteered to help, and the stash was temporarily stored in Ted's garage. Ted then contracted with Rick to build a permanent storage site for his treasure, a ten-foot-square concrete vault on a lot he owned in Pahrump. On July 4, 1998, Rick and his crew moved the treasure from Ted's garage and sealed it in the vault. By Ted's design, the vault was in plain sight, between a Burger King and Terrible's Town Casino, on the main highway connecting Pahrump to Las Vegas, where intruders were certain to be spotted.

Just days after the treasure was sealed, Ted revised his will. Though the bulk of his approximately $30 million estate was still to go to his daughter, he deleted the names of a number of old friends and bequeathed to Sandy $300,000, his home, and all of its contents. To make sure the new will was valid, Sandy had her own lawyer look it over. According to the arrest affidavit, she informed friends that she was also the beneficiary of Ted's $1 million insurance policy. Curiously, the flame of love was exhausted by the time Ted made this change. He and Sandy slept in separate bedrooms, and she admitted to several people—including Ted's gardener, Tom Loveday—that his drug habit made him unable to perform in the bedroom. "I'm twenty-six and I need sex," she confessed to Loveday. Sandy barely bothered hiding her affair with Rick. Records seized by prosecutors show that she bought him expensive gifts at Neiman Marcus using Ted's credit card and flew with him to Los Angeles, where they registered as husband and wife at the Beverly Hills Hotel.

By August Rick was in serious financial trouble. Checks issued by his company were bouncing all over town, an equipment-leasing company had sent a default notice of $67,000, the IRS was demanding back payments of $337,000, his company in Montana had defaulted on a $75,000 loan, and a $200,000 Nevada bank loan was coming due. According to several prosecution witnesses, Rick confided that he planned to kill Ted and steal the treasure and began to recruit coconspirators, including the foreman of Ted's ranch. He also contacted a longtime friend in Montana, a former Army Ranger named Kurt Gratzer, and told him of his plan to kill Ted and steal the money, jewelry, and silver in his home and the treasure buried in the vault. Gratzer later told the authorities that Rick promised to give him part of the insurance money and a new car if he would make the hit. Rick advanced several plans. First, he suggested that Gratzer use a sniper rifle. An alternate scheme had him doing it with one of Ted's antique guns, then rolling the body in a carpet and disposing of it in a rock crusher. When Gratzer nixed these schemes, Rick suggested that they force him to swallow a lethal combination of heroin and Xanax, a prescription drug that Ted took to help break his heroin habit. Gratzer telephoned another friend, a Montana pharmacist, and asked him to research the amount of Xanax needed for such an overdose. Like Gratzer, the pharmacist later told his story to Clark County prosecutors.

In the days just before Ted's death, according to the affidavit, Rick and Sandy each spread the word that Ted's drug habit was worse and speculated that one of these days he would kill himself with an overdose. Sandy was drinking a lot, behaving as if she were high on cocaine, and talking a blue streak. Several employees at the Neiman Marcus beauty salon overheard her rambling on about getting $3 million and the house when Ted died of an overdose of heroin, which she predicted would be very soon. Three days before Ted's death, Sandy and Rick again shacked up in Beverly Hills.

Even so, Ted seemed upbeat. He talked to attorneys about trying to get back his gambling license and to a real estate broker about buying several properties for potential casinos. He talked to a journalist about writing a book and a movie script based on the life of his famous father. He wrote a $1 million check to open a new investment account and donated $40,000 to Las Vegas mayor Jan Jones's campaign for governor. By this point Ted had guessed that Sandy was having an affair with Rick. He told friends that he was planning to "get rid of the bitch" and unloaded his guns, explaining to his maid that he was afraid Sandy might shoot him. On September 16, one day before his death, Ted called his lawyer and instructed him to "take Sandy out of the will, if she doesn't kill me tonight." Later that day, speaking to a ranch hand who was visiting his home, Ted pointed to Sandy and Rick seated in the next room and said, "They got me the best shit that I've had in a long time." The ranch hand assumed that his boss meant heroin. Late that evening Ted's regular dealer delivered twelve balloons of black tar heroin, and Ted tipped him with thirty tablets from the Xanax bottle he had just had refilled.

The following morning Sandy telephoned the maid and told her, "Ted isn't feeling well. Don't come to work today." About noon, Ted's real estate broker phoned and was informed by Sandy that he was still asleep and couldn't be bothered. Police officers now believe that by noon Ted was already dead and that Sandy was busy cleaning up the mess and staging the scene. At 3:47 P.M. Rick telephoned Sandy, and seven minutes later she dialed 911 and reported in a hysterical voice, "My husband has stopped breathing!" The authorities found Ted's body on a mattress on the floor of his den, partly covered with a sleeping bag. Beside him was an empty bottle of Xanax, and in the bathroom were some narcotics paraphernalia, including a knife and some pieces of foil like those Ted used when he smoked heroin. Police reports at the time indicated "absolutely no evidence . . . to suggest foul play."

Nobody who knew Ted bought the cops' theory. "Ted loved life way too much to kill himself," said Tony Cook, a former casino manager at the Horseshoe who had known him since high school. "He had such a knowledge of drugs and was such an active drug user, Ted wouldn't accidentally overdose," Becky said. Moreover, the scene itself was too pat, too sterile. "As soon as I saw the scene," Claiborne recalls, "I told them it had been staged." In fact, several things seemed suspicious, starting with the fact that nobody had ever known Ted to sleep on the floor, much less on a sleeping bag. The bruises and cuts and the position of the body suggested that it had been moved after death. Though there were traces of heroin on the knife blade, there was no trace of the drug on the pieces of foil. An autopsy revealed no heroin in Ted's lungs but high concentrations of both heroin and Xanax in his stomach. This alone should have suggested foul play: Nobody eats black tar heroin.

Prosecutors believe that Rick restrained Ted with handcuffs or thumbcuffs while Sandy mixed up the fatal cocktail in a wineglass. According to this theory, Ted was forced to drink the cocktail and then smothered. The wineglass disappeared, but prosecutors have a videotape filmed the following day that shows Sandy removing a wineglass from a kitchen counter and dropping it in her handbag. A subsequent inventory of the house revealed that a large amount of cash and jewelry were missing, as was a $300,000 collection of rare coins and currency that Ted had kept in his den.

In the early morning hours of Saturday, September 19—three days before they buried Ted—sheriff's deputies in Pahrump spotted Rick and two others using a backhoe to break into the vault. All of the silver except a single silver dollar had already been loaded into a tractor-trailer. Rick tried to convince the deputies that he was merely following Ted's instructions: to sell the silver and set up a trust fund for Ted's daughter, Bonnie, in case of his sudden demise. When that didn't fly, he made a crude attempt at bribery, claiming that Ted's will bequeathed $250,000 to the sheriff. The deputies took the three to jail and charged them with theft. Two days later Sandy bailed her lover out, pledging her Mercedes-Benz SL500 convertible and five pieces of jewelry as collateral.

After her initial hysteria, Sandy calmed herself and went methodically about the task of grabbing what she believed was coming to her. In addition to the $300,000 in cash, the house, its contents, the $1 million insurance policy, and $3 million in savings, she expected a fat check for the literary rights to her story. Things didn't work out that neatly, however. Ted had indeed obtained forms making her the beneficiary of the policy, but he died before signing them. A probate judge awarded Sandy the items stipulated in the will—Ted's call to his lawyer was too late—but lawyers for the estate appealed, and Becky filed a separate suit, claiming many of Ted's personal items. When lawyers at the probate hearing began asking embarrassing questions about Ted's death and the thousands of dollars in cash and valuables missing from his home, Sandy and Rick both took the Fifth.

While the police did little or nothing, the estate hired a private investigator, former Las Vegas homicide detective Tom Dillard, who turned up a trail of cellular phone conversations and secret meetings between Rick and Sandy, as well as evidence that they had told people about their plot to kill Ted. In December, three months after Ted's death, the chief deputy district attorney for Clark County, David Rogers, impaneled a grand jury as a tool to continue the investigation that Dillard had started. Over the next three months Rogers called dozens of witnesses and gathered volumes of information. In March of 1999 the Las Vegas coroner changed his finding to homicide. In June, the same day Sandy expected an appeals court to validate her take from Ted's will, she and Rick were arrested and charged with murder and conspiracy to commit murder and/or robbery.

The struggle for control of Binion's Horseshoe won't be officially settled until July 2000, when the $20 million note signed by Becky comes due. The wise guys are betting that she will default and that Jack will emerge triumphant. Jack's casinos in Mississippi and Louisiana appear wildly successful, attracting millions of dollars from Texas gamblers.

In the meantime, there are other issues to be resolved. When the Nevada Gaming Commission approved the sale of Ted's stake to Becky and awarded her a license, it issued explicit instructions that her husband, Nick, had to keep his hands off the business, as it had in 1978 when Becky was running the Silver Star. Many of Benny's old friends believe that Nick calls the shots at the Horseshoe and refuse to patronize it. So do many Vegas residents who used to be regulars. One of them, a high-stakes gambler named Bob Stupak, sued the Horseshoe because it refused to cash $250,000 in $5,000 chips, including one that he had donated to his church. Though Nick is not an officer of the corporation, Stupak named him as a defendant and charged that he "has done irreparable harm to the Horseshoe." Nobody is sure how many unredeemed Horseshoe chips are floating around. In January the casino redeemed $10 million in $5,000 chips but refused to cash another $1 million. Another $3 million in chips were discovered in the toolroom of Ted's ranch. Apparently, he took the chips along with the silver, though nobody knows why.

Benny's name may glitter in gold, but his soul has gone south. You can get a bowl of Horseshoe Chili for $2.75 at either of the two snack bars on the casino floor, and the late-night steak is still a bargain at $2.99, but Benny would be appalled to discover that somebody has added a Chinese restaurant. The players have lost the wild-eyed, foaming-at-the-mouth intensity that used to make every roll of the dice a life-altering experience. They look haggard and listless, as though they were killing time at a bus station — women with piles of orange hair and tight pants, guys in gimme caps and jeans soiled with the drudge of the oil patch. They look bored or maybe dead. What's missing is the no-holds-barred élan of the Wild West: dudes with suitcases of cash ready to play the bundle on one hand of Texas Kickass and the delicious possibility that Benny might suddenly appear to air-cool a bottom dealer. The nearest thing these days is a mounted collection of guns once owned by Cowboy and his pals. A Smith & Wesson .38 Special is identified as a piece "owned and carried by Benny Binion during the depression era in Dallas, Texas." But even that appears suspect. According to old police reports, Benny always used a .45.

The Sting | AUGUST 1996

The out-of-towner who introduced himself as John Clifford sounded too good to be true—especially in the winter of 1992, which was one of those down cycles that the aerospace industry has learned to expect in election years. Horizon Discovery Group, the small aerospace company operated by Neal and Karen Jackson, was struggling to stay alive. So were most of the other small subcontractors who orbited Johnson Space Center. The Jacksons, who were expecting their third child in the fall, had just learned that they were losing their funding on a long-term project with one of NASA's prime contractors, GE Government Services. They had talked about getting out of the business, maybe even leaving Houston. Then John Clifford phoned with a proposition that would change their lives. For that matter, it would change the lives of a lot of people at the Johnson Space Center.

Clifford talked with a southern drawl and described himself as a good ol' boy with more money than brains. He and his partner, Joe Carson, owned a number of companies, including Eastern Technologies Manufacturing in Maryland and Southern Technology Diversified in Atlanta. Eastern was developing a unique piece of hardware, Clifford said, and he wanted the Jacksons to represent the product and put him in touch with the right people. The new hardware was a lithotripter, an ultrasound device that smashes kidney stones without invasive surgery. Clifford's lithotripter was not the standard model found in hospitals, which is so large it has to be transported by 18-wheeler, but a portable model small enough to fit in a spaceship. The hardware sounded right for NASA. In the weightlessness of space, calcium leeches from the skeletal system and forms spiny stones that cause immense pain as they migrate toward an astronaut's bladder. Clifford made it clear that he was talking about both government and commercial contracts—hundreds of millions of dollars—and that he was offering the Jacksons a spot on the ground floor. He took notice of the impending birth of Karen's baby and personally guaranteed that by the child's first birthday the Jacksons would make at least $1 million. Dazed by the speed and magnitude of the offer, Neal and Karen made a down payment on a lot and hired an architect to design the $500,000 home they had always dreamed of owning.

The Jacksons were typical of the mom-and-pop entrepreneurs who lived in Clear Lake and the other NASA bedroom communities south of Houston. This was a close-knit group of scientists, engineers and businesspeople, well educated, ambitious, dedicated to the exploration of space. Some had arrived in Houston in the 1960s, the dawn of America's space program, but most had hitched their wagons to NASA in the seventies or eighties when they were still in school. Many had dreamed of being astronauts but had settled willingly for positions as support troops. Neal Jackson had ten years service as an air force pilot when McDonnell Douglas hired him in 1981 to train astronauts. Like others in the industry, Neal and Karen moved into a tidy middle-class neighborhood where names like Mercury, Gemini, Apollo, and Challenger seemed painted on every street sign, shopping center, park, or doughnut shop. From their patio gazebo they could look across a vacant field and see the sprawling campuslike Johnson Space Center complex with the rocket casings of historic missions scattered about like the art of a postutopian culture.

It was a homogeneous community. People belonged to the same trade groups, clubs, and churches. They ate at the same steak houses and drank at the same pubs. They perused the pages of *Commerce Business Daily*, a bulletin published by the Department of Commerce listing every potential government contract from toilet paper to space shuttles, and swapped information on who was bidding what contract. Life in the aerospace industry revolved around NASA contracts. Contracts were usually long-term, but subject to periodic renewal. When a big-ticket contract was up for renewal, the community came to a rapid boil. Résumés were updated and mailed. People jockeyed for position. Small companies like Horizon networked and formed alliances, and large companies worked the halls of Congress.

Eight or ten prime contractors dominated the process and set the agenda—giants like Lockheed, Boeing, General Dynamics, Rockwell, Martin Marietta, McDonnell Douglas and General Electric. When the contracts were awarded, the prime contractors farmed out pieces of the action to any number of subcontractors. At this point the scientists and engineers who had worked for the incumbent contractor simply switched badges and went to work for the company that had won the bidding. Switching badges was not so much a sign of corporate disloyalty as it was the method by which NASA maintained continuity. In the end, everyone worked for NASA.

Karen founded Horizon Discovery Group in 1985 while Neal was on active duty with the Air Force Reserve—upon his discharge, he became her first employee—and she was still the company's CEO in 1992 when the mysterious John Clifford came on the scene. In the argot of the industry Horizon was a "body shop." The company sought support and service subcontracts in fields where it had some expertise—e.g., writing a womb-to-tomb mission requirement document for the space shuttle—then hired from the available pool of "bodies" however many scientists, biomedical engineers, or market specialists a job might require. When the job was done, the bodies looked for work elsewhere. Prime contractors like GE dangled subcontractors like Horizon on a string, but such was life in the aerospace business.

Blond, pretty, pleasingly plump, Karen was a hardheaded business-woman with strong opinions and little tolerance for nonperformers. She was Horizon's organizational strength; Neal its technical expert. He was a good front man, an aerospace engineer from Texas A&M, an Aggie's Aggie, strong willed, macho, egotistical, a bull of a man with broad shoulders, curly steel gray hair, and fading good looks. A bullshitter, hand-shaker, and contact maker, Neal was also prone to indecision and slow with the follow-up. But his twenty years in the Air Force and his background training pilots for Boeing and astronauts for McDonnell Douglas made him a natural in the industry, as did his unabashed record as a patriot. When Operation Desert Storm erupted, Neal volunteered. Together, Karen and Neal gave Horizon credibility. You heard that word over and over in the aerospace industry—credibility. It was a small company's most valuable asset, and undoubtedly one reason John Clifford chose Horizon to represent the lithotripter. But there was another, more practical reason. By the fact that Karen owned and operated the company, Horizon qualified as a small disadvantaged business (SDB). Roughly $400 million, or 8 percent of Johnson Space Center's annual $5 billion budget, was set aside for SDBs. With that much money up for grabs, most small businesses found a way to be disadvantaged.

On April 1, about a month after Clifford's first telephone call, the Jacksons closed the deal at a meeting at Southern Tech's new office in a warehouse off Houston's South Loop. Clifford wanted to seal the bargain with a handshake, but Karen insisted on a written contract. This was her first face-to-face meeting with Clifford. He was younger than she expected, mid-30s, reddish blond hair and boyish good looks, a little arrogant, something of a show-off. At that first meeting Clifford went out of his way to impress on the Jacksons that he was a ruthless businessman who played by his own rules. If that bothered them, he said, now was the time to speak up. "Nice guys finish last," he said—to which Karen volunteered that she'd been trying to tell Neal that for years.

This was Clifford's proposition: Neal would guarantee his services as a contact man for the next twelve months, introducing Clifford and his company to the most important people in the community. Clifford mentioned in particular Carolyn Huntoon, director of the Life Sciences Division at the Johnson Space Center, who would have to approve the lithotripter project. In return, the Jacksons would be paid $7,500 a month for the first two months, then $10,000 a month for another ten months. In addition, they would receive 25 percent of any government contracts they brought in. This was chump change, Clifford made clear, compared to the millions that would come once the product was established. A deal with NASA was merely the seed money: the NASA "meatball" (logo) could be invaluable in marketing the product commercially. Karen was happy for the chance to shift the burden of running the business to Neal for the duration of her pregnancy, and also recognized an opportunity for Horizon to evolve to the level of a manufacturing contractor, where the big bucks resided. Nevertheless, she insisted on a clause that would require Clifford to pay out the full term of the contract regardless, and demanded a copy of Southern Tech's Dunn & Bradstreet Report. When Clifford handed over the first payment that afternoon—in cash—Neal danced around the room and waved the bills in the air.

Driving back to Clear Lake that night, the Jacksons joked that they were probably being followed. "We'd never been paid in cash before," Karen recalled. "It was legal tender for a legal contract, but still . . ." Things were moving faster than they ever imagined.

Of course they had never imagined that they were being set up. More than a year would pass before the Jacksons realized that they had been designated as the Judas goats of Operation Lightning Strike, an FBI sting designed to root out fraud and corruption among NASA employees and contractors. The wheeler-dealer who called himself John Clifford was really Special Agent Hal Francis, who had arrived in Houston the previous summer fresh from a similar sting in St. Louis called Operation Brown Bag. Francis was not all that different from the fictional Clifford, just a good ol' country boy who grew up in Mississippi and cultivated a gift of gab. Karen Jackson's initial impression was on the mark: Francis was a hot dog, ruthless in pursuit of his own cause.

Francis had served with the supersecret National Security Agency in the early eighties and joined the FBI in 1988. His reassignment to the Southern District of Texas in 1991 was fortuitous. The NASA Inspector General's Office needed help. It had investigated hundreds of complaints of contract abuse and kickbacks, many of them at the space center, but had yet to get a single conviction. Most of the complaints came from anonymous calls to the NASA hotline.

Sifting through the open cases, Francis and his boss Art Schultz, supervisor of the government fraud squad—together with agents from the space center IG's office and the Defense Criminal Investigative Service—created the elements of Lightning Strike. Francis would reprise his role as Clifford. A phony company, Southern Technologies Diversified, was created and given a financial history. When the Jacksons checked the company's financial rating, it showed that Southern Technologies had annual sales of about $45 million.

Over drinks at Fuzzy's, a downtown bar, the agents decided they needed something to sell, some kind of "black hole" project that would appear to suck government money into the tunnel of no accountability. Its true purpose, of course, was to lure greedy contractors into the trap. Francis came up with the idea for the miniature lithotripter. As a prop, the bureau purchased a 1983 model ultrasound device from Johns Hopkins Medical Center for $5,000. The company that supposedly manufactured the lithotripter, Eastern Tech, was a real company: Its president had cooperated in Brown Bag.

Once the covert operation was approved in December 1991, Francis went under cover. All of his conversations with targets were recorded. Francis regularly filed reports and placed his tapes into evidence, and he met each morning with Art Schultz. The two met weekly with Assistant U.S. Attorney Abe Martinez and other federal prosecutors. To target a subject, the government has to establish that the subject is predisposed to commit a criminal act. Higher-ups at FBI headquarters made the call on who was and wasn't predisposed, but Martinez had to decide when a target had sufficiently compromised himself to warrant prosecution.

Francis's initial targets were GE Government Services and the Life Sciences Division at the Johnson Space Center. In fact, he didn't contact the Jacksons until he had spent all of January and most of February having doors slammed in his face. Frustrated by an inability to crack this close-knit community or score with the corporate executives and NASA big-wigs, Francis decided to use Neal Jackson as bait. Once Jackson was under his spell, Francis began to construct a house of cards based on the belief that Jackson was predisposed to crime. This alleged predisposition rested on two anonymous complaints: that Karen was merely a front for their small disadvantaged business, that Neal was the real boss; and that Neal had attempted to influence government contracts by flying GE executives on hunting trips to West Texas. Neither complaint survives scrutiny, but that didn't stop the FBI.

Neal was the perfect instrument for Lightning Strike, a man so taken with his own abilities and ambitions that he would see what he wanted to see, hear what he wanted to hear. In the spring Jackson flew to Baltimore to inspect the manufacturing facilities at Eastern Tech. The plant occupied about ten thousand square feet of a strip shopping center and specialized in "black box" (top secret) electronics. Eastern had contracts with, among others, the National Security Agency, with whom Clifford claimed to have once served. Neal inspected areas where technicians were assembling circuit systems for robots, and he saw the prototype of the lithotripter. It was about the size of a desk, and fairly crude, as one would expect of a prototype. But Neal had researched ultrasound equipment and believed the device to be genuine.

A few weeks later both Neal and Karen flew to Atlanta to the headquarters of Southern Technologies. Clifford and Joe Carson (a fake name used by another undercover agent) met them in a Rolls-Royce convertible and treated them like visiting royalty. At NationsBank they watched Clifford sign a $1 million line of credit for the lithotripter. Always the southern gentleman, Clifford hurried ahead to open doors for Karen. Though she attached it no special meaning at the time, Karen remembered later giving Clifford a big hug and, for an instant, feeling him freeze. Months later she realized why—he was wearing a body mike.

Twice in the spring and summer of 1992, Clifford invited Neal to the Florida Keys for one of his boys-only fishing trips, aboard his fifty-four-foot cabin cruiser. There is a classic photograph, taken by Clifford, of Neal kissing a thirty-pound dolphin fish. The boat was one of the undercover agent's favorite toys, a method of helping targets relax and lulling them into compromising conversations. These trips usually included dinner at a fancy restaurant and an evening at a topless bar, another of Clifford's passions. Good ol' boy that he was, Clifford would knock down tumblers of scotch and expound on his philosophy of ruthlessness, how he'd steamroll anyone who got in his by-god way. He talked about accounts in offshore banks and volunteered to arrange one for Neal that even Karen wouldn't know about. Neal declined.

One night at a bar in Fort Lauderdale Clifford remarked that he didn't care if the lithotripter worked or not; his only concern was getting money out of NASA. This statement pushed Neal's button. His own tongue loosened by whiskey, Neal told Clifford to produce or get lost. "John, we don't enter these things lightly," Jackson said. "I'll tell you, you can take your money and your three-day boat trip and shove it up your ass . . ." When Neal thought about Clifford's cavalier attitude in the sober light of day, how Clifford went out of his way to make even the most innocuous transaction sound sleazy, he decided it had something to do with this good ol' boy's background as a spook with the National Security Agency. Neal was too much of a patriot to question the methods or motives of the NSA.

All that spring, Jackson introduced Clifford to the right people. Meetings or lunches were arranged with individuals and groups at NASA and with major contractors. On three separate occasions meetings were scheduled with Carolyn Huntoon, the space center's director of Life Sciences, but all were canceled for various reasons. Clifford did meet with some of Huntoon's biomedical engineers, but they didn't seem impressed by the lithotripter project.

At a division of Krug Industries, Neal introduced his boss to Jim Verlander, a fellow Aggie and business acquaintance. A research scientist, Jim Verlander had been with NASA since the Apollo program and helped train astronauts for moon landing. He was currently working on an ultrasound device for the space station. This alone made Verlander a potential target. But there was something else that made the scientist ripe for exploitation—his vulnerability. Verlander's pregnant wife suffered from cervical cancer, and the family had exhausted its savings.

When Clifford showed Verlander a brochure of the lithotripter, however, Verlander told him to forget about it. The machine was simply not on NASA's wish list. On the other hand, if this technology could be redesigned as a multitissue imaging system that could study all the organs of the body, Verlander believed that it might sell. No problem, Clifford assured him: the boys at Eastern Tech would get to work on it right away.

Clifford paid Verlander $5,000 to write an unsolicited proposal to the space center, extolling the wonders of the lithotripter—now referred to as a multitissue ultrasound imaging system, or MTUIS—and asking NASA to approve $600,000 to develop the prototype. This was a relatively small amount for NASA: Huntoon had the authority to approve it out of discretionary funds. Even so, getting the proposal into Huntoon's hands would be tricky without inside help. A few days later Verlander called Clifford offering to provide exactly that help. Verlander told Clifford that he had a "mole" deep inside NASA, very close to Huntoon, who could tell Clifford how to get the project funded. This service would cost $3,000. Clifford immediately agreed.

Though it now appears that there was no mole—Verlander invented the mysterious insider to improve his own stock with Clifford—Verlander did have a friend who worked in Huntoon's division. David Proctor, a pudgy, mild-mannered bioengineer with graduate degrees from Texas A&M and Texas Tech, had been at NASA since 1987. Along with other engineers, Proctor had traveled to Russia with Huntoon to work on the joint U.S.-Russian space station. It was a huge stretch, however, to claim that Proctor was tight with the director of Life Sciences, or even in her good graces. Proctor planned to quit NASA at the first opportunity and open a consulting firm with Verlander. The lithotripter could be their first big job.

Though he never met Clifford, Proctor worked for him as Verlander's partner, editing proposals and supplying costs for hiring engineers. Proctor's first legal mistake was sharing the money that the agent was giving Verlander, and his second was accepting the loan of a computer that he needed to fine-tune the proposals and do the future work that Clifford wanted. The deluxe computer that Clifford loaned Proctor was a $100,000 model, nearly as good as the one he used at NASA: using his computer at the space center for a private job would have violated NASA policy. A few months later Proctor was surprised to receive a $1,000 Christmas bonus from Clifford—again through Verlander. Manna-from-heaven was John Clifford's specialty, a fringe benefit that made it easy to fall under his spell.

In the weeks that followed, the undercover agent greatly accelerated his activities. He persuaded the Jacksons to incorporate another small disadvantaged business—Space, Inc.—with Karen as its CEO. Space, Inc. was conceived as an electronics manufacturing company, though it would depend on Eastern Tech for hardware. The Jacksons owned 51 percent of Space, Inc. and Clifford owned the other 49 percent. To give the new company instant credibility—and a history as a government contractor— Clifford agreed that 51 percent of Eastern's stock would be turned over to Space, Inc., though like many other promises from Clifford this never materialized.

The first thing Space, Inc. needed to qualify as a vendor for companies with NASA contracts was a financial statement. Neal pointed out that the company had no finances, but Clifford didn't see that as a problem. They would simply "create" one. After all, Eastern Tech, their partner, was well financed. Clifford offered to supply blank invoices or whatever else was needed.

They needed someone to draft the financial statement, and Neal thought of his friend Dale Brown. Brown, whose small company, Terra-Space, shared offices with Horizon, had met Clifford and was trying to persuade him to sink money into one of Brown's pet projects, a NASA theme park. Brown and his two partners at TerraSpace saw themselves as "the future captains of the aerospace industry" and believed that the wave of the future was the transfer of technology from the government to free enterprise. NASA had blazed this trail repeatedly with such inventions as the cell phone: the lithotripter would simply follow the same path. Assistant U.S. Attorney Abe Martinez regarded Brown as "a gnat who wouldn't go away," but Clifford saw another target and put Brown on the payroll. Brown recalls that he used numbers supplied by Clifford to cobble together a financial statement good enough to satisfy NASA's requirements. Clifford was so pleased that he promoted Brown to marketing director at $5,000 a month, plus 10 percent of the profits on the lithotripter.

In the summer and fall, Clifford elevated the profile of the project and lured more victims into his net. He commissioned the prestigious Washington consulting firm of Beggs and Associates to lobby the lithotripter at NASA headquarters in Washington and in Congress. The president of the firm, Jim Beggs, had been the top guy at NASA during the Bush administration and had convinced Congress to fund the U.S.-Russian space station. He had been indicted on charges of falsifying government contracts, but the charges were dismissed and the government issued a written apology. Nevertheless, the FBI and the Department of Justice believed that Beggs was dirty and gave Agent Hal Francis permission to move on him.

To give Lightning Strike real cachet, however, the FBI needed to snare an astronaut. Francis targeted two of them, one of whom turned out to be a friend and neighbor of Dale Brown. Dr. David Wolf, 36, was an expert on ultrasonic equipment and one of the inventors of a bioreactor that regenerates human tissue in three dimensions. More to the point, he worked directly under Life Sciences director Carolyn Huntoon. When Wolf learned of the miniature lithotripter from Brown, the astronaut agreed to review it and a dinner was arranged with John Clifford and his partner, Joe Carson.

The dinner developed into a drunken night on the town. In the company of Jackson and Brown, Clifford and Carson picked up the astronaut at his home in Clear Lake in a white stretch limousine. Drinks were poured on the way to the Rainbow Lodge in River Oaks as Clifford directed the conversations away from technical matters to a bull session about women they had conquered. At dinner many bottles of champagne were consumed, and a tab accumulated in the hundreds of dollars. Clifford waved off Wolf's attempt to pay his part, but the astronaut persisted and left some money on the table. The second half of the evening evolved at Rick's Cabaret, Houston's premier topless club, where Clifford hired two dancers to put on a private show. Long after the others were ready to leave, Clifford was still ordering drinks and paying the dancers.

They never got around to discussing the lithotripter. A few days later, on instructions from the undercover agent, Brown left a copy of the lithotripter proposal in Wolf's mailbox. Brown must have known that this was a dumb move: the proposal was a proprietary document—a trade secret—and any unauthorized person caught with it was committing a crime. Wolf claimed later that he threw it in the trash. Had he brought it to Carolyn Huntoon's attention—as Clifford hoped—the act would have ended Wolf's career as an astronaut and probably put him in jail. Clifford did not give up, however. On at least a dozen occasions in the months that followed, he tempted Wolf with offers of trips to the Florida Keys and other enticements. Fortunately for his career—and for the space program—Wolf turned him down every time. A few years later Wolf spent 119 days aboard *Mir*, the Russian space station, and on his return personally handed over the patch that he wore in space to President Clinton, as a gift for the president's daughter, Chelsea.

The FBI had deep pockets and Clifford knew how to use them. At the Space Expo Symposium at South Shore Harbor Hotel in League City in October, giant corporations like IBM, Martin Marietta and GE Government Services set up hospitality suites. So did little Space, Inc. With plenty of food and liquor being served by attractive hostesses, Space, Inc.'s suite was perhaps the most popular at the symposium, attracting among others former astronaut Buzz Aldrin. At Christmas, Karen planned a modest wine-and-cheese open house at the offices of Space, Inc., but Clifford decided instead to splurge for a black-tie affair at South Shore Harbor Country Club and invited the presidents and CEOs of all the top aerospace corporations. To speak to this group the undercover agent hired former NASA administrator Jim Beggs, who was by this time a primary target of Lightning Strike. Beggs selected a topic of interest to everyone: "NASA and the Clinton Administration." A month earlier, Clinton had been elected president. Many in the industry saw the 1992 election as a battle for the future of the Johnson Space Center; Clinton's victory almost assured that the center would endure. David Proctor recalled that his boss, Carolyn Huntoon, had boasted to her staff that if Clinton won, she'd be the new director of JSC. And so she was.

By the end of 1992, Karen was nearly out of the picture. Her baby, a third son the Jacksons named Colin, was delivered by emergency cesarean section in September. Complications followed. In December, the child almost died from a general seizure and spent two weeks at Hermann Hospital, suffering from a rare neurological disorder. Because the Jacksons had changed insurance companies after the child's birth, the illness was determined to be "preexisting." Hospital bills soon climbed above $100,000. On top of everything else, business was nonexistent.

As the Jacksons became increasingly vulnerable, the FBI made its move. In October Clifford and Joe Carson informed the Jacksons that the monthly payments of $10,000 would stop in November. In the future, Neal would be paid according to the number of contacts he introduced. Neal didn't understand what was happening, but Karen did: Clifford was breaching their contract. She wanted to take the matter to their lawyer, but Neal convinced her to wait. He still believed that by his baby's first birthday, Clifford would come across with the promised million bucks.

Early in January 1993 the Jacksons got a break, or so they thought. An executive for a Houston robotics manufacturing company, Automaker, called Neal about an item she'd noticed in *Commerce Business Daily*. The Tobyhanna Army Depot in Pennsylvania was taking bids on an assembly robot. Perhaps her company and Neal's could bid it jointly: Automaker as the prime contractor, Space, Inc. as the subcontractor. At a meeting with the Automaker executive, Clifford boasted that he had a friend in the Pentagon who could help land the Tobyhanna contract. Put off by Clifford's sleazy suggestion, the executive remarked that Automaker didn't do business that way. "If you don't bid it," Clifford told her casually, "we will."

The Jacksons were flabbergasted by this remark. The notion of Space,

Inc. as the prime contractor was ludicrous. But Clifford had it covered. Eastern would buy existing hardware, modify it to Tobyhanna's specification, then step aside and allow Space, Inc. to be the prime contractor, thus giving the small company instant credibility. Clifford told Neal to write a proposal using numbers that Clifford would supply from "an inside source." He reminded Neal that this was his final chance—that Space, Inc.'s future depended on getting the Tobyhanna contract.

After eleven months of frustration, the FBI was finally ready to spring the trap. In February, Clifford brought news that the chief of procurement at Tobyhanna, Joe Umbriak (who had been recruited to go along with the sting), was coming to Houston. He instructed Neal to show Umbriak the town, to "throw a couple of titty dancers in his lap." A fax from Umbriak arrived shortly, informing Space, Inc. that the price it submitted was a little high. Neal and Dale suggested lowering it by $5,000, but Clifford quickly vetoed that idea. "We're basically buying the contract," he said. "We don't have to lower the price." Later, he told Jackson that his friend had slipped $5,000 to his man in the Pentagon. In private, Clifford told Brown, "This is Neal's last chance. If this does not come off . . . Joe [Carson] will cut Neal off at the knees."

During preparations for Umbriak's visit, Clifford remained mysteriously out of town, but nevertheless directed the planning with frequent telephone calls. On March 4 Clifford called Neal, allegedly from Tallahassee, and told him that plans had changed. Umbriak wouldn't be coming to Houston after all but wanted them instead to deliver some "entertainment money" to a gay friend of his who would be staying at the Hobby Hilton. In return the friend would give them the bid price needed to win the contract. Neal was instructed to get together $400 or $500 in unmarked bills, seal them in an envelope, wipe off the fingerprints, and deliver the envelope to the hotel room.

After this conversation Neal sat in his office for nearly half an hour, trying to sort out the mess he was in: payoffs at the Pentagon, insider information on a government contract, and now bribes to a homosexual. Neal made no secret of his homophobia. Handing over money to a pervert was a sacrifice he could not make. Leaning on his longtime friendship with Dale Brown, he persuaded Brown to make the delivery.

A few days later, Clifford vanished as mysteriously as he had appeared fourteen months earlier. Neal didn't hear from him again until August 2 when Clifford phoned unexpectedly and asked Neal to meet him at the warehouse off Loop 610. Driving north on I-45 Neal thought of that day when he and Karen were returning home with $10,000 cash, that prickly feeling that they were being followed.

The warehouse was somehow different than Neal remembered. Walking into the foyer, he was met by a man he had not seen before, escorted to a small room, and told to wait. As his eyes adjusted to the light, Neal saw giant blowups of photographs propped against a wall. One was a photograph of the proposal he had written for the Tobyhanna contract. Another was the shot Clifford had taken of Neal kissing the dolphin. There were other candid shots of Neal, all of them seemingly innocent and yet somehow sinister and ominous in this Orwellian setting. A video machine with a TV monitor caught his attention. Neal realized suddenly that he was watching film of himself and Karen, signing the contract with Clifford. There he was, dancing around the room like a fool, waving a fistful of cash at a camera he didn't know was there, saying, "If the tapes are rolling we'll have to live with it!" Stacked nearby were boxes of audio and video tapes with his name on them. He lost track of how much time passed, then the door opened and four or five men with hard faces and Glock pistols on their hips entered the room. One of them was John Clifford. "My real name is Hal Francis," he said, flashing his badge. "I'm a special agent for the FBI and you're in a whole lot of trouble."

Dozens of aerospace professionals fell for Agent Hal Francis' well-crafted performance in the role of John Clifford, and those who fell hardest ended up in the warehouse. Of all the bells and whistles that adorned Operation Lightning Strike, the warehouse treatment was the most exotic and diabolical, a brilliantly executed exercise in coercive persuasion in which victims were systematically reduced to quivering masses of jelly.

Although the traps were sprung over a number of weeks, all the defendants recalled a common experience. Once Agent Francis had introduced himself, other agents unveiled large white poster boards on which were printed the "crimes" committed by the subject at hand. To one side was written the corresponding number of years in prison and fines. In Dale Brown's case, for example, there were twenty-one felony charges totaling sixty years and $1.25 million. Another agent then explained options. The subject could leave, in which case he would be arrested in a manner calculated to best embarrass his family. Or he could stay and help himself. None of the Lightning Strike victims had ever been arrested or ever imagined himself in such a predicament. Everyone elected to stay. Then they learned the ground rules. They could not contact an attorney; otherwise all deals were off. They couldn't speak of what happened to anyone except their wives and ministers. Before the day had ended, all except one had confessed to crimes so vague that they weren't sure they were even involved. Before the day was over, all of them were "flipped"—that is to say, they agreed to go under cover for the FBI and trap friends and associates.

As a final act of submission they were handed a telephone and instructed to telephone the next victim and lure him to this theater of hell. While the warehouse treatment may strike an average citizen as constitutionally dubious—uncomfortably similar to the North Korean method popularized in *The Manchurian Candidate*—this technique has been used for years by the FBI. Apparently it is as successful in this country as it is in North Korea.

Francis' and the government's position was that from the beginning of their dealings, Jackson and all the other defendants knew that the lithotripter was a fraud. The government released only a tiny portion of the thousands of hours of tape made during Lightning Strike. The available transcripts confirm that Francis/Clifford presented himself as a successful scumbag who made clear to everyone that his primary concern was getting money from NASA, that he could care less if the equipment worked. The Clifford character was a fountain of jabbering promises and mixed signals, but nowhere does he say the lithotripter is fake.

What is clear is that the undercover agent used all of his ample resources to establish himself as a legitimate businessman, and that he manipulated his targets and led them "down the slippery slope of impropriety," as Houston attorney Dick DeGuerin termed it. Francis worked for more than a year to manipulate Neal Jackson into committing a crime. At each stage, Clifford is the one who suggests the impropriety—paying in cash, hiding money in offshore accounts, creating a phony financial statement, trying to influence an astronaut to sneak their lithotripter proposal through the back door, using insider information to gain contracts. His back to the wall, his career and family in jeopardy, Neal Jackson finally agreed to pay a $500 bribe. Jackson may have been weak, greedy and stupid, but if he is a criminal it's because the government enticed him to be.

With Jackson in his back pocket, Clifford moved with relative ease. Seduced by the promise of huge profits from the lithotripter, the targets didn't ask a lot of questions, and many bent over backward to please Clifford. For example, Verlander was enticed to write a proposal by the promise of 25 percent of the lithotripter funding. Verlander brought his friend

David Proctor into the mix by lying that he had a mole planted deep in Life Sciences. No telling how many people Clifford had in his sights: Art Schultz says that the bureau eventually collected forty to fifty prosecutable cases, though only twenty-two were turned over to the U.S. attorney and seven of those were rejected for insufficient evidence. A bitter debate ensued among various levels of bureaucrats over who should and should not be prosecuted.

Frequently the government's requirement of predisposition came down to Jackson's word to Clifford that a suspect was "our kind of guy." Former NASA director Jim Beggs was targeted because Jackson remarked, "He knows how the game is played" and because another aerospace consultant (himself a target) confirmed that "Beggs and Associates knows how to spend your money without you winding up in jail." Beggs escaped the trap, but his consulting partner Jim Robertson pleaded guilty of accepting a proprietary document that he had repeatedly told the undercover agent he didn't want. An executive with Astro International fell for a similar trick. Clifford stuffed a brochure in this man's pocket, folded inside of which was bidding information for a contract the company had already lost. The executive told me that he pleaded guilty, on the advice of his lawyer, to try to avoid being suspended from doing government business. Most of those who dared speak to an attorney were advised of the hopelessness of their positions. Vince Maleche, a division director at GE Government Services who pleaded guilty to accepting $2,500 from Francis/Clifford in return for placing Eastern Tech on a "short list" of bidders, was told by his lawyer that these were his options: he could live out his life on a half-acre plot in Alvin and be found innocent, or keep what he had and plead guilty. "The economics of pleading innocent were astronomical," Maleche told me.

Once the warehouse treatment began, they fell like dominoes. Maleche gave up his boss, Tony Verrengia, a retired air force officer who had joined NASA in 1964 and was one of the first men assigned to the space shuttle program. Verrengia gave up Carter Alexander, a pioneer of the manned space program who was the civilian equivalent of general at Brooks Air Force Base in San Antonio and weeks from retirement after a distinguished thirty-one-year career. Alexander, at the FBI's direction, was helping set up Carolyn Huntoon when Lightning Strike was leaked to the media. Though Huntoon was not a target during the covert operation, she became one after Proctor and Alexander flipped.

The truism that an honest man cannot be bribed was put to the supreme test by a relentless agent with an unlimited expense account. Eventually, all the defendants succumbed to repeated temptations. They accepted cash for what appeared to be legitimate work and eventually turned over or accepted proprietary documents, at which time the cash became bribes. All of them did something that at least smacked of impropriety —including the corporations who allegedly accepted inside information. The $10,000 computer that David Proctor believed that he borrowed was viewed by the government as evidence that he took a bribe in return for using his influence to ram the lithotripter through NASA. This charge was particularly ludicrous: Proctor was a peon at Life Sciences. But convincing a jury that he was not the mythical mole of which Verlander spoke so freely would have been difficult. Even though Proctor cooperated and did everything the FBI asked—including illegally entering a building and copying a credit card number—Proctor was one of only two defendants to get jail time. His real "crime" may have been talking to reporters for CBS-TV. Ironically, long before Clifford showed up, Proctor was writing anonymous letters to the NASA inspector general reporting incidences of fraud and mismanagement and asking for an investigation.

Of the thirteen individuals who were ultimately fingered in Lightning Strike, Dale Brown was the only one who didn't cop a plea. Brown's rich uncle in New Jersey hired Dick DeGuerin, one of the few lawyers in Houston willing and able to challenge the sting. Once DeGuerin signed on, the government reduced the number of felony charges against Brown from twenty-one to one. The only charge they had any chance of proving was the $500 bribe to the man from Tobyhanna.

DeGuerin's defense was that his client had been entrapped. "If I show enticement on the part of the government," the lawyer argued, "then the government has the burden of proving that Brown was willing to commit a similar crime before being enticed by the government. If the enticement is great enough, then predisposition is not a factor." The judge didn't buy that argument. An appeals court might have, but the point became moot. The jury reported itself deadlocked, and a mistrial was declared. After interviewing the jurors, the government decided to drop the charge against Brown.

Lightning Strike accomplished several things, all of them negative. A brigade of federal agents worked twenty-one months and spent millions of dollars to trap such desperadoes as Jackson, Brown, and Proctor. Meanwhile, if there really were topflight executives indulging in fraud and corruption (as Proctor had tried to warn), they were free to try again. The sting did prove that the space center had problems in its Life Sciences Division. The FBI was able to bypass the procurement system and run its lithotripter proposal through—not just once but three times. Carolyn Huntoon (who refused to be interviewed for this article) has said that she rejected the proposal three times. Nevertheless, she lost her job as director of the space center in 1995. Reportedly a friend of the Clintons, she became NASA's representative at the Office of Science and Technology in Washington, D.C.

Hal Francis resigned from the FBI, embittered by what he believed was a political decision to halt the sting prematurely. Lightning Strike ended its covert phase in December 1993, a time when a major scandal could have seriously damaged the space center's attempt to fund the U.S.-Russian space station. Some FBI agents believe that a high-ranking politician with a vested interest in seeing the space center funded called the U.S. attorney and suggested in strong language that "enough is enough." Art Schultz, former head of the FBI's government fraud squad, says that the U.S. attorney's office lied to the FBI on several key points, including a promise to prosecute two corporations. Instead, GE and Martin Marietta were allowed to pay a $1 million settlement without admitting guilt. "They bought their way out, plain and simple," Schultz told me. "And they'll just write it off to the next government contract."

Finally, Lightning Strike ruined the lives and careers of more than a dozen people and their families. Several defendants required psychiatric care, at least two contemplated suicide, and Dale Brown suffered a heart infection that eventually proved fatal. All of them told me that they felt betrayed by a government that they had served for years, and all were barred from doing future government contract work. As confessed felons, they can't vote or own firearms. Some served probation and house arrest. Those who didn't retire were forced to accept lesser jobs. Neal Jackson eventually landed a job as a pilot for American International Airways. Carter Alexander, who has a Ph.D. in physiology and was once a Distinguished Professor at the Air Force Academy, got a job teaching science at Floresville High School.

Once the ordeal was over, a group of the defendants agreed to meet with me at DeGuerin's law office, even though the terms of their probation made it unlawful for them to gather in the same place. This was the first time they had seen each other face to face since the sting. One by one they stood and gave their names and a brief account of their "crime." A few took this opportunity to apologize to fellow aerospace professionals for ratting on them. All of them regretted that they had not demanded a jury trial. If they had exercised this basic right, they could have at least appealed. But having confessed to a crime, there was nothing to appeal. The despair in their eyes made it clear that they understood the ugly lesson of this entire affair—that the decision had been out of their hands from the beginning.

"Once the FBI has you in their sights, you're finished," one of them observed, and the others nodded in agreement, almost before the words left his lips. "Even if you could beat the rap, you can't beat the ride."

Touch Me, Feel Me, Heal Me! Exposing Psychic Surgery, or the Case of the Smoking Panties

DECEMBER 1986

I first heard about psychic surgery from my hairstylist, George Oberg, a chatty, gossipy reservoir of obscure information. George and his friend Robert had undergone treatment from a Filipino psychic surgeon named Angel at a small nondenominational church in North Austin in February 1986. A few weeks had passed, and George was happy to report that the neck and lower back problems he had previously experienced were much improved.

Except for a small amount of pressure when the surgeon's hands penetrated his body, George told me, there had been no pain. There had been some blood; a small scab formed, but it washed right away. The only time George was the least bit apprehensive was on his third visit, when Angel opened his chest wall and began to massage his heart. "I didn't actually see my own heart," George said as he snipped at my hair, "but I saw the opening and some watery-looking blood. I actually saw his hand go through the wall of Robert's stomach. Robert was supposed to be watching my operation too, but he couldn't see anything. Robert is the type who went to see *120 Days of Sodom* and closed his eyes at all the interesting parts."

George had been curious about psychic surgery since reading about it in *Wet*, an off-the-wall humor magazine. He was skeptical at first, but the experience with Angel turned him into a believer. Since faith healing was a fundamentally religious—in this case, Christian—concept and since I had never known George to concern himself much with Christianity, I expressed surprise. "There are a lot of unexplained, miraculous cures in this world," he said, somewhat offended by my attitude. George had no difficulty whatsoever believing that a surgeon could run his hand through a person's body, remove diseased tissue, and leave no trace of an entry wound. "That seems perfectly logical," he said. What was patently illogical, in his view, was space travel. He considered the moon landing to be a fraud of mind-boggling proportions and was convinced that the whole episode was filmed in a television studio.

In the days that followed, I started hearing a good deal about the Filipino faith healer, Angel Domingo, who had been working around Austin, Houston, San Antonio, and Lake Whitney. At least two other Filipino psychic surgeons had worked in Texas fairly recently; this type of faith healing is indigenous to the Philippines, though a few American practitioners of holistic therapy have taken up the trade in the last few years. Austin, I learned, is a mecca of psychic activity—an "energy vortex" where healers, psychics, and other denizens of the Twilight Zone come to recharge their metaphysical batteries.

Thousands and maybe tens of thousands of Texans regularly pay for a variety of psychic therapies, the most exotic of which is psychic surgery, or "bloody operations," as they are called. The operating room is usually in some off-the-beaten-path motel or private residence. The times and places are not advertised; advertising would be an open invitation to legal action. Word is passed along by an informal network of believers.

It didn't take me long to tap into this network. Seek and ye shall find is one of the tenets of the psychic world, and I've found it works for journalists as well. What surprised me was that the network included three of my oldest and closest friends—entrepreneur Segal Fry, Jerry Jeff Walker's wife, Susan, and writer Bud Shrake. I learned that they all had been treated by Angel Domingo last February when the healer did a one-day stint at "Willie World," as they call Willie Nelson's Pedernales Country Club retreat west of Austin.

Of the three, Shrake was the only skeptic. He had asked Angel to treat a blocked colon and had seen a pool of coffee-colored liquid well up between the healer's fingers as Angel removed what appeared to be a piece of hog tripe from Shrake's abdomen. When Shrake returned an hour later for a second treatment, he asked Angel to work on his foot, which had been broken years ago but had never healed properly. "He pulled what looked like a chicken bone out of my left foot," Shrake told me. He experienced no pain, other than the pain of a foot that had been constantly sore for years, nor did he notice any relief. Shrake acknowledged that this was possibly attributable to his lack of faith.

Susan Walker had four sessions with Angel and said that the leg cramps and pain that had been bothering her for eight years became much less intense. Susan had watched while the Filipino worked on a friend's liver. "I saw his hands go to her liver, saw this pulsing organ going around his fingers," she said. Though her husband had gone to another psychic surgeon and had not been helped, Susan was convinced that the concept was valid. "I saw him take that bone out of Shrake's foot. I frigging saw it," she insisted.

Segal Fry was no less convinced. He also suffered from a colon blockage; there was a knot in his lower abdomen that caused constant pain. He had been to a couple of doctors and found no relief, and he had tried alternative forms of treatment, among them a fast of lemon juice, maple syrup, and cayenne pepper. Angel removed something "gristly, nasty, and about the size of a thumb" from Fry's abdomen. "I still have colon problems," Fry told me. "He didn't cure that. But the knot is gone, and the pain hasn't recurred."

Fry had been treated by Angel at an apartment in the West Montrose section of Houston and had invited the healer to bring his show to Willie World, at the request of Willie's daughter Lana and other members of Willie's entourage. Angel accepted, apparently because one of his Texas contacts assured him that Willie Nelson was a famous entertainer who would probably want to take part in the healer's miraculous work.

Three months later Angel had again set up headquarters in a rented condominium at Willie World. He worked only two days, but at each session he treated between 150 and 200 patients, most of whom journeyed from Austin for the day. An operation takes only three to four minutes, and Angel treated two patients at a time. There was no set fee for the healer's services — as in the case of advertising, the collecting of fees could invite unpleasant encounters with the law — but patients were encouraged to deposit "love offerings" in a collection box just inside the door of the treatment room. The suggested offering was $30, and it was collected on each visit. Most of the patients made at least two visits to the treatment room, and some made four or five. One member of Willie's staff estimated that the daily take exceeded $5,000.

Angel's presence at Willie World sparked some serious debate among the musicians, promoters, and showbiz-fringe players who congregated there. One musician observed that inserting a hand through a stomach wall seemed contrary to the laws of physics. "What the hell do you know about physics?" someone asked, and the musician said, "I'm not saying you can't run your hand through someone's stomach, just that it takes a lot more velocity." Tom Gresham, a concert promoter from Austin, wasn't impressed. "This is piddling stuff," he said. "There are these two guys in

Vegas that make an elephant disappear, and they do it every night." The group members asked each other: "What do you think this psychic healing stuff is all about?" About $30 a minute, they decided. Even Lana Nelson and the country club staff members sympathetic to the healer were not altogether sure that the bloody operations were real. Angel had removed a two-inch piece of gristly tissue from Lana's stomach, and there had been a good deal of blood, some of which stained her panties. She had thought about having the stains analyzed. Some of the staffers were beginning to resent the healer and the assistants. Golf pro Larry Trader complained that the Twilight Zoners who came to see Angel felt no constraint about wandering aimlessly around the golf course; he kept chasing middle-aged housewives out of the club's sand traps. One of Angel's Austin contacts, a doctor of nutritional science named James Marlin Ebert, failed to endear himself to Willie World regulars, who thought he was pompous and overbearing. The staffers suspected that Ebert had convinced Angel that his main purpose in coming to Willie World was to cure Julio Iglesias' good friend Willie. Angel was not an educated man, but even in the mountains of the Philippines they recognized the names of Julio and Willie. Unfortunately, Willie was seldom around, so Angel didn't get to treat a single celebrity.

It became clear that the presence of the strange Filipino was dividing Willie's camp. Those who had faith stopped talking to those who did not. The believers thought that the nonbelievers were infidels, and the nonbelievers looked on the believers as kooks. After a while no one dared mention the subject of psychic surgery.

On a Sunday morning in late April, the last day that Angel was in town, I drove out to Willie World with a friend, Tom Athey, to join the horde of true believers in condo number 10. We sat around in our robes, looking a little sheepish and waiting to be called to the treatment room upstairs. We could clearly hear Angel's voice, praying or communicating with his patients. "Does it hurt?" he asked. "Can you stand the pain?" A girl squealed, or maybe it was a high giggle. Angel started to sing "How Great Thou Art." I looked at Tom, expecting to see his eyes roll, but my friend sat straight faced and silent.

Tom had become intrigued with psychic surgery ten years ago, when a healer helped a friend who had been seriously injured in a parachute jump. He had read numerous books on metaphysics and was comfortable with the jargon of the Twilight Zoners—terms like "chakra" and "karma" dropped smoothly from his lips. We had made appointments for two morning sessions, two hours apart. A woman from a group called the Light Association, which acted as a booking agent for the healer, advised us that we would need a minimum of two sessions and that recovery time of at least an hour between treatments was essential. "You'll be receiving so much energy your body can't take it all at once," she said. She also warned that Angel didn't do cosmetic work, though I couldn't conceive of anyone coming here expecting cosmetic improvements.

About twenty people were waiting when we arrived, and more filtered in and out all morning. At least half were older women who looked as though they had read a lot of books by Edgar Cayce, but some were young, holistic, New Age women with wholesome faces and startled eyes. I'd seen one of them recently at Austin's Whole Foods Market. There was a handful of men too, including a bearded, bald-headed young man in a Japanese bathrobe who was so weak that two women had to assist him to the sofa. Judging from the red blotches on his thighs, he had undergone chemotherapy recently. As the patients arrived they were directed to undress in the laundry room. One young woman who had forgotten to bring a robe was given a blanket.

A pretty, overweight woman named Jann Weiss Peterson checked our names with her master list and had us read and sign a disclaimer saying that the treatment we were to receive was religious rather than medical and that the healer—the "minister"—made no promises. Jann is the founder and spiritual commander of the Planetary Light Association. She asked us to form a circle and hold hands while she said a nondenominational prayer emphasizing peace, love, and faith. While Jann prayed, I studied the copies of ordination documents that were tacked to the wall behind the reception table. They were from the Lumerian Light Center and Our Church of the Garden, and were made out in the names of Angel Estaco Domingo and Dr. Star Johnson. Star Johnson, I learned, lived in San Antonio and acted as Angel's surgical assistant. Upstairs, Angel was singing "Spanish Eyes."

The waiting made me uneasy. I felt like a trespasser. Though I vowed to approach this experience with an open mind, everything I saw and heard eroded that vow. Clients in the waiting room avoided eye contact or, worse, gave such all-knowing stares that I wondered if I had remembered to put on clean underwear. They spoke in whispers, those who spoke at all, and many appeared to be meditating or praying or both. A tall silver-haired Hispanic wearing a VA hospital robe had cancer and had been to Angel a dozen times. He sat rigidly in a folding chair, his vacant eyes fixed on the fireplace as his wife and teenage daughter comforted him. I knew he didn't have long to live. Whatever Angel did or didn't do for this poor fellow, at least the experience couldn't damage him. But that wasn't true for many in the room.

Faith wasn't my problem—I'm a Christian, and I pray daily for miracles, some of which come about. I profess little understanding of cosmic forces, and my life is riddled with questions for which I assume there are no answers. I fully believe that faith can heal or, for that matter, move mountains. So can laughter. Former *Saturday Review* editor Norman Cousins made a convincing case that he cured his own crippling ailment by watching Marx Brothers movies. But sitting in this room, looking at the dreamy, innocent countenances around me, knowing that most of their wisdom came from reading tarot cards and casting the I Ching, I knew theirs was a faith I would never obtain. I was already having serious doubts that this psalm-singing Filipino hillbilly could cure hiccups, much less cancer. As Angel burst into a rousing chorus of "Beer Barrel Polka" even the hardiest of the believers and wackiest of the zonies were forced to smile.

Angel was a stocky little man with greasy black hair and baggy, weathered face. He wore a flowery short-sleeved shirt with the tail out, like a Tijuana cab driver. His assistant, Star Johnson, a tall woman with brown hair, watched closely as I deposited a ten and a twenty in the box of "love offerings." In a coolly efficient voice she commanded me to strip to my shorts and lie on the table. I caught a glimpse of the hospital robe folded away in the corner and realized that the naked body on the other table was the Hispanic veteran I had seen downstairs.

Another assistant, an elderly woman with a kindly smile, read a card I had filled out earlier and told Angel, "This brother has some kidney damage as a result of high blood pressure. Do you want me to do a scan?" Angel answered that he did, and she passed a small towel over my body. Then Angel held the towel to light as though reading an x-ray and said, "Blockage!"

As his assistants rubbed my chest and stomach with an aromatic balm, Angel directed me to face the window—the "light"—while he prayed for my recovery. I watched closely as he plopped a moist piece of cotton onto my belly, applying pressure with the fingers of his left hand. The fingers of his right hand fidgeted and probed, until one finger seemed to stab into my flesh and vanish for maybe two seconds. I didn't see any blood—he blocked my view with his stationary hand—and the next thing I saw was a small, stringy piece of gristle which he exhibited for my brief inspection before tossing it into the trash can behind the table. "See?" he said. "Blockage. No more bad blood."

Tom and I sat on a rock wall outside the condominiums after our sessions, discussing whether to blow another $30 on a second round. Tom's experience had been more disheartening than mine, because he had expected so much. Nevertheless, we went back for a second treatment. It was more of the same. Angel said more prayers, sang more songs, and extracted more gray meat from our bodies. Neither of us saw any blood. It wasn't even good sleight of hand. I didn't feel energized—I felt depressed and a little stupid.

When I called Tom five days later, he told me his throat had been sore all week. "I blame it on Angel," he said. "What a charlatan!"

"Have you changed your mind about psychic surgery?"

"No, I haven't," Tom said. "I still believe there are authentic psychic surgeons around."

"Maybe," I told him. "Either way, I intend to get to the bottom of this psychic surgeon stuff."

N inety percent of all psychic surgery is fake." That's the conclusion of Arsenia dela Cruz, daughter of the legendary Filipino healer Eleuterio Terte. Her father's bloody operations were the real article, she swore— as are her own—but most healers are mere sleight-of-hand artists with nylon blood bags hidden between the palm and the thumb. Genuine psychic operations, she said, require tremendous amounts of magnetic power. Any healer who pretends to perform large numbers of operations in quick succession is therefore a proven fraud; so says the daughter of Terte, the man who in 1925 came down from the holy mountains to perform the civilized world's first bloody operation.

Nearly every psychic surgeon in the Philippines claims to be related, directly or indirectly, to Terte, and hence to each other. Their methods and beliefs are usually self-taught, and their self-righteousness infamous. Though they all started life as Roman Catholics, their theologies have evolved into imprecise mixtures of Hinduism, Buddhism, voodooism, and maybe some other isms yet to be identified. Those who have visited Texas have definitely been exposed to zonieism, for example.

Some healers live aesthetic, saintly lives, but many raise hell at every opportunity. They get hangovers like everyone else. Their techniques are as varied as their personalities—some administer psychic injections from invisible syringes, some use spiritual x-rays, some even heal by long distance. A few limit their treatment to spiritual or magnetic messages—laying on of hands—but most accede to the wishes of the public, which seems to demand the so-called bloody operations.

"Angel gives people what they want, the same as Willie," said James Ebert, the Austin therapist who had accompanied Angel to Willie World. "He performs a service, like any other businessman. I doubt Angel could even tell you how he does what he does. He doesn't have the time or the intellectual inclination to analyze it."

Education and training inhibit faith healers. None of them study anatomy, or have even a mild curiosity about modern techniques of sterilization or anesthesiology. The material that they appear to remove from their patients' bodies is merely the "manifestation" of an illness, Ebert informed me. The gunk that was removed in the operations that I saw looked like human or animal tissue, but in rural areas of the Philippines it is common for psychic surgeons to remove rusty nails, pieces of wire, or bloody palm leaves. The healers claim to be instruments of God: It is the Holy Spirit that diagnoses and cures. Almost all of them agree that the purpose of bloody operations is to help the patient have faith. "If you can heal a patient with a trick," says dela Cruz, "the trick becomes legitimate."

There are about fifty practicing healers in the Philippines, and less than a dozen travel outside their country—usually under the sponsorship of groups like the Planetary Light Association or individuals like James Ebert. "People are literally throwing money at the healers," says Ebert, who practices what he describes as holistic rejuvenation. When I visited him a few days after my experience with Angel, Ebert was making plans for Angel's return to Austin in early June. He also books guided tours to the Philippines. His main business, Ebert made clear, is healing. "I do things for people, as opposed to to people, as is done by the medical establishment," he said, an enigmatic smile creeping across his pale, slender face. The services listed in his brochure include "bodywork," health and nutritional counseling, therapeutic massage, and spiritual healing. Ebert's "doctorate" comes from the Life College of Science, a correspondence school that operates out of a warehouse in South Austin.

Ebert had yet to perform an unassisted bloody operation, but it was only a matter of time. He confided that he has been personally tapped for ordination by one of the best-known healers in the Philippines, the man reputed to have been Ferdinand Marcos's private psychic surgeon. This illustrious psychic healer, whom I will call R., used to work out of Dallas until a couple of years ago, when the cops raided a house and took R. away in handcuffs. He was never formally charged, but the experience was so unnerving that he hasn't been back to this state since. These days Texans who desire R.'s services must travel to resort spas in Mexico.

Twilight Zoners understand the marketing potential of bloody operations. Nevertheless, many find it difficult to deal honestly with its gory particulars. They prefer to call the greasy gunk that the healers pretend to extract from their clients' bodies "congealed energy." Zonies are big on words like "energy" and "vibrations." Scientific tests of congealed energy are futile, I was informed, because the stuff will only dematerialize. I made a note to myself: "Get some of that gunk . . . have it analyzed."

Zonies love to bash the American Medical Association and indict Western culture for being too literal minded, yet their driving passion is an attempt to explain the unexplainable—to reduce metaphysics, you might say, to a science. Jann Peterson's husband, Art, an Austin chiropractor, told me that a healer's ability to penetrate a patient's skin without leaving a mark depends on the speed of the vibration of the electrons. "If you speed up the vibrations of the electrons in this table top," he said, rapping his knuckles on the surface, "you could stick your hand through it."

Zonies can explain away every doubt. The reason their number is growing exponentially, something they take as a given, is explained by "The One Hundredth Monkey Theory." It goes like this: a monkey discovers that yams taste better washed, and by the time this piece of information has been discovered by one hundred monkeys everyone is in on it. "The White Crow Theory" is the zonies' handy way of shifting the burden of proof to the nonbeliever—if you've never seen a white crow, how can you be sure one doesn't exist? One of the missions of the Planetary Light Association is to raise the vibrations of the Earth in preparation for its arrival into the Age of Aquarius, which I'm informed is scheduled to start any day now.

Another of the association's missions is to sell T-shirts, bumper stickers, "Be Your Light" buttons, mugs, and tapes in which a spirit named Anoah advises the heartsick and weary. Anoah, I was interested to learn, borrows the voice of Jann Weiss Peterson when he needs to speak. Jann, a professional medium or channel, is the only one who is in contact with the great Anoah—an old man with white hair and white robe who floats along, carrying a book titled succinctly "Wisdom." Another spirit who also uses the voice box of Jann Peterson is Elaina, a sort of spiritual Joan Rivers, who refers to Anoah as "the Big Cheese." Elaina is always trying to get the archangel Jeremiah to loosen up and tell a few jokes, but being unfamiliar with the ways of mortals, Jeremiah finds this difficult. Jann's more recent visitors are a group of extraterrestrials from the Octurian Federation. The Octurian Federation can be reached by traveling to the belt of Orion and hanging a left. Anoah and the whole gang are available on tape for $4 a copy, or can be heard live (so to speak) during a $40, half-hour personal counseling session with Jann herself.

Though I don't usually advertise the fact, I too possess psychic powers. I discovered these powers in a tough beer joint on Fort Worth's North Side, where to my astonishment I convinced four housewives who had stopped off for an afternoon cocktail that I could read nipples.

"That's right," I told them, my confidence boosted by numerous shots of tequila, "I said nipples! Laugh if you will, but it's a God-given gift, and I'd sooner burn in hell than abuse it." Before long, one of the housewives had produced a bare breast for my inspection. I had drunk enough by this time to really believe I could do it. As I studied the ripples and ridges of her pink nipple, careful to make any contact appear purely therapeutic, a voice I hardly recognized began to speak. The voice told the woman: "You are extremely intelligent and sensitive, but your husband doesn't understand you. But you alone realize that by following your instincts, you can discover your true self, the inner you, and with that find peace of mind."

I could tell from her reaction—from all their reactions—that I was on the right track. Two of the others were already unbuttoning their blouses.

I was thinking of the nipple-reading episode as I flew to Mazatlán, Mexico, to watch the miraculous cures of R. Those housewives had trusted me because we were in a barroom rather than carnival tent, and because I seemingly had nothing to gain by deception. The rest was easy. People expect to see tricks at magic shows—trying to spot the deception is half the fun—but those who visit healers come with some sort of belief or at least hope. In a nation where as many believe in lucky numbers as believe in the theory of evolution, this isn't surprising. There were a lot of questions I wanted to ask R., if indeed I got to see him at all. I had the gnawing feeling that his handlers were getting suspicious of my motives.

For the first two and a half days that I was in Mazatlán, R. managed to avoid me. Twice he agreed to interviews, and twice he failed to show up. "He's very paranoid," said Jann Peterson, who had been working with him for two years. "Just detecting a strange energy in a room causes him to freak out." R. had not forgotten what had happened in Dallas. A similar raid in Puerto Vallarta had disrupted the powers of another healer of R.'s acquaintance. Being led off in handcuffs must play hell with concentration. I told Jann that my purpose was to write about R., not arrest him. As far as I could tell, no laws were being broken anyway. Let the buyer beware. Jann's own psychic vibrations told her that I was okay. "If he agrees to give you an interview, will you agree not to use his name?" she asked. I agreed—hence my use of the letter R.

Jann was one of three psychics on R.'s staff in Mazatlán. The others were an astrologer from Connecticut named Lynn Files, and Belle Shiplett, the elderly woman with the kindly smile whom I had seen assisting Angel at Willie World. Late one afternoon, after R. had again failed to keep an appointment, I provoked the three women of his staff into a discussion of reincarnation. All zonies have experiences with reincarnation, or past-life regression, as some call it. Jann told us of her life as a Mayan priest in the seaside city of Tulum. Belle had been the son of an Indian chief in Texas and had witnessed her own funeral near Fredericksburg. Though it was a warm tropical night in Mazatlán, I could see goose bumps rippling up her arms as Belle told the story. Lynn was reproachful and of the opinion that Jann took herself too seriously. "Let's face it," Lynn told the other women, "a lot of people remember being Indian princesses, but there's only so many Indian princesses to go around." Nevertheless, I coaxed Lynn into admitting her belief that she had been a young German soldier killed in the early days of World War II. Despite Lynn's reproach, Jann took another turn. Speaking in an extremely animated, almost agitated voice (the voice of Elaina, I imagine), she told of her experiences hiding Baby Jesus from authorities in Cairo. "I seem to remember changing his diapers," she said serenely.

It was a Sunday, my last full day in Mazatlán, when I finally got to meet R. He was younger than Angel (who is a relative by marriage) and smaller—he looked like a jockey. His assistant healer, Dodo, looked like a Filipino bantamweight, bandy-legged and puffy-eyed. Dodo was much more relaxed and cheerful than R., and he offered all of us, including a woman dying of cancer, a Filipino cigarette. The brand name was Hope. A large room with a balcony overlooking the ocean had been chosen as the treatment place. Sheets of clear plastic were spread over two beds—like Angel, R. treated two patients at a time. Unlike Angel, love offerings weren't good enough. It was a straight cash deal, $80 U.S. for two sessions—no pesos, por favor! Ten patients awaited treatment this particular morning, including Belle, who would also be assisting.

Except for me and a young couple from Houston, all the patients were New Yorkers. Grace, a woman with frightened eyes, was dying of cancer. Nick, her son, a pious young man who walked with his hands clasped and talked almost exclusively of faith, remained constantly at her side. During orientation, Nick asked Dodo, "Do you believe that walking on fire increases faith?" Dodo looked as though someone had dropped a cobra in his lap. "Walk on fire?" he said incredulously. "Me?" Lynn tried to clarify the question for the Filipino. "He means his own faith," she explained to Dodo, pointing out that fire walking was popular among the zonies of the East Coast. "I happen to believe there is no limit to faith," Nick added. "No, no," Dodo said, waving his hands furiously. "No walk on fire! Burn feet!"

R. had much quicker hands than Angel; he put on a good show. I asked him to remove a small knot just above my wrist, what my doctor in Austin had called a ganglion. According to a folk remedy, if a ganglion is struck with sufficient enthusiasm by a family Bible, the blow will cause the knot to vanish. Compared with curing cancer and blocked colons, removing a ganglion seemed the simplest task in the Christian world.

R. rubbed oil on the knot, then shook his head—he didn't want any part of an affliction that would still be there when he was finished. Instead, he fluttered his hands in the area above my kidneys and produced a piece of gray meat. For the second time in less than a month, my high blood pressure had been cured, or so I was asked to believe.

As soon as my treatment was complete, Jann and Lynn tried to hustle me out of the room, but I resisted. R. must have sensed that I was ready to make a scene. Finally, the healer nodded that it was okay for me to watch as he worked on Belle. I knew by now that I wouldn't get an interview, but this was even better. In the dim light, I watched R.'s hands. His left pressed into the white flesh of Belle's abdomen, creating a small pocket, and his right flitted about, distracting attention. Suddenly, the pocket in Belle's abdomen filled with dark fluid, and just as suddenly R. produced several slivers of gristle. "You see?" he said, dangling the meat just out of my reach. The operation had taken about five seconds. Dodo was already cleaning away the mess. There was no trace of an entry wound on Belle's stomach. "Amazing," I said dryly. The truth was, if R. had tried to pass off this act on a carnival midway in, say, Wichita Falls, he'd be leaving town on a rail, covered not with glory but with tar and feathers.

Flying home to Austin, I experienced again the uneasy guilt of a trespasser. As fraudulent as I knew the bloody operations to be, the healing was another matter. Maybe it took displays of blood to trigger faith in certain people. On the other hand, I had sensed that beneath the conditioned reflex of faith, there was a deeper despair, a mute surrender to the inevitable. If the believers had indeed succeeded in damming up their fears and anxieties, it wouldn't take much to break the dam. I just hated to be the one to do it. Nevertheless, as a journalist my duty seemed clear: I had to get a piece of that "congealed energy" and have it analyzed.

I stopped off at the laboratory of the Austin Pathology Associates, where a doctor friend agreed to help my quest. He gave me a bottle of formaldehyde in which to preserve the suspect tissue. Then I telephoned James Ebert and made an appointment to see Angel, who was working that week out of a home in South Austin. I wasn't sure how the zonies would react when I made my play for the meat, so just in case, I took along two big friends, Bud Shrake and Fletcher Boone, owner of an Austin restaurant called the Raw Deal.

Star Johnson was the first to detect trouble. I was stretched out on the table, nearly naked, and Angel was humming and producing small pieces of gunk from the area of my kidneys, depositing them on my stomach. When I grabbed the gunk Star Johnson grabbed my fist, and we wrestled for control. Angel began to scream, "You'll destroy my power. All the thousands of people I have healed . . . Give it back. . . . I'll pray for you. . . . I'll heal you." All the color had drained from Ebert's face. "You're playing with fire," he warned me. "This is like giving a loaded .45-caliber pistol to a 4-year-old girl."

All hell had broken loose in the waiting room too. The woman at the reception desk covered her head with her arms and cried out, "Cover yourself with the white light . . . surround yourself with light before it's too late."

Ebert was waiting for me by the front door, but I knew he wasn't going to make any move to stop me. Instead, he said, "You'll regret what you did the rest of your life. It will follow you to your grave. It will haunt your karma."

As I raced out the door, I could hear Angel's voice at the back of the house, shouting: "Bullshit! This is bullshit!"

My fist was clenched so tightly around the piece of gristle that I wasn't even sure that I had gotten away with the evidence. But I had—it was a piece about the size of a pencil eraser. On the way to the laboratory, Shrake and Boone told me that as soon as I was out the door, Angel complained of a sudden headache, grabbed the cash box, and split. "But he did give me my money back," said Boone with a smile. I heard later on that Angel left town the same day.

The piece of meat didn't dematerialize, as had been predicted, but it might as well have. The lab report was inconclusive. The meat was a piece of connective tissue, but the preservative in which it had been stored prevented scientists from determining if it was of human origin.

I had about given up hope of cracking the case when Shrake called a week later. While playing golf at Willie World, he had learned of new and dramatic evidence—the panties that Lana Nelson had worn the day that Angel opened up her lower abdomen. She had been saving them for four months, meaning to have the stains analyzed. "Lana has graciously agreed to donate her panties to your investigation," Shrake told me. I sent the panties by messenger to the Bexar County Regional Crime Lab in San Antonio. The stain did turn out to be blood—bovine blood, apparently diluted with water. Not that it will make any difference to the believers, but I had bovine ranked third on my list of suspect tissue, behind chicken and goat, with cat moving up fast.

When I telephoned the news to Shrake, he said, "I guess you knew all along it would turn out this way, eh, inspector?"

"That is correct," I told him. "Henceforth, this caper will be known as 'The Case of the Smoking Panties.' "

The Bad Brother |

An EMS vehicle and units from the Hutchins Police Department and the sheriff's patrol clogged the street and blocked the drive in front of the beige brick house on the corner. It was one of those suburban residential streets on the south edge of Dallas County where people move to get away from this sort of trauma, a short block of modest brick and frame homes backing up to a cul-de-sac. Old cars and pickups in various stages of disrepair gave the street a jumbled working-class look, and an uneasy blend of races suggested that nobody lived here too long.

It was late on a hot, clammy afternoon in September 1982, and the neighbors who clustered in the street gawked at the television cameras and talked in whispers. A man in greasy coveralls strained to hear what the two black teenagers were saying to the police. The boys were eighteen and sixteen, large for their ages. Until recently both boys had worn their hair long and curly, but now their heads were shaved to a bare stubble. The younger boy, who had been crying, pointed in the direction of the backyard, where three large and menacing German shepherds strained at their ropes.

The house had been randomly ransacked to make the murder appear to have resulted from a burglar surprised in the act—a chair overturned, the contents of a bottle of bleach sloshed on the floor. Police found a television set in the backyard, and in the bedroom the body of a muscular black man in his early forties, tangled in bloody bedsheets.

A neighbor who worked for the City of Dallas knew the family. There were three boys, he told police, all named Matthew Donald Johnson, which was also the name of the dead man, who was their father. There was a girl named Tina. The two older boys discovered their father's body when they came home from Wilmer Hutchins High School. The 16-year-old ran to the neighbor's home and reported that his father had been shot two times through the head. Strange, but at this point the police had discovered only one bullet hole.

The reporters who bothered to check old files soon learned that Matthew Johnson had been one of the leaders of the radical wing of the Dallas civil rights movement in the sixties. He and a handful of other young black men in South Dallas had made up the local chapter of the Student Nonviolent Coordinating Committee (SNCC), an organization that had an important impact on the course of the nation and a brief, fiery run in Dallas. Despite the name, SNCC led the movement away from nonviolence and toward the ideology of Black Power, and so contributed mightily to the polarized politics of the late sixties and early seventies. In the summer of 1968 Matt Johnson and his brothers in SNCC had staged an impromptu "merchandise raid" on a South Dallas grocery store, and in the summer of the King and Kennedy assassinations and the Chicago convention, that was as close to a riot as Dallas ever got. Still, it seemed strange that a man involved in political matters should meet his end in what appeared to be a low-rent crime of passion.

But when Ernie McMillan, the leader of SNCC in Dallas—and in his own way a man even better known back then than Matt Johnson—read that Johnson had been ignominiously murdered, he wasn't surprised. That was about the way he'd figured Matt would end up. Ernie hadn't seen Matt since they both went to prison. He'd heard that Matt was working as a welder in a shop in South Dallas, but he didn't stay in touch anymore. Prison had done something to all of the SNCC brothers, but especially to Matt. Once he'd served his time he acted as though the black movement had never existed.

When Ernie thought back, it was plain to him that SNCC had never been quite the unified, disciplined organization that it seemed at the time, either to the brothers or to outsiders. Like any small and intense political movement, it had been an amalgam of all things good and bad, of purity and crookedness, idealism and cynicism, planning and scheming, rogues and saints, and all shades in between. When the brothers thought about Matt Johnson dead, they immediately thought: It figures! Matt had never been anything except a troublemaker in the old days, and yet Ernie and the others believed in him, thought of him as a committed radical, a man they might have laid down their lives for, had it come to that. Strange times throw people together in strange ways, and those had certainly been strange times.

Some of the older people in the South Dallas ghetto still remember "the SNCC niggers," as they called themselves, tearing around in Matt Johnson's funky '37 Pontiac or Fred Bell's red convertible, carrying shotguns and wearing tribal dashikis and Afros that bushed out like enormous black auras. They planned to form a self-defense force they would call the *Kaka Tahari*—Swahili for "ready brothers." Matt had brought the name back from California, along with the dashikis, the Afros, the blacker-than-thou lingo, and an obscure guide to black culture called *The Nigger Bible*, written by a friend of his in Los Angeles. Matt's wife, Dorothy Jean, remembered that they were the first couple in Dallas to sport Afros. "People at the barbecue stand used to ask if we were from Africa," she said. Ernie McMillan remembered that Matt was the first one of the brothers to adopt the African tribal regalia—Afro, dashikis, earrings, and conga drums. Quacy Williams, the youngest member of the brotherhood, recalled, "Matt had a gift for manipulating people. He could get a woman or money or anything he wanted with that line of jive. He could go to Highland Park and talk white people out of more money than any of us had ever seen."

The SNCC brothers could frequently be found around places like the Good Luck Drive-Inn on Oakland, passing out recruiting literature and haranguing customers with their bullhorn oratory. Matt was usually the loudest. Though he had no formal education after Madison High School, and probably hadn't read more than ten books in his life, he had the air of wisdom you might expect from a medicine man. Some of the brothers thought of him as their resident philosopher. He had absolute disdain for the whole history and collective wisdom of the black movement in America. Instead, he preached a line of almost mystical hatred of whites that even the blacks didn't understand. "Anything that had gone before didn't count with Matt," recalled Ernie McMillan. "If you wore your hair short or if you didn't wear a beard, you couldn't be trusted. You had to wear a dashiki and an Afro, the bigger the better. If you had a really big Afro, you had leadership quality."

I f Matt was the philosopher, the orator, for the movement, Ernie McMillan was clearly the intellectual. Born to a family of doctors, lawyers, and educators in the area now called Short North Dallas, Ernie had been one of the young followers of Martin Luther King Jr.

Ernie McMillan's great-great-grandmother was a slave in the household of James K. Polk in Tennessee. His great-grandfather was Chavis Lee Partee, one of a family of Huguenots, who married a slave in the McKinley household in Tennessee. Their last child, Chavis Jr., grew up and moved his own family to Dallas, to a community of former slaves near what is now Inwood Road. One of his eight children was Eva Partee, Ernie's mother. Eva married Marion Ernest McMillan, whose father, Walter R. McMillan, was one of the first black doctors in Dallas and the founder of one of the city's first black hospitals, at Hall and State Streets. Marion and Eva had four children. Their only son, Ernie, was born in 1945.

The McMillans and the Partees were among the best-educated, most influential black families in Dallas. Ernie's uncle, Cecil Partee, taught history at Madison and Roosevelt High Schools. Another uncle, Clifton Partee, helped found the Progressive Voters League. Eva McMillan was an organizer and precinct worker at the Hall Street Commissary. The Hall Street precinct, even in the days of the poll tax, had almost 100 percent registration.

"We were a close, tight-knit family," Eva McMillan remembered. "Two or three nights a week we'd have family and friends over to our house for discussion—politics, women's rights, the solar system, whatever. The kids would listen and join in, then we'd give them quizzes."

Ernie recalled, "Our home was a little oasis, a sort of cultural center for me and my friends."

Ernie grew up with some sense of black history and culture but hardly any recognition of the white man's world, though it lay only a few blocks away, in downtown Dallas. "I had heard about the poll tax and the job market and all those things," he told me, "and I could see that we lived a different way because of the color of our skin. I guess I learned about Social Security, the eight-hour day, unions, and Marcus Garvey, but none of it registered. As kids we were spoon-fed Booker T. Washington and George Washington Carver, education in the narrowest sense."

Ernie's mother worked in a laundry and his father worked as a postman, an elevator operator, and sometimes a preacher, though there was very little income connected with the ministry. One Thanksgiving Ernie found a basket of food on the front porch. "I had a sense of outrage, of embarrassment," he remembered. "In school we'd given charity baskets to the less fortunate. Only I didn't think of us that way."

There were books in their home—*The Grapes of Wrath*, *The Black Bourgeoisie*—and music that celebrated black culture and commemorated the tragic suffering of a people—such as Billie Holiday's "Strange Fruit," a 1940 antilynching song. Ernie remembered, too, being restricted to the few black movie houses and to the balcony of the Majestic Theatre downtown, and drinking from water fountains labeled "Colored," though the meaning didn't register at the time. He saw photographs of blacks hanging from trees or lying crumpled and mutilated on the banks of bayous, but these didn't register either until he heard members of his family talking about the lynching of 14-year-old Emmett Till in Mississippi. This was 1955, one year after the Supreme Court ruling outlawing segregation in education.

Something else happened about the same time that was discussed in the homes of the McMillans and the Partees. A black seamstress named Rosa Parks made national headlines by refusing to surrender her seat on a Montgomery city bus. Rosa Parks explained that she was just tired; and the following Monday, outside the Holt Street Church in Montgomery, a young black preacher named Martin Luther King Jr. aroused a crowd of four thousand with a speech in which he observed: "But there comes a time when people get tired."

In the late fifties Ernie's parents separated, and his father moved to Noonan, Georgia. Ernie joined him there after he graduated from high school. He enrolled in Morehouse College, in Atlanta, where families of the most smug, affluent blacks in America sent their sons to learn the consciously arrogant manners long associated with Morehouse men, among whose numbers was counted Martin Luther King Jr. Ernie hated Morehouse from the start. "It was that class thing all over again," he explained. "The college was only a few blocks from the ghetto, but students wouldn't go down there. They felt superior. Who your parents were and what kind of linens you had were the important things."

Later that summer word spread across campus that Martin Luther King Jr. was planning an unannounced visit to invite participation in his march on Washington. Although Malcolm X and other militants condemned the march as another example of blacks toadying to manipulate white interests, the march was a huge success, attracting more than 250,000 people. At the zenith of the event Dr. King delivered his "I Have a Dream" speech. Ernie McMillan couldn't afford a trip to Washington, but he organized a companion demonstration in the small town of Noonan.

When McMillan turned nineteen, his father signed a paper allowing him to become a full-time staff member of SNCC, at a starting salary of $9.64 a week. He went to work in what was considered at the time the lynching capital of America—Southwest Georgia. Counties had names like Terrible Terrell and Bad Baker, collections of mean little rural towns of sharecroppers and field hands existing in tin-roofed shacks along dusty side streets. Ernie learned firsthand about police dogs and clubs and fire hoses pressurized to strip the bark from trees and snap human bones. He knew about working alone, about living from house to house and getting meals wherever he could, and about ways to outwit local sheriffs who equated registering black voters with high treason.

"We were supposed to be nonviolent," Ernie recalled, "but we weren't stupid. We carried shotguns. That nonviolent philosophy scared me more than anything else. SNCC regulated us more than anything the white power structure ever did. They'd search us before a march or demonstration. If you were carrying so much as a pencil—a pencil was considered a dangerous weapon—you weren't allowed to march."

He remembered the leadership of SNCC too. "The leaders would start the march in front of the group—you know, the black preachers or the Andy Young types. When we got close to the fire trucks they'd disappear. The next time you'd see them would be back at the church, only they weren't wet or bloody like the rest of us."

In Georgia, Ernie met almost all the young black leaders of the time —John Lewis, Julian Bond, Andrew Young, Stokely Carmichael, Hosea Williams. Some of them were his friends, and some of them also became disillusioned with SNCC after passage of the Civil Rights Act. A lot of blacks thought the battle ended in 1965, but Ernie knew better. He returned to Dallas and enrolled at the University of Texas at Arlington in the spring of 1965. "After almost two years of fighting racism in the Deep South," he recalled, "it was a shock to come back to Dallas and realize that things were just like I had left them. Nothing had changed. Nobody in the black community was doing anything." By this time Ernie was calling himself a black nationalist, though, strictly speaking, he was not a disciple of Malcolm X, who was an outspoken enemy of Martin Luther King Jr. and the nonviolent program. Compared to other campuses around the country, UT Arlington appeared joltingly sedate, frozen in time. Students called themselves Rebels and celebrated Old South Week, during which the men dressed like Confederate soldiers and the women wore bonnets and layers of crinoline petticoats. Ernie joined a group that, though it was small, attracted so much attention with its protests that the school was eventually forced to abandon its "tradition" and drop the nickname Rebels. Ernie was suspended from school in 1966 for an insufficient grade point average.

Next, Ernie became involved in the Dallas antiwar movement. It never numbered more than a handful of people, but it got a lot of media attention. One volunteer was a former member of Students for a Democratic Society (SDS) and a self-proclaimed Marxist. When the Dallas newspapers exposed this, and Congressman Joe Poole promised an investigation by the dreaded House Un-American Activities Committee, the group scattered like seeds in a gale. "I was alone again," McMillan said. "That's when I seriously thought of forming a SNCC chapter and working with Dallas blacks on black problems."

The conservative Dallas establishment automatically assumed that Ernie McMillan was a subversive, an outside agitator sent to foment revolution. Newspaper accounts sometimes identified him as "the son of an Alabama college professor"; hardly anyone remembered him as the one-time commander of the Booker T. Washington drill team.

Dr. Emmett Conrad, the first black to win election to the Dallas school board, spoke for the establishment when he said, "The majority of the Negro people in Dallas want to bring about change in the same way we have always done it in the past—through discussions with the white leadership and, if necessary, through the courts." The majority of the blacks, in fact, seldom thought of change. Al Lipscomb, who had been a black leader before most of the SNCC members were even born, said, "We'd go downtown with our hats in our hands and talk to the establishment. The establishment would appoint some superspook leader. You'd see the same names on all the boards and commissions—'the more responsible Negroes,' as [Mayor] Erik Jonsson used to call them."

The Dallas police accumulated an impressive file on Ernie McMillan. His mother recalled that unmarked police cars used to cruise their block, especially at night. "We had the only house in Dallas that didn't have to worry about burglars," she laughed. "The scariest times were during the antidraft movement. I'd hear Ernie early in the morning getting ready to go demonstrate, and I'd shake all over. I knew he had to do what he was doing, but I was still his mother. When he'd leave the house the police would trail him and find some excuse to give him a ticket. For a while he gave up driving—started walking. They'd still stop him. They'd give him a ticket for using profanity or something. Every week, two or three times a week, we'd have to go get him out of jail."

The rallying cry of "Black Power" was catching on, even in Dallas. Stokely Carmichael, the new chairman of SNCC, started it by asking at a rally held during a march through Mississippi, "What do you want?" The answer, supplied by Willie Ricks, who had worked with Ernie in Thomasville, Georgia, came back: "Black Power!"

Black Power was condemned by King and the moderates, but it was powerful medicine to the SNCC workers. Carmichael and H. Rap Brown advised a crowd in Cambridge, Maryland, to "burn this town down," and nearly twenty buildings were destroyed. By the summer of 1967 there had been major riots in dozens of cities. The black revolution was a reality, and it was no longer limited to the South.

I n retrospect, it seems remarkable that Dallas remained calm for as long as it did, given what had been happening elsewhere. Every time Bull Connor turned his dogs or his high-pressure hoses on marchers, every time the mayor of Birmingham spoke of "the nigger King," every time George Wallace advised authorities to "knock some heads," every time a church was bombed and millions of Americans watched tiny caskets being paraded across their TV screens, there were new converts to the movement —and the converts grew increasingly militant.

Ernie McMillan formed his SNCC chapter in Dallas in 1967, but it attracted almost no members until the assassination of Martin Luther King Jr. and the aftermath of bloody rioting in April 1968. McMillan appeared on a locally produced television show and declared Dallas to be "the epitome of all racism in this country." In May 1968, a month after the assassination, McMillan appeared at a send-off rally at Fair Park for the Poor People's March on Washington, advising blacks, as Malcolm X had done five years earlier, that the march was a waste of time. "If this country doesn't meet our needs," he warned, "we're just going to have to burn it down and start over." McMillan's reputation as *the* black leader in Dallas was established.

McMillan's television exposure attracted a hard core of new talent to SNCC. Matt Johnson, Quacy Williams, Fred Bell, and Charles Beasley all joined within the next few weeks.

By this time Matt Johnson had served a hitch in the Navy, had gotten married, and was working as a metal cutter for a furniture manufacturer in Los Angeles. Matt's father, whose name was also Matt, operated a small paint and body shop in South Dallas. He had settled there during World War II when a lot of farm families moved to the city looking for work. The senior Matt Johnson was from Freestone County, east of Waco, and his wife was from the adjacent county of Limestone. "We grew up on farms, chopping cotton, picking corn, whatever had to be done," recalled Tinnie Mae Johnson, a small, frail woman. Neither of Matt Junior's parents had much education; they probably had never heard of racism and certainly never dreamed of demonstrating against it. Matt Junior was a husky, aggressive kid who played football at Madison but otherwise was a student of no distinction. He joined the Navy after high school, and when he was discharged he married Dorothy Jean and moved to California. "When he come back from California in '68," his mother remembered, "he had changed. He had all that long hair and talked in some funny way where we couldn't hardly understand him. My husband thought for a while he was off his rocker, but I guess it was just a generation thing."

Quacy Williams grew up a few blocks from the O.K. Supermarket— a supermarket that would go down in history as the scene of the beginning of the end of the Dallas SNCC chapter. Quacy remembered that they made the best barbecued bologna sandwiches in town. Quacy was a street kid in Dallas, but he spent a lot of time with his grandmother in East Texas. In 1966 he dropped out of Lincoln High and joined the Marines. Less than two years later he was back in South Dallas, broke and unemployed. "I remember I was waking up one Thanksgiving morning in a motel on Oakland with this whore, after eating reds and drinking wine the night before, wondering if this was all there was to my life," he told me. He got a job as a butcher's assistant, and a few months later he happened to look out the window of a city bus and saw "this bunch of niggers in Afros and dashikis picketing O.K." He jumped off the bus and joined them. That's the way things happened in those days in the South Dallas ghetto.

Fred Bell, who was usually identified as McMillan's bodyguard, was a tall, athletic, and intelligent man, a prelaw student and an orator. As SNCC's director of defense, he was absorbed by military discipline and machismo.

Charles Beasley, called Foots because of his large feet, was quiet and self-contained, yet physically intimidating. He harbored as strong a hatred for the white man and his system as anyone in the movement.

Viewed through the eyes of the old-guard Dallas establishment, SNCC must have looked like the apocalypse unchained. But it was actually never more than an alliance of young blacks with vague ideologies and a notion that the system had to be changed.

"We had no real structure," Ernie McMillan recalled. "We operated on the run. Whatever had to be done had to be done now. Everyone had his own idea. One of us stressed the community patrol, the need to arm, the military training. Matt had a mystic philosophy of manhood and self-defense. The black man was absolute king—that may have been the only thing we agreed on. We weren't very strong on women's rights."

"Ernie and Matt were usually at odds," recalled Quacy Williams. "Except when we were actually doing something—then they were together. Ernie was completely dedicated to the movement, to the brothers and sisters. Matt was a hell of a dude, but he was inflexible. Some of the things we did, I shake just thinking about it now—seven or eight of us in a car with shotguns and bandoliers! Matt got his hands on some money and went out and bought what he called our new organizational car—a two-seat Corvette!"

Some of Dallas's old-time black leaders admired the SNCC bunch. "They fascinated me," admitted Al Lipscomb. "I helped them picket, raise money, sit in at welfare. They made things happen." Other blacks thought they were hotheads, or worse. They didn't have jobs, and they were a threat to the jobs of those who did. They dressed like freaks and probably used drugs. Some of them were thieves and bullies.

During the spring and early summer of 1968 the SNCC leaders were being hauled into jail regularly on a variety of charges. McMillan was arrested for violating an antinoise ordinance by using a sound truck to promote a political candidate. McMillan and Bell were arrested for allegedly threatening the owner of a black security service who refused to join SNCC and attempted to run them away from the Good Luck Drive-Inn. Johnson was arrested for theft—specifically, theft of a security guard's side arm—after he tried to snatch the guard's gun from its holster. None of the charges amounted to anything, but it wasn't unusual for the SNCC people to spend four or five days in jail, usually in an isolated psychiatric cell. "Every time they raised a little money," Eva McMillan recalled, "they'd have to spend it on bail and lawyers." These nagging misdemeanor charges wouldn't get the SNCC people off the streets, but the *Times Herald* reported that an unidentified assistant DA hoped to find reasons to file felony charges and put them away for ten years.

New members were proving hard to come by, and so were new ideas. The brothers started a newspaper—a pamphlet, really—called *Black Disciple*. It featured articles with such titles as "The Awareness of Being Black" and "They Call Us Communist." Although Quacy's marine service hadn't taken him anywhere near Vietnam, he wrote a regular "letter" from the combat zone. Matt Johnson contributed such articles as "Nigger—Open Your Eyes and See!"

During one of his trips to Atlanta, Ernie McMillan ran across the strategy of organizing an economic boycott. The idea was to target a business or chain of businesses that was ripping off blacks and apply the squeeze through the use of tactics like picketing, harassment, and "basket boycotts," in which protesters would fill shopping baskets, then claim to have forgotten their money. The Dallas SNCC workers targeted the O.K. Supermarket chain, eleven small stores, ten of which were in South Dallas. They complained that the stores operated under poor sanitary conditions, employed blacks at a pay scale lower than that for similar jobs in other parts of the city, and sold inferior produce at prices 15 to 20 percent higher than fair market value. The O.K. at Oakland and Pine had a reputation for raising prices on the day welfare checks arrived. "Most of the people on welfare were old and didn't have transportation," Eva McMillan said. "They didn't have any choice but to shop at O.K. The only time I ever went in there I came home with a dozen rotten eggs."

The boycott appeared to be succeeding. Word got out that the absentee owners were willing to sell, and Ernie attempted to set up a black economic development corporation to buy the chain. "We saw this as a great victory," he recalled. "The chain wouldn't be owned by SNCC; it would be owned by the community. We weren't talking about extortion, we were talking about actually changing ownership. We didn't realize it at the time, but we'd become a genuine threat to the business community." Even so, some of the SNCC leaders thought the strategy was too slow, too passive, and they demanded more aggressive and immediate action.

On the evening of July 1, 1968, thirty to forty blacks attended a meeting at the Hope Presbyterian Church and decided to descend on the store at Oakland and Pine and carry out a giant basket boycott. They were cautioned against violence and vandalism, and all carried money in case anything was broken.

What happened at the store was described by one lawyer as being "like the food-fight scene in *Animal House*." Someone left a freezer door open, and someone dropped a bottle of milk. Matt Johnson smashed a watermelon on the floor. Ernie McMillan smashed some eggs and crushed some tomatoes. The whole thing was over in a couple of minutes, but the floor of the market was littered with broken glass, eggs, fruit, sugar, flour, and assorted condiments. The ruined merchandise was valued at between $143 and $211. Johnson and several others offered to pay, but the manager apparently refused to accept the money. "We went back to SNCC headquarters feeling very good about the boycott," McMillan said. "The manager didn't seem upset. We even went back later that night and bought some beer. It never occurred to us that we had committed a criminal act. We saw ourselves as the vanguard of the community, defending our people against the bloodsuckers."

The following day McMillan and Johnson were singled out for prosecution and arrested on charges of destruction of private property valued at more than $50—a felony punishable by up to twenty years.

After considerable shuffling of dockets, the case against the two SNCC leaders ended up in the court of the district judge James Zimmerman, a former Dallas County prosecutor who had played a minor role in the Jack Ruby trial. Zimmerman had been appointed to the bench following the death of the Ruby trial judge, Joe B. Brown, and had just won the Democratic primary; however, he faced stiff opposition in the November general election. Both defense attorneys charged that Zimmerman rushed the proceedings to trial because he needed a "high-profile" case to assure his election, a charge that Zimmerman denied.

When I interviewed him fifteen years later, Zimmerman didn't recall that the atmosphere in Dallas was "particularly supercharged" that summer. But it was. The entire nation was virtually on red alert for a potential race war. A casual glance at the headlines of Dallas's two dailies reveals the atmosphere: [CHICAGO] FOOD STORE STORMED BY NEGROES . . . DETROIT GAINS NEW REALISM LACED WITH FEAR, LETHARGY . . . NEGROES IN MIAMI GO ON RAMPAGE . . . NEGROES STAGE MARCH ON L.A. POLICE STATION . . . LOUISVILLE AREA LOOTED: POLICE PELTED . . . TEXAS GUARDSMEN READY 'IF' . . .

An AP survey showed that since the bloody Newark and Detroit riots of the previous summer police had been stockpiling armored vehicles, helicopters, and high-powered rifles and were sending undercover agents into the slums and recruiting civilians as ready reserves. The Dallas Bar Association had a contingency plan whereby its members would be pressed into service as judges and prosecutors in the event of big trouble.

The Dallas City Council, without bothering to consult a single black leader, passed a sweeping antiriot ordinance. The Dallas establishment appeared genuinely surprised by the sharp reaction from blacks. The Reverend O. H. Lakey called the ordinance "a blatant act of tyranny," and the *Times Herald* remarked in an astonishingly naive editorial that it was "most difficult to understand how they [black spokesmen] could believe the ordinance is directed at the Negro community." One question in a poll published in the *Dallas Morning News* asked, "When a race riot starts, what do you think should be done?" The question everywhere wasn't *if* there would be a riot but *when*.

Chief prosecutor Doug Mulder personally took charge of the case against Johnson and McMillan. The hardest of hard-nosed prosecutors, Mulder made his reputation by persuading Dallas juries to hand down sentences of 800, 1,000, 1,500, and finally 5,005 years. Appearing for the defense were two young lawyers who were just starting to make a reputation for themselves, Vincent Perini and Frank P. Hernandez.

Attorneys Perini and Hernandez correctly anticipated that they would be stuck with an all-white jury, and that Judge Zimmerman would deny most of their motions. At the trial, several dozen grimacing blacks in dashikis and Afros dominated the spectator section. The interior of the courtroom was rimmed by armed guards.

Perini, who had been out of law school less than two years, now admits that he made "a young lawyer's mistake" when he compared the raid on the O.K. with the Boston Tea Party during his final argument. He invoked the memory of Paul Revere, John Hancock, and Samuel Adams, "sometimes known as the father of the American Revolution," and asked, "Was there evil intention in those American patriots" when they dumped thirty-five thousand pounds of tea in the bay? Chief prosecutor Mulder recalled, "When I heard Perini talk about the Boston Tea Party, I couldn't believe my ears. Okay, let's identify them for what they are: revolutionaries. Imagine what the British government would have given Samuel Adams back then." The prosecution suggested to the jury that the event at the O.K. was the "beginning of a revolution" and asked, "Do we want a revolution in Dallas County—do we want to begin here?" In affirming the conviction, the Texas Court of Criminal Appeals called this an "indeed telling argument."

Members of the jury obviously agreed. In a deposition taken later, juror Mary Elizabeth Farrar told how the jurors discussed that if "these boys" were released on probation "there would definitely be riots. . . . There was much talk that we didn't want any Carmichaels or any Rap Browns or any Kings here in the city." The jury quickly found McMillan and Johnson guilty and sentenced them to ten years.

"That was the end of the black movement in Dallas," Al Lipscomb said. "That broke the back of the group."

When the appeals were exhausted and it was time for Matt Johnson to go to prison, he was close to a nervous breakdown. The brothers heard that Matt had thought of hanging himself right after the trial, during the six weeks he spent in county jail awaiting bond. Ernie volunteered to spend an extra six weeks in jail so that the first bond money raised by the members of the movement could be used to reunite Matt and his family.

A lot of things happened in the weeks and months following the trial, almost all of them bad. Fred Bell, possibly overcome by his promise that the defense lawyers would be paid, was arrested and charged with being part of a gang that had robbed a bank in the small Northeast Texas town of Ladonia. Now Fred was on his way to prison. Foots Beasley was charged with the same robbery, but he vanished. Some months later the brothers read that Foots had been arrested in Montreal trying to hijack a plane to Cuba. A guard at the county jail warned Ernie that a "pine box" was waiting for him at Huntsville. Ernie's mother organized a campaign of telephone calls that she hoped would convince Sheriff Bill Decker that the black community was aware of the threats on her son's life. "One of the first things I did when I made bail," Ernie recalled, "was buy a .30-caliber rifle with three banana clips." The gun was confiscated a few days later in a sweeping police raid on the homes of McMillan, Johnson, and another SNCC worker. Incredibly, Ernie was charged with illegal possession of a firearm. He was also indicted for draft evasion because he had refused to take an army physical the previous spring. Quacy Williams was stopped one night driving across a bridge between South Dallas and West Dallas, and a search of his car conveniently turned up a matchbox of marijuana, which at that time could get him life in prison.

In June 1969, almost a year after the raid on the O.K., Ernie and Quacy traveled to Greenwich, Connecticut, to speak to a meeting sponsored by the National Council of Churches. Although Ernie had cleared the trip with authorities, he heard from his lawyer in Dallas that his bond was about to be revoked. "My lawyer thought the FBI was planning an ambush," he said. "He advised me and Quacy to take a circuitous route back home."

The circuitous route they decided on went through Africa. Fugitives now, they were on a mission to locate Stokely Carmichael, who was living in Guinea. Quacy remembered turning 21 "in the Motherland." As a kid Ernie had dreamed of an almost mystical Africa of tribal kingdoms "where a great people lived with an empire when the English and Europeans were still living in caves." But the Africa he discovered was not the land of his dreams. "There was nothing romantic about it," Ernie told me years later. "I had thought of one people, one nation, but I learned there were something like two hundred fifty different languages, tribal wars, and economic chaos."

Quacy remembered, "I loved the people but not the political systems. We saw corruption and blacks oppressing blacks."

After about a year they had had enough. "We finally realized that this wasn't our place," Quacy said. "We were Afro-Americans. That's when we decided to go home."

They disappeared into the underground of the black movement in Chicago and were not captured until December 1971 when a platoon of police and FBI agents cornered them in Cincinnati. Some of the charges against them had been dismissed by then. Quacy pleaded guilty and was sentenced to five years' probation. Ernie was sent first to federal prison in Leavenworth, then to the Texas Department of Corrections at Huntsville.

Prison certainly didn't change Ernie McMillan. He served much of his sentence working in the fields and he led a sit-down protesting an order to work on Father's Day. For this he was beaten and thrown into solitary. In December 1974 he was released, partly through the efforts of State Representative Eddie Bernice Johnson of Oak Cliff, who had arranged for him to testify before her House Prison Reform Committee.

Shortly after his release, Ernie went to work for Eddie Bernice Johnson. Later he worked in Dallas for the Opportunity Industrialization Center, and then for a bleach factory, where he became a union organizer. In 1979 he joined the United League of Mississippi, a civil rights organization working in the heart of the Delta, birthplace of the White Citizens Council, and stronghold of old-time white supremacist Democrats.

Ernie was working in Sunflower County, Mississippi, just a few miles from the spot where Emmett Till was lynched, when he learned from his mother that authorities in Dallas were about to revoke his parole. A district attorney in Indianola, Mississippi, had alerted authorities that McMillan was suspected of being an accessory to a robbery. "I knew I hadn't done anything," he recalled. "But the DA gave me a choice of either leaving the state or being prosecuted and having my parole revoked. I decided to go home to Dallas and sort things out in my mind." Charges were never filed, nor was his parole revoked.

Ernie's first marriage ended in divorce while he was still in prison. His wife, Felicia, who had been pregnant back in 1968 when the Dallas cops and the FBI kicked in the door to their apartment, had at one time planned to join Ernie in Africa, but instead she suffered a nervous breakdown. Now she had remarried and moved to Michigan with their son. His life in shambles, Ernie moved to Houston in 1980. "I felt we were on the eve of a new movement," he said. "Houston had the largest concentration of

Afro-Americans in the South and a history of worthwhile struggles under people like Barbara Jordan and Mickey Leland. I decided that's where I belonged."

While he was reassessing the movement, Ernie ran across something that shed new light on the tumultuous sixties. It was a photograph of two old arch-enemies, Martin Luther King Jr. and Malcolm X. They were shaking hands.

Ernie married again a few years ago and lives with his second wife, Marionette, and their newborn daughter in a duplex not far from the Texas Southern campus. His beard is neatly trimmed and flecked with gray, and his hairline is receding—he's only 38, but he looks older. He still sees Quacy and a few of the others, and he keeps up with what is happening in Dallas through his mother. He is no longer bitter or angry about what happened in 1968, only a little disappointed. "The things we fought for bought off a lot of people," he told me. "A lot of activists of the sixties were channeled into jobs with [government] agencies, into the nine-to-five syndrome. The only thing they worry about now is their paychecks."

Matt Johnson became a model prisoner. His wife, Jean, recalled that he was terribly depressed for months. "A man in his cell hung himself because he got a Dear John letter," she said. "But after a while Matt seemed to adjust." Jean speculated that her husband "made some kind of deal in prison," but she never knew what.

There was speculation, too, about some missing money that a wealthy Highland Park playboy had given Matt Johnson. The money was supposed to have been used to build the community center on Forest Avenue, but it disappeared. Jean recalled that some months before Matt went to prison, he had spent a considerable sum on clothes, a new Jaguar, and a gift to his parents. "He never confided in me where he got the money," she said. "He never confided in me about nothing."

Judge James Zimmerman was instrumental in Matt Johnson's parole. The judge visited Johnson in Huntsville when he learned that parole was being considered, and he was greatly impressed with the convict's record and attitude. "I was impressed with his dignity," Zimmerman recalled. "He didn't appear beat down or broken. He wasn't wild or hostile or aggressive. He gave me his word that he would get a job and never embarrass anyone."

Defense attorney Perini observed a similar transformation. "Matt went to prison and took his licks and became a model prisoner," Perini said. "He apparently turned out to be a very deep person."

But Jean Johnson saw something else. "Prison twisted him," she told me. "He became an absolute terror. Right up till the day he died."

Purely by chance, Quacy Williams ran into Matt last September, just a few days before Matt's murder. Quacy had gone to a welding shop in South Dallas to check on a bus used to transport families of prisoners to and from Huntsville on visiting days. And there was Matt Johnson, trying to look pleased at this accidental encounter. Matt's hair was traced with gray, and some of the muscle had turned to fat, but Quacy thought he hadn't really changed.

Matt asked about the movement—he must have known that Quacy was still involved. He said, "Anytime you need me, brother, I'll be there." Of course he didn't mean it. Matt didn't care about the movement now. There wasn't anything in it for him; the years hadn't transformed the brothers' basic characters, but it had transformed their needs.

"Call me," Matt said as Quacy was leaving.

"Okay, Matt, sure," Quacy said. But he didn't ask for Matt's phone number.

True to the promise of his parole, Matt Johnson never fooled with the movement again. When he was released from prison he moved with Jean and their four children into the home of his parents, who had bought a small farm near Hutchins in the southern part of Dallas County. Matt had learned welding in prison, and he worked in his father's paint and body shop for a time. The old man had finally realized his dream—he had opened not one but two barbecue places, one in South Dallas and the other in Oak Cliff. They were called Matt's Barbecue.

"Matt and his daddy were always arguing about something," Jean recalled. "It was a strain living there." Matt found another job as a machine welder, then in 1974 went to work for Glifford-Hill-American, a manufacturer of high-pressure concrete pipes, as a tap welder and later as a troubleshooter. He told Jean he had been laid off in June, but after his death she learned that he had been fired.

A few years ago Matt and Jean made a down payment on the beige brick house on the street with the cul-de-sac. It was a short drive away from his parents' farmhouse. Matt and Jean argued constantly, and he frequently beat her. She left him seven different times, but she always returned. "There was nowhere else to go," she confessed, the misery permanently etched across her face. Matt never talked about his days in the movement, and Jean never brought it up. Not long after they moved into the new house, Matt joined a motorcycle club, the Buffalo Soldiers, sublimating part of his deeply embedded machismo in powerful machines and a new brotherhood. He also took a lover. When she learned of the affair, Jean was actually relieved, sensing that this was an opportunity to spend time away from her abusive husband.

Jean Johnson knew that it had to end, but until she arrived home from work last September 21 and saw the police cars and television cameras and the yard full of neighbors, she never dreamed it would end in disaster.

When she left for work that morning, the children were fixing breakfast; Matt was still asleep. He hadn't worked since June. She called home about an hour later to remind him that he had an appointment at the unemployment office, but she didn't really believe he would get dressed and go. She tried to call him several more times, but there was no answer.

Jean left work about four, stopped at the bank, then drove home to Hutchins. As she approached the street with the cul-de-sac and saw the commotion, she thought, "Oh, dear Lord! He's finally hurt one of the children." Then she saw her 16-year-old, Donald. He was crying. "Daddy's dead," he sobbed, throwing his arms around her.

This didn't surprise her, though at the time she couldn't make any sense out of it. In a perverse way that she couldn't bring herself to admit, it was almost as though God had answered her prayers. Living with Matt had become unbearable. He had been beating her for years, and beating their children as well. Her 18-year-old, Matthew II (called Two), and Matthew III (Donald) had run away some months ago after their father slapped them around. There was an ugly scene in juvenile court—the judge almost held Matt in contempt for his outburst. Lately, Matt had been picking on the 6-year-old, Matthew IV (called Punkin), because the boy couldn't learn to count. Punkin had asthma and a nervous stomach that caused him to lose his breakfast almost every morning.

Donald, even more than the others, developed an obsessive fear of his father. Matt seemed to take a special delight in attacking the big, slow, awkward boy, who was timid and painfully reticent. Donald was left-handed, which Matt took as a sign of weakness. He tied the boy's left hand behind his back, and beat him with a stick and an extension cord. There was a time when Donald couldn't take off his shirt at school because of the slash marks on his back. The boy developed a stutter and high blood pressure.

Donald was a candidate for the varsity football team at Wilmer-Hutchins, but when he came home with failing grades in the spring, his father refused to allow him to play. Matt then apparently forgot about his injunction, because in late August he jumped the boy and demanded to know why he wasn't at practice. Jean said, "He slapped him against the wall, then dragged him in the bathroom and shaved his head with an electric razor, shaved it as naked as the palm of my hand." Several days later Matt blew up because Two hadn't put away his tools; he shaved his head also.

"I felt like I couldn't report him to child welfare," Jean said. "Matt had been through so much. He detested whites; so you can imagine what I'd be doing to him by putting him through the white man's system of justice again."

Matt was constantly issuing new mandates: Jean was forbidden to wear earrings, for example, or to attend church. The children had never been baptized. About a week after the head-shaving incident, she decided to disobey him. She took the children to church for the first time and made plans for their baptism.

A few days later Matt was dead.

Jean's in-laws turned against her, and she was virtually penniless and without friends. She didn't even have enough money to bury her husband. The motorcycle club and Matt's parents paid the bill. Her father-in-law was still holding Matt's van and his motorcycle.

A day after the funeral Jean learned the awful truth: Donald confessed to her that he had murdered his father. He had walked his little sister, Tina, to the bus stop that morning, then sneaked back into the house and hidden in a closet until the other children left for school. He took one of the rifles from his father's gun collection and walked to the bedroom. "He didn't remember firing the first shot," Jean explained later. "It was like a dream. But the noise of the gun brought him back. He fired the second shot because he was afraid . . . his daddy would get up and kill him. He said he just couldn't stand to see me hurt no more, and he couldn't stand to see Punkin growing up like he had."

The authorities weren't certain how to handle the case against Donald Johnson. He wasn't a killer, though he had committed a murder of mythological significance. In a report to Judge Pat McClung of the 305th Family District Court, a probation officer took note of the frequent beatings and abuse and observed that Donald Johnson "does not possess the sophistication or 'street knowledge' expected of an eleventh-grade student reared in a lower-middle-class environment." Except for the time he ran away, the boy had never been handled by the police, nor was there any indication he had used drugs or exhibited antisocial behavior.

Jean took Two, Punkin, and Tina to California to live with her sister, then returned to Dallas with Donald. He transferred to another high school, joined a boys' club, and was active in a church group. He remained in his mother's custody until January 3, when Judge McClung, in a ruling that stunned nearly everyone, ordered that Donald Johnson should be prosecuted as an adult and set bond at $10,000. Jean Johnson wasn't able to afford that kind of money, so the frightened and bewildered 16-year-old remained in county jail for six weeks while the authorities debated how to dispose of his case. No one was willing to make a decision.

Attorney Tom McCorkle, appointed by the court to defend Donald Johnson, said at one point, "I would take ten years right now. You have to realize this is just a game they play called the criminal justice system. The system is not interested in saving the boy's soul."

The following February, however, a Dallas grand jury chose not to indict Donald Johnson and the 16-year-old was released to his mother, who moved her family out of state to start a new life.

Gila Hell | NOVEMBER 1993

This will be our routine, I'm sorry to report. Very early every morning, at an hour when the Mogollon Mountains are still velvety silhouettes against the star-smeared sky and the predawn tranquillity of the Gila Wilderness has swallowed us into the deepest valley of our dreams, we will be jarred awake by the abrasive voice of the Cougar, reciting one of his incessant rhymes. "Grab your britches and get ready to go./We're packin' into the Sapillo," he sings out, beating a spoon against a tin cup as he stalks through camp, calling his followers to action. Those who drift back to sleep risk the shock of a bucket of cold river poured into their sleeping bags. The Cougar hates malingerers and slugabeds.

This is the first morning of our adventure in the Gila Wilderness, half a million acres of rugged mountains, steep canyons, and nearly inaccessible meadowlands straddling the continental divide in southwest New Mexico. The Cougar, whose real name is Alex Cox, is 83 years old and far too stubborn to act his age. Even in a place as isolated as the Gila Wilderness, he is a menace to society. Nevertheless, part of our group will follow him down Sapillo Creek this morning, through a dangerously narrow box canyon that is sometimes inhabited by bear, stray cattle, and cougar — the relatively harmless four-legged kind. Though the U.S. Forest Service considers the box canyon impassable even in the relatively dry month of June, the Cougar has been hiking it for over forty-five years. The trip has become a ritual, the central theme of a personal myth that he has created and enjoys perpetuating. The few of us who are fool enough to follow him become accessories to that myth. The Cougar claims this is his final hike through the box canyon, his swan song, but then he said the same thing a year ago. We'll see.

The members of our party who chose not to risk the box will travel by horseback over the Mogollon ("Muggy-own") Mountains, leading a caravan of pack mules that will haul most of our equipment and be used for day trips and for the return to civilization five days from now. In all, about fifteen of us are sharing this adventure. With the exception of me, my wife, Phyllis, photographer Wyatt McSpadden, and his 13-year-old son, Trevor, everyone in the group is a relative or close friend of the old man's. They live either in Corpus Christi, where he lives, or in Houston, Dallas, or Waco. Most have done this trip before. The Cougar's son, Kim Cox, a Corpus Christi attorney, made his first trip up the box canyon thirty-four years ago, when he was just 6. Now Kim's wife, Susan, and his two daughters, Whitney, 12, and Mallory, 9, are enduring the same adventure, apparently with anticipation.

Our starting point is Rick Cheney's Lake Roberts Motel and Outfitters, a hard hour's drive northwest through the mountains from Silver City. From Lake Roberts, we will follow Sapillo Creek along its westerly course through a seven-mile-long canyon to the creek's confluence with the Gila River. Our base camp will be another hour's walk upriver, on a grassy meadow near the trailhead to 7,752-foot Granny Mountain. From there we will make daily explorations of the wilderness. We will examine the cliff dwellings and ancient ruins left by a race of the Mimbres people, who lived here a thousand years ago and mysteriously vanished around A.D. 1270. We will search for signs of the legendary bear hunter Ben Lilly, who in the early part of this century lived in the Big Thicket and later in the Gila Wilderness and was the subject of a book by J. Frank Dobie. Mostly, we'll just test ourselves against nature—and against the Cougar's unbending standards.

An adventure in the Gila Wilderness is not to be confused with, say, a trip to Yellowstone or Yosemite. Except for two winding mountain roads, one to the Gila Cliff Dwellings National Monument and the other to Lake Roberts, there are no roads into the wilderness and few on the periphery. There are no trails, no picnic tables, no campgrounds, and no water except the river, the creeks, and the springs. The only concessions to civilization are a few trail markings and an occasional corral left by some forgotten rancher. This is not a trip for the fainthearted, as the Cougar will remind us repeatedly.

The Cougar is as lean and spare as a buggy whip, a condition he attributes to the fact that he has never smoked or had a drink of alcohol in his life. He's never even tasted coffee or Coca-Cola. He was the captain and star of the University of Texas track team in 1934—he held the UT quarter-mile record for twenty-four years. While he is not especially pious in his temperance, he does take a perverse pride in obstinacy. He is unfailingly polite, even courtly (I never heard him use profanity), but for reasons known only to himself, he delights in flaunting his political incorrectness, in particular his deliberate use of racial slurs. His attitude can drive you mad.

The Cougar hits the trail up the Sapillo wearing khaki pants, a long-sleeved dress shirt, and a pair of rubber-soled shoes that probably came from Payless. Everyone else spent hundreds of dollars in recent days at Oshman's and REI, purchasing the finest boots, backpacks, and outdoor gear available, but the old man is dressed for puttering in his garden. He carries his lunch—a can of C rations that he picked up for a few pennies at some surplus sale—in his pants pocket. A canteen of water that nobody ever sees him drink is slung across his bony shoulder. He can hike for hours without resting or even looking back to see if anyone is following. In this same box canyon two years ago, the Cougar's group was attacked by a wild bull, which so unnerved one woman that when they finally pitched camp hours later, she went to her tent and cried hysterically. "We were in serious danger of getting gored or even killed by that damn bull," recalls the woman's husband. "But old man Cox just watched it all and laughed." The Cougar has been known to strip naked and scamper like a goat up the side of a cliff, just to shock his companions. Those who have made trips with him in the winter say that his idea of a high old time is breaking ice in a frozen lake or pond and diving in for a morning bath, then rubbing himself dry with moss, which he claims gives him the proper smell of bush. On this trip he carries a small tent and blanket, but he prefers to sleep in caves, using a plastic garbage bag he fills with leaves as his only bedding. His habit of "denning up" in caves or hollow logs is the reason this group calls him the Cougar.

As we start into the canyon, the Cougar sets the pace, his gait stiff and jerky but his resolve that of a man possessed. I quickly lose sight of him, but I can hear him far down the trail, cackling:

We take no gripe, we take no bitch.
Or we'll pack you out with a diamond hitch.
And if we do, you ain't coming back
'Cause we'll meet you at the road with a rubber-tired hack!

By the time the sun finishes crawling above the mountains, we have walked for several hours, crossing Sapillo Creek a dozen times as it winds downstream from canyon wall to canyon wall. The canyon is still a hundred yards wide, and in places the cottonwoods, piñons, and junipers grow so thick that the trail disappears, at which point it becomes necessary to wade along the creekbed. The water is ankle-deep, cold but refreshing in the summer heat. *Sapillo* is Spanish for "little toad," and hundreds of thumbnail-size toads skitter about on the slick green rocks. On the cliffs high above, violet-and-green swallows practice their takeoffs and landings. The air smells sweet and spicy.

Deeper into the canyon, giant ponderosa pines and Douglas firs crowd out the smaller lowland vegetation and in places blot out the sky. The air is cool and moist. The silence overwhelms; the only sounds are heavy breathing and the scuff of boots, in harmony with the rattling of the breeze in the boughs. The terrain is becoming much rougher. The floor of the canyon is strewn with rocks—rocks the size of baseballs, grapefruits, watermelons, armchairs. You can't move your foot without stepping on a rock. Tangles of brush, stumps, and fallen logs in all stages of decay block the trail and must be negotiated at some cost of time and energy. The Cougar has slowed the pace a little so that those of us at the rear can catch up. He walks like an old turkey gobbler, waddling and leaning slightly forward. Sometimes he stumbles and falls, as do we all. One of my knees is already bloody, and the heel of my right hand has been skinned raw. The canyon starts to narrow and eventually the trail disappears entirely. We follow one side of the creek until it meets the canyon wall, then cross over and follow the other side, back and forth more times than I can count. In some places the only way to move forward is to wade the creek. The water here is waist-deep, and we step carefully among the slippery rocks, probing with our walking sticks for unseen holes in the creekbed.

After five hours we stop to rest. I glance at Phyllis and see that she is losing her normally sunny disposition. Me too. Soaked to the waist, I sit on the trunk of a fallen ponderosa and pour gravel from my hiking shoes. It occurs to me that I've been so busy watching my step that I've neglected to enjoy the scenery, which is magnificent. Behind me is a tree stump that must be four feet in diameter. I try to calculate its annual rings but lose count. This old fellow was already an impressive size in the 1830s, when the Apache leader Geronimo was a boy growing up along the Middle Fork of the Gila River. I wonder if it's okay to eat lunch. From the way the others are looking around, I can see they are wondering the same thing. After several minutes we start nibbling tentatively on sandwiches and fruit. The

Cougar crouches on a large rock, watching us patiently through thick eye-glasses, taking no sustenance, proffering no rebuke, offering no encouragement. How much farther is it? Not far, the Cougar says mildly.

By midafternoon we can no longer see the sun or feel the warm rays of summer. We are seriously into the box: No turning back now. The exquisitely carved walls of the canyon—mostly slate gray, except for patches of moss and fern—bend and twist and loom above us like the corridors of a city of permanent shadows. As the walls close in, we can almost reach out and touch both sides. A sycamore tree grows sideways out of sheer rock two hundred feet above our heads, and above that a cave as large as a living room yawns like a hungry black mouth. The only sound is our feet on the rocks and the gurgling of the creek as it eats away at the barrancas. In places, the stream riffles into rapids, then quietens into shimmering pools. The scale is spectacular. Boulders as large as boxcars rise out of the streambed, sometimes one on top of another, sometimes piles of them, deposited like enormous cannonballs millions of years ago by the eruptions of volcanoes a hundred miles away. Our progress is made mostly hand over foot, up one pile of boulders, down another, back into the water, slipping, sliding on our tails down chutes of rock, trying to brake ourselves, looking for places to plant a foot or lock a hand.

The water is getting deeper, more treacherous. In the narrowest passages, the creek is twelve to fifteen feet deep. Our choices are to climb the cliff and detour around the deep water—or swim. Most of us elect to swim, even though we are not certain how far we'll have to go before we can touch bottom. But even with our heavy boots and packs, swimming seems safer than scaling a cliff and inching along a ledge so narrow that you're not sure it's even there. The Cougar seems spooked by the deep water. He has never seen it this deep, he tells us, blaming the new dam upstream at Lake Roberts for trapping the gravel and sediment that once filled these deep holes.

At a particularly difficult spot, where the creek cascades over an enormous sheet of rock—a sudden drop of about twelve feet—most of us decide that it is wiser this time to take our chances on the cliff. Fifty feet above the creekbed, we begin creeping along a narrow ledge, maybe ten inches wide, pressing our bodies against the rock, feeling along the wall for pockets to hold on to. Fortunately, Kim Cox is an accomplished mountaineer, and he leads the way, helping us across the most hazardous stretches by extending his walking stick for us to use as a handrail. When we are past the waterfall, we work our way back down to the safety of the canyon floor—all except the Cougar. For some reason, he elects to continue along the cliff face, though the narrow ledge is about to peter out. "You can't make it," Kim calls out to his father. The old man pays no attention. He reaches blindly along the wall, his fingers searching for a handhold. As he tries to shift weight from one foot to another, loose gravel spills down the cliff and he seems about to lose his balance. For an instant I think that the Cougar might plunge to his death, and in a rush of professional curiosity, I wonder if photographer Wyatt McSpadden has him in focus. But the old man manages to regain his footing. After more urging from those of us below, he listens to reason and comes down—refusing the hands that are offered to support his descent.

The final half mile of the box is the most difficult. Progress is measured in feet and yards. To negotiate one stretch, we are forced to rig a rope over an outcropping of rock and hoist our packs and cameras overhead before swimming a span of about fifty yards. Beyond this pool, the canyon bends sharply and the terrain appears less hostile. One wall recedes into a shallow cave, partially concealed by a waterfall. The water flows from a spring somewhere within the canyon wall and is cold and pure. Standing waist-deep in water, we hold our nearly dry canteens under the flow, gradually realizing that the water here is much colder than the water we've grown accustomed to. Shivering in the deep shadows, teeth chattering and skin turning blue, we push on toward a patch of sunlight. Soon the canyon begins to widen, opening into a small valley of boulders and trees. After eight hours of extremely hard traveling, we've made it to the end of the canyon.

Zigzagging through a forest of pine, we come eventually to a large open meadow at the confluence of Sapillo Creek and the Gila River. This particular spot is as close as one gets to a landmark in this forbidding wilderness. Here, the river bends to the southwest, carving a U-shaped corner out of a promontory of rock as tall as a ten-story building. At least as far back as A.D. 1000, humans have lived on this stretch of the Gila. The caves in the cliffs above us were occupied by the Mimbres, contemporaries of the Anasazi. The most famous cave ruins are ten miles upstream—the Gila Cliff Dwellings—but there are many lesser-known caves, uncataloged, inaccessible, and virtually unknown. From the riverbed, we can make out masonry and see the ends of the pine-pole rafters, the smoke-blackened ceilings, and even a few faded paintings of lizards and turtles. In the mid-1800s, six hundred years after the Mimbres people vanished, the Apache lived along this river, and in the early part of the present century, some unknown rancher built a cabin and a corral on this site. The walls and part of the roof were still intact when Alex Cox first discovered the place in 1948, but hardly a trace of the structure remains now. Apparently the old bear hunter Ben Lilly used the cabin for a time, because Cox found some 1920s-era bank statements from a bank in Silver City made out in Lilly's name. Lilly, who became nationally known in 1906 when he took President Theodore Roosevelt on a hunting expedition, lived in the Gila Wilderness from 1912 until his death in 1936, most of that time in caves and shelters above the river.

Exhausted and battered, we fall onto a grassy slope, tired beyond words. Both of Phyllis's knees are bruised and swollen, and there are tears in her eyes. In another hour the sun will start sinking below the mountains. Our campsite is still three miles upriver, but the Cougar takes no notice of the time or our pathetic condition. Seeing this place again has rejuvenated him. He dances about, looking for relics of the past, excited as a schoolboy showing off a secret place. A horseshoe driven into the trunk of a giant cypress catches his eye: The cabin where he found Ben Lilly's bank records was over by that tree, he says. Later he had located one of Lilly's caves. "It's upriver a ways," he says, and for a moment I'm afraid he's going to insist that we go there right now. Instead, he says, "Let's climb up there," pointing his stick at the caves a hundred feet up the side of the cliff. "There's some Indian ruins I want to show you." I tell the Cougar that I'll join him, just as soon as hell freezes over.

Long after dark we make camp, eat a cold supper, and crawl into our sleeping bags. The night is crisp and clear. For a few seconds I lie on my back, looking at the three-quarter moon through a window in our tent, listening to the chirping of crickets and the babbling of the river, feeling the weight of the day in my aching joints and bones. Then I fall into a dead, dreamless sleep. The next thing I know, the Cougar is stomping through camp, beating on a cup, and singing out,

I'll tell you now if you can't keep pace.
Get some water and wash your face!

Must be the start of another glorious morning.

Thehe Cougar has brought along a packet of photographs and memorabilia, as well as copies of four books that he has written about his service in World War II and his hunting and exploring ventures. Over the next four days I read through the material, enlightening myself about Alex Cox and his generation. I know something about his generation already. It was my parents' generation too, a time of sacrifice and hardship, when the frontier was still a living reality and nature was sometimes regarded as the primary enemy of man. I am not surprised to learn, therefore, that Cox is a hunting enthusiast, that hunting in his view is more than just a sport; it's a religion. Born in 1910, Alex grew up listening to tales of how his great-grandfather and family came by wagon from Arkansas to Texas in about 1850, surviving off the game they shot along the way. He has hunted animals all over the world, some of them Boone and Crockett record-book kills, and he makes no apology for the slaughter. One of his favorite hunting tales concerns the time he shot an Indian bull elephant twenty-seven times in the ear with his army-issue M1 rifle and then hacked off its jawbone and tusks with an ax. In one of his books, he tells of a bear hunt in Mexico in 1938 that culminates with Cox—barely able to walk because of injuries sustained in the rough mountain terrain—tenaciously tracking down and shooting a mother bear while her bewildered cub watches, then trying to shoot the cub too. Cox seems puzzled that anyone might find this insensitive. He reminds me that the pioneers lived on what they were able to shoot, then tells what is probably an apocryphal story about a young woman of his acquaintance who refused to eat freshly killed dove but experienced no problem gobbling up a bucket of fried chicken. "Now you tell me," he says, a twinkle in his eye, "what's the difference?"

Already in his thirties when World War II broke out, he was commissioned into the Army as a second lieutenant and sent to the China-Burma-India theater, where he trained a Chinese tank battalion and led it across the Burma Road. Though he was never in combat, Cox (by then a captain) was decorated for valor by the Chinese army. "When they sent me to India, I thought I was going off to war," he laughs, "but it turns out I landed in the heart of one of the greatest big-game hunting areas in the world. During the week, I lectured on tank-warfare, but I had every weekend off. I checked out a Jeep and a rifle and ammunition and went hunting." A photograph in one of his scrapbooks captures perfectly what he did during the war. It shows Cox and two buddies in a blood-stained Jeep, surrounded by the carcasses of leopards and bears.

After the war Cox returned to Corpus Christi and formed a partnership with his father and brother to build low-cost prefabricated homes for "niggers and meskins." The old man knows that his racist remarks offend everyone in our group and that's why he says them—to appear mean and recalcitrant. On the other hand, many of the homes that he built in the Molina area in southwest Corpus Christi are still standing forty-five years later, worth five or six times the $5,000 the owners originally paid. Old-timers in the Molina area, most of them veterans of World War II, remember Mr. Alex fondly.

His writings exhibit an eye for detail, a sense of humor, and a sensitivity to the human condition. Only one of his books has actually been published, *Deer Hunting in Texas;* the others are bound collections of letters written home during the war and memoirs of hunting trips. Recurring themes are his obsession with the pioneer spirit of America and his need to constantly test himself by those standards. Consciously or unconsciously, the Cougar has modeled himself in the image of Ben Lilly, challenging the high country in winter without a coat or a blanket, sleeping in caves or hollow logs, bathing in icy streams, rejecting anything easy, convenient, or modern. Ben Lilly was a bounty hunter and made it his life's business to track down and kill wild animals, to the exclusion of nearly every other pursuit in life. J. Frank Dobie, who greatly admired the old hunter, nevertheless referred to Ben Lilly as "a brutal exterminator." In the area of Louisiana where Lilly lived in the 1890s, he killed all the bears except one, then moved to the Big Thicket, where he stayed until almost all the bears there were dead. Wherever he traveled—Matagorda Bay, the Big Bend, northern Mexico, southwestern New Mexico—Lilly contributed heavily to the annihilation of that area's population of bear and mountain lion. According to Dobie, the most satisfying period of Lilly's life was from about 1912 to 1927, the time he lived in the Gila Wilderness. The old hunter died at roughly the same time that New Mexico's population of grizzly bears became extinct.

Dobie observed that Ben Lilly went out of his way to make himself conspicuous, blatantly fueling his own legend. Similarly, these yearly trips to the Gila Wilderness are designed to celebrate the legend of the Cougar. He lays down the rules and exercises the discipline. As an initiation ritual, he sometimes requires rookie campers to gather rocks from the river and scrub them clean. At night the entire group gathers around the campfire and listens to the old man read from a well-thumbed book of poetry by Robert W. Service, the Shakespeare of the Yukon. As he drones on about the shooting of Dan McGrew and the cremation of Sam McGee, the youngsters grow restless and whisper to their parents that they don't understand why they have to listen to Uncle Alex read this stuff again. The answer is a glare: Because they do, that's why.

The Cougar's innate curiosity and zest for competition have been passed along to his son Kim and his two granddaughters, and while these traits have not diminished with each generation, they have changed direction. Kim Cox is a life master bridge player as well as a mountaineer, and although he hunted as a young man, he confesses that he would rather shoot game with a camera than a rifle. A lawyer by profession, Kim is also an avocational anthropologist and archaeologist. In the seventies he photographed the Indian pictographs of the Gila Wilderness and turned over his work to the National Park Service. Both of Kim's daughters are trained in wilderness survival, though neither has much interest in hunting. Whitney is named for Mount Whitney in the Sierra Nevada, and Mallory is named for George Leigh-Mallory, who died in an attempt to conquer Everest in the twenties. On a day trip downriver, Mallory was knocked off the mule she was riding when the animal bolted into a tangle of low-hanging tree limbs. Fighting back tears—she obviously didn't want to show fear or weakness in front of her grandfather—Mallory brushed herself off and got back on the mule. The old man never looked back or inquired after her well-being.

"The Cougar likes to test people," says Parnell McNamara, a regular member of this group. "He thinks that because he can do something, everyone else should be able to do it too." Parnell and his brother, Mike McNamara (if the name sounds familiar, it is because they are the U.S. marshals from Waco who led the search for killer Kenneth McDuff last year), have been following the Cougar into places like this for years and have the scars to prove it. The first time that Parnell ventured up the Sapillo, the temperature was twenty-five degrees. Before they reached the box, McNamara slipped on the ice and ripped his knee open to the bone. "I didn't think I could make it," he recalls. "But the Cougar showed no mercy. He told me, 'You have two choices. You can walk out with me, or you can stay here and die.'"

For some, the highlight of this trip comes on the third day, when party or parties unknown—Parnell McNamara's daughter Mandy is a prime suspect—plant a talking alarm clock in the grass behind the Cougar's tent. Half an hour before the old man would normally awaken, a recorded voice of impressive volume begins bellowing: "Wake up! Rise and Shine!" followed by an extended bugle call. For a full hour, as the message repeats itself, the Cougar stumbles about the woods, frustration mounting as he is unable to determine the source of the ungodly racket. Once the recording has run its course, the old man makes his usual tour of camp somewhat subdued but nevertheless determined to get in the final word:

Hear ye! Hear ye! Lord, I wonder
Who would try to steal my thunder.

It's good to see that the Cougar can take it as well as dish it out.

The Cougar conducts daily wilderness expeditions, during which nothing is too trivial to escape his notice. See those scratches on the trunk of that aspen? A black bear stopped within the last three days to sharpen its claws and mark its territory. A hungry elk has nibbled bark and rubbed velvet from its antlers on that spruce. The Cougar sniffs the air tentatively and informs us that there are no deer or elk nearby at the moment. His eyes are usually trained on the ground; he is so absorbed with the floor of the forest that he occasionally bumps into tree limbs. From time to time he stops to inspect an animal track or examine a rock, which, if it looks interesting, he drops in his pocket. A jawbone discovered under a bed of pine needles is from a deer that died before the age of 2, he explains. Exploring a pine forest, he introduces us to the mysteries of the pine knot, a club-shaped chunk of wood that is found near the decaying trunks of fallen pine trees. The knots are the oil-filled joints where the limbs connect to the tree; long after the tree has died and rotted away, the knots remain. Indians used them in a variety of ways, including as medicine. The Cougar raps a pine knot against a rock to knock off the top, exposing its interior, then shaves off a sliver of oily pulp and lights it. It burns fiercely, filling our immediate vicinity with scented perfume. "You can start a fire in any kind of weather with one of these things," he tells us.

On a horseback trip to Ben Lilly's cave, I realize that my feelings for the old man have undergone a metamorphosis. In the four days since we started out, I've gone from a palpable loathing to a grudging admiration. He grows on you. He's like the wilderness—unpredictable and unapologetic, one of a kind. In his way, this old man has taught us a lesson about rocky trails and wild places, and about our own capacities to survive and endure.

We've been talking about the trip to Lilly's cave all week, but none of us has the slightest idea if it's an hour's ride from camp or if we'll be gone all day. It's not far, the Cougar says, which means bring a lunch. We follow the river downstream, past the confluence of the Sapillo and the Indian caves, turning southwest at the U-shaped bend where we rested the day we came out of the box canyon. I am constantly amazed at the rich and complex diversity of the wilderness ecosystem, how it harmonizes and makes peace with its own violent geophysical history. Ancient riverbeds of rock and brush fan out toward the mountains whose hardscrabble southern slopes are tangled with piñon and juniper and contrast starkly with the moist northern slopes that are dense with ponderosa pine and fir. Giant cottonwoods and willows arch along the high-pitched banks of the Gila, amid patches of fern and wild mint.

We ride across grassy valleys where wild cattle graze, and through oak woodlands. Wild turkeys eye us with suspicion and then scamper into the trees. A solitary hawk watches from the charred steeple of a pine zapped by lightning. At higher elevations we pass by groves of curiously deformed aspen, their trunks twisted from the compressive effect of high-country snowdrifts that overlap the growing season. In places, the summer sun drills down unimpeded, bleaching the country in its hard glare. Then we climb a long ridge and without warning are swallowed into a cool primeval forest that looks as if it has been undisturbed for a thousand years. Some of the fir and spruce are more than one hundred feet tall, eerie and mystical with their gray green beards that look like moss but are really lichen. Occasionally we spot the remains of a campsite, usually a semicircle of rocks arranged around some charred pieces of wood, reminding us that others have been here in recent times, that even our own footprints demean the wilderness in small but perceptible ways.

After about two hours, a rider appears over the mountains to the east, eventually crossing the river to join us. The rider turns out to be Sue Kozacek, the ranger in charge of the wilderness district. She has heard of Alex Cox and wants to meet him. She, too, has wondered about the location of Ben Lilly's cave and asks permission to ride along. The Cougar mumbles his consent, then without another word turns his mule up a steep hill and continues his relentless quest. Having no choice, we follow. I'm seriously wondering if he knows where he is going. I've lost all sense of direction. There is no sign of a trail, no landmark except the river, which we see only occasionally. We climb long slopes, level out along narrow ridges so thickly forested that you can't see the rider in front of you, then descend again down perilous slopes to the river, which, for no discernible purpose, we cross from time to time.

At one point we start up a canyon, then the old man changes his mind and turns back toward the river. The canyons in this part of the wilderness are some of the wildest and least accessible, heavily forested and teeming with bear. Many of the caves contain Indian ruins that only the Cougar and those under his command have explored. "If you dug into the floor," Kim Cox tells us, "I'm sure you would find bodies and a lot of pottery." At one site we find shards of the distinctive black-on-white pottery crafted by the Mimbres people, scattered among flakes of shiny black obsidian used to make arrowheads. Mimbres pottery is considered the most beautiful and vital (and expensive) Indian pottery in the Southwest, depicting geometric forms, fish, humans, insects, and composite creatures. "They were the only North American Indians that I know of who depicted figures in motion," Kim says. "The difference between these people and other Indians of the Southwest is similar to the difference between the Romans, who painted figures in motion, and the Greeks, whose drawings were stiff and rigid."

We cross the river again and stop below a limestone cliff to inspect what Kim calls the Art Gallery—an entire wall of pictographs. Though the drawings are badly faded, some almost imperceptible, we can make out lizards, turtles, snakes, and the thunderbird rain god, with lightning bolts and cornstalks sprouting from each of his sides. "Everything on this wall has something to do with the river and water," Kim says. "You find pictographs exclusively near the river. Maybe they hoped the magical power of this art would keep the river running." Though nobody knows why the Mimbres people vanished from the Gila, drought and the drying up of the river are suspects.

After another hour of riding, Ranger Kozacek decides that the old man is lost. We stop to check a map, unaware for the moment that the Cougar has continued without us. Then we see him far downriver, bobbing along on his mule, looking neither to the left nor to the right, supremely confident that he is headed in the right direction. "Mr. Cox is certainly a stubborn man," Kozacek observes. We exchange glances, then spur our mounts and follow. Presently, the Cougar stops in midstream to study the terrain. Suddenly he jabs his heels into the mule's flanks and urges him up a steep embankment. This must be the place.

We dismount in a grove of willows, tired and hungry, assuming that we'll look for Lilly's cave after lunch. But the Cougar didn't come all this way to eat. "C'mon," he says, thrashing his way into a thicket of underbrush. "It's up here." No sooner have the words fallen from his mouth than he loses his balance and tumbles backward. Ranger Kozacek's instinct is to help him to his feet, but she thinks better of it, and the old man is allowed to regain his footing while we pretend we didn't notice what happened. Part of the group has lunch as Kozacek and a few of us follow the Cougar, climbing over rocks and fallen logs, wading through high grass. The cliff where the cave is located is straight ahead, but first we have to cross a ravine about fifteen feet deep. While we are looking for a way across or around, the Cougar studies the situation, remembering something from long ago. "There it is!" he yells, indicating the trunk of a long-dead tree that has toppled across the ravine. "That's where we used to cross!" The rest of us have already found an easy path to the other side and are waiting for him there but the Cougar is dead set on tightroping his way across the log bridge, just like he did forty years ago. The log is obviously unstable and probably rotten, and we call out for him to take the long way around. But he ignores our pleadings. Arms out for balance, he starts across. Again, I'm sure we are about to witness a tragedy, but he makes it safely to the other side, then begins climbing on all fours up to the cave.

Ben Lilly's famous cave is nothing more than an overhang. There's not even room to stand up. Two poles once used to dry hides lay against the back wall. The only other signs that someone lived here are the remains of a bed, a few rusted tin cans, and a hearth of blackened rocks. Ecstatic to have found this place again, the Cougar strikes a pose for the camera.

When we have returned to where we tied the horses—the Cougar again by way of the rotten log—the old man acknowledges that, yes, he does feel the need for some nourishment. He removes from his pants pocket an olive-drab one-ounce tin of army-issue peanut butter and a slightly larger tin of crackers, both of which were probably packed about 1938. To no one's surprise (except the Cougar's), the peanut butter is rancid. I ask him if he would like some of my trail mix. He gives me a dark look and says, "What's trail mix?" Maybe he's putting me on, but I don't think so. I offer him the bag of raisins and nuts, and he takes a small handful and eats them without comment. That's all he wants. Time to start back.

Reading from his book of Robert W. Service poetry our last night out, the Cougar has a catch in his voice. "The kid that handles the music box was hitting a ragtime tune," he reads aloud, stumbling over the words. The light from the campfire flickers in his glasses, and his eyes look moist. Maybe it's the smoke. Someone has tossed a pine knot into the fire and the woods are filled with its sweet fragrance. The sky is a tapestry of light, cooled and swept clean by an afternoon rain shower and illuminated by a full moon. At the edge of the clearing, a fox pokes his nose from behind a tree, gives us the eye, then trots off into the shadows.

It's raining the next afternoon as the Cougar packs his saddlebag and mounts his mule. The ride out is perilous but much quicker and far less difficult than our hike through the box canyon five days earlier. We climb steadily for nearly an hour, the heroic little mules and horses slipping and sliding on bare rock, heaving under the weight of their riders and the strain of the steep grade, stopping to catch their breath every few seconds before lunging up another short stretch. The final fifty yards to the top of Falls Canyon is sheer rock, tilted at a forty-five-degree angle, with the mountain on one side and a drop of hundreds of feet on the other. Some of us dismount and lead our horses to the top, but the Cougar stays astride his mule. The view at the top is stunning. To the north we can see Granny Mountain and to the west the whole Mogollon range.

As the others mount up and start down the opposite side, the Cougar pauses for a moment, wiping the rain from his glasses and allowing his eyes to roam across the hazy blue-gray top of the wilderness, wild and untamed and timeless as the earth itself. "Every year when I reach the top of this canyon," he says to no one in particular, "I always wonder if I'm packing out for the last time." Then he turns his mule toward home and doesn't look back again.

The Innocent and
the Damned

Most of the people in the small meeting room at Cicada Recovery Services in South Austin were therapists, and all of them had patients who had been diagnosed as victims of satanic ritual abuse—including some of the children allegedly savaged at an Austin day care center two years earlier. In the fall of 1993, the therapists met monthly at Cicada to discuss satanic ritual abuse (SRA), which they regarded as the most menacing evil of our age. Most victims are children, though in some cases they are women, who, in the course of therapy, have recovered memories of abuse twenty or thirty years earlier. The stories that the victims relate to their therapists— stories now being discussed and analyzed at the meeting—are strikingly similar and seem to have boiled up from a Stephen King nightmare.

The tales of satanic ritual abuse usually started with touching or fondling, then progressed to oral, genital, and anal penetrations; forced injections of mind-altering drugs; monsters or witches enacting bizarre rituals that included defecating and urinating on their victims' heads and forcing them to eat feces and drink blood and urine; and finally torture, mutilation, and murder. The rituals were almost always filmed. The victims were forced to participate in the murders and often made to eat the flesh and drink the blood of those who had been sacrificed. These were not merely the sadistic acts of pedophiles but the sophisticated techniques by which devil-worshiping perpetrators programmed and controlled victims, ultimately turning them into *Manchurian Candidate*-style robots. The perpetrators were often the parents and grandparents of the victims. The cults went back many generations and were as powerful as they were secretive, including among their ranks doctors, lawyers, the clergy, police officers, and prominent business and political leaders.

"They have infiltrated the legal, medical, and law enforcement professions with their agents," reported Karen Hutchins, one of the therapists at Cicada. "The male agents tend to end up in the criminal justice system and the females in state hospitals." Hutchins is the secretary-treasurer of this watchdog group, which calls itself the Travis County Society for the Investigation, Treatment, and Prevention of Ritual and Cult Abuse. It is part of a statewide organization headed by Dallas psychologist Randy Noblitt. Hutchins and the others believe that satanic cults are widespread throughout Texas and the United States. They believe that cults induce multiple personality disorders in their victims to control them. These cult-created alternate personalities, or alters, behave like mental robots, programmed to follow orders. Robots have been strategically placed to sabotage our institutions and to recapture and return to the cult those who have somehow escaped—in other words, those whom the therapists are attempting to deprogram. This is nothing less than a battle to the death for the soul of America.

Psychologist Pam Monday had brought to the meeting copies of secret CIA documents supplied by Cory Hammond, a Utah psychologist and leading theorist on the satanic menace. The document, which Hammond had gotten through the Freedom of Information Act, comprised mainly lists of names of people connected to a satanic-influenced mind-control experiment that the CIA conducted following World War II called Project Monarch. "This will give you some sense of how big the cover-up is," Monday said, passing the lists around. "Some of these names will blow your mind." They included Albert Einstein, Wernher Von Braun, Lyndon Johnson, Fidel Castro, Karl Marx, and Mao Zedong.

Hammond frequently lectured at seminars and had convinced many therapists—including those at this meeting—that satanic ritual abuse was an international conspiracy involving the CIA, former Nazi scientists, and a mysterious Dr. Greenbaum. According to Hammond, Greenbaum was a young turncoat from the Nazi death camps who saved his own life by giving the Nazis the secrets to the cabala. After World War II, the CIA brought Greenbaum and the Nazi scientists (who were satanists) to this country and hid them at military bases. In the years that followed, the scientists continued to perfect the mind-control techniques they had started in the death camps. Greenbaum was educated in psychiatry and positioned as the centerpiece of the satanic order. What was the purpose of all this activity? "My best guess," Hammond told audiences, "is that they want an army of Manchurian candidates—tens of thousands of mental robots who will do prostitution, engage in child pornography, smuggle drugs, engage in international arms smuggling, snuff films. All sorts of lucrative things. Robots who will do their bidding. And eventually the megalomaniacs at the top believe they will create a satanic order that will rule the world." Hammond thought that the satanists had already penetrated high levels of government. Part of his evidence was the frequency with which the name "Greenbaum" was spontaneously and independently mentioned by patients being treated for multiple personality disorder in therapy sessions across the United States.

Karen Hutchins had several patients who had spoken of Dr. Greenbaum and who recalled being subjected to mind-control experiments on military bases. Patients suffering from multiple personality disorder sometimes appeared quite normal, but their alters were capable of amazing and often supernatural feats. A client of Hutchins's, whacked-out on drugs almost to the point of being comatose, was driven to the Cicada Recovery center one night by one of her alters, who turned out to be completely drug-free. It was common for an alter to have different-colored eyes from its host's. Scars that appeared on one personality could not be detected on another. During therapy, rope burns might suddenly appear like stigmata on wrists or necks. Therapists referred to these apparitions as body memories—an evolving theory asserting that memories could be stored not only in the brain but also in cells of the body. In *Michelle Remembers*, the 1980 book that introduced satanic ritual abuse, a photograph of an asymmetrical rash on Michelle's neck was labeled a body memory of the "devil's tail." The book was written by a former Catholic priest who is now a psychiatrist and his wife and former patient, Michelle. Under hypnosis, Michelle recovered bits and pieces of memories in which the former priest discerned satanic motifs. Though there was no evidence that anything Michelle remembered was true, the book became a nonfiction bestseller. Within a few years, the FBI was getting reports from women all over the country who claimed that they had escaped from devil-worshiping cults.

Ritual abuse cases usually involved day care centers, which seemed only logical in the opinion of the members of the Travis County Society for the Investigation, Treatment, and Prevention of Ritual and Cult Abuse. "You start with preschool-age kids," said Hutchins. Everyone in the room was familiar with the November 1992 prosecution of Fran and Dan Keller, the middle-aged couple who operated Fran's Day Care Center in the rural

Oak Hill area south of Austin: Hutchins was now treating two of the three children allegedly abused in that case. Fran and Dan were each serving sentences of forty-eight years, and two Travis County law enforcement officers had also been indicted and were awaiting trial. Dozens of additional conspirators were still at large, the therapist believed.

Although the allegations of torture, mutilations, and murder in the case of Fran's Day Care Center seemed unbelievable—and indeed there was hardly a trace of physical evidence—they fit precisely with a pattern of charges that had emerged in earlier highly publicized day care cases in California, North Carolina, and Florida. Dozens of people had gone to prison. Families had been wrecked. Children too young to understand what was happening had been permanently scarred with memories of unspeakable assaults. The damage in human terms was incalculable. SRA had spawned a cottage industry among therapists, child-protection workers, cops, writers, lecturers, radio talk show hosts, and others who bought into the SRA story line. This country hadn't seen anything like it since the Salem witch trials.

Most of the parents who took their children to Fran's Day Care Center were baby boomers, dedicated to their careers and their children and drawn irresistibly to the day care's rural isolation and rustic, idyllic setting. The one-story fieldstone house, which was also the Kellers' home, was nestled among cedar trees and rolling hills, as tidy and pastoral as a cottage in a fairy tale. Behind the house was a playground, a shallow swimming pool, cages of rabbits and doves, and a corral with a resident pony named Dancer. This part of Oak Hill was sparsely populated, with small homes, trailers, and century-old family cemeteries. The Kellers' neighbors were working people, fiercely independent and likely to drive pickup trucks. Lawn decor usually featured iron kettles, rusted farm equipment, fieldstone walkways. Strings of deer skulls hung from the limbs of live oaks, armadillos and raccoons roamed freely, and hawks and turkey buzzards rode the invisible currents of the placid blue sky.

Dan and Fran Keller didn't look like monsters, though it is true that there are no demographic profiles of pedophiles, much less satanists. The Kellers had no history of drugs, mental illness, or sexual abnormalities, but neither would pedophiles necessarily. Pedophiles are narcissistic and exhibit what therapists call cognitive distortions, or the inability to recognize that even the vilest act is anything except normal behavior. That description didn't fit the Kellers. Nor did they appear to be victims of low self-esteem, as many child molesters are said to be. Indeed, those who knew Fran suspected that she suffered from high self-esteem. The word usually used to describe her, even by friends, was "bitch." She was a woman of strong opinions and clearly the dominant partner in her marriage to Danny. Danny had retired from his job with a Travis County road crew to help Fran run the day care, which opened for business in September 1989, two years before charges were filed and the day care was ordered to shut down.

Fran was 42 and had three grown children from a previous marriage. Dan was 50. Fran was his fourth wife, and he had four children. Together they had seven grandchildren. Neither of them had ever been accused of molesting a child or of any other crime for that matter. A ninth-grade dropout, Danny Keller had worked most of his life with bulldozers and heavy equipment. Before marrying Fran in 1987, he supervised the Precinct 3 road crew. In his off-duty hours, he enjoyed riding patrol with the Travis County Sheriff's Office deputies who worked the three-to-eleven shift. "After our shift, we all gathered to drink beer and cool out, what we called choir practice," recalled Janise White, one of the deputies and later a constable at the precinct. "Danny was like part of the family." After Danny married Fran, he no longer hung out at choir practice, but Janise White remained his friend and Fran's too, a relationship that eventually cost all three of them dearly.

Aside from the location of Fran's Day Care, what made it attractive to many parents was Fran herself. She was at once stern and good-hearted. She took it on herself to buy large stocks of children's clothes from Goodwill so that when kids soiled their own clothes during the course of the day, she could send them home wearing fresh and dry things. Fran had worked with children all of her adult life. Children sensed that she could not be intimidated or manipulated, that she was the clear and undisputed boss. Unlike most day care centers, Fran's Day Care accepted children with emotional and behavioral problems, including those who had been abused. This was a small operation, with about fifteen kids in attendance each day.

One of the children she cared for in the summer of 1991, when the ritual abuses supposedly took place, was the daughter of Suzanne Chaviers. Suzanne was going through a bitter divorce and had accused her husband in court of physically and emotionally abusing their child, which he denies. The Chaviers girl, who was not quite four years old, had exhibited behavioral problems since the couple separated two months earlier. Fran accepted her anyway. But, according to testimony, after two weeks at the day

care, the child had become almost unmanageable at home: biting, screaming, kicking, pulling her mother's hair, destroying things, trying to stab
the dog with a barbecue fork. Fran quickly observed that the little girl was
a liar and manipulator who attacked other children and accused them of
attacking her. Suzanne Chaviers made hardly any effort to discipline the
child, having been advised by a previous therapist against "setting limits."
Suzanne was an interior designer who worked out of her home: Until
the child started going to Fran's Day Care, she had always stayed at her
mother's side. The Chaviers girl clearly did not like this new arrangement.

Danny Keller was the antithesis of his wife, soft and easygoing, patient,
almost comically professorial with his gray hair and beard. Danny was
handy, good at fixing and creating things. He enjoyed making toys for
the children—bows and arrows, Indian drums, capes on which he painted
the likenesses of Ninja Turtles. Sometimes Danny would hitch a trailer to
his riding lawn mower and give the kids rides around the property, with
the pony, Dancer, prancing behind. Almost all of the kids enjoyed riding
Dancer, except the Chaviers girl, who complained after her first day that
the horse frightened her. Suzanne Chaviers told the Kellers to keep the
child away from the horse, which they did. Though the Chaviers girl attended the day care from May 8 until August 15, 1991, she was considered
a drop-in, not a regular. In all, she attended Fran's Day Care only thirteen
times.

En route to her appointment with her therapist on what turned out to
be her final day at Fran's, the Chaviers girl told her mother that the Kellers
had molested her. She was the first of three children to make accusations
against the Kellers. Within a matter of days, Earl and Carol Staelin and
Sean and Sandra Nash also charged that the Kellers had sexually abused
their children. By the first week in September, authorities had closed the
day care. In December, a few days after the grand jury indicted the Kellers,
they fled. They were arrested a few weeks later in Las Vegas, where Fran
Keller's eldest daughter lived. They have been in jail or prison ever since.

In the months after the day care was closed, the parents began to suspect that the Kellers were satanists, and the allegations of simple child
abuse escalated to monstrous proportions. In light of their new set of
beliefs, everything looked different to the parents who had leveled the
charges. The pastoral, commonplace backdrop that had made Fran's Day
Care so attractive in the beginning now appeared sinister. The seemingly
innocuous middle-aged couple now looked evil and malevolent. Sandra
Nash, who had a 5-year-old son and an infant daughter at the day care,
had originally regarded Fran Keller as "a warm, loving woman." Later,

as she looked back on events of the summer of 1991, Sandra remembered that Fran's personality had changed, that she suddenly became "very cold-hearted . . . a very different and aggressive woman." Many parents remembered occasions when their children would be wearing different clothes in the afternoon from those they wore when they were dropped off that morning. At the time, these incidents didn't seem important, but now they suggested unspeakable acts—at least to the parents who believed their children had been molested. Sandra Nash recalled the day she dropped in unexpectedly at the day care and found her son's hair wet. She was told that Fran had had to shampoo the boy's hair because when Dan and the boy had been goofing around, Dan had put styling gel in the boy's hair. But the Nashes came to believe that it wasn't gel in the boy's hair but semen.

The Ninja Turtle capes and other toys that the children brought home from Fran's became—in the parents' minds—diabolical "triggers," planted to call the children back to the cult. Many months later, Sandra Nash told investigators, "They gave my son drums so he could call Satan at home." Carol Staelin, whose 4-year-old son had suffered emotional and physical problems most of his life, including frequent asthma attacks, believed that the boy's severe asthma attack two weeks after starting at Fran's Day Care was because the Kellers had put horse manure in the boy's nebulizer. "Every aspect of these kids' lives, they twisted and perverted," she said. "They tortured a bunny in front of the kids and told them it was the Easter Bunny. They kept a flock of doves—doves, the symbol of Christianity. They would break a dove's wing, then bury the wounded dove and the children in a casket in the cemetery." Danny supposedly buried the children, then Fran dug them up seconds before they ran out of air and told them, "Satan has spared you." Even Dancer was seen as part of the satanic plot. As Carol Staelin reconstructed the events, the Kellers initiated the children on their first day—taking them on horseback to the woods, abusing them sexually, torturing them by applying electric shock to their genitalia, and threatening to kill their parents and burn down their homes if they told.

Most of the ritual abuse allegations came months after the initial claims of molestation. Understandably, the prosecution tried to avoid the satanic aspects of the case. It was far easier to sell the abuse than the ritual, and the jury heard only bits and pieces of the lurid details. The Kellers denied each and every allegation, but the jury did not believe them, partly because they had fled and partly because Fran Keller came across as such a cold, hostile witness. Several members of the jury told investigators and prosecutors later that Fran's demeanor in court was the main reason they convicted the Kellers.

"They painted us as monsters and ogres," Fran Keller told me about a year after her trial, during an interview at the Hobby Unit of the Texas Department of Criminal Justice, near Marlin. "On the witness stand, I told them that the little girl [the Chaviers child] was a liar and a manipulator, and the prosecutor jumped me and said, 'Don't you think it's an uneven match, a 40-year-old woman taking on an emotionally disturbed child?' Let me tell you something. I was as scared as that child. It was my life and my husband's life they were ruining. We have lost everything we ever owned or cared about because of that little girl."

At the Clements Unit, in Amarillo, Dan Keller spends much of his time trying to figure out what happened to the life he once knew. "I know God has a reason to have me in here for something I did not do," he wrote. "Is it to test my love for Him? As I write this, I notice only one set of footprints outside my cell door, and I remember that He said: 'When you notice only one set of footprints, that is when I carried you.'" The Kellers are not eligible for parole until 2004.

The following is based on trial testimony, the official police investigation, and interviews with parents and therapists.

When Suzanne Chaviers picked up her daughter at Fran's Day Care that final time on August 15, 1991, she had a lot of things on her mind. And one of them was sexual abuse. The 39-year-old University of Houston graduate was in therapy, trying to come to grips with her own memories of being sexually abused by a drunken father, who died when she was 18. The therapy had induced new, heretofore unknown recollections of that traumatic time nearly thirty years ago. On top of that, she was struggling through her second divorce. As in the first one, she claimed in legal proceedings that her estranged husband, Rick Chaviers, had intense and uncontrollable outbursts of rage, that he had physically and emotionally abused their daughter. Rick Chaviers denied this. But in the first months since the couple's separation there had been talk of a "bad daddy," which reinforced the image of an abusive father who pulled down the child's panties and beat her with a belt. On the advice of her therapist, Suzanne had taken the child to a pediatrician for a vaginal examination on May 7, one day before she started at Fran's Day Care. No signs of sexual abuse were detected, but Suzanne was still not convinced that her daughter hadn't been molested.

A psychologist who did a court-ordered psychological evaluation of the Chaviers in June 1991 wrote in his report, "This is a pathological family system . . . [the daughter] stood as the battleground and lightning rod for tension . . . between the parents. The mother seems to have a great deal of anger, of which she is only marginally aware . . ." The psychologist speculated that Suzanne Chaviers "unconsciously encourages others to act out her anger for her."

If Suzanne was subliminally attempting to transfer her repressed hostility to her daughter, the little girl appeared to be receiving the message loud and clear. More recently, the child's out-of-control behavior included her insistence that she was a dog—walking on all fours, barking, eating out of the dog bowl, defecating or urinating like a dog, licking herself like a dog. Sometimes she defecated or urinated on the floor in front of guests. On one occasion, when Suzanne's sister and her boyfriend came over for dinner, the little girl took off her clothes, climbed onto the boyfriend's lap, and began kissing him, then relieved herself on the floor. The child had started using profanity too, some of it extremely rough and vulgar. As for the no-limits program recommended by a previous therapist, obviously it wasn't working. Therapist Donna David, who had been seeing the Chaviers since May 21, had suggested setting some limits, noting that while the child appeared to have the ability to control her behavior, she "seems to be struggling for control and testing mother's limits continually."

On the day that the Chaviers girl made her allegations, mother and daughter were on their way to see Donna David to discuss the child's latest outrage—the ice cream truck game. The previous Sunday at The Kids Exchange—a court-supervised facility where parents involved in custody cases go for visits with their children—Rick Chaviers and the supervisor on duty were shocked by the child's behavior. Spreading her legs far apart, the little girl pretended to run a toy truck into her vagina, saying, "Here comes the ice cream truck." Donna David testified that she had observed similar behavior in earlier sessions, when the girl would stuff beans into the various orifices of anatomically correct dolls. Suzanne Chaviers had reported that several times she had caught the child hiding behind the couch, sticking marbles and crayons into her vagina. In a therapy session a week before the incident at The Kids Exchange, Rick Chaviers told Donna David that his daughter had exhibited "loving behavior" for him even before the separation, pulling down her pants, looking for things to insert.

On the way to the therapist on that fateful day, the Chaviers girl told her mother that she did not want to go back to the day care. Why not? Because Danny had hurt her, she said. How? He had pulled down her panties and spanked her. Suzanne was shaking all over by the time they reached Donna David's office. In her notes from that session, David wrote that the child had told her mother, "[Danny Keller] spanked her like her daddy used to and it hurt. . . . 'He hit me with a belt.' When asked where, in front or in back, she said, 'Front.' . . . She continued saying that Danny pulled her pants down and played with her and that 'he pooped and peed on my head,' and when asked if someone washed her hair, she said, 'Fran did,' and when asked further details, she said that it did not happen." The therapist produced an anatomically correct doll and asked the child to demonstrate what Danny Keller had done. The Chaviers girl stuck a ball-point pen in the doll's vagina. David informed the mother that she would have to contact Child Protective Services, and from there the case began a long, tortuous journey through the criminal justice system.

But something else happened that evening that virtually nailed the case shut. The Chaviers girl called to her mother from the bathroom and said that it hurt to urinate. When questioned, the mother would report later, the child told her, "Danny put his pee-pee in me and got glue in me, and it was warm and yucky, and Fran washed it out." Nearly overcome with anxiety, Suzanne took her daughter to the emergency room at Brackenridge Hospital. The physician on duty that night discovered two small tears in the hymen, which he judged to be less than twenty-four hours old. This medical discovery became the single piece of physical evidence against the Kellers.

In a second session with the therapist a few days later, the Chaviers girl gave more-graphic descriptions of what happened at the day care, this time involving Fran in the story. In her notes the therapist wrote, "When asked if Fran did anything to her . . . she said that Fran [kissed the child's vagina] and 'ate me all up,' making smacking lip sounds and using her mouth to imitate the movement of Fran's mouth on her vagina."

By coincidence, Carol Staelin happened to telephone Suzanne Chaviers the night of the Chaviers girl's allegations. Carol had called to invite Suzanne to a meeting of her twelve-step recovery group. Carol was a recovering alcoholic and believed the group could help Suzanne deal with her own post-traumatic stress of growing up with an abusive and alcoholic father. In getting acquainted, the two women sometimes talked about their children and about their common problems and experiences. Both had gone through troubled marriages: Carol and her husband, Earl Staelin, were still trying to work things out. Suzanne had previously suffered from severe allergies, and Carol suffered from a similar ailment diagnosed as environmental illness. Carol frequently followed Suzanne's lead. Suzanne was the reason that Carol has chosen Fran's Day Care and the reason that she now planned to send her son to therapist Donna David. The child had been in therapy two years earlier, suffering from a trauma induced by the sudden resignation of his nanny. Lately, he was showing new signs of emotional and physical distress.

When Suzanne Chaviers told Carol what her daughter said had happened at Fran's Day Care, Carol went into what she described as "automatic denial." Later she would explain, "At first I was sure that the abuse was limited to Suzanne's daughter, that my son wasn't involved. Though my intelligence was telling me otherwise, I was just saying, 'Thank God it wasn't my son!'" But two weeks later, after a session with Donna David, Carol was firmly convinced that the boy had also been sexually violated. It was an area in which she was painfully familiar. Like Suzanne, Carol also had memories of being sexually abused as a child. The memories had been "recovered" in therapy, nearly thirty years after the abuse supposedly happened.

Earl and Carol Staelin both had law degrees and had moved to Austin in 1981 looking for alternative lifestyles. For twelve years Earl Staelin had worked as a staff attorney for the public defender society in Toledo, Ohio. One thing that attracted them to Austin was the city's perceived New Age persona, particularly its commitment to nutritional, homeopathic, and holistic approaches to life's problems. A second reason was that the Staelins wanted to adopt a baby, and Texas offered more opportunities than Ohio, where they would have had to wait eight years just to qualify for a home background check. The Staelins were already older than the preferred adoptive parent: He was 41 and she was 33 when they moved to Texas. Earl Staelin was a great admirer of Gandhi's, and both were fascinated with Indian culture, so when they heard that it was possible to adopt a baby from an international agency in India, they jumped at the opportunity. Their son was four months old when he arrived at their home.

After moving to Austin, Earl quit his law practice to become a nutritional counselor, but the career change didn't work out, and in 1982 he returned to law. Carol had already decided to give up her own law practice. She wasn't sure what she wanted to do with her career, and this bothered her. Austin hadn't worked out the way she planned. Since the move, their lives had been in constant crisis. Carol had problems with alcohol, problems with overeating, problems with her liver, problems with her career, problems with her marriage. And problems with her son. Constant problems. And now the experience at Fran's Day Care. It was almost as if life had conspired against her.

After her son's first visit with Donna David on August 29, Carol recalls that the therapist gave her instructions to question her son until he told the truth, because "these people" customarily threaten and warn their victims against telling secrets. "Tell him that we don't know what happened at the day care," the therapist said. "He needs to tell us. He needs to protect the other children." (David denies that she said these things to Carol.) Later Carol attempted to get the boy to tell by admitting her own terrible childhood experiences. "When I was little like you," she said, "I was hurt in my private parts. I didn't like it—but now I can talk about it." The boy didn't respond, either that day or in any of his next several visits to the therapist.

The more the boy resisted, the more determined Carol was to get to the bottom of things. She tried to impress on him that other children had been hurt too, that by not speaking out he was putting the lives of other children in danger. That didn't work either. He wasn't talking. Moreover, he was exhibiting some of the same symptoms as the Chaviers girl's— out-of-control behavior, clinging to his mother, and using baby talk. He was destructive, using profanity, wetting the bed, having bowel movements in the bathtub, making improper sexual gestures—trying to touch his father's penis, for example, and looking up his mother's skirt. Once when he looked up his mother's dress, Carol asked him, "Did someone teach you to do that? Did Fran teach you to do that?" The boy nodded yes.

By late September, a month after the Travis County Sheriff's Office began its investigation, the Staelin child still hadn't said anything specific. But little by little, Carol Staelin was forcing the issue. One day, as she was washing the boy's hair in the bathtub, he suddenly threatened to cut her head off. "I thought this was very odd," she explained, "so I led him. I asked, 'Did Danny tell you he would cut your head off if you told secrets?'" The boy nodded. Four days later, again as she was washing his hair, the boy said, out of the blue, "Pee-pee in your hair." This sounded suspiciously like what the Chaviers girl had told her mother. Carol asked her son if anyone had ever peed in his hair. He smiled and hesitated. "Was it Danny?" she prompted. The boy nodded. "And how did you feel?" she asked. "Bad," he said. Then he changed the subject.

An incident on October 6 convinced Carol that the devil had possessed her son. For no apparent reason, her son hit his pet cat with his fist. "Did anyone teach you to do that?" she asked, her voice trembling. He nodded. "Who was it?" she demanded. He wouldn't say. "Was it Fran and Dan?" He told her that it was, then put his finger up the cat's anus and began to strangle the animal. At that moment, it crossed Carol's mind that the Kellers were satanists. The next day she telephoned a friend who said she herself had experienced satanic abuse; and a short time later Carol received in the mail a ritual abuse checklist compiled by a child protective group called Believe the Children. Carol gave the group's address to Suzanne, who later ordered her own checklist. In due time, every one of the twenty-eight indicators on the checklist was matched by an allegation against Dan and Fran Keller.

Carol had also spoken with Sandra Nash, the third mother who would level charges against the Kellers. The two Nash children, a 5-year-old boy and his infant sister, attended Fran's Day Care from March 25 to August 22, when Sandra learned from Fran Keller that charges of sexual abuse had been made against Dan. Like Suzanne Chaviers and the Staelins, Sean and Sandra Nash were college educated and middle class. Both parents were busy with their careers. Sandra Nash was a landscape architect who had been recruited to Austin from Colorado eight years ago by the engineering consulting firm of Espey Huston. She had been laid off during the bust of 1987 and had more recently been on maternity leave, but by the summer of 1991, she was working up to seventy hours a week. Sean owned a small, struggling moving company, largely subsidized by his wife's income, but he expected business to improve.

The allegations against Fran's Day Care hit the Nashes even harder than they had hit the other families. "When Sandy came home that day and told me what had happened," Sean Nash told me later, "I was sitting down and I nearly fainted." They immediately placed their son in therapy with a psychologist, who noted the "suspicion of abuse" and observed that the boy showed "anger at the Danny doll." Afterward, the Nash boy admitted to his mother that he knew a "secret" about Dan and Fran, but he couldn't tell.

By the early fall of 1991, all three of the children had been interviewed by therapists—hired by the Travis County Sheriff's Office—who videotaped the sessions. Despite a barrage of leading questions—Did Danny ever put his penis in your mouth? Has Fran ever asked you to touch her pee-pee or poo-poo?—the children revealed very little. The Staelin boy did acknowledge that Danny put his penis in the boy's mouth, but when the interviewer asked him to show what happened using the dolls, the boy said, "You tell me." On the first of three attempts to interview the Chaviers girl, the therapist couldn't even certify that the little girl knew the difference between a lie and the truth. The child identified the doll's penis as a nose and the vagina as a foot. The Nash boy admitted that "we heard" that the Chaviers girl and the Staelin boy had been harmed. He had obviously heard this from his parents, who had heard it from Suzanne and Carol.

By November, the third month of the investigation, the parents were becoming impatient and occasionally angry, pressing the investigators to move more quickly. They were on the telephone weekly, demanding to know why the Kellers hadn't been arrested and held without bail: The parents believed (correctly as it turned out) that the Kellers were about to flee. Someone from the district attorney's office told them they couldn't make an arrest until the grand jury indicted. Nobody knew when that would be. The parents began to suspect a cover-up or worse.

The Staelin boy's emotional state continued to worsen and so did his mother's. On November 20, Carol wrote in her journal, "For the past several days I've tried to find a therapist for myself, without success. Today my son has pneumonia again, an ear infection and asthma. I'm very upset about the grand jury situation. Today my son was acting out worse than ever. I had to call two (separate) hot lines for help at one point to make it through the day. At 7 P.M. I lost it and nearly hurt my son. Instead I shoved a wooden chair across the floor and shouted: 'I can't take it anymore!' I cried hysterically and then shook for half an hour, and panted heavily in a dog pant. Then I told Earl, 'I want my doll.' " The next day the Staelin boy was placed in a hospital, where he stayed for three weeks, followed by two more weeks in a day care program at the hospital. Since the Staelins couldn't afford to have two family members hospitalized, Carol settled for outpatient treatment. Around the same time, Carol's dark suspicions were confirmed. Both a nurse at a psychiatric hospital and a policeman who had worked on a cult task force assured her that Austin was a hotbed of satanic ritual abuse. Indeed, all of Texas had been invaded by satanists, Carol's informants told her.

On January 28, 1992, the Nash boy watched television footage of the fugitives Dan and Fran Keller being returned to Austin in handcuffs and chains, and afterward he began to talk about Satan. He told his parents that Dan and Fran were on Satan's team, and that Dan read out of Satan's bible and put spells on people. He told how Dan shot people, pushed their bodies into holes, then waved his staff in the air and called to Satan. A short time later, Carol Staelin reported that her son was also talking about Satan's bible. The Nash boy said that he couldn't see the cover of the bible because it was always concealed behind a magazine. But Carol Staelin's son described it as a large blue book, about the size of a telephone directory, with illustrations of clothed adults abusing naked children. In his scenario, Fran would ask Dan, "What do I do to [the Staelin boy] next?" and Dan would look it up in the book and read her the instructions.

Once the children started talking about Satan, the parents began seriously researching the massive amounts of literature available on the subject of ritual abuse, pressing the children to reveal more and more secrets. The Nash boy started talking about "bad sheriffs" being part of the satanic team. He described a blond woman named Pam who wore a brown uniform and a man named Lee who wore a similar uniform. Both "bad sheriffs" had tattoos. Deputy constable Janise White, who had known Dan Keller from their Precinct 3 days and who occasionally socialized with the Kellers—Fran Keller was the matron of honor at Janise's wedding—immediately became the suspected female conspirator, though she in no way matched the Nash boy's description and hadn't worn a uniform for nearly eighteen months. Investigators showed the Nash boy four photographs of female officers, two of which were Janise. The boy most likely had seen Janise on at least one occasion, when she visited Fran's Day Care with some coloring books and deputy sheriff stick-on badges for the kids. He also must have seen her wedding photograph, which sat on a table in the living room of the Kellers' home. Not surprisingly, he picked Janise from the photo lineup. From a much larger group of eighty photographs of male officers, the boy picked out a captain in the Travis County Sheriff's Office, who was later polygraphed and cleared. At a second photo lineup, the boy picked two deputy sheriffs. They were also cleared. Eventually, the investigators decided that the male suspect had to be Raul Quintero, Janise White's partner. Their reasoning: Quintero resembled the three cops that the Nash boy had misidentified in the photo lineups.

In March 1992 the investigation was taken away from the Travis County Sheriff's Office, which in seven months had discovered almost nothing in the way of evidence, and turned over to two detectives from the Austin Police Department, Sergeant Larry Oliver and Detective Rodney Bryant. Later, two Texas Rangers and an investigator from the district attorney's office were added to the task force. The parents of forty additional children who had attended Fran's Day Care over the past two years were questioned, but no other complaints of abuse were reported. Since the Nash boy was shaping up as a key witness, Larry Oliver asked Sandra Nash to come to his office and make a statement. "I knew that her statement would be very important," he told me. "Under Texas law, the first person a child reveals something to can testify in court. It's an exception to the hearsay rule." Oliver had heard some horrible, almost unbelievable tales in his years on the child abuse beat but nothing even remotely like the stories that Sandra Nash related. Danny Keller had urinated and ejaculated on the boy's head and made him brush his teeth with feces, Sandra reported. Her son had been forced to kiss his baby sister between the legs with his tongue out while Danny took movies and Fran held a gun to the boy's head. Danny had pretended to cut off the boy's penis. All the children had been baptized with blood and taken to the cemeteries where, with the help of two "bad sheriffs," they dug up bodies. After Oliver's first of several interviews with Sandra Nash in April 1992, he told her, "First, I believe you. And second, this scares the hell out of me."

As the parents continued their research into satanic ritual abuse, they bombarded Oliver and Bryant with ever-more-amazing reports. The Staelin boy talked about killing people, cutting them up with chain saws, skinning them, and putting the skins in the children's socks. The kids told stories of people in multicolored robes, carrying candles, sacrificing cats and dogs and sometimes babies. The Chaviers girl had been talking about killing babies all along, but now she was going into details. An elderly neighbor woman had brought a newborn baby to Fran's for sacrifice, the girl told her mother. The baby's name was Rachel. Suzanne Chaviers remembered the matter-of-fact tone in the child's voice as she related the grisly details, almost as if she were watching it on television: "And then, Mommy, they cut baby Rachel up the middle so I could see her insides, and she started crying. They cut her throat, and she quit crying. They put her little heart in my hand, and it was bloody and it went thump, thump, thump. Then they cut her up, and Fran held me, and Danny made me drink the blood."

According to the parents, Fran's Day Care was a working brothel. When customers appeared, the Kellers lined up the children like cuts of meat on a display shelf. Customers paid cash up front to Danny, then took the child or children of choice to the playroom. One customer wanted all the children and agreed to pay Danny's price of $2,000. Before the children were taken to the playroom, Fran drugged them with needles to the anus or toes. Lookouts carrying two-way radios warned the satanists when someone was approaching the day care, at which time Fran Keller and Janise White turned the satanic pictures to the wall, revealing the Christian paintings on the other side.

Frequently the children were driven to other homes or businesses in and around Austin, where they were abused by people dressed as monsters and werewolves. At the sheriff substation and Precinct 3 road maintenance complex—where both Danny Keller and Janise White had worked—the children were supposedly abused by men and women in black uniforms. The orgies were often filmed. The Nash boy reported an incident in which Danny Keller delivered ninety gift-wrapped packages (apparently of pornography tapes) and collected $10,000, which he spread into piles on the floor of the day care for all the kids to play with. An investigator suggested to the parents that the Kellers were part of an international porno and prostitution ring. This explained why, at the advanced age of 50, Danny Keller found satanism so attractive. He was in it for the money.

The children also told of being flown on jets to Mexico and taken to military bases like Camp Mabry, home of the Texas National Guard. These reports squared with the satanic checklists and other satanic ritual abuse information the parents were gathering. Carol had discovered the airplane scenario in a book titled *The Franklin Cover-Up: Child Abuse, Satanism, and Murder in Nebraska*, recommended to her by Pam Noblitt, the wife of Dallas clinical psychologist Randy Noblitt, the president of the Society for the Investigation, Treatment, and Prevention of Ritual and Cult Abuse. (Randy was a guru and adviser to a number of Austin therapists.) The book makes wild and unsubstantiated claims that some of Omaha's top business, academic, and political leaders conspired in a network of pornography and ritual murder. Girls and boys were flown to a number of cities, including Austin, where they were subjected to unspeakable sexual abuses by devil-worshiping old men in satanic hoods and then murdered during the sex acts while a cameraman filmed and Hunter S. Thompson directed.

Since her son had talked about cemeteries, Sandra Nash obtained a geological survey map of the area with all the cemeteries marked and took the boy to three of them. The Nash boy described and reenacted a memory of Danny pushing a man into a grave and riddling him with bullets. In time, each of the children pointed to graves where they had seen people buried or dug up. Sergeant Oliver noted in his report that the surfaces of the older graves appeared "disturbed," that the dirt was suspiciously soft rather than hard-packed as one would expect. Twice during the summer of 1992, the task force conducted land and air searches of a cemetery, using a Department of Public Safety helicopter equipped with an infrared camera. Nothing was detected the first time, but during the second search, the camera picked up "hot spots," which might indicate recent burials. However, only one of the hot spots was a place the children had pointed out. Oliver wanted to get a court order to dig up the grave, but he was overruled. "I still think a crime was committed there," Oliver told me eighteen months later. "There should have been more of an investigation, but that was a decision I had to live with." In fact, there was more of an investigation. Drew McAngus, a former Travis County deputy sheriff who was hired as a private investigator by lawyers for the Kellers, talked to the families of people buried at the cemetery. None of the graves had been disturbed. "A lot of those graves were old and were sinking with age and erosion," McAngus told me. "The families would go there periodically and add fresh dirt. Nothing really mysterious about it."

Sean Nash was conducting his own investigation, jotting down license numbers of vehicles at homes or businesses where the kids told of being abused and taking pictures of suspected satanists during pretrial hearings. Exploring the woods behind the day care center, Nash discovered what he considered evidence of satanic activity—fire circles, a doll with the arms and legs ripped off, and some bones of small animals, which he had analyzed at the Balcones Research Center. Carol Staelin suspected that District Attorney Ronnie Earle was involved in satanism. Unable to get Earle's home address from the DA's office, she looked it up in the county clerk's records. She discovered that he lived on Hamilton Pool Road, not far from Fran's Day Care. On her way to check out Earle's home, she passed a large goat farm—"Goats are used in satanic ceremonial rituals," she observed—then came to the walled compound of county buildings that included a sheriff substation and the Precinct 3 road maintenance headquarters, places where her son said the kids had been taken. "Imagine my shock when I saw that cozy little arrangement," she told me later. "But that was nothing compared to what happened next. I backed out of the driveway and continued down the road, and to my shock, the first driveway I came to was his—Mr. District Attorney himself. I literally started shaking all over."

The big break in the prosecution's case came in July 1992, almost by accident. Sally Whitley, who was the DA's representative on the task force, knew the two "bad sheriffs," Janise White and Raul Quintero. Before joining the DA's staff the previous spring, Whitley had worked with the two suspects in the Precinct 3 warrant division. Whitley also knew Doug Perry, a road crew truck driver who had married Janise White about a year earlier but was now divorced from her and apparently bitter about the experience.

At the moment, the investigation was stuck—there was not sufficient evidence to indict White or Quintero—but Whitley had a hunch that Doug Perry was the key to dislodging it.

Debbie Dorrance, a deputy constable at Precinct 3, recalls that on July 8 Sally Whitley told her of a plan. "She told me they were going out to see Doug, Janise's ex-husband," Dorrance says. "She said if we tell Doug that Janise and Raul have already given statements and 'ratted' on you, he'd probably sign a statement on them. Sally said that she thought Doug was dumb enough to fall for it." (Whitley admits that the plan was hers but denies saying Doug was dumb.) The plan worked better than anyone at the DA's office had dared hope. After submitting to two polygraph tests and undergoing several hours of intense interrogation by Texas Rangers, Perry implicated not only Dan and Fran Keller, Janise White, and Raul Quintero in the sexual abuse of children but also himself. This was the final brick that the prosecution needed to build its case—an adult eyewitness.

The following day, after obtaining a lawyer, Perry retracted his statement. But the damage was done: He later pleaded guilty and was sentenced to ten years' probation. Perry claimed that the Rangers had intimidated and pressured him, insisting that they could prove that he was part of the conspiracy and warning him what happened to child molesters in prison. "I was scared," he said. "I didn't know what I was doing." A polygraph expert testified that Perry was lying when he said he didn't know what went on at Fran's Day Care. In fact, Perry was lying—about that at least. While he was still married to "the bad sheriff," Janise White, he had read a copy of the offense report against the Kellers.

Perry's statement described in graphic detail a textbook example of pedophilia: how he and the Kellers and Raul Quintero did terrible things to a boy and girl (later identified as the Nash boy and the Chaviers girl), while Janise White took pictures. There was nothing ritualistic or ceremonial in his description, no robes or candles or satanic bible: It read like a page out of *The Story of O*. But the statement was made-to-order for the case the prosecution was planning.

By the time the trial of Fran and Dan Keller started in November 1992, prosecutors Judy Shipway and Bryan Case thought they had an excellent case, much neater than most of the child abuse cases they had tried. The plan was to sidestep the sensational allegations of satanic ritual abuse and restrict the case to a single child-victim, the Chaviers girl, who had made the initial accusation and for whom there was medical evidence of abuse. It didn't matter that after hours of interrogation the little girl had told authorities almost nothing. They needed her only for show: this pristine child pitted against the evil Kellers. The hearsay exception in child abuse cases cleared the path for her mother to testify in lurid detail. The judge also agreed to allow the therapist, Donna David, to give hearsay testimony.

The Chaviers girl's testimony was an exercise in futility. The child appeared more silly than frightened, waving her lollipop at Shipway and popping the microphone with her hand. She denied that she even knew anyone named Dan and Fran or that she ever went to a place called Fran's Day Care. She denied that she ever told anyone that someone touched her in a way she didn't like. When Shipway asked, "Did you ever tell Donna that Danny did something to you?" the girl replied, "No way, Jose"—one of her mother's favorite expressions.

Carol Staelin even speculated that it may not have been the Chaviers girl on the witness stand, but one of her programmed alters. Randy Noblitt, the Dallas clinical psychologist who was being paid $120 an hour to research satanic abuse for the state and another $140 an hour to testify, had warned that this might happen. Satanists often use hand signals to control their victims, he said. What most people in the courtroom took to be the defendant's running a hand down the side of his face, Noblitt interpreted as a signal that meant "You saw nothing, you heard nothing, you will say nothing." An Austin television station later ran a special report that showed Keller flashing a hand signal as he was led away from the courtroom. It looked like he was forming the letter *c* with his thumb and forefinger, and Noblitt told the TV reporter that this was a satanic message. Most likely, Keller was saying hello to the boys in C Block, where he had been confined for the previous nine months.

The Nash boy was called as a witness to rebut Fran Keller's claim that all of her troubles could be attributed to one lying little girl. He was not required to sit in the witness box as the Chaviers girl had been but was allowed to testify in a separate room, on closed-circuit television. He appeared primed and thoroughly prepared. When Case began questioning the boy about Fran's Day Care, the boy interrupted and said, "You mean Hate Care Center." "Why would you say that?" Case asked. "Because they hate kids," the boy replied. After that, every time the prosecutor mentioned "day care," the boy corrected him and said, "You mean 'hate care.' " The Nash boy was a far better witness than the Chaviers girl had been. In a clear voice he told the jury that he had watched as "Danny pee-peed glue on [the Chaviers girl's] head . . . and Fran washed it off."

The defense, not the prosecution, introduced satanism into the trial. The court had appointed two attorneys to defend the Kellers—Dain

Whitworth for Dan Keller, Lewis Jones for Fran Keller—but had given them little money to hire investigators or bring in expert witnesses. Whitworth and Jones didn't know about the satanic allegations until after the trial started. They found out about them almost by accident when the judge allowed them to subpoena Donna David's worksheets. They took a calculated risk that the jurors would find the satanic allegations so incredible that they would doubt the validity of the simpler sexual abuse charges. The gamble didn't work.

The prosecution made the most of Fran Keller's defiant personality and implied that the mere fact that the Kellers had fled was proof of guilt. One of the Las Vegas cops who had pushed their way into the Kellers' motel room the previous January told the jury that Fran had refused to cooperate, that she had an "attitude." Fran claimed that he had forced her to stand naked while being questioned. Fran told the jury that she and Dan had left town because "we were scared and humiliated." Also, at the time of their indictment, their lawyer hinted that the court would set a bail they could not afford. Above all, their long-term outlook appeared bleak. Fran had read about the prosecution of other child-care workers around the country and feared that they couldn't get a fair trial. It was a fear with some foundation: Conviction rates in day care cases are about 85 percent. The jury in Austin bought into the mainstream view, just as juries had in other cities and states.

A year later, charges against the two "bad sheriffs," White and Quintero, were dropped. The reason cited by the district attorney was that the children had stopped talking. To this day the parents continue to believe that dozens, maybe even hundreds, of coconspirators walk free to continue Satan's work. Sean and Sandra Nash have filed a civil suit against the Kellers, White, Quintero, Doug Perry, and others.

The fear of cults is part of a recurring pattern in our society, surfacing time and again during periods of widespread social upheaval. Satanic ritual abuse is to the 1990s what McCarthyism was to the 1950s and what the Salem witch trials were to the 1690s—a mythic expression of deep-seated anxiety over complex changes in family and values. Child abuse is the demon of our generation. Without question it is widespread. But are we to believe, as statistics indicate, that it is nineteen times more likely to occur today than it was thirty years ago? Or is it something else happening? Essayist and retired psychiatrist Charles Krauthammer argues that the helping professions—child-protection workers, therapists, child-abuse police—have convinced themselves that the abuse is epidemic and "have encouraged a massive search to find cases, and where they cannot be found, to invent."

Child-protection workers and therapists are caught in the middle of this controversy. They are not expected to be impartial investigators but advocates for children. They commonly act on a presumption that children have been victimized, that their real job is to gather evidence to support prosecution. An independent therapist hired by defense attorneys to review the videotapes made of the three victims in the Keller case counted eighty-nine leading questions. The problem with this, aside from the inherent injustice, is that well-intended child advocates may inadvertently trap a child in a contradiction. If a child denies being abused, the denial is taken as evidence that the child is repressing memories of terrifying experiences. If a child expresses anxiety—as one would expect after repeated interrogation—the anxiety is regarded as evidence of repressed memories. Dr. George K. Ganaway of Emory University writes, "[A] substantial portion, if not all, of the newly acquired SRA trauma memories and cult-related alternate 'personalities' eventually will prove to be products of a mutually shared deception between patient and therapist, serving the narcissistic needs of both."

The first and still best known SRA investigation began in 1983, when a mentally ill mother told Los Angeles County authorities that her child had been abused at the McMartin Pre-School. As it happened, this allegation coincided with a hotly contested reelection campaign for the office of district attorney, in which the primary issue was child abuse. Following the first accusation, the police department mailed out two hundred letters to parents of McMartin preschoolers, listing specific questions to ask their children to determine whether or not they had been molested. All of the children denied having been abused. But at the suggestion of prosecutors, frightened parents sent their children to Children's Institute International, a clinic that specializes in sexual abuse therapy. The CII staff suggested ritual abuse scenarios to the kids and warned that if they didn't tell us the "yucky secrets," people would think they were stupid. This technique is almost identical to the Child Abuse Accommodation Syndrome, a catch-22 theory authored by Roland Summit, M.D., which says, in effect, if there is evidence of sex abuse and a child denies it, this is only further proof that it happened. In which case, a therapist should use any means necessary to help the child talk. Of the 400 McMartin children interviewed, the CII staff suspected that 369 had been molested. The McMartin trial went on for nearly three years, without a conviction. But it led to a rash of satanic ritual abuse reports around the country, of which the case against Fran's Day Care is among the most recent.

Sensationalized by the media and by far-fetched theories put forward by psychologists such as Cory Hammond, many people now accept that our nation and world is under siege by a multigenerational international megacult. So-called cult survivors have appeared on television talk shows like *Oprah Winfrey* and *Geraldo*. And after each television appearance, fresh allegations surface. Accounts of satanic ritual abuse have also appeared in countless articles, books, and made-for-television movies such as *Do You Know the Muffin Man?* Though *Muffin Man* was total fiction, its ending was straight out of the true believer's handbook: Parents discover day care teachers worshiping the devil and piles of kiddie porn. Thousands of women—most of them in their twenties, thirties, and forties—have come forward in the past ten years with accusations that they were sexually abused as children. One of the most popular self-help books on sexual abuse, *The Courage to Heal* (which Carol Staelin read during therapy in 1989), advises, "If you are unable to remember any specific instances [of childhood sexual abuse] . . . but still have a feeling that something abusive happened to you, it probably did. . . . If you think you were abused and your life shows the symptoms, then you were."

Almost all "recovered memories" begin with vague recollections that something happened. Carol Staelin's first clue, for example, came in group therapy, as another woman was describing her own recovered memory of childhood abuse. "Suddenly, my body started shaking all over, and I started crying," Carol told me. "I went into an altered state. My body was remembering something." Later, in a one-on-one session, her therapist suggested that her many physical and emotional problems were caused by repressed memories of childhood abuse. "It was the therapist who planted the idea in my mind," she admitted. "I had no idea." Gradually, with the help of her therapist, Carol began recovering the memory. It came in bits and pieces—flashbacks of a room, a shadow, a feeling. In these flashbacks, she looked down on the scene of her abuse as though she were a camera mounted on the ceiling.

But the theory of recovered memory contradicts the way memories actually work. Our brains are not cameras, indiscriminately recording everything in view. We selectively record and distort to suit our needs. And memories are not film—not true, unchanging renditions of reality. Over time, these already distorted renditions are reworked and integrated with other memories, each of which is also distorted and changed over time. "Memory is basically a reconstructive process . . . [a way] to 'make sense' of the present," says Robyn Dawes, a professor of psychology at Carnegie Mellon University. "The fit between our memories and stories enhances our belief in them. Often, however, it is the story that creates the memory, rather than vice versa."

Some professionals claim that the similarity of satanic ritual abuse cases around the country is proof that they are true. More likely, the similarity results from the questions posed by professionals, who are familiar with the well-publicized cases. Most of the police officers whom I talked to either bought the story line without reservation or rejected it entirely. "The danger of all these wild allegations is that they could hurt legitimate child abuse cases," one Austin-area detective told me. "Ritual abuse is such an emotional area, it defies credibility. There's a core group of law enforcement officers who feel that they are on a mission from God, that ritual abuse is the ultimate battle of good versus evil." The FBI has been consulted in hundreds of cases involving allegations of ritual abuse and concluded that there is far less there than meets the eye. Kenneth Lanning of the FBI's Behavioral Science Unit has been widely quoted debunking reports of satanic ritual abuse. "We now have hundreds of victims alleging that thousands of offenders are abusing and even murdering tens of thousands of people as part of organized satanic cults," Lanning wrote. "And there is little or no corroborative evidence." Not a single body or body part has been produced. If the cults are real, Lanning observed, they constitute the greatest crime conspiracy in the history of the world.

It is important when investigating allegations like those against the Kellers to distinguish between sexual abuse and the far more bizarre satanic ritual. The incredibility of the latter should not reflect on the possibility of the former. Assistant district attorney Bryan Case conceded that Fran and Dan may have faked the ritual part to conceal and confuse their true intentions, but he believes that the children were abused. His belief is supported in part by the children's bizarre "acting out" behavior in the summer and fall of 1991. Although the Chaviers girl and the Staelin boy had previously demonstrated behavioral problems, the problems appear to have greatly intensified after the children started at Fran's Day Care. But are these problems indicators of sexual abuse or indicators that the parents lacked the will to discipline their children? It is necessary too to factor in the influence of the therapists, whose education and training are in social work, not medicine, and who have a substantial financial interest in identifying and sustaining a malady for which there is no quick cure. The Nash boy exhibited few behavioral problems until *after* he had been in therapy—and asked to reveal secrets—for four or five months. There is certainly evidence that the Chaviers girl was sexually abused—the medical report, Doug Perry's statement, the child's own allegations, which were unusually lurid and detailed for such a case.

What started as a simple accusation—"Danny hurt me"—became an avalanche of charges that overwhelm the senses. District Attorney Ronnie Earle told me, "We've learned from long experience that these stories often get embellished. There is usually a kernel of truth at the core, but over time it gets covered with layer after layer of things we're not sure really happened." But what if the kernel at the core is not the truth? What if it's a lie? What if a distraught mother, obsessed with fears of sexual abuse, and an emotionally disturbed and manipulative child somehow conjure up a tale that never happened? And what if a therapist too ready to believe in satanic ritual abuse picks it up from there, and it just snowballs until nobody can really say what happened?

In every satanic ritual abuse case that I've read about, there is evidence of overprotective parents' pressuring children to reveal "secrets" and planting ideas in their minds. A mother in the highly publicized Little Rascals Day Care case in North Carolina refused her child dessert until he told her what she wanted to know. Carol Staelin admits asking her son leading questions: She simply wouldn't take no for an answer. When the Chaviers girl was being videotaped by a therapist at the sheriff's office, her mother interrupted the process at one point with promises of a "special treat" if she would cooperate. When that didn't work, she tried another approach, telling the child, "They need to know what happened because you're the only big girl that can protect the other children because what Fran and Danny did was very, very, very mean."

For at least nine months before the Kellers' trial, the parents and investigators relied on material from groups such as Believe the Children (which was started by the parents in the McMartin case in California) to answer the unanswerable questions. For example, how did such an apparently unsophisticated couple as the Kellers learn the rituals or master the mind-control techniques credited to them? Was all that covered in the satanic bible? "I learned that the cults send people around the country to teach [these rituals] to child-care workers," Sergeant Larry Oliver told me. He learned this from Dee Brown, a special education teacher, television reporter, and self-proclaimed satanic ritual abuse expert from California. Also, with the repeated rapes, electrical shocks, and screwdrivers up the anus and urethra, how was it that the children showed no cuts and bruises? According to the gospel of Cory Hammond, that wasn't the Chaviers girl, the Staelin boy, and the Nash boy who underwent such assaults, it was their alternate personalities, or alters.

Much of what the children said—or, more accurately, what the parents reported they said—is either demonstrably false or inherently unbelievable. In the beginning, the children talked about Fran Keller's little dog, Sissy, who had mysteriously disappeared. As the story evolved, it became more demonic. The Staelin boy related how Danny Keller had clamped the dog's lips together, poked its eyes with pins, shot it full of drugs, then strangled it. The Nash boy put his own spin on the story, relating how the Kellers axed Sissy to a pulp. By talking to neighbors, private investigator Drew McAngus discovered that Sissy had been hit by a car: Danny buried her but spared his wife's feelings by letting her believe that the dog had run away. In another tale, the Kellers kidnapped a baby gorilla from Zilker Park, after which Fran cut a finger off the gorilla and drained the blood in a water bucket. But there has never been a zoo at Zilker Park, much less a gorilla.

Doug Perry's confession is hard to refute but nevertheless puzzling. Even if Perry wasn't the brightest guy in the world, it is hard to imagine anyone admitting such brutal behavior. On the other hand, none of the children identified Perry as one of their abusers, nor did they describe a scene like the one in his statement. The Austin-area detective who complained that many fellow officers believe they are on a mission from God also speculated that Perry's confession may have been tailored to fit their preconceived notion of how these scenarios were supposed to be played out.

The physical evidence that the Kellers committed a crime—or indeed that a crime was ever committed—seems suspect. Asked at the trial if the tears in the girl's hymen could have been caused by her having inserted marbles, pinto beans, toys, and crayons into her vagina, the physician who examined her replied, "Could have." Another physician testified that it would have been "highly unusual" for the child to injure herself in such a manner, but then many things about the Chaviers girl were highly unusual. Lost in the general atmosphere of hysteria was this question: While even a small tear to the hymen would have caused a stinging pain each time the child urinated, how was it that she didn't report the pain until almost eight hours after she left Fran's Day Care? Did she wait that long to void her bladder? Or was it something else? In the report of his initial investigation at Brackenridge Hospital shortly after the girl was examined, Travis County Sheriff's Office detective Roger Wade wrote: "The complainant

[Suzanne Chaviers] said she caught the victim [her daughter] taking her panties off behind the couch." This statement did not appear in any subsequent reports, nor was it mentioned at the trial. But it appears that shortly before the onset of pain, the child was playing an old familiar game.

A conventional wisdom has emerged that children are innocent beings who do not lie. Children under the age of 6 probably do not recognize the difference between the truth and a lie, but they are extremely suggestible. A review of a scientific study of children's suggestibility published in *Psychological Bulletin* concludes that police officers, child-care workers, and therapists who specialize in ritual abuse have a preconceived notion of what happened. "In the course of questioning [they] suggest it to the child, who then reports it as though it were true," say the authors of the article, Maggie Bruck, a psychologist at McGill University, and Stephen Ceci, a psychologist at Cornell University. "The more often you ask young children to think about something, the easier it becomes for them to make something up that they think is a memory."

Austin therapist Vivian Lewis Heine, who has testified an estimated five hundred times in child abuse cases (almost always for the prosecution), told me that young children hardly ever give false accusations without the influence of an adult. "The majority of the time when a child falsely accuses someone," Lewis Heine said, "there's a coconspirator. It's usually a parent involved in a divorce case or an adult who suffers from post-traumatic stress disorder, someone who was either abused as a child or believes she was abused." She cited an article in the *Canadian Journal of Psychiatry* that listed four warning signs of false accusation: (1) the presence of post-traumatic stress disorder in the adult, (2) the presence of serious psychiatric disorder in a parent and evidence of a disturbed mother-child relationship, (3) an ongoing custody dispute, and (4) a professional committed prematurely to the truth of an allegation. Three of the four warning signs were clearly evident in the Keller case.

Only a small percentage of therapists (or police officers) buy the satanic ritual abuse and multiple personality disorder material put out by theorists like Hammond and Noblitt. In a nationwide survey of mental health professionals in 1991, 70 percent of those who responded had never treated a case of ritual abuse or multiple personality disorder. Of the sample who did report such cases, 2 percent were responsible for a majority of the cases, each reporting more than one hundred victims. One individual reported two thousand cases. Austin therapist Karen Hutchins, who for the past seven months has been treating the Chaviers girl and the Staelin boy, estimates that about half of her fifty patients have been ritually abused and suffer multiple personality disorder. She can usually spot a victim after one visit. "I can feel an energy change," she told me. To date, Hutchins had identified in the Staelin boy fifteen to seventeen personalities, including Jacob, an assassin alter, and Poopsie, a 56-year-old man who can have bowel movements on command. Carol Staelin regards Poopsie as final proof that the child was ritually abused. "Having a bowel movement at 9 P.M. when your pattern is every other morning, you can't fake that," she concluded.

The Chaviers girl has eight personalities, Hutchins claims, including a violent alter named Crystal. At the appropriate age, Hutchins has determined, the child is programmed to be called back to the cult as a breeder, meaning that she will bear a child that will be sacrificed to Satan. The Chaviers girl was supposedly programmed to kill herself on her sixth birthday, in November 1993, but she did not. According to his therapist, the Staelin boy said he is supposed to kill himself on his eighth birthday.

The Nash boy is seeing a psychiatrist rather than a therapist, and at this point, multiple personality disorder has not been diagnosed. The boy continues to show great anger and confusion. He has achieved a blue belt in karate so that, he says, "when they come and get us, I'll be ready." Full recovery for the boy (and for all the children) may take years: They may be in therapy for the remainder of their lives. Except for the continuing obsession with getting to the bottom of this tragedy, life has virtually stopped for Sean and Sandra Nash. Sean's moving company is operating only part-time. Sandra has been on disability leave since the time of the trial. Their savings are long gone. "Our children's emotional needs are such that we have no choice," Sandra told me. "We just take it one day at a time."

What happened at Fran's Day Care Center was a tragedy. If the Kellers did even a fraction of what was alleged, they got what they deserved. If they didn't, then the tragedy is compounded beyond measure, because the children believe that the stories of humiliation and torture that they were encouraged to tell are real and also because innocent people are in prison, their lives and the lives of their families wrecked. Stories of unimaginable horrors have been told and repeated and refined so many times by parents, therapists, and law enforcement authorities—told with such passion and conviction—that they are permanently planted in these children's minds. In that respect, some form of ritual abuse obviously took place.

The Longest Ride of His Life

MAY 1987

How the Dallas Police Nearly Murdered Randall Adams

It has been almost eleven years since that bitter-cold November night when Dallas police officer Robert Wood was gunned down by the driver of a car he had stopped for a minor traffic violation. The murder case went to the U.S. Supreme Court and back in a futile search for justice. Eleven years after the shooting, the case still rustles the memory and haunts the conscience of Dallas.

The only one who got a good look at the killer was Robert Wood, and for all practical purposes Wood was dead before he hit the ground. For several days the police searched for the wrong make of car, and for several weeks they assumed that the killer was Hispanic or black. The intensity of the investigation and its strange twists and quirks attracted considerable media coverage and aroused the city of Dallas to unaccustomed passion. By the time a suspect was arrested a few days before Christmas, 1976— three weeks after the shooting—Wood's murder had become the longest and certainly the most embarrassing unsolved cop killing in the city's history. When a jury convicted the suspect, Randall Dale Adams, the following May, and sentenced him to death, there was a genuine feeling of exhilaration within the law enforcement fraternity, a belief that the painful affair had finally been put to rest.

But it didn't rest. It couldn't as long as Adams remained on death row— which, ironically, was also the home of the real killer of Officer Wood. The good and sound reason that this case continues to haunt the conscience of Dallas is that Dallas convicted the wrong man.

A group of attorneys who worked for next to nothing—with the assistance of filmmaker Errol Morris, and to a lesser extent my research into the case for *Texas Monthly*—turned up new evidence and uncovered dramatic insights into the old evidence. The shame of Dallas is that it took more than a decade to free a man whose only crime was to be in the wrong place at the wrong time.

This is the story of Randall Dale Adams and how Dallas almost killed him.

The four-day Thanksgiving weekend was winding down that frigid Saturday night in 1976. Shortly after midnight, Officer Robert Wood and his partner had stopped at the drive-in window of a Burger King on Hampton Road, which runs along the river bottom just west of downtown, through a high-crime district of warehouses and dreary housing projects. Wood's partner was Teresa Turko, one of the first females ever assigned to street patrol. She had been on the force for only about a year and, like the other women assigned to the dangerous job of patrolling the streets, was under unusual scrutiny and pressure to perform. Wood and Turko were being served coffee and a milk shake when they spotted a dirty blue compact car traveling near the Hampton Road viaduct with only its parking lights on.

A less conscientious cop might have stayed put and finished his coffee, but Wood flashed his red lights and gave chase. When he climbed out of his patrol car and walked toward the blue car, Wood apparently intended just to warn the driver; he left his ticket book on the seat. The standard procedure was to radio the vehicle's description and license number to the dispatcher, but most two-officer patrols ignored the procedure, and Wood ignored it too. It was also standard procedure for the second officer to stand at the right rear fender of the stopped vehicle, but investigators concluded later that Turko either stayed in the patrol car or at best stood beside its open door, drinking her milk shake. When Wood was shot, Turko dropped her milk shake and managed to fire several shots as the killer sped away. She immediately radioed for help, and within five minutes another unit was on the scene and others were on the way. But the killer's car had disappeared.

Badly shaken, Turko could supply only a skimpy description. The killer drove a blue Vega, she thought. She had gotten just a glimpse of the back of his head; he wore a heavy coat with the collar turned up, and his hair was dark and medium length. She saw only one person in the car, and she couldn't tell if he was black or white. For several days her description was all the police had.

That night and most of the following day, the investigation centered on Turko. She was taken to headquarters, stripped of her gun and identification, and placed in a tiny room that was used to interrogate prisoners. Sergeant Gus Rose, probably the best detective on the force, questioned Turko repeatedly, once for four solid hours; still, she was unable to supply additional information. Wood had been the second cop in less than a month to fall victim to a wanton and seemingly random shooting, and the fear, anger, and frustration that pervaded the ranks gave the new affair the irrational quality of a witch-hunt. Though an internal affairs investigation eventually concluded that Turko had done the best she could have under the circumstances, the consensus among senior officers was that the one cop who could have prevented Wood's death—or at least apprehended his killer—had failed her baptism of fire. Even so, the way Turko was badgered made a lot of cops uncomfortable. She was relieved of patrol duty until the completion of the investigation. She agreed to take a lie detector test, but the results were inconclusive. She also agreed to undergo hypnosis, and an expert was flown in from California.

"They treated her like a common criminal," recalled Dale Holt, one of the internal affairs investigators. "Gus Rose was one of the finest detectives I ever knew, but, frankly, I got into it with him over how they were treating Turko."

Five days after the shooting, the police got their first break. A woman waiting at a stoplight next to an off-duty cop rolled down her window and volunteered the information that the police were looking for the wrong make of car. "The newspapers said it was a Vega," she said, "but it was a Ford product"—a Mercury Comet, as it later turned out. The surprise witness was Emily Miller, a 36-year-old white woman married to a black man, a self-described "nosy type" who happened to be driving down Hampton Road with her husband, Robert, at around 12:40, the moment Officer Robert Wood was confronting his killer. Both of the Millers recognized Wood, who had befriended the family when Mrs. Miller's daughter was caught driving without a license. Emily Miller said that even though it was dark and the Millers' car was traveling in the opposite direction on the four-lane road, she took a hard look at the driver because she thought he might be her son-in-law. Her son-in-law, who was Hispanic, drove a similar car and wore his hair in an Afro, the same as the man in the driver's seat. She described the driver as "a Mexican or a light-skinned black." Robert Miller didn't give a statement until nearly five months later, after jury selection began. Any man who would kill a cop, Miller warned his wife, would not hesitate to kill a witness.

Despite Emily Miller's eyewitness account of the crime, the investigation stalled. A $10,000 reward offered by an association of concerned citizens was bumped to $20,000, then to $25,000, and the police let it be known that information in the case could buy an extraordinary measure of what one detective called "goodwill." Then, a week before Christmas, there was a development so dramatic that within three days Dallas had its killer, or at least the man it still maintains shot Wood. The break came in Vidor, a small town near Beaumont, where the police arrested a young hoodlum named David Ray Harris. The 16-year-old had been bragging to friends that he had blown away "a pig in Dallas." Harris, who was already on juvenile probation, admitted that he had burglarized a home, stolen a car—a blue Mercury Comet, in fact—and driven to Dallas the day after Thanksgiving to dispose of his loot. Part of the loot was a .22-caliber pistol, which turned out to be the gun that killed Robert Wood. Harris still had the gun when he returned to Vidor the day after the murder. He gave it to a friend, then borrowed a rifle, which he used to rob a convenience store. Harris freely admitted the burglaries and the robbery, but told investigators that the part about killing a cop was a lie. He proposed a deal: if the Vidor police would drop all charges, he would tell them who had really killed the cop in Dallas.

Elated by the sudden break, Sergeant Gus Rose hurried to Vidor to interrogate David Harris. If one takes into account Harris's record, his boasts about killing a Dallas cop, and the fact that he had the car and the murder weapon, the story Harris told seems childishly far-fetched. On the day of the murder, Harris said, he picked up a hitchhiker named Dale, who helped him pawn some stolen tools. They spent the afternoon together, drinking beer and smoking pot. That night, as they were returning to Dale's motel from a drive-in movie, a patrol car stopped them. Dale was driving, Harris said, and when the cop approached the car window, Dale grabbed the pistol from under the front seat and pumped five slugs into the startled officer. Harris remembered being told, "Forget what you saw." The mysterious Dale did not fit Emily Miller's description— he wasn't black or Hispanic, nor did he wear an Afro. Harris remembered that Dale had bushy, shoulder-length hair, and a Zapata-like moustache. That was close enough for the Dallas cops.

Since Dale had signed his name on the pawnshop receipts, locating him was routine. The following day Dallas authorities issued a warrant for the arrest of Randall Dale Adams on a charge of capital murder. The 28-year-old construction worker was picked up at Forest Hills Pallet Company, near the abandoned air terminal that used to be called Amon Carter Field. Thanks almost entirely to the testimony of David Harris, Officer Teresa

Turko, Robert and Emily Miller, and another witness who had driven by the murder scene, Adams was convicted four months later and sentenced to die.

Nothing in Randall Dale Adams's unremarkable life suggested that he was a candidate for death row. He grew up in a good blue-collar home in Columbus, Ohio. His only brush with the law was a DWI conviction as a teenager, for which he paid a fine of $100. His father, a coal miner in West Virginia before the family moved to Ohio, worked the last ten years of his life for a grocery chain. Randall's mother raised five children, and when her husband died, she went back to school and got a degree in nursing. Family life was typically middle-American—two cars, a large home, a membership in the Brown Road Community Church in Columbus.

Randall played sports in high school and always had some kind of job but never a trade. Basically honest and sincere, Randall wasn't driven by personal ambition. "Clever" was not a word that came to mind in describing Randall Dale Adams. On his employment application for the construction job, he had listed his nonreligious activities as "dogs, football, basketball, women."

That Adams was in Dallas at all was a quirk of fate. Two months earlier, Randall and his older brother Ray had left Columbus with the idea of heading for California and warm weather. Randall had done a hitch with the 82nd Airborne from 1969 to 1972 and developed problems with his knees, finally diagnosed as rheumatoid arthritis. Cold climates became unbearable. The previous winter, he had been barely able to climb out of bed.

Randall and his brother had several hundred dollars between them when they arrived in Dallas in early October. They had intended to stay only a few days, but Randall found a construction job the next morning, then Ray found work, and after a few weeks Dallas started to feel like home. The room they rented at one of the drab little motels tucked among the used-car lots and fast-food joints on Fort Worth Avenue was warm, with a bed, a roll-away, a TV set, and a tiny kitchen. By Thanksgiving the two brothers and another construction worker were making plans to rent an apartment in Fort Worth. Randall did piecework, constructing wooden pallets, and worked six days a week by choice. When he drew his pay the day before Thanksgiving, the foreman told him that Friday was a holiday but work on Saturday was optional.

Randall Adams's fate was sealed before daylight that cold Saturday morning when he woke at the usual time, dressed, and drove to work. But the foreman apparently had changed his mind: there was no one else at the job site. Adams waited about forty-five minutes, then drove back to town. Having paid another week's rent at the motel, he was short of cash. His car was almost out of gas, and he decided to pawn his stereo speakers and a box of cassettes at a pawnshop on Fort Worth Avenue. Unwilling to accept the pawnbroker's offer, Adams walked back to his car and had just pulled away from the curb when the car ran out of gas. He walked about a quarter mile to a service station, carrying a plastic jug, but the attendant told him it wasn't legal to put gasoline in plastic jugs. Adams stood there in the cold, weighing his options. At that moment a blue Mercury Comet pulled up, and a pleasant young man wearing a heavy coat with its fur collar turned up offered Adams a ride. It would turn out to be the longest ride of Adams's life.

At first, David Ray Harris seemed likable enough. He was bright and personable, traits that Adams admired. Harris had just come from Houston, he said, and was looking for work. Clothing and other items were piled on the back seat, including some tools, a rifle, and a pistol. Harris never mentioned that the goods were stolen, but he did ask Adams to help pawn them. Adams agreed to pawn the tools but not the guns. Adams had never cared for guns: his father refused to allow guns around the house.

With one spectacular exception, Adams's memory of what happened that day corresponds with the story that Harris told the police. They visited at least four pawnshops before agreeing to a broker's price for Harris's tools and Adams's stereo equipment, and then they drove out Texas Highway 183 to Adams's job site. Adams thought his boss might give Harris a job, but there was still no sign that anyone was working. They drove around, drinking beer and sharing a joint: Adams did most of the driving, partly because he didn't trust Harris at the wheel. At one point Harris unexpectedly fired the pistol at a stop sign. Adams yelled for Harris to put the damn gun under the seat. That's where it remained until Robert Wood's murder. As they were bumming around a shopping mall in Irving, Adams began to reevaluate his new friend. "He started acting crazy," Adams recalls, "lifting up girls' skirts, pinching them, yelling. He was acting like a kid, a youngster. It made me uncomfortable."

It was dark when they left the shopping mall. Both Adams and Harris remember that they sat through part of a soft-porn double feature at an Irving drive-in theater. Neither remembers the exact time they entered or left, though they agree that they left during the second feature, *The Student Body*. It is at this point that the two men's stories don't match up. Adams recalls driving back to the motel without incident, taking the Inwood exit off Highway 183 and crossing the Hampton Road viaduct to Fort Worth Avenue. Harris says they made one stop along the way, at which time Adams cold-bloodedly murdered Robert Wood.

Both men recall that when they arrived at the motel, Harris asked if he could crash there for the night. In a moment of decision that would forever haunt both men, Adams refused. Locked away now in a wire cage on death row, Adams has passed countless dark hours speculating about how different the future would have been if only he had said yes: if Harris had spent the night in Adams's motel room, Harris wouldn't have been out on the road at 12:40. And Officer Robert Wood would be alive today.

One of the first things Sergeant Gus Rose did after he interrogated David Harris was arrange for a lie detector test. Harris passed. Adams failed a similar test a few weeks later. Rose was absolutely certain by this time that Adams was their man. "The timing and the sequence of events is exactly right for Adams to have left the drive-in, gotten to the river bottom, and killed Officer Wood," Rose told me eleven years later. "Adams admits that he was driving the car. There is no conflict in the sequence of events, except that Adams claimed to have conveniently blacked out at the moment Wood was killed."

Blacked out? I had read Adams's statement and all the police reports just a few days before my conversation with Rose, and there was nothing about Adams's "blacking out." But Rose insists that he is certain that Adams used that term during interrogation. Rose, who retired from the police department in 1981 and is now the chief deputy constable of Precinct 3 in Garland, tells me: "I worked more than two thousand murder cases during my twenty-one years in homicide, and I'm telling you it's not unusual for a suspect to remember every detail of a murder except the most important part."

I resist an urge to tell Rose that from my own observations as an investigative reporter, it is not unusual for a homicide detective to demonstrate that same peculiar failing. It has to do with wish-fulfillment, I imagine.

On its face, the case that the Dallas police turned over to the district attorney's office was badly flawed. It depended primarily on a jury believing David Ray Harris, hardly a model witness, and on the testimony of Officer Teresa Turko, who had been wrong about the make of the car and had initially said that its single occupant had dark medium-length hair and wore a heavy jacket with the collar turned up—not a bad description of

David Harris. Harris and Turko were the only major witnesses on the list that chief prosecutor Doug Mulder tendered to the defense. On the other hand, Adams's attorney, Dennis White, had at least three—and maybe as many as half a dozen—witnesses who had heard Harris brag about killing a Dallas cop.

But most lawyers who had gone up against Mulder knew from bitter experience that this was the perfect situation for an ambush. In his twelve years as the chief prosecutor for District Attorney Henry Wade, Doug Mulder never lost a capital murder case, and he sent maybe two dozen men to death row. That his unblemished record would have been broken by a cop killer was unthinkable.

Doug Mulder had the personality, the flinty eyes, and the exquisite vanity of a marine drill instructor, a man of infinite patience and self-esteem who would as soon starve out an enemy as snap his spinal column. His machete-like tongue could carve up an opponent with a minimum of bloodletting. Nobody could analyze a situation or read a jury or know exactly when and where to frame a point of law better than Doug Mulder. Mel Bruder, one of Dallas's best appellate lawyers—and the man who would later argue Adams's case before the Supreme Court—said of Mulder: "He is one of the finest pure prosecutors I ever saw. He is thorough, he is heartless, and once the objective is made known to him, he pursues it at all costs." The objective here, of course, was to send Randall Adams to the electric chair.

Dennis White, the attorney Adams's mother hired to save her son's life, was almost organically mismatched for Mulder's kind of combat. White had taken a degree in economics at Harvard before returning to his hometown of Dallas to study law at Southern Methodist University. A classmate of Doug Mulder's, he graduated in 1964 and, like many young Dallas attorneys, served a short apprenticeship as one of Henry Wade's prosecutors. White didn't claim to have Mulder's passion for infighting. He was a gentle man, courtly almost, intellectually and emotionally inclined to see the best in people. Though he had been in private practice for nearly ten years, his experience in criminal cases was limited and spectacularly without distinction. White had gone head-to-head with Mulder only one time before—in the Mandy Dealey kidnap case, in which his client had received 5,005 years.

Mulder quickly established his domination in the case against Randall Adams. He won the first battle (and maybe the war) in the pretrial, when he convinced Judge Don Metcalfe that Harris's past and present criminal record should be kept from the jury. Dennis White was stunned by the ruling. Harris's well-documented criminal background not only destroyed his credibility as a witness, it supplied an excellent motive for him to point the finger at Adams. In a single stroke, however, Mulder had neutralized it. White was certain that a deal had been made with Harris, but unless he could get across to the jury that Harris faced robbery and burglary charges and a probation revocation, there was no way the jury would understand how much Harris had to gain by testifying for the state. Nor would the jury comprehend that Harris's boasts that he had killed a cop were more than ego bursts from an excitable teenager, that they were more likely the remarks of a young man well on his way to becoming a career criminal.

White correctly cited the U.S. Supreme Court decision in *Davis* v. *Alaska*, which determined that a juvenile's criminal record can be admitted as evidence if it is needed to demonstrate "bias and motive." But in framing his motion for the court, White failed to use those specific words—"bias and motive." On that technicality, Judge Metcalfe ruled against the defense. It was a narrow interpretation, but later upheld by the Texas Court of Criminal Appeals.

Mulder couldn't have asked for a better judge than Don Metcalfe, a longtime acquaintance and admirer of the chief prosecutor. A deacon in the First Baptist Church and a trustee of the Criswell Bible Institute, Metcalfe was conservative and proprosecution. He was a stickler for the letter of the law, an area in which Mulder excelled—and that Dennis White tended to overlook. Metcalfe approved Dennis White's pretrial motion that Mulder be required to turn over any documents favorable to Adams or inconsistent with the state's theory of guilt. But when Mulder failed to produce just such a document late in the trial, the judge let it slide.

White also neglected to ask if any of the state's witnesses had undergone hypnosis, although, in fairness to White, no one could recall a case in Dallas in which hypnosis had been used. Strict procedural safeguards are adhered to when witnesses have been hypnotized, but White didn't think to request them, and Mulder, of course, didn't remind him. Mulder claims that he didn't know about Turko's hypnosis. He did know about the police department's internal affairs investigation of Turko, however, and he knew that a few weeks after the killing, a report sent to the chief of police suggested that Turko had been coached to provide information that fit the investigators' scenario. Mulder didn't conceal that from his adversary, but he persuaded the judge to keep it from the jury.

Turko told the jury that she was standing at the right rear fender of the killer's car when her partner was gunned down. Then she added a startling piece of evidence that, as far as the police records show, she had never revealed to anyone and that was inconsistent with her earlier description—she said that the killer had bushy hair. Mulder had been harping on Adams's bushy hair since his opening argument, and now he made sure that the jury understood its significance. David Harris was brought into the courtroom so that Turko—and the jury—could see that Harris's medium-length dark blond hair didn't fit Turko's description. Though Adams had cut his hair before the trial, Turko looked at a picture of him at the time of his arrest and agreed that his hairstyle was "very similar" to that of the killer.

The revelation didn't seem all that dramatic at the moment, but as Mulder's strategy unfolded, it became the essential plot point in the prosecution's scenario. When Mulder cross-examined Randall Adams, he zeroed in on the bushy hair. "You got a new hairstyle, I notice, Adams," the prosecutor said for openers. Adams said he had gotten a haircut. "I said a new hairstyle," Mulder snapped. He had Adams step down from the witness stand and approach the jury, and he said, "It is not bushed out like it is in the photograph here, is it?"

Mulder had Adams read aloud the statement he had made to the police. Near the end of the statement, Adams said that he had driven the car from the drive-in to the motel, taking the Inwood exit off Highway 183. Then the statement concluded with this abrupt sentence: "I do not remember anything after I took a right off Inwood until I was turning left on Fort Worth Avenue." Though disjointed and confusing, the statement said nothing about blacking out; it read less like a narrative than a response to specific questions. Nevertheless, Mulder agreed with Sergeant Gus Rose's assessment: the statement—with its disclaimer about "not remembering anything"—was tantamount to a confession. A blackout at a key moment, how convenient! Mulder glanced toward the jury as Adams read it aloud, and when the defendant got to the last sentence, the prosecutor said, "You just want everybody to kind of believe that you blacked out . . . that it was so horrible." Mulder went on about Adams's alleged blackout, how convenient, how self-serving, all this despite Adams's insistence that he never meant to suggest a loss of memory.

Mulder's cross-examination had had its intended effect on the jury. Still, when the two sides had called all their primary witnesses, Dennis White was certain he had won his case. Mulder had apparently put all his marbles on David Harris. At least that's what he had led White to believe. Now it was time for Mulder to spring the trap: he called his first rebuttal witness.

Detective J. W. Johnson, the officer who had arrested Adams and helped with the interrogation, told the jury that he had gone to Adams's workplace looking for "a man with bushy hair" and had arrested Adams and taken him downtown. Then, like Turko, Johnson supplied a piece of information that had not appeared in any report or statement. Whereas Adams had told the jury he got back to the motel before 11 P.M., an hour and a half before Wood was killed, Johnson said that Adams admitted that it was closer to 1 A.M. Even if Adams had actually made such an admission—and Adams denies that he ever did—that type of oral statement during rebuttal was not admissible under Texas law. But Dennis White failed to object, and the damage was done—doubly so, since without a timely objection there was no basis for appeal. That fumble paled, however, in comparison with White's next legal blunder.

Mulder had three more rebuttal witnesses—Robert and Emily Miller and a third motorist who happened to pass the scene seconds before the murder, a tall salesman named Michael Randell. Dennis White had never heard those names before. Incredibly, he didn't have a clue as to the identity of these people, or what they were prepared to say. Though the judge had ordered Mulder to supply the defense with his list of primary witnesses, Mulder had not included rebuttal witnesses. Rebuttal witnesses are usually witnesses whose testimony cannot be anticipated, witnesses who become relevant only because of something that happens in the course of the trial. Three eyewitnesses to the scene of a murder hardly fit that definition, especially since Emily Miller's tip was what started the cops looking for a "Ford product." That tip led directly to Harris, and then to Adams. Holding key witnesses until the rebuttal stage of the trial is legal ambush, a way to prevent the opposition from learning the identity of witnesses until it is too late to prepare for them. That was a tactic Mulder had used before, and White should have known it. White could have asked for a continuance, which would have bought him a few days to investigate. But he didn't.

All three surprise witnesses said two men were in the car and substantiated Officer Turko's latest allegation that the driver had bushy hair. Emily Miller pointed across the room to Randall Adams without the slightest hesitation or doubt. "His hair is different, but that is the man," she said. Robert Miller, though less impressive as a witness, was no less certain in his identification of Adams. Nor was the third witness, Michael Randell, who earlier had picked out Adams in a police lineup. Outside the presence of the jury, Emily Miller said that she too had identified Adams in a police lineup. That was a lie. Dennis White should have caught it—there is no record that either of the Millers had even viewed a lineup—but White elected not to pursue the matter.

White's biggest problem with Emily Miller was that he had no idea that she had made a prior statement identifying the killer as a Mexican or a light-skinned black. Despite the judge's pretrial ruling requiring him to do so, Doug Mulder had neglected to tender that document to the defense. He simply forgot, Mulder claimed later, adding that in his opinion Emily Miller's prior statement would not have assisted the defense anyway. Dennis White did not specifically request a prior statement from Emily Miller—he assumed that wasn't necessary. He was wrong: in affirming Adams's conviction, the Texas Court of Criminal Appeals held that White had failed to make a timely request for that vital piece of exculpatory evidence.

Both sides rested their cases on Friday, April 29. On Saturday, White learned of Mrs. Miller's prior statement from a newspaper reporter. When White demanded the following Monday that the court recall Mrs. Miller, Doug Mulder said that the Millers had checked out of the Adolphus Hotel, where the state had been keeping them, and he had been told that Mrs. Miller had gone to Illinois. Mulder convinced Judge Metcalfe that it would be improper for the jury to hear the prior statement, since Mrs. Miller wasn't available to explain the contradiction. But Mrs. Miller was available. She appeared on local television that same evening, standing in front of her room at the Alamo Plaza Motel.

Numbed by that final setback, White watched helplessly as Metcalfe sent the case to the jury. Notes from the jury room over the next several hours demonstrated that jurors were having problems with the testimony of the rebuttal witnesses. Six of eight notes asked for clarification, and each time the judge refused. One note even asked if Mrs. Miller had made a prior statement; apparently at least one juror had read about it in the *Dallas Times Herald* months before the trial.

Not long after Adams was convicted and sent off to death row, Dennis White filed a lawsuit and a grievance with the Dallas Bar Association, accusing Mulder of prosecutorial misconduct; neither action got anywhere. The sad truth was, White had blown it. He had believed so strongly in his client's innocence that he forgot his lawyerly objectivity. Crushed by the experience, Dennis White never accepted another major case. Eventually he phased out his law practice completely and got into real estate.

In 1979 the Texas Court of Criminal Appeals affirmed Randall Adams's conviction. If his future had seemed bleak before the appeals court review, it seemed nonexistent afterward. And yet a confluence of unexpected and seemingly unconnected events were working beneath the surface, slowly destabilizing the house of cards that the state had constructed in making its case against Adams. Haunted by his failure, Dennis White continued to investigate, and so did three other attorneys who eventually became involved—Dallas appellate lawyer Mel Bruder and his associate George Preston of Dallas, and Houston appellate lawyer Randy Schaffer.

Bruder was appointed by the court after Adams's mother, Mildred, exhausted her life savings on the trial. In all the nightmare months since Adams first arrived in Dallas, this appointment was his first break. Bruder had an impressive track record in capital murder cases. In 1972, he had argued *Branch* v. *Texas*, one of four cases that persuaded the Supreme Court to overturn all the death penalty statutes in the United States. Adams would become his second landmark reversal. Three years after Adams was sent to death row, the Supreme Court overturned his sentence on a technicality. A section of Texas law requiring jurors to swear that the possibility of a death sentence would not influence their deliberations on issues of fact was found unconstitutional. This meant among other things that Adams was entitled to a new trial. A confident Dallas district attorney Henry Wade immediately informed the media that Adams would be tried—and convicted—a second time.

But Wade was bluffing. By this time Adams's team of lawyers had collected considerable evidence to discredit key state witnesses, including Emily and Robert Miller, and Michael Randell. Dennis White learned that Emily Miller lied when she testified that she drove past the murder scene minutes after leaving her job at a Fas Gas service station. Records from the station showed that she had been "terminated" fifteen days prior to the murder, after shortages in her account were discovered. Two Fas Gas employees also revealed to White that Robert Miller had admitted to them that he never saw the driver that night. Why had Robert Miller been so positive in identifying Adams from the witness stand? One of the employees remembered hearing the Millers talking about the reward money. The other rebuttal witness, Randell, had also lied. He told the jury that he drove by the scene after playing basketball at a city-owned court, but records showed the court was closed that night. Randell also led the jury to believe he once played in the National Basketball Association, another misrepresentation. Though White had presented this new evidence in his motion for a retrial, Judge Metcalfe denied it. In a second trial, however, the defense could demolish all three rebuttal witnesses. "I think it was obvious to the district attorney that the Adams case was dirty," Bruder explained.

But the state was about to find yet another way to screw Randall Adams. Before the Texas Court of Criminal Appeals could order a new trial, Henry Wade persuaded Governor Bill Clements to commute the sentence to life in prison. Removing the death sentence meant that the conviction was otherwise without error. Though spared execution, Adams was still doomed to a life behind bars, unless other appellate roads could be developed. By this time Bruder and George Preston were handling Adams's appeal pro bono—the $5,000 that the state had paid Bruder to take the appeal had been depleted long ago.

Meanwhile, Mildred Adams, dissatisfied with the pace of her son's appeal, decided to bring in another attorney, Randy Schaffer, a first-rate Houston lawyer who went to work for famed trial attorney Richard "Racehorse" Haynes while still in law school and now had his own practice. Fascinated by the case, Schaffer agreed to accept low monthly payments from Adams's mother. In February 1984 he filed an application for a writ of habeas corpus, in which he asserted that crucial evidence had been suppressed and that new evidence, which would have impeached witnesses, had emerged. He knew it was a long shot. Even if a federal magistrate granted a hearing, the lawyer would have to prove that Adams had been railroaded: guilt or innocence was not an issue. In other words, Schaffer would have to establish that the prosecution *knowingly* withheld key evidence.

Schaffer began to sniff around. In an old detective magazine, he stumbled across an interesting item that had not been revealed to the defense at the time of the trial—to help her recall the events of that fatal night when her partner was gunned down, Officer Turko had been hypnotized. The hypnosis also had been reported in the *Dallas Times Herald* months before the trial—White apparently missed it. But what about the prosecutor, Doug Mulder? If reporters for two such diverse publications had uncovered Turko's hypnosis, how was it Mulder hadn't known? The prosecutor was required by law to reveal such vital investigative techniques to the defense. It was now abundantly clear that Turko didn't have a clue about the killer's hairstyle until her day with the hypnotist.

Schaffer was on a roll. He developed evidence proving that Emily Miller had indeed told Doug Mulder that she was checking into the Alamo Plaza Motel. Mulder swore that he didn't know that the Millers were still in town, but he could not explain why a receipt showing that the Millers made 135 local telephone calls from the Alamo Plaza was in his case file. Schaffer also learned that robbery charges against Emily Miller's daughter, which were pending in Judge Metcalfe's court at the time of Randall Adams's trial, were dismissed five days after Adams was sentenced to die. A payoff for Miller's testimony? It made you wonder.

Several things happened in the fall of 1986 to suggest that Adams's spectacularly bad luck was about to change. Most important, U.S. Magistrate John Tolle of Dallas granted the writ hearing that Schaffer had requested. For the first time, Schaffer and Bruder would be allowed to present new evidence. They would also be able to shed new light on old evidence, thanks partly to a totally unexpected source—New York filmmaker Errol Morris. The award-winning filmmaker, who had achieved critical acclaim and cult status with such previous documentaries as *Gates of Heaven* and *Vernon, Florida*, met Adams and got interested in his case while researching a project on death row inmates.

In the weeks following their meeting, Morris accumulated an impressive amount of information on the case, not the least of which was the district attorney's file. Henry Wade would never have given that file to the defense, or to me, or any other journalist. But he offered it up in its entirety to the famous filmmaker. Morris tracked down and interviewed nearly all the investigators and witnesses—including David Harris, who had vanished but was traced through a parole officer in Orange County. Since testifying against Adams, Harris's life had been a continuous trail of crime. Free of legal problems, he joined the Army six months after the trial. Within a year he was convicted of burglarizing a house trailer in Germany and was sent to the federal prison at Leavenworth, Kansas. Paroled in June 1979, Harris went to California, where he was charged with burglary and robbery the following November. The police also suspected that he had kidnapped a hitchhiker and forced him to take part in the crimes, though Harris was never charged with that offense. Sentenced to six and a half years in San Quentin, Harris was paroled again in December 1984. He returned to Vidor, where Morris found him the following summer. "He was an engaging young man," Morris told me, "not menacing or frightening. My main concern was to do a film interview, so I didn't press him just then with any tough questions."

A few months later, Morris was shocked to hear that Harris had been arrested again and charged with capital murder. This crime was right out of the sociopath's handbook: Harris had broken into a Beaumont apartment, dragged a young woman naked and screaming to his car, then pumped five slugs into her boyfriend as he attempted a rescue.

Schaffer visited David Harris on death row and found the young killer surprisingly candid. Harris admitted that he had lied at Adams's trial when he swore that nobody had promised him a deal. Not only had Doug Mulder promised to "take care" of Harris's pending charges in Orange County, Harris would later testify, but the prosecutor had also instructed Harris to lie about the deal if he was asked in court. Harris stopped short of admitting that he also lied about Adams's killing the cop, but he went out of his way to leave that impression. Confronted with Harris's statement, Doug Mulder denied any knowledge of a deal, but some kind of deal was obviously made: Harris was never prosecuted for the robbery and burglary charges or for his probation violation.

It was Morris the filmmaker, however, who supplied the most convincing and dramatic proof that Adams was framed. The evidence was outtakes from his film, *The Thin Blue Line*, which documented the case against Randall Dale Adams. The film wasn't yet completed—it wouldn't be released for another eighteen months—but Morris agreed to screen some of his interviews for Adams's lawyers as they prepared for their hearing in federal court in the fall of 1986. The filmmaker's technique is to have his subjects speak directly into the camera, telling their stories and whatever else comes to mind, with few interruptions from the camera crew or director. In such an atmosphere, people are amazingly revealing, if not forthcoming. Clips of interviews that he did with Emily Miller and Michael Randell put a sharp new focus on their testimony in Adams's trial.

Mrs. Miller, who appeared before Morris's camera wearing a scarlet dress and long platinum hair (her hair was black at the time of the trial), clearly saw herself as the heroine in this drama. She revealed that her lifelong fantasy was to be a girl Friday to a famous private detective like Charlie Chan or Boston Blackie. Even before Officer Wood's murder, she explained, she had been an eyewitness to an incredible number of murders and acts of violence. "When something like this would happen . . . I would go see if I could solve it before anyone else could," she said. The most significant thing that Mrs. Miller said, however, was that she and her ex-husband, Robert, had indeed viewed a live lineup at the police station. That was an extraordinary revelation, because no police lineup identification forms were in the case file, as is required by law. In the film interview, she admitted that not only had she and her husband viewed a lineup, but they also had failed to pick Randall Adams. Robert Miller couldn't pick anyone, and Emily picked one of the decoys. And that wasn't all. As they were leaving the lineup room, Emily Miller recalled that a policeman pointed out the man she should have picked—Randall Dale Adams.

Therefore, to Mrs. Miller's way of thinking, it wasn't a lie when she told the jury at Adams's trial that she had identified him at a police lineup.

Schaffer and Bruder already knew that the other rebuttal witness, Michael Randell, had lied about playing basketball the night of the murder. Watching Morris's film clips they learned where Randell had really been that night: He had been drinking at the Plush Pub in Fort Worth and he was hurrying home because the woman in his car wasn't his wife. "My wife . . . would've tore my head off if she knew I was out that night with another woman," he says in the film clip. Randell insisted, however, that he had identified the right man. Being a salesman, he made it his business to study people and situations: he had developed, he said, the rare gift of total recall. In his fantasy, at least. Randell apparently saw what he wanted to see and remembered what he wanted to remember. Subpoenaed a year after his interview with Morris, and required to testify at the writ hearing in the court of U.S. Magistrate John Tolle, Randell couldn't even remember if he was married at the time of the murder.

I became involved in Adams's case shortly before the hearing. By this time Adams had written me three long, handwritten letters proclaiming his innocence. I get similar letters addressed to me at *Texas Monthly* nearly every week, many of them from death row inmates. A cynic might conclude that our prisons are full of innocent people. There was something about Adams's letters, however, that prompted me to at least telephone Randy Schaffer, who I knew by reputation. "Just do one thing," Schaffer advised me, "read the transcript and the police reports. Then let's talk."

After reviewing the case and talking to the principals, I was convinced that the police and prosecutors had nailed the wrong man—and that they had done it deliberately to expedite a successful conclusion to the murder investigation of Officer Robert Wood. My conclusion was based partly on my own experiences in murder cases, but mostly on common sense. The vast majority of murders are acts of impulse, committed in moments of great anger or grief, usually by someone who knows the victim. It takes a unique personality to shoot a cop five times for no apparent reason. Given the two candidates, Adams and Harris, who seemed the more likely shooter? Who had a record? Who had a motive? The police and prosecutors based their case on Harris's testimony and on the results of the lie detector tests, but Harris's testimony was clearly self-serving, and lie detector tests are famous red herrings. Anyone who could kill a cop in cold blood could lie to a polygraph examiner without breaking a sweat. Investigators put little or no stock in the polygraph process, unless the results fit a convenient theory. Of all the mistakes Dennis White made, allowing

Adams to take a polygraph test was probably the worst, because the results gave the police the momentum they needed to go forward with their investigation.

The murder of Robert Wood struck at the heart of police work, defined its limits, arbitrated its priorities and responses. *Somebody* had to die for this one, and it couldn't be David Harris. Under Texas law, juveniles cannot receive the death sentence. Here was the situation Dallas authorities faced: Harris was willing to say that Adams did it. All Adams could say was he didn't even know a murder had taken place. This point was lost on both the judge and the jury. The judge, Don Metcalfe, told me during an interview: "Something I've always wondered about this case is, why didn't Adams just say he was in the car and that Harris did the shooting?" The possibility that Adams wasn't in the car—that he had already been dropped off at his motel at the time of the murder—never occurred to the judge.

Detective Gus Rose was equally certain that David Harris told the truth. Hardened in Rose's memory was a clear portrait of this grown man, this drifter, "showing off for the kid." In his memory, the kid is always fresh-faced and innocent, in contrast to the dark and menacing Adams. First, Adams helps the kid dispose of his loot, then plies him with beer and marijuana, then treats him to an X-rated movie. "Wait a minute!" I tell Rose. "It was Harris, not Adams, who had money for beer, marijuana, and movies. Adams didn't even have money for gas, remember?" Rose doesn't hear me. He's "remembering" Adams's final act of depravity, hearing the five shots, watching a fellow officer fall dead by the side of the highway. It was a scene he had replayed thousands of times.

In a murder case, a defense attorney's first job is to develop his own scenario of the time and sequence of events. Dennis White had failed, but as I framed my own scenario I discovered that the time and sequence of events virtually proved that Adams was telling the truth. The second feature at the drive-in movie ended at 11:49 P.M., fifty minutes before Wood was killed. Adams and Harris both remembered leaving partway through the movie. That could easily have put them back at the motel before 11 P.M. Nowhere in Adams's statement is any mention of what time he got home. Nobody asked him, Adams told me. His brother Ray was no help. He had awakened briefly when Adams came in, but had not noticed the time. Adams's failure to pin down the time that he and Harris arrived at the motel makes sense only when you consider that he didn't realize for several days (he didn't even have a lawyer for the first week) that murder was even the focus of the investigation. Adams thought he was being held as an accessory to burglary. His statement, dictated after hours of questioning, contains not a word about murder. Even so, it was extremely naive of Adams to attach such little importance to the sequence of events.

But Adams *is* naive, as I discovered when I interviewed him at the Dallas County Jail before his hearing in magistrate John Tolle's court. Now 38, Adams came across as a nice guy, though somewhat slow and strangely passive. He had been on death row for more than a decade, but he showed no anger or righteous indignation, posited no clever conspiratorial theories or alternatives. All he could think to say in his defense was that he didn't do it.

After talking to Adams, I visited David Ray Harris on death row at the Ellis Unit outside Huntsville. Harris was 26 but looked five years younger —his blue eyes still sparkled, and there was still a boyish charm behind his grin. I asked Harris if he ever thought of Adams and how different both of their lives might have been if only Adams had invited him to spend the night at his motel. It was a loaded question. I knew from conversations with Adams that his answer would have special meaning: if he said yes, it would be an acknowledgment that Wood was killed *after* Harris had left Adams at the motel room.

"I think about it," Harris said, and the memory seemed to touch something deep. "If he'd just said, 'Come on in . . .' "

"Then what?"

Harris didn't reply, but the answer was obvious.

"Adams didn't kill that cop, did he?"

A thin smile played along his lips, as though he were pleased that I had guessed his little secret. He shook his head no.

"Did you kill him?"

He thought about the question for a while. Then he said, "I can't answer that."

"It can't hurt you now," I said, though I knew that wasn't necessarily true.

"It can't help me either," he said. "But if it ever gets to the point where they're strapping me on that gurney to die, stand by for a statement."

In December 1986, Judge Tolle heard all the new evidence and the reflections on how old evidence had been twisted. Adams's lawyers called both Millers and Randell to show that none of the rebuttal witnesses had a story that would stand up. Other testimony demonstrated that David Harris had indeed gotten a deal for his testimony against Adams. Though the judge would not permit the screening of clips from *The Thin Blue Line*, he made one exception. After detective Gus Rose told the court that Adams had never denied the murder, a clip from an interview was shown in which Rose made clear that Adams "kept saying over and over" that he didn't do it.

Tolle didn't rule on the motion for a new trial for nearly eighteen months. When he did make a ruling in the summer of 1988, the motion was denied. Adams's lawyers finally won their long and frustrating fight the following December when a state judge in Dallas heard the evidence and dismissed the case against Adams. Suddenly it was over. The ending was almost as stunning as the beginning, and nearly as inexplicable.

Ironically, the reason that Adams was finally set free wasn't the evidence but the climate. Errol Morris's brilliant film had become a box-office hit in the weeks just prior to the state hearing and was about to be nominated for an Oscar. The movie changed the climate in a way that my magazine story never could. "Adams was tried in a climate of hate and animosity," Schaffer reflected. "But the movie showed dramatically that they not only convicted the wrong man, they framed him. The public was convinced. In this new climate, it was okay for the judge to grant Adams relief."

The relief came with no apology, not even an admission of error. Though Adams got to tell his story on the talk show circuit and even testified before the Senate Judiciary Committee, he eventually faded into obscurity back home in Ohio. Neither Dallas nor the State of Texas ever paid him a penny for those twelve years that he lost. Adams didn't even get the usual $200 that the prison system hands out when a prisoner is released. Technically, he wasn't released from prison. His case was simply dismissed.

Turn Out the Lights
Dallas Cowboys
Old-Timers Reunion

I recognized Alicia Landry as soon as she walked into the party, but I had to get closer before identifying the man with her as her husband. Tom Landry seemed to have shrunk; either that or the floor was tilting. The 72-year-old founding coach of the Dallas Cowboys appeared surprisingly frail and stooped, as though he carried on his back the wreckage of countless careers and ambitions. For the first time in the thirty-odd years I had known him, Tom looked his age. So did a surprising number of people at the Dallas Cowboys old-timers reunion.

The idea for the reunion had originated with the wives of such former Cowboys as Lee Roy Jordan, Tony Liscio, Don McIlhenny, and Jerry Tubbs. For me, the party came at an auspicious time. Once, the Cowboys had been a big part of my life. From 1963 to 1967 I covered the team on a regular basis for the *Dallas Morning News*, and since then, I have written dozens of magazine articles about them. Like so many fans, though, I've had about all I can take of the Jerry Jones—Barry Switzer—Michael Irvin—Leon Lett follies. It was easy to love the teams of the sixties and seventies. They had an unspoiled innocence, even a certain nobility. That began to degenerate in the eighties and nose-dived into abject depravity by the nineties. Apparently others have the same feeling. Two new books looking at the early Cowboys—*Cowboys Have Always Been My Heroes*, by Peter Golenbock, and *Cotton Bowl Days*, by John Eisenberg—are scheduled for publication in August, just as the current team will be staggering into its uncertain future.

Still, when I got my invitation to the reunion, I wasn't sure that I should go. Some of the things I had written about the Cowboys were critical and some complimentary, but I knew from experience that while the players and coaches might forget the criticism, the wives never would. Sure enough, shortly after I arrived, Alicia Landry approached me while Tom stopped to chat with a couple of old players. "I hope you're not going to write anything nasty about us," she said in a stage whisper. Before the evening ended, two more wives made remarks similar to Alicia's. Sorry, ladies. One of the predictable things about reunions is that everyone falls back into old roles.

The old-timers reunion was limited to players, coaches, and staff—and a few sportswriters—who had been part of the coming-of-age years, 1960 to 1980, two decades in which the team emerged from a ragtag group of castoffs that nobody took seriously into the most fabled franchise in sports. The site was The Ranch, a party barn near the Dallas Convention Center, decorated for this occasion with blue and white balloons and banners that looked curiously dated. So did the players themselves. Most of them wore the same kinds of boots and Western-cut shirts they had worn thirty years ago, in keeping with the country and western theme. This was strictly a family affair, with children and grandchildren predominating: Nothing makes you feel as old as meeting the grandchild of a contemporary. One section of the room was lighted as a makeshift photographer's studio, where family groups took turns posing for pictures. On the opposite side of the large, open room, a western swing band played tunes that were familiar and easy for dancing. Families helped themselves to generous heaps of barbecue, beans, and potato salad. The cast of characters whose nighttime escapades led teammate Pete Gent to write *North Dallas Forty* could not have been more sober or low-key.

In the dim light of the party room, worn eyes squinted to read name tags, arthritic hands reached out to greet old friends, and reconstructed knees tried gamely to do the cotton-eyed Joe. At every table and in every group, tales of small defeats, near misses, and glorious triumphs gained nuances with each telling. At the bar, I ran into Tex Schramm, the executive who put together five Super Bowl teams and created the image of America's Team. Over the years I'd run into Tex countless times at countless bars, and our conversations had been unfailingly stimulating. But tonight, for some reason, talk was flat and awkward. We were forced to confront how much has passed—not only time but also the Cowboys' magic. Yet I heard not a word about the current Cowboys at the party; there was no common bloodline.

Looking around the room, I allowed random memories to surface in my consciousness. Pettis Norman, an unknown second-year tight end, deeply absorbed in a Bible, taking a solitary stroll at twilight across the campus of the training camp in Marquette, Michigan. Defensive tackle Rocky Colvin, pounding his fist into a steel locker in the Cotton Bowl dressing room, getting mentally ready for a game against the Giants. Bob Lilly, the Cowboys' first Hall of Famer, and his dove-hunting parties: drinking cases of beer and firing at dragonflies or anything else that moved. That charter flight home after a big win in New York in 1965, when rookie Bob Hayes's two touchdown receptions gave Dallas the right to participate in its first postseason game, in Miami—and the stricken look on Landry's face when Hayes, fortified by champagne, got on the airplane intercom and sang "Moon Over Miami."

Watching Tex return to his table, I noticed that he walked with a slow shuffle, his dancer's poise gone with time. I spotted Lee Roy Jordan, the great linebacker, across the room: Most of his hair had turned silver. Most of Jim Boeke's hair had vanished. Cornell Green, in my memory the ultimate warrior—a cornerback lithe and ribboned with muscle—had gone to lard. It's the fourth quarter for all of us.

Even the great Lilly appeared somewhat enfeebled. "When there's a chill in the air," Lilly complained, "my lungs ache and my fingers sting like someone is driving nails through them." This is a legacy of playing in the thirteen-below-zero conditions of the 1967 NFL championship game in Green Bay, forever to be known as the Ice Bowl. A number of Cowboys were treated for frostbite that day, and all of them have similar complaints. "Anytime the temperature drops below forty degrees," Jethro Pugh said, "my hands and feet feel like they're on fire." Lee Roy Jordan remembered that when the mercury had dropped during a hunting trip a few years ago, the pain got so severe that he actually cried in front of his son.

There were essentially two groups of players in the room—those from the Don Meredith era (1960—68) and those from the Roger Staubach era (1969—79), and they didn't mingle. A few, such as Lilly and Jordan, bridge the gap, having played under the leadership of both quarterbacks. The difference between the two groups, aside from age, is that those who played with Staubach wear Super Bowl rings, while those who played with Meredith missed out on two rings by a total of two yards. Football, the cliché goes, is a game of inches.

The Staubach group congregated near the front of the party room, where Roger, his wife, and Tom and Alicia Landry sat. Near the back of the room, out of the limelight as always, were offensive linemen Boeke and Liscio, along with Colvin and several other veterans of the sixties. They laughed about the time that Meredith bought drinks for the entire team at a posh hotel in Miami and signed Tex Schramm's name. Meredith's enduring popularity and his toughness and resiliency of spirit were the subject of many a conversation, but the key ingredient was missing—Meredith himself. Perhaps it would have been a different party if he had been in attendance, but nobody there had seen him for a long time.

A number of old teammates wrote Meredith a few weeks before the reunion, urging him to attend. But they never heard back. "I question if he ever got my letter," one lamented, shaking his head in despair. "I've heard that his wife Susan pretty much runs his affairs." Others have heard the same story, that Dandy Don's third wife is so protective that even agents and movie producers have tired of trying to contact him. In his day the most gregarious and approachable of the Cowboys, Meredith has become a recluse. Financially secure, he lives half the year in Palm Springs, California, half in Santa Fe, New Mexico. He gives out no address, just a post office box and a fax number. When former governor Ann Richards and her friend Bud Shrake visited him last winter in Santa Fe, Meredith appeared in good health, but his notoriously spindly legs were so fragile that he required a pair of $2,000 custom-made shoes to walk straight.

Meredith gives no interviews, responds to no queries, disdains the card-show circuit, and makes almost no personal appearances. But it's not the physical damage that causes him to shun the spotlight; it's the damage to his psyche. Nine bittersweet seasons in Dallas apparently have changed him. Meredith made a rare public appearance last December, signing autographs at a Kmart in New York as a favor to his friend, Kmart chairman Floyd Hall. He told a *New York Times* reporter, "I don't miss the limelight, not at all. I'm just more comfortable out of it." He had long since stopped answering to the name "Dandy Don." "Dandy is somebody else," he told the reporter, no doubt plaintively. "He wasn't a bad guy."

A couple of hours into the party, Landry began to look at his watch, and someone whispered to the photographer to get cracking on the official reunion photograph. When players, coaches, and staff were asked to take their places on the makeshift bleachers prepared for the occasion, the irrepressible Hollywood Henderson nudged his way around several players and slid into the seat next to Landry. Tom tried his best to smile. Henderson threw both arms around the startled coach's neck and plopped his legs into Landry's lap. Tom's face appeared on the verge of cracking, but not into a smile.

My wife and I left just behind Tom and Alicia. I'm glad I went, but I don't think I want to do it again.

Perhaps the reason that Meredith's failure to show up cast such a pall on the party—as if the class president hadn't attended the high school reunion—is that it reminded everyone of his unexpected and premature decision to retire after the 1968 season. It still haunts and puzzles these Cowboys, because it robbed them of their destiny to become the game's finest team. In 1966 and again in 1967, under Meredith's leadership, the Cowboys lost the NFL championship to the Green Bay Packers in the final seconds. In retrospect, these two near misses reflected the growing pains of a still immature franchise, but at the time, they devastated the Cowboys and prompted some finger pointing and blame shifting. As usual, Meredith was the designated goat. A hometown boy who twice played to All-American honors at Southern Methodist University, Meredith was the first big name to sign with the Cowboys. He got a five-year contract for $150,000, an enormous amount of money in 1960, and Dallas fans, being rank novices to the pro football experience, assumed that it guaranteed the team and the quarterback instant success. When they realized how dreadfully wrong they had been—that first Cowboys team went 0-11-1—they took it out on Meredith. No athlete in Dallas has ever been so maligned and abused by fans, sportswriters (including myself), and even coaches. John Eisenberg, a sports columnist for the *Baltimore Sun* who followed the Cowboys as a kid growing up in Plano, writes in *Cotton Bowl Days*, "Someone had to serve as a laboratory rat as the city developed the harder edge that came with the pros. It was [Meredith's] destiny to become the sacrificial figure on whom Dallas lost its innocence as a sports town."

Meredith set the tone for the sixties, playing with pain and an incredible assortment of injuries, shouldering the blame for defeats, deflecting the credit for success, defying and mocking Landry's somber, bloodless approach to the game. "Meredith had more fun playing the game than anyone I ever saw, and it made it fun for the rest of us," former running back Dan Reeves, now the head coach of the Atlanta Falcons, told me after the reunion.

Landry used to lecture his players on the subject of character, which he claimed was gained through adversity. But time after time, when adversity visited the Cowboys during a game, Landry pulled Meredith from crucial situations. Football stopped being fun for Meredith when Landry removed him from the 1968 playoff game against Cleveland after a couple of interceptions. The interceptions were not Meredith's fault; he was following the "keys" that Landry had given him—believing that the Browns' defense would react in a certain way, and if he threw to the right spot, the pass would be completed for a handsome gain. Unfortunately, the Browns failed to cooperate with Landry's game plan. And Landry rewarded Meredith's faith with a spot on the bench.

"Meredith shouldn't even have played in that game," Bob Lilly told me in a telephone interview following the party. "He had just gotten out of the hospital with a punctured lung. He didn't have a very good game, but then none of us did. The players felt that Tom should have defended him, but Tom got so focused on a game he didn't know if a player was hurt or not."

When Meredith went to Landry's office to tender his resignation after the season, he fully expected—and desperately wanted—Landry to reject it. The quarterback was only 31, just reaching his prime. After years of building, the Cowboys were finally putting all the pieces together. The offensive line was respectable, the defense was the best in the league, Meredith was comfortable with Landry's multiple-set offense and had mastered the art of picking apart a defense, and the players loved and trusted him. But Tom made no attempt to change Meredith's mind. Instead, he said, "Don, I think you've made the right decision." No blitzing linebacker ever crushed Dandy Don Meredith the way Tom Landry did that day.

As things worked out, Landry was able to replace Meredith the following year with a 27-year-old rookie named Roger Staubach. After a couple of seasons of sharing time with Craig Morton, Staubach got Dallas its first Super Bowl championship. Had Meredith elected to keep on playing, Staubach, as he has been the first to admit, probably would have left for a less-talented team, not content to be a backup. Game of inches, right? Say Landry had made the tiniest effort to talk Meredith out of retirement. Everything might have been different. Meredith might have been front and center at the 1997 old-timers reunion, and Roger Staubach would have been the answer to a trivia question.

Cowboys fans got to know Meredith mostly through the media, and the media often reflected Landry's point of view. Meredith's congenital good humor was one of his many unique qualities the Cowboys coach was unable to appreciate. Landry was an engineer by training and he viewed the game of football as a set of physical laws grounded on his own two innovations—the multiple-set offense and the flex defense. In Tom's scheme of things, players were as interchangeable as the parts of a machine. As long as a quarterback could operate the multiple-set offense, one player was no better or no worse than the other. Even after Staubach took over as the starter, Landry continued to juggle quarterbacks, with the result that the team sometimes panicked and lost confidence. The difference between Staubach and Meredith was that Roger never snickered when he talked back. What Landry found hard to accept in Meredith was exactly what made him so beloved by his teammates: No matter how grave a situation, he refused to lose his sense of humor.

At the reunion the old-timers told stories of how Dandy Don would waltz into the huddle singing a Willie Nelson song. Or he would interrupt the snap count at the line of scrimmage and tell an opposing player like Redskins linebacker Sam Huff, "Hey, Sam, you're in the wrong position!" It was his way of saying, "Stay cool, baby." In the 1966 NFL championship game, after the Packers jumped in front 14–0 before the Cowboys' offense ever got on the field, Meredith looked around at the grim faces in the first huddle and cracked, "Men, we're in a shitload of trouble!" By halftime the offense had responded with two touchdowns of its own and the score was tied. Latter-day Cowboys no doubt had great respect for Staubach, but the feeling that the sixties Cowboys had for Dandy Don Meredith went way past respect. "We would have done anything for him," Boeke told me. "Anything!"

I was a greenhorn 26-year-old sportswriter in 1960 when both the Cowboys and the Dallas Texans of the AFL started up business. For the next seven years, I covered pro football, first as the beat man following the Texans for the *Dallas Times Herald* (1960 — 62), then as the beat man following the Cowboys and a columnist for the *Dallas Morning News*. It was one hell of an education.

My influence on the Cowboys was minimal but not entirely nil. In 1964 I started writing about the "Doomsday Defense"—for no particular reason except it sounded sexier than flex defense—and the name caught on. My counterpart at the *Times Herald*, Steve Perkins, and I started a campaign to force Landry to move Mel Renfro from defensive back to offensive running back. Landry believed that Renfro's slight build couldn't take the pounding at running back, but our daily reports from training camp so fervently pleaded our cause—we called it MOO, short for "Mel on Offense"—that Landry finally relented. Unfortunately, in the season opener against the Giants, running back Renfro broke a bone in his foot. He subsequently returned to defense, where he made the NFL Hall of Fame, and Perkins and I found something else to bitch about. When I left Dallas in 1967, the Cowboys gave me a going-away party and a plaque, which is still on my bedroom wall. Mounted on the plaque is a kicking shoe and engraved beneath the shoe are the words "Just for Kicks," celebrating the time that I kicked a universally despised radio reporter down a flight of stairs at the Cowboys' headquarters on North Central Expressway.

Although I remain, however grudgingly, a Cowboys fan, my favorite memories of the team are still of those years—not just because I covered the team, but because I felt I was watching an absorbing sports drama. The Cowboys had great potential and great flaws, and you never knew which was going to win out. When the Golenbock and Eisenberg books arrived, I read them avidly to see if their recollections of the early years matched mine.

Eisenberg's book, *Cotton Bowl Days*, paints an accurate and often moving portrait of the team, reflecting both the researching skill of a veteran sportswriter (the author worked at the *Times Herald* before moving to the *Baltimore Sun*) and the memories of a boy who grew up believing in God, country, and the Dallas Cowboys. From 1960 until the present, Cowboys football was a family affair for the Eisenbergs. John's grandfather, Pop, originally purchased ten season tickets in 1960 and "lorded over them with patriarchal sway."

Golenbock's *Cowboys Have Always Been My Heroes* is a different matter. Though the book is billed as "a definitive oral history" of the Cowboys, the author's technique of running long, unchallenged quotes from former players, interspersed with just enough writer's narrative to move the story along, is anything but definitive. The oral history depends on interviews with a relative handful of players. And a disproportionate amount of the quotes on the turbulent 1965 season come from two infamous malcontents, Pete Gent and Buddy Dial. I should know. According to Golenbock's book, one of the main things they were malcontent about was me.

I remember the 1965 season all too well. It was a gut-wrenching rollercoaster ride that carried the Cowboys to new lows and new highs. The team finished with a respectable 7–7 record, the first time in their six seasons that the Cowboys had not had a losing record, and earned a trip to a playoff game. The ride was seldom pleasant, however. Landry benched Meredith unceremoniously during a losing streak and compounded his poor judgment by alternating two rookie quarterbacks, Craig Morton and

Jerry Rhome. After a fifth straight defeat, in a hushed locker room in Pittsburgh, Landry broke into tears as he admitted to the team that perhaps the fault was his. Bob Lilly recalled the moment for me: "He just started to cry, and nobody knew what to do. But we saw the real man that day. He was crying because he felt he had let us down. We never forgot that moment. It was the turning point for the Dallas Cowboys." A few days later, Landry pulled himself together and announced that Meredith would be his starter for the remainder of the season. But the team hadn't yet bottomed out.

The Cowboys moment that will forever live in infamy arrived a couple of weeks later in the Cotton Bowl against the defending NFL champion Cleveland Browns, with the first sellout crowd in Cowboys history looking on. Though the Cowboys were overmatched, they outplayed the Browns most of the game. Trailing by a touchdown with eighty-three seconds remaining, Dallas owned the ball on the Cleveland one-yard line. Seventy-six thousand Cowboys fans were on their feet; after six seasons of frustration, their team was about to tie or beat the best team in the league.

On first down Meredith dropped back to pass, read the reactions of the defenders as Landry had taught him to do, and threw the ball—straight to the Browns' middle linebacker. My game story in the *Dallas Morning News* the following day began with a takeoff on a famous passage written by Grantland Rice about the 1924 Army—Notre Dame game:

Outlined against a grey November sky, the Four Horsemen rode again Sunday. You know them: Pestilence, death, famine and Meredith.

Golenbock devotes four pages of his book to the reaction of four Cowboys receivers—Gent, Dial, Frank Clarke, and Pettis Norman—to my "Four Horsemen" story. All of them insist that the interception was Landry's fault, not Meredith's, and say that the players were so outraged by the story that in a team meeting they decided to give me a savage beating. Gent recalls, "We had a private team meeting without the coaches over Cartwright. They all wanted to kill him, and Meredith kept saying, 'You can't. It's his job. He's just doing his job like we're doing ours.' " Norman says the story was typical of "the sour grapes that really made the Gary Cartwright Era in Dallas." Dial, the onetime Rice All-American, calls me "a wormy little old devil . . . [who] breathed an ill wind."

There was no Gary Cartwright Era, just as there was no beating. To settle the question of my alleged thrashing and determine once and for all who called the fatal play that November day in 1965, I checked newspaper stories of the time and telephoned several players on the team, including Lilly, Reeves, and Bob Hayes, as well as Landry. None of the players I spoke with remembered a team meeting or talk of physical violence against me. "No, that never happened," Lilly said. "Now, Landry would come into the locker room with newspaper articles sometimes and say, 'Here's a scathing article and it's true, that's where we are, right there!'" Reeves, who is now the dean of NFL coaches, remarked that Gent had often reworked facts to fit his own agenda and said of the controversial play: "Really and truly, that play wasn't Meredith's fault. He only had three plays to choose from in our goal-line offense, two passes and a wedge where he hands off to the fullback going low over the top." In that case, I asked, shouldn't Landry have defended Meredith to the media? Reeves, who still refers to Tom as "Coach Landry," paused for a moment, then told me, "That's one of the things a coach has to consider when the quarterback is choosing the play." Though Reeves's reasoning was intentionally ambivalent, it's meaning was clear to me: he meant that Landry wasn't entitled to have it both ways, that when the Cowboys coach decided that he would call the plays he also agreed to accept the blame if those plays failed.

Landry didn't return my call. But in the dressing-room interview published in the *Morning News* the day following the game, Landry made it clear that the play was Meredith's doing. Then he added, disingenuously, "I don't second-guess my quarterback." There was a phrase, also borrowed from Grantland Rice, that you used to hear around the Cowboys locker room after a losing game: "It's not whether you win or lose, but who gets the blame."

Many of the players quoted in Golenbock's book (and Eisenberg's) are critical of Landry, not necessarily for the way he handled Meredith but for the way he handled the entire team. "Even when we won, Tom Landry would go to the media, and you'd think we'd lost," says Cornell Green. "Tom had trouble saying we played a good game. He had a problem with that." Even Lee Roy Jordan comes down hard on Tom: "The players always had to take the blame for the losses. If Tom had a bad game plan or if he called a bad play, it was always the players' fault."

Looking back, I realize that I allowed myself to become emotionally involved with the Cowboys. My reaction to a game was not much different from that of an ordinary fan, except that I got to talk to the players and coaches before blowing off steam. At a downtown fan club luncheon a few days after the loss to the Browns, a hard-core fan asked Landry why the team allowed me to write such uncensored garbage. Landry replied,

"You have to remember, when the game is over and we're all feeling terrible about losing, Gary is the one with the typewriter." I've always been grateful to Tom for understanding my role.

I don't regret the Four Horsemen story, but I do regret writing in my column later that Meredith was a loser. I have committed a lot of stupid opinions to print, but none as stupid as that. Timothy McVeigh is a loser. Don Meredith was an extraordinarily gifted and complex man, at once whimsical and introspective, and no one ever worked harder or under more pain or pressure to prove himself as an athlete. Reading Golenbock's book, I regretted all over again not getting straight my feelings for Meredith.

Several players described flying home from Washington a week after the Four Horsemen episode. Meredith's daughter, Mary Donna, was sitting in his lap. Apparently overcome with a sense of failure, Don began crying and saying out loud, "I'm not a loser." I had never heard that story before, and reading it nearly brought tears to my eyes.

After the 1965 season I spent several days talking with Meredith for what became a cover story in *Sport* magazine. It was as complimentary as the Four Horsemen had been abrasive. Meredith predicted that the Cowboys would continue to improve until they won more consistently than any team in history. The reason, he said, was Tom Landry. "I've learned one thing: Tom is right," he told me. "You get tired of a guy being so right so often, but that's the way it is. The hardest thing to do with Tom's system is believe it."

After he retired, Meredith went on a binge of self-destruction, literally trying to kill himself. In *Cowboys Have Always Been My Heroes*, Gent tells Golenbock about a drugs-and-booze-besotted trip that he and Meredith took to Baja California in 1969 as guests of the Jantzen swimwear company. On the trip, Meredith insisted on swimming in shark-infested waters, challenged a cantina-ful of bad Mexicans to a fight, and rode his motorbike into a ravine, dislocating his shoulder and fracturing an arm. In a local hospital, he almost died from an overdose of morphine. Until then, Gent says, Meredith and the Cowboys were talking about his coming back for the 1970 season. Instead, Meredith became one of the stars of ABC's *Monday Night Football* and eventually made peace with his past.

John Eisenberg traces the decline of the Dallas Cowboys as a team worth loving not to the arrival of Jerry Jones or the departure of Jimmy Johnson or to any other recent event, but to the abandonment of the Cotton Bowl in 1971. There is wonderful nostalgia in his recollections of the ratty old Cotton Bowl: "a big concrete tureen, a Depression-era project incorporating none of the amenities that would become standard features." The bathrooms were little more than outhouses, hot in the summer and cold in the winter, and the stadium's general-admission seats were separated from the reserved seats by strands of chicken wire. It was a blue-collar stadium, where blue-collar fans watched a blue-collar team, which for five seasons lost many more games than it won.

The concept of pro football as a social event didn't arrive in Dallas until 1971, Eisenberg reminds us, when Clint Murchison Jr. defied the civic leaders of Dallas and built Texas Stadium in suburban Irving. "The Cowboys had always cultivated a mildly snobby character with their multiple-set offense, reliance on computers, and Landry's unemotional approach," he writes. "But moving to Texas Stadium pushed their elitist reputation to a new zenith." In 1993, after Eisenberg's grandfather died, his 74-year-old father somehow forgot to mail the renewal for the family's season-ticket allotment, which by then had dwindled to a single pair. The old man telephoned the Cowboys' office, certain that they would forgive the minor oversight from a family that had been ticket holders since 1960. A sharp-tongued assistant eventually renewed the seats but warned him that he was on "probation" and that if this ever happened again, his tickets would be forfeited. "[This] was emblematic of the attitude searing pro football's soul," Eisenberg writes. "Teams no longer wanted fans: They wanted clients."

It is impossible to compare the teams of my generation with the present Cowboys. Everything is different—the game, the expectations, the money, the fans, the owners, even the sportswriters. If some of the old-timers thought I was a tough critic, how would they deal with Randy Galloway or the acerbic current crop of Dallas–Fort Worth talk show hosts?

The self-commodification of pro football has bred an atmosphere of nihilism and greed in which players jump from team to team, teams jump from city to city, and fans pay through the nose and damn well like it. The old Cowboys had no agents, no business managers, no limousines waiting to take them to the practice field. After every game they signed autographs for hours—without charge, of course. In the early sixties, players like Lilly and Meredith would show up at Dallas Cowboy Night at a bar called Bud Shrake West and, for a fee of a few free beers, talk directly to fans for a couple of hours. People felt like they knew them personally. Most of the players had regular jobs in the off-season: Landry sold insurance, and Meredith worked for a stockbroker. In 1958 the entire payroll of the twelve-team NFL was $3 million, about what Cowboys defensive tackle Leon Lett was making before his drug suspension. There was a loyalty to team and teammates unknown today, a willingness to sacrifice, and a devotion to the game itself.

It's ironic to remember that one of Landry's last top draft picks was Michael Irvin. Someone at the reunion asked Landry if he could coach today's game. "I probably could," Tom said, "but I wouldn't." A lot of us know that feeling.

"I Was Mandarin . . ."

I had been in some strange places and listened to some strange stories, but none of them had been as bizarre as this.

"Neither of us slept very well the night before the assassination," she said, snubbing out one cigarette and lighting another. "He kept tossing and turning, and finally I asked him how he could go through with it. He said 'Honey, it's like war. The President is a national security threat. If I don't do it, we'll be in a nuclear war very soon.' 'But he's got two children,' I told him, 'just like you.' But he said, 'Honey, matters were taken out of our hands a long time ago.' Then he turned over and pretended to be sleeping, and I started to cry. . . ."

We were seated in the living room of Geneva White Galle's modest home in Odessa, and she was telling me how her late husband, Roscoe Anthony White, killed President John F. Kennedy. The story was shot full of contradictions and wildly implausible coincidences—if this had been a book I would have thrown it away after page one—and yet there was something interesting in the way she told the story. Like the heroine of a soap opera, she was able to weave the most intimate details of history into the fabric of everyday life and make it sound, well, not exactly believable, but compelling.

I already knew that at least two parts of the story were true. First, Roscoe White was in the same military division as Lee Harvey Oswald—the First Marine Air Wing. So were about seven thousand other marines. Geneva swears that her husband and Oswald were friends, but except for her word, there is no proof they even knew each other. Second, in the fall of 1963, Roscoe White was a Dallas policeman, and Geneva worked for a few weeks as a hostess in Jack Ruby's Carousel Club. Geneva's story is that she overheard her husband and Ruby plotting to kill the president and that when Ruby caught her listening outside his office door, he threatened to torture and kill her two children, Tony and Ricky. Rock White, as Roscoe was called, suggested an alternative: that she undergo a series of shock treatments, calculated to obliterate her memory. Starting in 1964, Geneva submitted to four separate sets of shock therapy. The final treatment was in 1975, four years after Rock White was killed in a mysterious explosion.

"Rock looked like a whipped dog when he went to work that morning," she continued. "He didn't touch his breakfast. I was bathing the kids when I heard on TV that Kennedy had been shot. Then they said that a policeman had been shot, and I thought, 'Oh, my God, it's Rock!' But then he came home around seven, just like always. I put the kids to bed around nine and made a pot of coffee, and we sat in the kitchen, talking for a long time. He said, 'Honey, I never dreamed it would come to this.' "

She stopped, as though that were the end of the episode and began shuffling around the room, pointing to paintings, woven baskets, and ceramic figurines that she had created. They overwhelmed the tiny room. "I play the piano too," Geneva told me. "Or used to when I felt better." The cord of her oxygen breathing tube trailed behind, and from time to time she pressed the nostril piece tight, making little rattling noises as she inhaled. She told me that she was dying, and ticked off a list of diseases faster than I could take notes—diabetes, lupus, emphysema, cancer of the intestine, several others. "I shouldn't smoke like I do," she said, reaching for another one. Geneva had shown me photographs of herself when she was in her early twenties, including one in which Jack Ruby is leering as she lifts her miniskirt. She was a real looker twenty-seven years ago. Apparently her life had been a chapter from hell.

"The assassination," I reminded Geneva. "You were about to tell me what happened on Saturday."

"Sunday was Ricky's third birthday," she said, picking up the story line, "so on Saturday I baked a coconut cake and got the party favors ready. That night Ruby came over for supper. We sent the kids outside to play with Ruby's dog . . . what was her name? . . . Sheba or something like that. Rock cooked steaks on the grill, and I made baked potatoes and a salad and strawberry shortcake—that was Rock's favorite. After dinner I was washing the dishes and I heard them talking in the living room. Ruby was bragging about killing Kennedy, flying high like he was drunk, only he wasn't drinking. He talked about killing Oswald the next day and said it wasn't going to be any problem because he'd get a signal when they were ready to move him. He said something about the magic bullet, how one of them had left the magic bullet at Parkland—"

"He used that term—'magic bullet'?" I interrupted. The phrase wasn't even coined until after the Warren Commission report declared that the bullet found on a stretcher at Parkland Hospital was the same bullet that had passed through the bodies of both Kennedy and John Connally—a truly remarkable conclusion because the bullet would have had to travel through seven layers of skin, shatter one of John Connally's ribs, shatter a bone in Connally's wrist, and emerge in nearly pristine condition. Magic was the only word to describe such a bullet. "Are you sure they said magic bullet?" I asked Geneva again.

"I'm positive."

"Mama, that can't be right," her son Ricky interrupted. In the four and a half years since he had read his father's amazing confession in an old journal he had found in a footlocker, Ricky White had become familiar with the details of the assassination.

"I get confused," Geneva admitted. "It's been a long time."

Roscoe White's journal is no longer available for our inspection. Ricky says the FBI took it. For the moment let's accept on faith that there was such a journal. The alleged journal was an interesting mix of the familiar, the convenient, and the ludicrous: It must have read like a C-grade movie script, and yet it was a scenario that nearly every critic of the Warren Commission wanted to believe. As Ricky recalls, the entry for November 22, 1963, started like this: "I was Mandarin, the man behind the stockade fence who fired two shots. Lebanon was the man in the Book Depository who fired two shots. Saul was the man in the Records Building who fired two shots." Oswald wasn't mentioned by name, but apparently he was the patsy, not one of the shooters. Mandarin's spot behind the stockade fence at the crest of the grassy knoll would have been the perfect position for a sniper. From that vantage point a marksman could have picked off the president with a pistol.

Though the Warren Commission maintained that no shots came from the grassy knoll, dozens of eyewitnesses thought otherwise. So did Sheriff Bill Decker, and so did a number of Dallas policemen, who rushed up the hill immediately after the shots were fired. Almost all of the doctors who worked on the president at Parkland thought the head wound indicated a shot from the front.

Anomalies like these are what keep the mystery of the assassination alive—and have brought the otherwise unremarkable American Gothic family of Roscoe and Geneva White into the public light.

Who was Roscoe White, and what was there about his life that made anyone suspect he was an assassin in the employ of some renegade intelligence organization? For one thing, he fit the profile. He grew up on a farm outside the small town of Foreman, Arkansas, a model boy who loved football, God, and country, who did what he was told and didn't ask questions. The speech that Roscoe White made to his graduation class at Foreman High School, warning of the international communist conspiracy and advocating a strong national defense, was a remarkable declaration of patriotic fervor, touching in its innocence but unquestionably sincere. This was a young man waiting to be molded, prepared to make any sacrifice in the cause of the Cold War.

After graduation, Rock worked in his grandfather's sawmill in East Texas. "He was lean-mouthed," recalls Kenny Slagle, who worked with him. "He didn't say much about his personal life. But he was a worker. We worked on Saturday without any kind of supervision, stacking lumber until it was stacked right." At age 21, Rock married Geneva Toland, who was just 15. A year later, he joined the Marines.

In August 1957 he sailed aboard the USS Bexar, from San Diego to Yokosuka, Japan. One of his shipmates was Lee Harvey Oswald. For the next five and a half months, White and Oswald were assigned to the First Marine Air Wing, first at Atsugi, Japan, and later at Subic Bay in the Philippines. Oswald was a radar operator in Marine Air Group 11, and White was an auto vehicle operator in Marine Air Group 16. The two groups may have been quartered miles apart, but Oswald and White probably drank at the same enlisted-men's club. Being Texans a long way from home, there's a good chance the two met. Atsugi, incidentally, was one of the bases from which the CIA operated its ultrasecret U-2 reconnaissance flights.

In 1959 White reenlisted for six years but inexplicably changed his mind in 1962 and applied for a hardship discharge. In the meantime, Oswald had also received a hardship discharge, had defected to Russia for thirty-one months, and then was allowed to return to the United States without so much as a debriefing by U.S. intelligence. Oswald's odyssey stretched credulity beyond all reason: Many of his marine buddies just assumed that Oswald was an American intelligence agent. Early in 1963, Roscoe White moved his family to the Oak Cliff section of Dallas, where Lee Harvey Oswald was living.

Geneva White remembers her husband's talking about a friend from the Marine Corps named Lee, particularly a story of how Lee got drunk one night and kept falling down a flight of stairs. Among the memorabilia that Rock brought home after his discharge was a photograph of a group of marines waiting to board a ship in the Philippines: Oswald is clearly identifiable in the foreground. Geneva says that the marine in the background, whose face is shaded by the bill of his cap, is her husband. The same photo, cropped differently, was published in *Life* magazine three months after the assassination. Another souvenir was a .22-caliber two-shot derringer. Geneva remembers that Rock told her, "Keep this in a safe place. It'll be worth a lot of money some day." The derringer is similar to one that fell out of Oswald's barracks locker in 1958, wounding him in the arm.

Geneva recalls being introduced to Lee Oswald a few months before the assassination at a rifle range near the Grand Prairie Naval Air Station, where White and Oswald were practicing marksmanship. A few weeks later, she saw Oswald in a grocery store near their home in Oak Cliff. "I saw your friend Lee today," she told Rock, who became irritated and told her to never mention that name again. About the same time, Geneva caught her husband in bed with a woman named Hazel, an act of infidelity that severely strained their marriage. Rock promised that the affair was over, Geneva recalled, but when she happened to overhear Jack Ruby mention Hazel's name one night at the Carousel, she stopped outside the door of his office and eavesdropped. She heard Ruby tell her husband: "Hazel is the contact." Ruby said something about the Bay of Pigs and said how Kennedy had betrayed them. The longer she listened, Geneva claimed, the clearer it became that her husband and Ruby were talking about killing the president. This, at least, is the memory of a dying woman with a history of shock treatments.

Policemen who worked with Rock White find the mere suggestion that he was involved in the assassination ludicrous. "Let me put it this way," said W. L. Bernard, now retired from the Dallas Police Department, "Roscoe was one hundred percent jarhead marine, just like me, trained to follow orders. Now do you suppose a man like that would kill the Commander in Chief of the United States of America?" John T. Williams, another former Dallas policeman, said, "The whole story is unbelievable. Rock never told anyone that he was personally acquainted with Oswald or knew anything about the assassination." White quit the police force in October 1965—two years to the day after he signed on—telling fellow officers he was quitting because of financial and marital problems.

In the six years that followed, Rock White made a number of unexplained trips to New Orleans and other places. "I was never sure what was happening," Geneva says, "but I was raised to let the man do the thinking and not ask questions." In 1968 White moved his family to Mountain Home, Arkansas, supposedly to work for the post office. But nobody at the Mountain Home post office remembers him, and postal employment records don't go back that far. Later that same year the family returned to Dallas, and White became the assistant manager of a five-and-dime store in Richardson.

"The family appeared to have money," recalled the Reverend Jack Shaw, who was their pastor at Central Park Baptist Church. "New car, new home. As I recall, Roscoe pledged $10,000 to our building program." White's sons, Ricky and Tony, had new bicycles and go-carts, and the family purchased a cabin on a lake in Central Texas. Rock continued to mess around with other women, and Jack Shaw counseled the couple and prayed with them on several occasions. "Rock poured his heart out to me," Shaw said. "He told me he had sinned against his God, his country, and especially against his wife. He told me he had taken human life on foreign soil and here at home. I knew he had been in the service and had been a policeman, and I didn't press him for details."

In the summer of 1971, shortly after Geneva returned from a trip to New Orleans, she suffered an emotional breakdown and was hospitalized for about a month. Jack Shaw was surprised that the family hadn't sought his spiritual guidance but sensed that there was some reason for their reluctance. Years later he learned that on the trip to New Orleans, a strange and sinister man had approached Geneva in a nightclub, reminded her about Rock's part in the Kennedy assassination, and told her: "We have another job for Rock. Tell him he has forty-eight hours to get in touch." Apparently White never got in touch with the man.

By this time White had a better-paying job at M&M Equipment Company. But in September he was fatally burned when a leak in an acetylene torch flamed up, causing a can of chemicals that was stored under his workbench to explode. On his deathbed White told Jack Shaw that the explosion was no accident. Shaw assumed that there would be a criminal investigation, but there wasn't. White's family eventually reached an out-of-court settlement with the chemical manufacturer for $57,000.

Not long after that, Geneva and her two sons moved back to her parents' home in Paris, where she remarried. Jack Shaw didn't see or hear from her again for nearly twenty years.

Ricky White bounced along like an overgrown puppy, leading a film crew to the shed behind his grandparents' home in Paris. "People don't realize it yet," he said, opening the door and pointing to the place where he had found the footlocker that contained his father's journal, "but this is a hysterical location." Ricky sometimes got his words mixed up, saying "hysterical" when he meant "historical" and talking about "Daily Plaza" (Dealey Plaza) and how things were "unnormal" or "obvient" (obvious).

There was a shaggy, good-natured innocence about Ricky White, a bubbalike quality that made you want to pat him on the head. He had been a football player and a vocational agriculture student at Paris High; he still raised pigs, chickens, and geese at his rural home outside of Midland. His standard dress was boots, jeans, and a grimy oil-field gimme cap that he wore night and day, indoors and out, pulled down around his ears so that the tufts of cream colored hair splayed around the rim like spaghetti. It was always "yes, sir" this and "no, ma'am" that with Ricky. Though he was nearly thirty, older people invariably called him the kid or the boy. When someone asked a question that required coupling two or more independent thoughts, the look of bewilderment that shadowed Ricky's face was truly childlike. If the Roscoe White story was a hoax, I decided early on, Ricky was its victim, not its perpetrator. He no more could have invented or even acted out a hoax of this sophistication than he could have explained the theory of quantum physics.

By the late summer of 1990, Ricky had become a minor celebrity. The print media had pretty much dismissed the story after a few days, but Ricky was in demand as a guest on talk shows, at civic club luncheons, and in college classes. A British producer named Nigel Turner brought a film crew from New York to document the story, and American producers sent out feelers. In public appearances Ricky was always escorted by one of the founders of the JFK Assassination Information Center in Dallas, who booked his appearances and screened the tips and leads sparked by the Roscoe White story. All this exposure couldn't have been easy on the family of Roscoe White, this constant demand that they acknowledge that a beloved father-husband-brother committed one of the most heinous crimes in history. Yet in some curious way the family seemed proud of

Roscoe's accomplishments, or at least reconciled to them. "I think he was the Oliver North of his time," said Roscoe's sister, Linda Wells. "He was just doing what he thought was best for our country."

Ricky didn't find his role as minor celebrity altogether distasteful, even though it caused some dissension within the family. His wife, Tricia, complained that when Ricky was invited to New York to appear on the Morton Downey television show, she didn't even get to go. "I was there the day we found the journal," she said, "but nobody ever asks me about it." Ricky tried hard to placate Tricia, but privately he believed she was being unreasonable. "It wasn't her daddy that killed Kennedy," he said. Geneva was also a problem, but for the moment she seemed content to let Ricky do the talking. But the story always went back to Geneva. She was the validator, the institutional memory. She was the one who said that Rock knew Oswald. She was the source of the stories about Jack Ruby. Everything that Ricky and Tony knew about their father and about Dallas and the strange happenings of 1963 came from Geneva. Even the journal had her fingerprint in that she was the only one who could vouch for its authenticity.

Ricky and other members of the family discovered the footlocker in 1982, on the day of Geneva's father's funeral. It contained not only the journal but also Roscoe White's service record and other memorabilia, including an unmarked safe-deposit-box key and what appeared to be a receipt for $100,000 in negotiable bonds. Ricky took the contents of the footlocker to his home in Midland and puzzled over them for months. He studied photographs from his father's military days and read bits and pieces from the journal, trying to grasp a father who had died before Ricky had a chance to know him.

For reasons that Ricky is still at a loss to explain, almost four years passed before he got around to reading Roscoe White's journal entry for November 22, 1963. Stunned by what he had read, Ricky drove to his mother's house in Odessa and showed Geneva the passage dealing with the assassination. "She read for a few minutes and started crying," Ricky said. "Then she told me it was all true."

Maybe Geneva planted the idea in his head—or maybe it got there by itself—but Ricky was overwhelmed by the belief that his father had meant for him to find the journal, that it was some kind of message from the grave. The journal seemed to him the centerpiece of a puzzle, extending back . . . he tried to remember how far. The mystery must have started, Ricky decided, after his father's death, when an old family friend appeared at their home in Paris with a mysterious packet of photographs. The family friend—let's call him Bill X—had been hiding the packet for Roscoe, or at least that's what Geneva led her children to believe. Then she locked the packet in a cabinet in her bedroom and allowed no one to see it.

As a teenager, Ricky knew only that the photographs seemed important. One day when Geneva was away from the house, Ricky and his friend Lance Nicholson forced open the cabinet and looked at the aging photographs. They were surprised and a little disappointed to discover that the secret treasure was nothing more than pictures of people, places, and physical evidence connected with the assassination of President Kennedy. Included in the forty photographs were a picture of Oswald's naked body on a morgue slab; numerous photos of Oswald's personal possessions, including selective service and marine service cards issued to Alek Hidell, Oswald's alias; and a variation of the famous photograph of a smirking Oswald posing in a backyard with a rifle, a side arm, and copies of communist newspapers.

There should have been no mystery concerning the origin of these photographs. On the day of the assassination Roscoe White had been assigned to the identification bureau of the Dallas Police Department and had no doubt copied the pictures from the evidence file, as had other policemen. But that explanation didn't satisfy—or even occur to—Ricky White. Nor did it explain why his parents put such a high value on the photographs or why Bill X, who had known Geneva before she had met Rock, had kept them until Rock's death.

A few months after Ricky first viewed the photographs, something else happened that deepened the enigma. Two men broke into the White home in Paris, beat up Geneva, and took, among other things, the packet of pictures. The men were arrested a few days later in Florida on an unrelated charge, and FBI agents sent the pictures to Washington, where they were turned over to the Senate Intelligence Committee, which was investigating the government's relations with the intelligence community. The packet was eventually returned to Geneva, but the mystery didn't end there. In December 1976 staff members from the House Select Committee on Assassinations (HSCA) showed up at Geneva's home in Paris and again collected the packet of photographs and other items of potential evidence, including a rifle stock that had belonged to Roscoe White. Shortly before the HSCA report was issued in 1979, the old family friend Bill X approached Ricky outside a grocery store in Paris and told him confidentially that the report would name his father as one of the conspirators. People in Paris believed that Bill X was a former agent with navy intelligence, though there was no proof. At any rate, his story turned out to have no credibility, and Ricky forgot the incident—until the night he read his father's journal entry for November 22, 1963.

In the weeks that followed, Ricky spoke of the journal to several close friends and acquaintances, but none of them actually saw the book. The only people who say that they have seen the journal are Ricky, his mother, his wife, and a woman named Denise Carter, who read parts of the journal while babysitting with Ricky and Tricia's two children. Ricky also told some of his story to Midland district attorney Al Shorre: He wanted Shorre to give him legal advice and to help locate the bank that went with the safe-deposit-box key from the footlocker. Shorre's chief investigator, J. D. Luckie, made several trips to Dallas but couldn't find the bank. In the meantime, Shorre told the FBI what Ricky had told him.

In January 1988 two FBI agents hauled Ricky and the contents of the footlocker to their office in downtown Midland and questioned him for five hours, copying some of the material and making an impression of the safe-deposit-box key. All his belongings were returned, but later that same day one of the agents came again to Ricky's house, supposedly to retrieve a notebook he had accidentally placed with the other material. A couple of days later, Ricky and Tricia discovered that the journal was missing. Agents of the FBI categorically deny that they saw—much less that they stole—Roscoe White's journal.

Only after the journal vanished did the story suggest commercial possibilities. Ricky was working for the Orkin Exterminating Company at the time, and he enlisted the support of a fellow worker, Andy Burke. The two of them began investigating the journal's allegations and interviewing people who had known Roscoe White. Burke, who had a flair for promotion, convinced Ricky and his family that the story was worth a lot of money and attempted to line up writers, publishers, and film producers. In July 1989 Ricky and Andy took a trip to New York and spoke to an editor at Viking Penguin. But publishers weren't interested: Without the journal Ricky had nothing to sell. Obviously Ricky and Andy needed to do a lot more research. But research was expensive and time-consuming, and neither could afford to quit his job. On top of everything else, this effort of trying to prove that his father was a ruthless killer was putting an enormous emotional strain on Ricky White, who began to wonder if he really wanted to know the truth.

Meanwhile, Geneva, who faced staggering medical bills and was several months behind in her house payments, lined up her own writer—a professor at the community college—and began to dictate her story. By this time, Ricky was so distraught that he spoke of taking all the evidence he had collected and burning it. Geneva suggested that he simply bury it in the same coffin that she expected soon to occupy.

In January 1989 Geneva, Ricky, and Tony agreed to act in concert. The instrument that brought the White family together was an offer from a consortium of Midland oil men who agreed to fund the research in return for a share of any profits that might be forthcoming. Incorporated under the name of Matsu, the consortium retained a literary agent from San Antonio and searched for a writer in Dallas to draft a synopsis. Later, members of the consortium bought out Andy Burke's interest for $16,000. But the problem was the same as it had always been: There was still no hard evidence to support the story, nor did anyone in the group know how to go about gathering evidence. By the spring of 1990 many of the investors were beginning to have serious doubts.

In desperation, Ricky went to see Larry Harris, a freedom of information officer for the U.S. Immigration and Naturalization Service in Dallas and coauthor of a book on the assassination titled *Cover-up*. Ricky and Andy Burke had talked to Harris on four previous occasions, without really explaining what they had in mind. "Burke had done most of the talking," Harris recalled. "All Ricky told me was that his father used to be a Dallas policeman, and he was trying to gather information about his life. But this time he came out with it. He said in this real low voice, 'Larry, I think my father was one of the men who killed President Kennedy.'"

Harris, who had spent fifteen years investigating the assassination, was impressed by Ricky's sincerity and by his obvious emotional dilemma. As it happened, Harris and Gary Shaw, a Cleburne architect and coauthor of *Cover-up*, had just opened the JFK Assassination Information Center in Dallas. The center was conceived as a project to educate the public about the mysteries of what its founders regarded as the greatest unsolved murder in the nation's history, and to analyze data and act as a clearinghouse for new tips and leads. Shaw and a third partner, a builder-developer named Larry Howard, set up shop on the third floor of the West End Marketplace, an old warehouse converted into a shopping mall three blocks north of Dealey Plaza.

In the spring of 1990 Ricky White and the JFK center seemed a match made in heaven.

The exterior of the JFK center's three thousand square feet of exhibition and office space has the macabre facade of a wax museum. On one side of the entrance, video highlights of the assassination run continuously from eleven in the morning until ten at night, and on the other side life-sized photographs of Ruby and Oswald loom like giant ogres. Above the picture of Oswald, in large letters, is the famous quote—and the center's central message—"No, sir, I didn't kill anybody. I'm just a patsy." On another wall, above a montage of photographs, is an equally interesting quote, this one from New Orleans crime boss Carlos Marcello, who was singled out as a prime suspect in the assassination by the House Select Committee: "Three can keep a secret, if two of them are dead." Marcello is said to have this exact quote on his office wall.

There was a quixotic quality about Shaw and his partners that was both a necessity to the center's operation and a detriment to its survival. Shaw and Larry Howard had quit lucrative professions to work full-time at the center. One or both were usually there seven days a week, answering phone calls and dealing with people who walked in from the mall with tales to tell or questions. Gary Shaw, who had been investigating the assassination for twenty-six years, was a mild-mannered, thoughtful man, respected among assassination researchers for his knowledge and for his ability to keep the peace among rival factions. Like other disciples of the assassination-conspiracy theory, they accepted that the Warren Commission was the Antichrist. Beyond that, the scenario was anyone's guess. The problem was separating the nut from the shell, and in an environment in which the nuts tended to predominate, the pitfalls were deep and treacherous.

The partners wanted to believe the Roscoe White story, wanted it too much. It was their hottest lead since the House Select Committee issued its report eleven years earlier, and it fit nicely with their need to establish that the fatal head shot came from the grassy knoll. They recognized the potential for fraud—indeed, paranoia ran shoulder deep at the JFK center—but they made themselves believe that the story would rise or fall on its own merits. Ricky volunteered to take a lie detector test, which he passed, and agreed to turn over all his father's papers to the center. If the partners had stuck to their original plan—to keep this new batch of evidence to themselves until it could be either proved or disproved—the story might have had a happier ending. But three months into the investigation, fearful that the FBI might swoop down and confiscate the evidence, or that one of their sources might compromise it, they decided to go public long before they had the story nailed down.

Once that happened, the center was flooded with calls and letters, some of them intriguing, most of them crazy or pathetic, few of them apparently helpful. An ex-marine and soldier of fortune named Gerry Patrick Hemming remembered that on a trip to Dallas in 1963 to raise money for Cuban exiles, he met Roscoe White, who tried to sell him some rifles. A woman who didn't sign her name wrote that she believed her husband was part of Roscoe White's assassination squad. Another woman from Fort Ord, California, wrote that Henry Kissinger had arranged Kennedy's murder to avenge an insult and that he kept the dead president's brain pickled in a jar in his basement. At one point, Gary Shaw and I flew to St. Louis to interview a man who claimed that the assassination plan used to kill JFK was the same plan he had drawn up in 1954 to kill Harry Truman. After listening to the man for three hours, I was convinced that his was the most stupid, simpleminded, and outrageous concoction I had ever heard. But Gary Shaw wasn't so sure. "Why would he lie?" Gary asked. That was a question I couldn't answer. Maybe the man thought he could sell the story as a book or a movie plot. Maybe the telling had made him feel important. Maybe he was lonely. Maybe he was nuts.

I came to realize that Gary Shaw's real mistake was in not keeping the Roscoe White story within the confines of his own organization. Shaw decided, however, to include on the investigative team an outsider, a Houston private investigator named Joe H. West, who had been working with Shaw on other aspects of the assassination. Shaw's partners didn't trust West. They saw him as reckless, comically secretive, and self-aggrandizing —a buffoon who unfailingly introduced himself as a "certified legal investigator licensed by the State of Texas," as though that were something truly special. West had approached Shaw two years ago and declared that he wanted to spend the remaining days of his life solving what he regarded as the greatest mystery of all time. "I gave him some leads to follow, and he did a pretty good job," Shaw said. "He tracked down a Mafia hit man who claimed that he had delivered some stolen rifles to Jack Ruby a few weeks before the assassination." In the spring of 1990, Shaw convinced his partners that the team needed a man as aggressive and innovative as Joe West, a decision they would soon regret.

West almost immediately justified Gary Shaw's faith, however. The team was having problems with Geneva: She seemed confused about the events of 1963. West decided to solicit the help of Reverend Jack Shaw (no relation to Gary), who had counseled Geneva through many emotional problems and who had been at Roscoe White's side when he died. When Ricky and Andy Burke called on Jack Shaw months earlier, Shaw had refused to help, but the minister was impressed with Joe West's credentials and agreed to join the team. Shaw's ministry had greatly expanded in twenty years. He now operated the Marketplace Christian Network in Plano, and counseled members of the flock for a fee of $100 an hour. West himself was a former minister, and the two men formed an instant bond.

A few days later Jack Shaw flew to Odessa for a reunion with his one-time parishioner. While other team members waited outside, Shaw talked to Geneva, regaining her confidence. Eventually he would record more than forty hours of interviews, but that day, after only a few hours, he achieved a partial breakthrough. "Oh, my God!" Geneva called out suddenly. "I can't believe I'm remembering that!" and she began talking about her trip to New Orleans and the sinister man who had approached her. Geneva thought the name of the man she met in New Orleans was Netti, or something similar. Joe West assembled eleven photographs and asked Geneva if any of them was the man she remembered. She selected a picture of Charles Nicoletti, a gangland enforcer who was the key man in the CIA-Mafia plots to kill Castro.

There was a major development in the investigation in early June when Ricky recalled that the journal spoke of a witness-elimination program and hinted that the material from the footlocker contained other clues. One inexplicable item discovered in the footlocker was a paper sack containing some strips of cedar bark. Ricky, and later Geneva and Tony, remembered that Rock had buried a box near a large cedar tree beside their lake cabin. That had to be it . . . the message from the grave.

On June 6 the team located the cabin, now deserted, and for three days proceeded to dig up the backyard, first with shovels and picks and finally with a backhoe. But they found nothing. Bitterly disappointed, they returned to Gary Shaw's home in Cleburne to regroup. As Ricky was driving back to Midland, he stopped in Ranger to buy gas and telephone his wife, who told him that his mother had been trying to reach him. Geneva had found another clue. On the inside of the paper sack that had contained the cedar bark, she discovered a barely legible notation, some Roman numerals similar to a house framer's code, and in even smaller print the word "Paris." "I think your daddy was telling us there's something hidden in your grandparents' old house," Geneva said. Ricky turned around and drove back to his hometown of Paris.

I t was late that night when Ricky reached the old house, which had been partially destroyed by fire. After breaking the lock on the front door, he searched the house by flashlight, first the downstairs and then the attic. Behind a piece of plywood he saw a heavy aluminum canister, sealed tight.

"My heart was beating something awful," Ricky told me. "I'm a pretty stout old boy, but I had to use a crowbar to pry it open."

What he found were his father's Marine Corps dog tags, negatives of old family photographs, a faded green textbook with newspaper pictures pasted over the pages, and three cables covered in protective plastic. The cables professed to be orders from navy intelligence, addressed to Mandarin, using Roscoe White's serial number. A cable dated October 1963 instructed Mandarin that his next assignment was "to eliminate a national security threat to world-wide peace." At the bottom of the cables was the code name RE-rifle, which was strikingly similar to ZR/RIFLE, an ultrasecret CIA project during the Kennedy administration, formed to recruit assassins to murder foreign leaders.

The green book, or the witness-elimination book, as it came to be called, frightened Ricky White more than all the other pieces of evidence put together. Though the contents of the book hardly supported such a conclusion, Ricky saw it as proof that his father had murdered repeatedly. Ricky believed that this was some sort of ghoulish scrapbook, apparently compiled at random and embellished with numerical code and hieroglyphics. Inside the front cover was his father's name and serial number, and the words "players or witnesses." Pasted to each page were old newspaper photographs. Some were easily identifiable—Ruby, Oswald, Jack and Robert Kennedy—but others were faces without names. One of the more obscure faces turned out to be Perry Raymond Russo, who once testified that he had attended a meeting in New Orleans where the plot to assassinate President Kennedy had been discussed; also in attendance was Lee Harvey Oswald. Written below the picture were the words, "Big Mouth you talked after all."

On another page was a copy of the famous Mary Moorman photograph, taken at the instant the president's head was blown open. An X drawn across a spot beside the stockade fence marked the place where Mandarin would have stood. Below the picture were these words: "Mandarin kills K uses 7.65 Mauser in assassination." For three days after the assassination, the Dallas police, the district attorney, and even the CIA believed the murder weapon was a Mauser. One of the pieces of evidence that Ricky turned over to the research team was his father's 7.65 Mauser.

The contents of the canister stunned Ricky White. It was nearly a week before he told any member of the team what he had discovered, and even then he didn't mention the green book. But Joe West seemed to know that Ricky was hiding something. West confronted Ricky one night after they had interviewed an old friend of Roscoe's. Ricky remembers feeling emotionally overwhelmed and on the verge of tears. At that moment he decided to show West the canister and its contents—all except the green book—and to give it to West for safekeeping. But rather than share this new evidence with other members of the team, West took it to Houston and locked it in his safe-deposit box. He eventually supplied the others with copies of the cables, but the originals remained locked in his bank box until Matsu filed a lawsuit. West countersued, charging that he had been libeled and his life threatened.

When Gary Shaw discovered that his partners had been right all along, that Joe West was a loose cannon, he terminated his relationship with the Houston investigator. But it was too late. Joe West—and his new associate, the Reverend Jack Shaw—were pursuing a separate investigation. Apparently West had appointed himself custodian of the evidence. Gary Shaw and his partners had Ricky and the green book, but West had the cables. And even more important, with Jack Shaw on his team, West had Geneva.

From the start the team had worked too slowly for Joe West's taste, not being aggressive enough with potential witnesses and missing what he regarded as obvious clues. West outraged Ricky by claiming that Roscoe White's old friend Bill X was a member of the assassination squad. Gary Shaw worried that West would compromise their investigation and maybe subject the JFK center to a slander suit. Such petty considerations did not bother Joe West, who vowed he would pursue Kennedy's killer until his dying day. "Like a mighty army marching across the land," West proclaimed grandly, "when justice is done, that will be my payday."

West claimed to have a Mafia informant who told him that five Mafia big shots were in Dallas on the day of the assassination, and from this he extrapolated another gunman on the grassy knoll. Even before Geneva identified Charles Nicoletti as the man she had met in New Orleans, West reached the conclusion that Nicoletti was one of the Kennedy assassins. On May 11 he called a press conference in Galveston to make this startling announcement. But this was just a warm-up for the big event.

In mid-September 1990 West sent out press releases announcing another press conference and hinting that at long last he was about to produce the smoking gun. It seemed that a *second* Roscoe White journal had surfaced. Geneva had found it two weeks earlier, found it quite by coincidence when she happened to knock over a book titled *Presidents of the United States*. It was hidden under "Kennedy, John F."

I had to wonder why Geneva hadn't mentioned this remarkable discovery to me when I interviewed her just a few days after she allegedly found the second journal. She hadn't even mentioned it to the other members of her family. Instead, she had turned the journal over to Jack Shaw and Joe West. And though it wasn't exactly a quid pro quo, she simultaneously received a payment of $5,300, part of it a gift from film producer Oliver Stone and the remainder from Jack Shaw's ministry.

Standing with his back to a banner proclaiming "Truth, Inc.," West told a large gathering of media that he was "only a certified legal investigator licensed by the State of Texas, not a documents expert," and therefore couldn't vouch for the authenticity of this new piece of evidence. But the fact that he had gone to all this trouble to make it public suggested otherwise. The night before the press conference, Jack Shaw had spoken of this breakthrough as "one of the most historically important events of the twentieth century." Apparently, Shaw changed his mind, because the next morning he pleaded with West to postpone the announcement until experts could examine the document. But West's mind was made up, and wild mustangs couldn't have dragged him off the rostrum. Halfway through the press conference Shaw slipped out of the room and flew back to Dallas.

Almost everyone who saw the journal believed that it was a fraud. John Stockwell, the CIA-agent-turned-author, pronounced the work "a crude fabrication," pointing out that though the journal was supposedly written between 1957 and 1971, it appeared to be written in the same felt-tip pen. Felt-tip pens weren't used until the early sixties. A more obvious flaw was a mention on the next to the last page of Watergate—apparently Watergate was to be Roscoe's last assignment, which he refused. The problem with this—other than believing that a man who had killed the president and numerous others would dig in his heels at the idea of taking part in a two-bit burglary—is that the break-in at the Watergate complexes didn't occur until ten months after Roscoe White died. The scandal that we now know as Watergate wasn't called that until weeks after the break-in. When I mentioned this to Joe West at the press conference, he became indignant and gave me a lecture about how the term "watergate" is more than two thousand years old and appears in the third chapter of the Book of Nehemiah.

The new journal fractured the tentative harmony within the White family. "That's not my daddy's handwriting," Ricky protested. "And that's not the way he wrote." There was a whiny, cringing, self-pitying tone to the prose, strikingly unlike Rock White's lean, spare style. The language was turgid, overburdened with regrets for what a rotten husband he had been, and gushing with appreciation for Geneva—"God thank you for Geneva. I've got me one hell of a woman. Thank you thank you God."

Ricky, Tricia, and nearly everyone else believed that Geneva created the journal. To me, this was a given. Considering her nearly hopeless financial situation and the constant admonitions of others, imploring her to come up with some new piece of evidence—something else—the creation could be viewed more as an act of desperation than a hoax.

The irony of the second journal was that it completely discredited the original journal. If the entire Roscoe White story was a hoax—and I'm convinced that it was—the hoax was the work of someone with an impressive knowledge of assassination details, a good grasp of intelligence operations, and some insight into organized crime. Maybe Roscoe White himself perpetrated the deceit. Or maybe it was the work of his mysterious friend Bill X, with some help from Geneva.

Considering all the bizarre happenings since 1963, the scenario appears rather tame. If you want to fault the Roscoe White story, fault it first for its lack of imagination.

How to Have Great Sex Forever

JULY 1998

Forget Bob Dole's confession on live television. To me, the proof that Viagra has become part of the national fabric was demonstrated conclusively in a conversation I overheard at Big Steve's Gym in Austin. Some hypermacho bodybuilders in the 50-year-old age group—more than half of whom would be statistically likely to suffer from some degree of erectile dysfunction—were openly discussing the famous blue pill and marveling at the way it had restored the prowess of their teenage years. One remarked that he was having sex three or four times a day, thanks to his Viagra-induced erections. Another told of having sex before church, only to discover shortly before noon—as his attention began to drift during the doxology to more-temporal matters—that his erection had returned. "Shaking hands with the preacher at the door," he confided to his companions with evident pride, "I was crossing my legs and trying to cover the damn thing up with my Bible."

Like millions of others my age, 63, I can testify from personal experience that Viagra is everything those guys say it is. For the first time we have a pill that can restore sexual function to men suffering from erectile dysfunction (ED), or impotency, as it was known to earlier generations. Other dependable remedies have been on the market—from penile injections and inserts to the still-handy vacuum pump—but none as cheap or as easy to use as Viagra: Pop a fifty-milligram pill and in less than an hour you're ready for action. And it's only going to get cheaper and easier to treat impotency. Other drugs are already being tested or are awaiting Food and Drug Administration approval, including a pill called Vasomax, which was developed by Zonagen, a biopharmaceutical company located in The Woodlands, north of Houston. If all goes well, Vasomax will be on the market by the summer of 1999. At least two more potency therapies are being tested in pharmacology laboratories in other parts of the country. In a few years Viagra may become as generic as aspirin—itself once a trade name wonder drug—and hopefully as inexpensive.

Viagra's real contribution to the common psyche is that it has coaxed out of the closet the most embarrassing of all male sexual problems. Thirty million American men have at least occasional problems achieving or sustaining a full erection, but until the avalanche of publicity brought on by the Viagra revolution, less than 5 percent had summoned the courage to consult a physician. My generation came of age at a time when nobody talked about such delicate problems. A power lifter at Big Steve's was more likely to acknowledge that he squatted to pee than confess he had occasional trouble getting it up.

What little we knew of the problem came from reading Hemingway: Impotency was the reason Jake Barnes couldn't connect with Lady Brett Ashley in *The Sun Also Rises*. It was something you got in the war or something psychological. Though seemingly remote from our own lives, impotency was the most terrifying of prospects: It destroyed the sufferer's claim on manhood. Worse still, the condition was permanent, or so most men were taught. Our forefathers believed that poor erections were simply nature's way of telling us that people aren't supposed to have sex once their reproductive years have waned. And so they faded softly into the night, never dreaming that men (and women) can enjoy sex well into their nineties—with a little help from medical science and a few practical hints about romance.

Remarkably, only in the final decade of the twentieth century have we agreed that most sexual impotency—including a woman's inability to have an orgasm—is physiological, not psychological, and that most often it should be treated as a vascular problem. The same vascular ailments that lead to heart attacks, strokes, and numbness in the legs—clogged arteries, high blood pressure, hardened vessels, and damaged nerves—contribute to sexual malfunctions by depriving the penis and the clitoris of oxygen-rich blood. A small percentage of impotency is attributable to injury or trauma-induced nerve damage, and other afflictions are indicators: Men who have had their prostate removed and people who suffer from diabetes or hypertension will more commonly experience sexual problems. ED is also made more acute by drinking, smoking, stress, and physical inactivity.

There are, to be sure, psychological aspects to the problem. "We grow up with the myth that a real man can always get an erection," Harry Croft, a San Antonio psychiatrist, sex therapist, and lecturer told me. "When a man fails to have an erection, these myths surface. He begins to speculate on future failures and gets anxious thinking about his sexual performance." Masters and Johnson, the sex therapist pioneers under whom Croft trained in the seventies, called this situation performance anxiety. Even after the primary causes of ED are addressed, fear of failure may continue to take the starch out of a guy.

It took me a long time to figure it out, but sex isn't about erections; it's about relationships. My libido has always been excessively active, even more so after I married my sex-bomb wife, Phyllis, twenty-two years ago. Both of us had been married multiple times before, and we came together with no illusions. We each knew of the other's adventurous past and were open and honest about our needs and desires. In acknowledging a bond of selfishness and weakness for the flesh, we advanced our own love affair in new and exciting directions. That's the way we viewed it—as a love affair, with all the attendant risks, thrills, plateaus, and challenges the term implies. We made out on moonlit beaches, in cornfields in the shadows of interstate highways, and in darkened 747s over the Atlantic. We had been searching separately and shamelessly for fulfillment all those years, and we found it in each other, as one finds an answered prayer.

About ten years ago I noticed that my erections were less dependable, and that orgasms took longer and were less intense. I didn't regard this as a major problem. We factored it into the act, allowing ourselves more time for foreplay and finding erotic diversions to stimulate desire and performance. I knew that part of the problem was fast living and made some concessions to a healthier lifestyle, though, in retrospect, not nearly enough. I was already being treated for hypertension, and in 1988 a mild heart attack sent me to the emergency room, where I subsequently learned that I needed quintuple-bypass surgery.

On the night before I was scheduled for surgery, Phyllis chased the visitors out of my hospital room and worked a dresser into position to block the door. Showtime! If I was going to die on the operating table, neither of us wanted me to go out horny. In a matter of minutes we were lost in passion, oblivious to the wires, tubes, and catheters that secured me to my bed. We were approaching nirvana when an alarm bell began to shriek above our heads, alerting the orderlies and nurses that my IV bag needed to be replaced. A team of medics burst through our barricade and with a show of tactful professionalism changed the IV. Then an angel in the uniform of a head nurse stood guard outside the door, in case anybody else had any bright ideas about interrupting her patient.

Bypass surgery momentarily interrupted our sexual routine, but only for three or four weeks, after which time things returned to normal. Nevertheless, my erectile problems got gradually worse over the next four or five years. The libido was as strong as ever, but the equipment frequently failed. Achieving an orgasm wasn't a problem for me, but I was never sure about Phyllis. Fear of performance edged at the margins of my consciousness.

Instinctively, we began to explore new and more-inventive measures. Though we were by this time a bit long in the tooth for amour in cornfields and tourist-class seats, we discovered that we could restore the old heat by slipping out of town for romantic weekends. Long vacations were even more therapeutic. An apartment in the Marais section of Paris, a villa on the Amalfi Coast of Italy, and a hotel room in Frankfurt, Germany, with an antique bathtub as deep and as spacious as the back of a pickup are among the selections in our Love Wallow Hall of Fame.

We also addressed the fantasy factor, collecting a wardrobe of seductive costumes and giving each a name appropriate to its suggestiveness and inauguration. An early favorite was the Warden's Daughter, a white see-through blouse with white lace panties. My corresponding outfit, a black jockstrap, was dubbed the Escaped Prisoner. A long, silk, black gown with a low-cut neckline and a split up one side became known as the Black Maria. We bought Monique's Paris Slip in the fall of 1995, during that unforgettable week in our Paris apartment. That was the week we started calling each other Frenchy and Monique, noms d'amour that we use to this day.

Paris did something to each of us, something permanent. For the first time, we fully understood the distinction between love and sex, and romance became a continuing affair. Phyllis resisted no impulse to surprise me with exotic gifts. No longer did I wait for Valentine's Day or birthdays to bring her flowers or scribble love notes or pathetic attempts at poetry. We shared secrets and revealed naughty episodes from our pasts. Acts of altruism were invariably rewarded—sometimes with wild monkey love, followed by candlelight dinners with wine and music, and sometimes with simpler, more subtle expressions of love: a look or a touch or an act of kindness that worked some subliminal pleasure point deeper than the libido. Lovemaking became much more than the act itself. It became a long, periodically interrupted, almost subconscious tease that went on for hours or even days. The much-celebrated climax became, in many ways, anticlimactic, the swan song of an interlude. And life was finally revealed as nothing more than a series of unbearably sweet interludes.

A few months after we returned from Paris, I finally admitted to myself that ED was a problem that would only get worse. With some trepidation I called my urologist for an appointment. I had been reading and filing away articles on the subject, the most dramatic of which was an account of a medical conference in Las Vegas. A 57-year-old British physician had presented a paper on a new injectable drug to treat ED, and then demonstrated its effectiveness by dropping his pants and displaying his fully erect organ. The full monty in Vegas was more than a landmark event; it was a cultural epiphany. The drug that caused that famous erection was papaverine, which had previously been used to lower blood pressure. Other researchers had observed that some drugs designed to treat high blood pressure and other vascular diseases could, when administered in large enough doses, cause male patients to get an erection. One such drug was alprostadil (a naturally occurring form of the hormone prostaglandin E-1), which was used to treat a rare heart defect. Another was Viagra, which was originally designed to treat angina.

The connection between the heart and the penis should not have been such a surprise. The physiology of an erection depends on a series of interacting electrical and chemical impulses, starting with up-close personal contact or some observed or remembered sexual image. Once this registers in the brain, a message is sent to the penis, causing an increase in the production of the chemical cyclic GMP, which is normally broken down and kept in check by the enzyme phosphodiesterase type 5 (PDE5). The additional cyclic GMP causes muscles in the erectile tissue to relax and the arteries to expand. As blood rushes into the newly opened spaces, the penis stiffens and expands. Simultaneously, veins that normally drain blood away from the penis are squeezed shut, facilitating full erection. After orgasm, or when arousal subsides, the equilibrium between cyclic GMP and PDE5 is restored. Impotency strikes when cyclic GMP is in short supply—and when the penis has been soft for so long or the erectile tissue is so defective it can't expand enough to close off the veins. Men who suffer from mild cases of ED can often achieve a semierection through arousal, but the blood drains away as quickly as it arrives: It's like trying to fill a bathtub with the drain open.

In July 1995 the FDA approved the nation's first drug for impotency, Caverject, the trade name for a product that consisted of a disposable needle and syringe of alprostadil. Injected into the base of the penis with a fine-gauge needle, the drug relaxes the smooth muscles surrounding the penile arteries, causing them to dilate and permit an increased flow of blood.

As expected, my initial visit to my urologist was awkward. First, a female therapist asked a lot of questions about my sex life with Phyllis. How often did we do it? How satisfactory was it? This was followed by a physical exam, and finally a small-dose injection of alprostadil to determine if I would have any bad reaction to the drug. Apparently I passed the tests, because I left with a prescription for ten Caverject, at $18 a pop.

The first time I used the needle, in the privacy of my walk-in closet, I recalled my army lessons in marksmanship: Take a deep breath, let a little out, hold it, and squeeze (don't jerk) the trigger. It worked: I felt a tiny pinprick and after a few minutes a nearly forgotten surge of blood in my groin.

"How's it going?" Phyllis called from the bedroom.

"Does the term Louisville Slugger ring a bell?" I replied, stepping from the closet for my debut. We both erupted into uncontrollable laughter. This spontaneous levity shattered what might otherwise have been a tense moment. It also set a precedent. After that, the Slugger became our little joke, our way of agreeing that while penile injections were not the desired beginning of foreplay, they appeared to make a most valuable contribution.

Treating impotency requires more than a pill or a needle; it requires a sense of humor. If I didn't already know this, I certainly discovered it while researching my book *HeartWiseGuy*, which deals with bypass surgery, hypertension, impotency, and other ordeals of aging. Between 1995 and 1997, I tried all the ED gadgets on the market except one: the penile implant. Back in the eighties the implant was considered the gold standard, even though it required expensive and potentially dangerous surgery and didn't always work as advertised. The most popular model today consists of two inflatable cylinders that are implanted surgically in the spongy tissue of the penis, a fluid reservoir placed in the pelvis, and a pump affixed inside the scrotum. Squeezing the pump forces fluid into the cylinder, thereby making the penis rigid; a release valve reverses the process. But a friend who had had this model installed—on the advice of a golfing buddy who assured him that his own implant made airline stewardesses faint with pleasure—found that it indeed rarely worked as advertised. In fact, it hurt all the time. Then one morning at his office he discovered he was sitting in a pool of blood. The operation had led to an infection that ruptured his scrotum and caused him to hemorrhage. The condition was complicated by diabetes; his doctor had not warned him that diabetics are particularly at risk with this procedure. His only recourse was to have the implant surgically removed, again at considerable expense. Later, when he decided to try Caverject, he discovered, to his horror, that the implant had destroyed the erectile tissue in his penis. It was gone and could not be replaced.

"My God!" my friend screamed at his doctor. "Are you telling me I'll never have another erection?"

"You're nearly seventy," the doctor reminded him. "You've screwed enough."

In November 1996 a new therapy called the Medicated Urethral System for Erection (MUSE) hit the market, with predictions that a new gold standard had been established. MUSE is a disposable catheter that inserts a BB-size pellet of alprostadil into the urethra. Essentially the same vasodilator therapy as Caverject, it spares the user the dreaded needle. But I learned, as did most others who tried it, that MUSE is less reliable than Caverject. Harin Padma-Nathan, a clinical professor of urology at the University of Southern California, reported in an article in the *New England Journal of Medicine* that only about 30 to 40 percent of his patients got a rigid erection using MUSE.

The simplest and most efficient therapy is the ErecAid, a handheld pump that creates a vacuum and draws blood into the erectile tissue; the blood is dammed there with rubber tension rings attached to the base of the penis. The pump and attachments come in a carrying case about the size of a shaving kit and cost about $375. Unlike the alprostadil therapies, ErecAid does not require refrigeration and can therefore be taken on the road. Be warned, this is a clumsy piece of equipment, about as romantic as a tire jack. But here's where the sense of humor comes in. If you incorporate the ErecAid into your foreplay, make it part of the ritual of lovemaking—think of yourself as a magician and his assistant, for example—the results are impressive. Even with Viagra in the house, the ErecAid remains a mainstay in our arsenal.

Without question, Viagra is the current gold standard. And its potential may have been barely tapped: Some scientists believe it may also improve the sexual response of postmenopausal women. Little research has been done on women's sexual problems, even though older women have even more sexual dysfunction than men. Therapists suspect that the chief complaint, a lack of desire, really reflects women's problems dealing with their aging bodies—vaginal dryness, the increased time needed for arousal, and difficulty reaching orgasms. Since the clitoris, like the penis, becomes engorged with blood during sexual arousal, Viagra may soon wind up on both sides of the medicine cabinet.

Viagra is a capacity drug, not a desire drug. Men still need to be aroused before anything can happen. It works by prolonging the effects of cyclic GMP—making a little go a long way—until it is sufficient to overpower the killjoy PDE_5. Since healthy erectile tissue accepts only a finite amount of cyclic GMP, men with normal erectile ability won't notice any effect from Viagra, no matter how many pills they take.

None of the ED therapies can rejuvenate an affair that has lost its spark, which calls up an extremely important issue. Men need to pay more attention to the quality rather than the quantity of sexual experiences. "Starting in puberty," says Harry Croft, "men somehow get the idea that all a woman needs to be happy is a good, stiff member. That's a male conceit. What women are interested in is romance, touching, caressing—sex is something that comes later. When men begin to experience problems with erection, a lot of couples withdraw from kissing and hugging and all forms of intimacy, fearing that they are making promises they can't keep."

Couples who have not had sex for a long time are bound to have feelings of anger and frustration that can't be addressed by the little blue pill. Reawakening sexual desire requires a reacquaintance with romance. I read recently about a middle-aged couple who lay quietly in bed waiting for Viagra to work and eventually fell asleep. Apparently they had forgotten about foreplay. Similarly, a guy who pops a Viagra, calls his wife at the office, and demands that she hurry home for a big surprise is in for a surprise of his own: You can't kindle the flame of love with a pill.

The Last Roundup

Everyone had prayed for rain, but this was ridiculous. After almost three years of drought, two full growing seasons, fifteen inches of rain pounded the ranching country in the Davis Mountains one night in June 1985. Fifteen inches was an average year's supply. The rain hit with the force of a runaway train, washing out nearly every bridge across Limpia Creek and stranding families in the high country around Alpine and Fort Davis. The normally placid little creek raged like a river at flood tide, a hundred yards wide and sixteen feet deep in places, gobbling huge chunks of its bank, uprooting ancient cottonwood trees and utility poles and sections of Texas Highway 17.

Chris Lacy, the boss of the Kokernot 06 ("oh-six"), was awakened about three in the morning by thunder and rumbling so terrible that he thought it was a tornado. From the front porch of his ranch house he could see a tree as large as a bull elephant being dragged under and thrashed about like a toothpick. A lesser rain several days earlier had washed out the bridge leading from the 06 to the highway into Fort Davis, but that was nothing compared with what was happening now. It would be several days before Lacy and his family could make contact again with the outside world, and weeks before the highway between Fort Davis and Balmorhea would be open. The worst storm in five years caused hundreds of thousands of dollars in damage—and still no one was ready to say the drought had ended.

Droughts do freaky things to ranchers. The emotional effects are sometimes deeper than the ecological effects on the land itself. Droughts drain the human spirit and open it to the ravages of pessimism. There is, of course, much to be pessimistic about in this fragile and volatile country. Life here is a cycle of natural disasters, predator attacks, failing markets. The history of ranching out here is documented by tears and heartaches; droughts and flash floods are landmark events, the same as marriage and childbirth and death. Old-timers remember the drought of the thirties, when cattle starved or died of thirst or disease in such numbers that finally, in desperation, government agents drove the survivors into a canyon and shot them. "It was a mercy killing," recalled Hallie Stillwell, the 87-year-old matriarch of the Stillwell Ranch, south of Marathon. "Still, it was sad." Natural disasters were part of this country's fatal charm—part of a compromise and contract made more than a hundred years ago when men like Herbert Kokernot Sr. began amassing the land to create their great West Texas ranches.

Though the price is immense in terms of human suffering, it is part and parcel of the romance, allure, majesty, and solitude that make the challenge of high country ranching so irresistible. It explains why most ranchers cling so tenaciously to their old and honored traditions—to their way of life. They regard change as a betrayal, knowing deep down that change is also inevitable. In other areas of Texas many of the largest ranches survived because of oil; the discovery of petroleum reserves on those ranches, in effect, subsidized the cowboy traditions. But in the highlands of West Texas, there have never been any significant oil finds. High country land isn't good for anything except ranching. Its value is measured by what it can produce for the dinner table—beef. And the price of beef is just about the only thing that hadn't skyrocketed in recent times. In 1985, beef on the hoof sold for about 65¢ a pound, the same as the year before, and the year before that. Cowboys' wages tripled in the last decade, as did almost everything else the rancher needs to survive. At the same time, thanks to an influx of new, rich, mostly urban buyers, land values have gone out of sight, from $20 an acre as recently as the sixties to $80 an acre in the seventies to $200 an acre and more today. Traditional wisdom in the highlands has it that each cow requires forty acres of range—each 640-acre section (ranchers out here always talk in terms of sections, not acres) supports no more than twenty head. If some rich oilman is willing to pay $200 an acre, a rancher has to be crazy to raise cattle on it.

These so-called corporate, or recreational, ranchers became a taproot for new sources of rancher pessimism. The irony was bitter as skunkweed: The high country still hadn't discovered oil, but it had discovered oilmen. Oilmen—and bankers and lawyers and other urban creatures—bought land the way they bought objects of art. Most of them were more interested in hunting deer and antelope than in raising cattle, and those who did get into the cattle business usually approached it without regard for the old traditions and without love of the land. They "modernized." They "experimented." They wanted to make money. Indeed, to them money was the whole point of the enterprise. Money might be an object, old-line ranchers conceded, but it was far from the point. The point of ranching was ranching.

Chris Lacy, though only 36, was an old-style ranch boss who ran an old-style ranch—the o6 was one of the oldest brands in Texas. Lacy ran his operation well. The o6 made a healthy profit during good years and was stable enough to survive bad years. When Lacy and his cowboys talked about the loss of tradition and values and a way of life (and they talked about it constantly), they weren't just talking in general terms. They saw an example of it next door. Their neighbor on the next ranch over was one of the newcomers. He was an Aggie and an oilman and a banker, a multimillionaire from Midland who represented in clear and stark terms all the things the old-liners had come to hate—the modernizations and experimentations and heightened concerns for the bottom line. The neighbor's name was Clayton Williams, and not only did he disdain the cumulative wisdom of ranching tradition but he was wildly successful while doing so.

After nearly a week of isolation, Chris Lacy and his family took an alternate route over the mountains and into Fort Davis. Thunderheads were building off to the west. Lacy met Joel Nelson, one of his top cowboys, at Sutler's Boarding House restaurant, where Nelson was drinking coffee and talking to a young bronc rider named Shot Branham. A student at Sul Ross, Branham was looking for part-time work breaking colts. The o6 had one of the largest herds of working horses in the country, close to 150. Because the terrain was so rugged, the cowboys did most of their work on horseback. "Frankly," Lacy explained, "we prefer it that way."

Chris Lacy was the fourth generation of his family to manage the o6 brand. The brand was registered in Calhoun County about 1837 and had been in the Kokernot family since 1872. Chris had managed the ranch since 1971, when his grandfather, Herbert Kokernot Jr., stepped aside. Though the original o6 had been divided after the death of its founder, Herbert Kokernot Sr., in 1949, it remained one of the most notable and massive spreads in Texas. Many of the great ranches had been broken up and distributed among offspring for tax purposes and because subsequent generations failed to see the romance of the cattle business. Before

Herbert Senior's death, the 06 sprawled over 450 sections—288,000 acres of the best grazing land in the state. The 200 sections of high country west of the rim, which was still called the 06, went to Herbert Junior, and the 250 sections of less desirable low-country range, now called the Leoncita, went to one of Herbert Senior's two daughters (the other daughter inherited enough money to buy her own ranch near San Antonio). Herbert Junior and his wife, Golda, continued to live at Casa del Monte, the original house at ranch headquarters, and the old man still set overall policy, but Chris made the day-to-day decisions and worked side by side with the cowboys.

The 06 was an awesome, spectacular spread: 220 square miles of lush, rolling pastures, sheer rimrock bluffs, and jagged canyons stretching across the top of the Davis Mountains from just north of Fort Davis to the city limits of Alpine, thirty miles to the south. The native brush and grasses were as pristine now as they were in 1535 when Cabeza de Vaca camped here. Other than Chris and Joel, the 06 regularly employed only two or three full-time cowboys, but cowboys all over the country knew the ranch as one of the last holdouts for cowboy traditions. Modern electric pumps and elaborate systems of water pipes were largely disdained in favor of windmills and old-style concrete stock tanks. There was a minimum of cross-fencing (that is, fencing within the boundaries of the ranch); a cowboy could ride from dawn to dusk without encountering a fence. The 06 was one of the few ranches that still used a chuck wagon for spring branding and fall roundup, though in a rare concession to the twentieth century the wagon was now pulled by a pickup instead of a mule team. Calves were still roped and dragged to fire for branding. Cowboys from as far away as Montana and Idaho kept in touch with the 06 and were hired on when extra hands were needed for branding or roundup. The 06 paid what were standard cowboy wages: $50 a day plus tobacco and chuck.

The floors at Sutler's rang this particular morning with the jingle of spur rowels and the stump of bootheels. It was too wet to work, but even during the drought there wasn't a lot to do this time of year except get ready for roundup in October. Roundup was always the major event in the life cycle of any ranch—it was the accounting, the grand finale of the yearly cycle. Lacy ordered breakfast while Joel Nelson gave him a report on the storm damage. Most of the water gaps would need replacing, but overall the rains had been a great asset. The drought wasn't necessarily broken, Joel was quick to point out, but it was cracked for at least eight or nine months. "We're in good shape for winter," he said. "We got another year's leeway."

There was something else that Joel wanted to talk about. It sounded petty, and it probably was, but Clayton Williams had padlocked his gates again, forcing the 06 cowboys to go miles out of the way to reach their pastures in the top country. It was a perfect example of what was happening to one of the old traditions—neighboring. Ranchers had survived the hardships because they shared them with the past and with each other, and the sharing had been institutionalized into a system called neighboring. It worked for one because it worked for all. But the communal trust had been violated, or at least abridged, and that showed up in things like padlocked gates. In the old days nobody locked gates. It didn't make sense to. Property lines were irregular and interlocked like clasped fingers; at the margins of a ranch you could never be certain, really, of whose ranch you were on. Williams's Brangus ranch was horseshoe-shaped, surrounded on three sides by the 06; it was necessary to cross Williams's ranch to get to the 06's Willow Springs camp or to gain easy access to the top country, just as it was necessary to cross a part of the 06 to reach Williams's ranch house. Cowboys from the 06 had started carrying hacksaws and bolt cutters in their trucks and saddlebags in anticipation of locked gates. A ranch cook sawed off a chain on one of Williams's gates, coiled the chain neatly on the ground, and decorated his display with a bowel movement. "Clayton probably didn't even know it was padlocked," Joel said. "Of course, that's his trouble."

Williams had bought the old Henderson Flat Ranch, adjacent to the 06, eleven years ago, and there had been a running battle of philosophies ever since. There were arguments over property lines, over water rights, even over the right to host wild parties. Some of the complaints were ludicrous, as when one Fort Davis merchant charged that the oilman raised black cows rather than the red Herefords that were traditional to the area. Williams had been blamed, too, for introducing helicopters to the serene highlands, but in fact the first helicopter in those parts was owned by a rancher named John Rice.

More serious was the quarrel over water. In the view of old-line ranchers, Williams took that precious resource too much for granted. Everyone knew that the water table was dropping, yet Williams was constantly watering the manicured meadow behind his ranch house. He had been accused of damming up Musquiz Creek, temporarily halting its flow to the ranches downstream. (Williams said the dam was there when he bought the ranch.) Clayton and his wife, Modesta—Claytie and Desta to their friends—often invited large numbers of guests to their ranch, particularly for their annual party and cattle auction. On the morning of the auction, tank trucks were sent out to water down the twelve miles of road between their house and the front gate.

Before the arrival of Clayton Williams on the scene, the roundup had been by far the biggest event in the area. Now there were two such events; Williams's big bash, held every August, had become the second. It was the subject of much gossip and speculation and anticipation, but it was also the focus of much resentment. There was a sense among the old-style ranchers that Williams was using his party to rub their noses in his success. The party had become a kind of antisymbol to them, a crystallization of everything that was wrong with the newcomers' approach to ranching. The idea of paying hundreds of thousands of dollars for a single bull seemed as absurd as having bulls wear real pearl necklaces, which Clayton had done at an auction held in the lobby of his ClayDesta National Bank in Midland. The battle of lifestyles reached its peak when a group of ranchers and local politicians complained to the Texas Liquor Control Board about the all-night drinking, singing, and carrying-on at Williams's party. There apparently was a technical violation: Though Williams's front gate was in wet Brewster County, the ranch house, where the party took place, was in dry Jeff Davis County. If the complaint seemed small-minded, so did Williams's response: He circulated a petition asking that a precinct of Jeff Davis County vote itself wet. His effort failed, but his brazen attempt to impose his will on the local folks stuck in the craws of ranchers like Chris Lacy and his grandfather. Most of the old-timers thought that Williams's disregard for tradition would eventually settle the score in their favor; he would run out of grass or out of water or out of luck.

Tradition had served the 06 well. In Lacy's thirteen years as boss, his ranch had not failed to show a yearly profit. There had been lean times, of course, especially since the onset of the drought. But the great highland ranches like the 06 or the Lykes 02, owned by the family that owned the steamship line, or the Reynolds X or the Paisano thrived almost in spite of themselves. The land had been in the families for years, long ago bought and paid for, and so had the breed stock. Most ranches ran basic cow-calf operations. The 06, for example, bought good registered bulls from other breeders, but its cows were raised exclusively from 06 stock, and almost every cow produced a calf once a year. The new calves were branded in the spring, then rounded up and sold in the fall, usually to large feedlots that would fatten them for another year before sending them to slaughter. Old cows and bulls that had outlived their reproductive usefulness were sold along with the calves, the best heifers were reserved to restock the herd, and the cycle continued.

Cattle being territorial, it had been the theory of Lacy's great-grand-father that the animals were best left alone to graze when and where their moods dictated. Despite the absence of cross-fencing, the same 06 cows were found, year after year, in the same 06 pastures. The first and last rule was, and still is, Let nature have her way. There was a reason it rained only fifteen inches a year. Native shrubs and grasses grew here for a reason. Nature understood conservation far better than man did, and it was the wise rancher who understood nature and bent to her will. Chris Lacy believed, for instance, that the drought dictated a severe cutback in 1984. He expected to ship fewer than one thousand cattle in October, as opposed to at least twenty-five hundred in normal years. But the cutback seemed vital; it would allow the range to recover.

"Basic cow-calf operations like ours take what they can get," he explained, "30¢, 60¢, 70¢—whatever they're bringing. Good years, we can make improvements. We're not extravagant. Bad years, we have to cut back. My grandfather is very conservative. He owns the land and he owns the cattle. Otherwise it wouldn't be possible to stay in business. This is a simple operation, a good operation, a safe operation."

It was midmorning before Lacy left the Sutler, and the rain stopped. A piercing blue sky illuminated the mountains. The great highland pastures swept off in all directions, clean, bright, and suddenly, magically, emerald green, as though the storm had transformed the world from black and white to Technicolor. Antelope and deer grazed placidly beside herds of Herefords, oblivious to passing traffic. "You're seeing this country in its Sunday best," Lacy told me.

There was some irony in the 06's resistance to change, because the Kokernot family had built its fortune during some of the most dramatic and violent changes in modern history. Originally from France, the Kokernots fled to Amsterdam at the time of the French Revolution. Herbert Senior's grandfather David Kokernot immigrated to New Orleans in 1817 and later served as a scout for Sam Houston at the Battle of San Jacinto. David's son Lee served with Terry's Texas Rangers during the Civil War, and later Lee Kokernot and his brother John bought the 06 brand and started a cattle business in Gonzales. When the newly built Southern Pacific Railroad was extended to the high country in the 1880s, Lee sent his son, Herbert Senior, to Alpine to buy, sell, and trade land. Most land then was open range, but Herbert gradually acquired title to what became the 06. Many of his holdings came from repossessions—he would rather have had the money, but the economics of the times got him into the cattle business. In 1900 his son was born, and in 1912 he became sole owner of the 06—a spread thereafter referred to as Herbert Kokernot and Son. Another landmark event occurred about that time. Kokernot brought the English-bred Hereford to the ranch and helped pioneer its development in the region. The whiteface, now referred to locally as the highland Hereford, was said to be ideally suited to the cool, rugged mountain climate. Newcomers to the highlands who have introduced Brangus and other breeds are looked on as fools, though the truth is that the case for the Hereford as opposed to any other breed is rooted in tradition, not cold, objective fact.

"A little Brahman would probably do good out here," Chris Lacy admitted, turning his four-wheel-drive pickup off the highway. "But my grandfather says keep it 100 percent the same breed—and you know what breed he means." Chris found a shallow place to cross Limpia Creek, hubcap-deep now and as clear and clean as its name suggested. The house where Chris and Diane Lacy and their two children lived was on high ground not far from the creek bank, flanked by barns, sheds, a trailer, and a corral. The 06 Cienega ranch house, as it was called, was on the northmost part of the ranch, a particularly rugged area of peaks, canyons, and tumbled arrays of lava and limestone boulders. Chris stopped at the house to pick up Diane and their 9-year-old son, Lance. Their 11-year-old daughter, Kristin, was away at a girls' camp.

Chris and Diane seemed an odd pair to be running one of the oldest and largest cattle operations in Texas. He grew up in Waco, the son of a banker—but first and foremost the grandson of a Kokernot. He spent every summer and most vacations at the 06—he and his third cousin, Tom Beard, who now ran the Leoncita, learned to be real cowboys when other boys their age were still playing with stick horses. Chris played football and studied ranch management at Texas Christian University, where he met Diane, who had grown up in San Antonio. They married in 1971; she was a 21-year-old bride when they moved to Alpine and took charge of the 06. "I barely knew how to ride," she recalled.

Chris wanted to check on some colts, so we drove toward Grapevine Canyon, along a rutty, muddy trail climbing above the floor of a vast valley of yellow, blue, and orange wildflowers. Diane pointed to a dull, dusty green flower and identified it as locoweed. "It can poison and even kill cattle," she said. "Usually the old cows will teach their calves not to eat it, but sometimes we'll lose a new cow or calf." A rhyolite cliff, pale red in the midday sun, towered far above us—this was what they called Arkansas

Pasture, twenty to twenty-five sections of rimrock country that was used for pasturing horses in the winter. Few cattle ever climbed up this far, and those that did were too wild to be rounded up.

Near a windmill called Taylor Mill, and not far from the ruins of an old kiln where soldiers had fired the original bricks used at Fort Davis, we spotted four of the meandering colts. They looked up from their grazing as Chris stopped the truck and walked toward them. When they finally started to move, it was in our direction. Diane touched each one and called it by name.

In her thirteen years at the o6, Diane had learned not only to ride but also to cut calves from a herd, handle a branding iron, and do almost anything else a working cowboy did. "Out here your values change," she told me. "You come in contact with the real basics—the weather, the animals, yourself. You learn patience. You learn to think like an animal." Diane had also, in that time, developed a few strong opinions about her neighbor Clayton Williams. "We've done a lot of things for him," she said. "He had no antelope, so we helped him round up some of ours and put them in one of his pastures. He overgrazes, and he root-plows the native grasses and replants with hybrids from Texas A&M. His trouble is he has no feel for the land. Feel is everything. We don't grow cattle, we grow grass. We don't feel we own this land. We're just leasing it during our lifetime. The land is fragile. It doesn't take that long to use it up."

Diane noticed that one of the colts had a nasty cut on his foreleg. She examined it tentatively. "Do you think it was a lion?" she asked.

Chris said he didn't think so. "Likely got it scuffling with the other colts," he said. "I'll come back later and put something on it."

The following morning, a Saturday, Mr. Kokernot, as Herbert Junior was always called, made one of his infrequent appearances. Though he had been a Jeff Davis County commissioner for sixty-two years—the longest continuous tenure of any officeholder in Texas—he was otherwise rarely seen in public. He had come out this morning to watch Lance, his great-grandson and potential heir to the o6, play baseball. Diane and Chris, who coached the team, were extremely attentive to the old man's needs and went out of their way to make him comfortable, but you could tell he would rather have been somewhere else. He was 84, bent and slender as a twig; he looked as though he might blow away with the next gust of wind. Hardly anyone recognized the old man in the crushed cowboy hat, necktie, brown slacks, and scuffed street shoes, or realized that he was the virtual patron of Alpine. Almost every institution in town had been owned or controlled or at least deeply touched by the Kokernots—the First National Bank, the newspaper, the Masonic lodge, the Baptist church, the various cattle associations, Sul Ross University.

The baseball field where the children were playing was once a part of the 06, as was Kokernot Field, which was adjacent to it and which had been the home field for the Alpine semipro team in the forties and fifties. For the last sixty years baseball and church had been the extent of Herbert Junior's social life, and after he disbanded the team in the late fifties, baseball no longer interested him. As he watched his grandson play, Herbert Kokernot Jr. seemed content that the 06 would remain as unchanged for the next hundred years as it had for the past hundred. "This is the kind of country that doesn't adapt itself much to change," he told me, responding in a minimum of words to my rather detailed and layered question.

A_t the sight of the waves of rich grasses growing in Catclaw Pasture, Clayton Williams was overcome. The opening bars of the Aggie War Hymn rattling from his lips, he slammed on the brakes and flew out of his Bronco, waving his arms and shouting, "Oh, man! I just gotta walk through this." So this was the enemy. He didn't act like the character I had heard described, a man with wanton disregard for the land. He seemed to care. He seemed to care passionately. The pasture bristled with black, blue, and hairy grama grasses and tender young tumbleweed sprouts, all of which thrive naturally in the high country, and with Johnson and Klein grasses that Williams had introduced after root-plowing the pasture and replanting it to suit his purposes. The most amazing thing about Catclaw Pasture was that there wasn't a catclaw in sight.

Across the fence, however, on the flats of the 06, there was an abundance of catclaw, a vicious, spindly shrub that sucks up water and shows its appreciation by tearing open the hides of cows, and sometimes cowboys, with spiked-clawed stems that grow as tall as ten feet. There was mesquite too, and black brush and some scattered strands of gramas. Cowboys on the 06 shared a sort of masochistic fondness for catclaw and even asserted that some of their fattest cattle came from catclaw country, but Williams hated the shrub with an inordinate, almost demonic intensity. He called it "the invader" and had spent the better part of nine years eradicating it from this particular pasture. "When I die," he said, "the catclaw of the world will hold the damnedest celebration you ever saw."

To put it bluntly, Clayton Williams did not believe in bending to nature. He believed with every bone in his Aggie body that with the proper application of modern ranching techniques, you could force nature to do the bending. Almost all the pastures on Clayton Williams's Brangus ranch had been improved, either by root-plowing the native grasses and replanting with hybrids or, at the very least, by poisoning the catclaw and other brush. Some of the improved pastures were failures, in the sense that they hadn't paid for themselves, and some had been plowed and replanted more than once. On the one hand, it didn't make that much difference if a few of Williams's experiments didn't work out. He was, after all, a wealthy oilman, and though he didn't admit it—especially to himself—that gave him a tremendous advantage over the old-style ranchers. Williams wasn't dependent on the land for his livelihood the way the others were. He could play by his own rules because he could afford to. If things didn't work out, well, it wasn't the end of the world. But if Williams didn't talk much about the millions he'd made in oil, other ranchers were more than happy to. "What it amounts to," one of them said, "is that he's subsidizing beef with oil."

But Williams was no dilettante, a character trait that distinguished him from many of the newcomers. He took ranching seriously. His competitive business instincts pushed him to make his ranch operation profitable—and it was. The annual cattle auction alone brought in several million dollars a year, and while no one knew how much his commercial cattle operation brought, everyone knew it was plenty. According to Williams, his books proved that his modern techniques made money. By spending $10 an acre on improvements, he said, he could at least double the number of cattle that grazed there. He pointed to the Hill Pasture, where a fork in the road led to the o6's Willow Springs camp, and explained: "This is one of the weakest pieces of land on my property, but for three years now I've been able to run forty-five cow units per section rather than the fifteen most people think is the limit."

The grass had an intrinsic value too, beyond its traditional purpose of fattening cattle. Another pasture had cost $35 an acre to plow and replant, but the first year after the improvements Williams pocketed $28 an acre baling and selling hay, and the second year he made $25 an acre. Baling hay, much less selling it, was as foreign to the o6 operation as selling zebras— something else Clayton Williams had done. Cowboys hated plowed land, just as they hated potted plants, artificial insemination, embryo genetics, and anything else not directly rooted in the past. Clayton Williams did not claim to be a cowboy, however, or even a rancher. "I'm a cattle entrepreneur," he bragged. "Kokernot is at one extreme of the beef production business, and I'm crowding the other extreme." Far from being subsidized by oil, for the last five years Williams's cattle business had been putting money into his oil business.

When Williams bought forty-three sections of the old Henderson Flat eleven years back, for $82 an acre, most ranchers thought he was crazy. The land was considered poor and overused. Then he bought four more ranches in the Davis Mountains, three near San Antonio, and three in Wyoming—he also owned an old family property, an irrigated farm near Fort Stockton. All in all, his ranch holdings were considerable. He ran a cow-calf operation, though it was only a small part of the business. He bought yearling steers from other ranchers and fattened them, either on one of his ranches or—depending on market conditions and rainfall—in feedlots or on leased land. The most spectacular aspect of his ranching business was his registered Brangus business. "That's another game," he said. "It twirls up there by itself." The jet-setting ranchers who attended his annual party and auction had paid hundreds of thousands of dollars for a small share of the semen rights to a single bull. Such prices made absolutely no sense to the traditional ranchers, but they made enormous sense to Clayton Williams.

Henderson Flat, the property next to the 06, was his showpiece. Although it was less than a quarter of the size of the 06, Williams ran two or three times as many head of cattle on it. "I have twelve thousand head on my Alpine operations this year," he said. "Some years I have only two thousand. Some years I have none. I can move with the market, with the grass." He went on: "A lot of ranchers like Kokernot are keeping their lights [steers under 350 pounds] to fatten them and wait for the market to jump. But smart guys like me are buying steers right now, today, instead of taking it like it is."

From Williams's vantage point, the drought was the best thing that could have happened. Williams was an eternal optimist, to be sure, but this was where his oil fortune came into play: When nature compelled the less fortunate to sell, it inspired him to buy. "A lot of ranchers around Austin and San Antonio were forced to quit or sell when the market was way down," he told me. "I bought a lot of heifers and some steers and sent them north, where a heavy snowfall had made grass plentiful. I bought another fourteen thousand yearlings in South Texas and seven thousand in Mexico. I sent some to the Colorado cornfields and some to the Arizona desert and some more to Wyoming. Cattle cycles are supply and demand, pure and simple. When prices go up again, ranchers will be buying heifers to replenish their stock. I'll be selling heifers back to some of the same people that sold them to me. I usually make about $7 an acre here, triple what most cow-calf operations make. This year I estimate I'll make $20 an acre. Next year, who knows? I might decide to let the grass grow."

Clayton Williams, like his neighbor Herbert Kokernot Jr., was a graduate of Texas A&M, an Aggie right down to his boots, which displayed the emblem of his alma mater, as did the swimming pool at his ranch in Alpine and many of his other earthly possessions. Texas A&M was the central fact of his life: He prided himself on being the little Aggie who could. Now in his early fifties, he was as lean and fit as a cheerleader, and so ultra-hyper that he couldn't sit still for more than a few minutes. His pet word for conditions was "hardscrabble," taken from the title of John Graves's book, which he talked about constantly. Graves wrote of a previous generation of God-fearing men from "the days of big grass," men who used up the land and moved on, "without heed or knowledge of such soil-saving measures as contour plowing, crop rotation, . . . terracing, stripcropping." When the land wore out and became naked, the brush that Graves had dubbed "the invaders" moved in. In Clayton's view, that described what had happened to Herbert Kokernot and other ranchers. They hadn't tried "to mold the land into new forms of usefulness but [had molded] themselves to its shrunken possibilities." The drought wasn't the reason they were losing; the drought was their excuse.

It was a hot July day, and Clayton opened a can of beer from the cooler behind the seat, surveying his ranch, pride radiating from his face like a fresh coat of lacquer. "I paid $82 an acre for this," he told me. "The original Kokernot paid $5. He got a lot of it by repossessing land. The present Kokernot inherited his. To his credit, he didn't lose it like a lot of them, but he hasn't improved it much either. The fact is, it's not like it was fifty years ago. They're playing make-believe. Me, I'm very intense in my business. I like to make money."

Williams grew up in hardscrabble, catclaw country. His father owned a ranch and an irrigated farm near Fort Stockton. He lost the ranch during the drought of the fifties, even though he pumped so much water from the city's natural spring that it didn't flow again for many years. But Clayton recovered most of his father's holdings after making his fortune in oil.

"A big part of our ranch was converted to cotton farms," he recalled. "This had been old, rough, used-up ranchland, but because of government subsidies farmers were able to irrigate and grow some cotton. But it was marginal. The only reason there was a market at all was because of government subsidies. Farmers went broke anyway, because it was not economically feasible to farm cotton out there. The government created a false economy. The drought relief just let the farmers go deeper and deeper in debt and ruined the land too. The farmers kept taking government handouts and devoted the best, most productive years of their lives to . . . what? To chasing a false idol. They should have listened to nature. Nature tells us when it's time to sell and get off the land."

It didn't take a psychiatrist to see that something didn't square here; any old-time rancher would have been willing to point it out. The lesson Williams said he had learned from his father's ranch—that one had to listen to nature—was in direct conflict, not only with his father's greed-driven experience in pumping the local springs dry, but with Clayton's own hardscrabble philosophy of "molding the land into new forms of usefulness." Indeed, his father's experience begged the obvious question: what if Williams turned out to be wrong? His operation was showing a handsome profit now, but he had been in the ranching business for only a decade, which in ranching terms was a blink of the eye. What if in the long run his hybrid grasses didn't thrive? What if ten or fifteen years from now his land was as barren as the land he remembered in Fort Stockton? Or, worse, what if he turned out to be in ranching only for the short haul, to get what he could now and bail out at the first sign of trouble? What if he was the one who was chasing the false idol? In their heart of hearts, all the old-style ranchers believed that that was how things would play out before it was over. What they also knew, though, and what embittered them, was that even if Williams did turn out to be wrong in the end, as they all hoped, he would simply write off the experience and go somewhere else. The land would remain.

Williams steered his Bronco through another pasture where twelve hundred head of commercial cattle grazed on new grass. Most ranchers would have limited a pasture this size to a few dozen head, but most didn't subscribe to Williams's theory of rotation grazing. "I'll keep them here for thirty days," he told me. "Then I won't use this pasture again until it's been plowed and replanted. I'm kind of radical, as are most people who love the land. That's what ol' Hardscrabble Graves and I have in common. Cowboys love cattle. They believe that only the tenderest grass is nutritious. But what's best for cows is not necessarily best for grass in the balance of management. Grass needs time. It grows logarithmically. Leave it alone and in a month there will be ten times as much grass as before."

Williams drove past some Hispanic workers who were terracing a section of pasture to catch runoff that otherwise would have disappeared into a ravine. Similar "spreaders" were located all over the ranch; the 06 also constructed spreaders, but there were fewer and they were not as well maintained. There were no windmills on Williams's property. "I trust electricity more than I trust wind," he said.

It surprised Williams that so few people understood what he saw as the basic economic facts of ranching. It galled him that the o6 got away with romanticizing a way of life that was fast becoming an illusion. Television crews, moviemakers, wildlife artists, writers — it chapped his Aggie ass to see them fawning over the o6. David Hartman and a crew from *Good Morning America* had shown up at the o6 roundup the previous October. The year before, it was a British movie outfit filming a piece called *My Heroes Have Always Been Cowboys*. The documentary starred Waylon Jennings, who had just been released from a drug treatment center and could barely stand up, much less ride. "The way I hear it," Clayton said, "the o6 pays its cowboys $20 a day, unless they bring their own camera, in which case they get $25." Singer Charlie Daniels had actually worked an o6 roundup — he was a pretty fair hand, they say. Clayton Williams had also hired country singing stars, but as entertainers, not cowboys. Nothing romantic about it. Just good business.

Opening another can of beer, Williams wheeled the Bronco back toward his ranch house and headquarters — the Cove, it was called. A giant antelope buck (imported apparently from the o6) galloped parallel to the Bronco for a few hundred yards, then shifted gears and raced across our path and out of sight. On the hill above the Cove, just beyond the o6 property line, stood a massive sentinel of rimrock called Polk's Peak. Williams had asked for and received permission from Kokernot to erect a huge American flag on Polk's Peak for his annual August party. He described the party as "Woodstock without sex." His guests were going to pay some fancy prices for cows, and Clayton wanted them to enjoy the experience.

The Willow Springs ranch house, where Joel Nelson and his wife, Barney, lived, sat on a finger of land along Musquiz Creek, near the center of the o6, and yet isolated by Williams's ranch from the o6's Cienega camp far to the north and the o6's Berrendo Flat camp well to the south. Willow Springs was one of the oldest camps on the o6, a throwback to the days when cowboys lived year-round in line camps on remote sections of the great spread. Except during branding or roundup, line camps were seldom used anymore, but Cienega, Willow Springs, and Berrendo Flat — along with Casa del Monte, where Mr. Kokernot and his wife lived — were permanent bases.

Joel and Barney Nelson were themselves throwbacks, remnants of a distant past buffeted by the clamor and confusion of modern times. They appeared to be plain and simple people, a cowboy and his wife, but there was a certain grandeur in their style, a formality of manner and attitude nearly forgotten. Joel had a degree in forestry and range management from Stephen F. Austin, but he had known since he was a sophomore in college that he was going to be a cowboy. Barney was a photographer, an author, and a graduate of Sul Ross; she still worked full-time in the university's department of range animal science. The ranch house where they lived was a turn-of-the-century model of western architecture and culture, and an archive of cowboy paraphernalia: antique saddles, branding irons, hackamores, swivel rings, ropes. The house was supplied by the 06, as were utilities, long-distance phone service, and all the beef they wanted. There was no television, no air conditioner, no clothes dryer—nothing except splendid isolation. "This is the center of the earth to us," Barney told me. "This is what satisfies us."

Sitting in their old-fashioned country kitchen one day in late July, eating steak and drinking iced tea out of tin cans, they talked about their life not as a means of accomplishment but as an end in itself, something done well for its own sake. Few people stood comfortably on tradition or felt inured to its timeless process. Few people cared enough about their job to make it their lives. The cowboy was a vanishing breed, but so were the things the cowboy stood for—humility, sensitivity, pride, reverence for what had gone before. Barney sometimes said, half joking, that if Clayton Williams wanted to make a real contribution he should set up a wildlife preserve for cowboys. There was something to that suggestion besides sentiment. Ted Gray, an old cowboy survivor and ranch owner, had said it eloquently in a passage from Barney's book, *The Last Campfire:* "If you talk to an old man sometimes, you can learn something it maybe took him forty years to learn. You might learn it in one minute." That was the kind of sentiment the new breed of ranch owner would not understand, a romantic notion that flew in the face of technology and quantum leaps but that went to the heart of what Joel and Barney believed. Cowboys worked hard because they believed in the redemption of hard work. Barney said, "It's the only job I know where you can turn a man loose and not see him for days at a time and know that he's been up every morning before daylight, just waiting to get started again." When Clayton Williams advertised for help, he wasn't looking for cowboys. He was looking for pickup drivers, swimming pool maintainers, weed poisoners.

Joel was making about $9 a day when he first met and married Barney in

1971. As newlyweds, they spent their free time dreaming of owning their own small spread. He was making considerably more than that now, but the dream had mostly vanished because of the influx of newcomers and the corresponding rise in land prices. "It's not possible anymore," Barney said. "We couldn't even make the down payment."

But the dream had not died completely. Joel used the Texas Veterans Land Program to buy 20 acres near Fort Davis and leased 640 acres in an adjacent state park, where he ran a herd of about eighteen cows, heifers, and steers. He owned another seven head that ran with the o6 cattle at Willow Springs. Though Joel was loyal to the highland Hereford, he wasn't dogmatic about it. His cows were Herefords, but they ran with a mixed breed of steers. "Every breed association will tell you their breed is best and give you statistics to prove it," he told me.

I was curious as to how Joel and Barney felt about Clayton Williams's annual bash. In a few weeks their splendid isolation would be shattered by several thousand jet-setting ranchers, traveling past their front gate to pay ridiculous prices for cattle, stuff themselves with barbecue, and spend the night drinking and listening to top-dollar country music. "We usually go," Barney told me matter-of-factly. "Clayton's our neighbor."

"I read that this year's guests of honor are General MacArthur's daughters," I said. "I wasn't aware the general had daughters."

Joel laughed out loud. "General MacArthur's a bull," he informed me. "His daughters are embryo donor cows. That's the big thing these days."

"They get a million dollars and more for some of those bulls," Barney said.

"There's no way you can make money on beef cattle paying a million dollars for bulls," Joel said. "There's nothing in the world wrong with up-grading cattle, but you can't put beef on the table running that kind of operation. We pay up to $2,000 for a good, practical range bull, but we're not afraid to kick him out in the pasture and not see him for a couple of months. You can't do that with a million-dollar bull."

"That's what's hurting the ranch business," Barney added. "People who don't have to worry about making ends meet. Everybody is jumping on the bandwagon. Ranching is getting to be a business where people have less faith in experience than in new, untried methods. I guess they get tax write-offs. Clayton plows the ground and raises tumbleweeds. He hires people to run around and . . . I don't know what."

"It gives them a lot to talk about on the golf course and at the country club dance," Joel speculated.

"You know what the difference is between a calf from a breed's top line and a calf bred from average stock?" Barney asked. "About ten pounds."

It rained again that night. Joel had planned to ride up to the top country to check on some young horses, but it was too muddy. Instead he decided to hitch a livestock trailer to his pickup and visit his friend Jack Saunders's ranch, south of Marfa. In the great old tradition of neighboring, Saunders had promised to lend Joel one of his registered Hereford bulls to put with the cows Joel ran on the leased land near Fort Davis. "Jack is short of grass," Joel explained. "Besides, it's good advertising. I wouldn't have seen his stock otherwise. He knows if I'm impressed I'll encourage Chris to buy some of them."

The bull that Joel was borrowing was big-boned, with a straight top-line, a broad, well-muscled rear end, and huge shoulders—near-perfect conformations. "Keep him till January," Saunders told Joel after they had loaded the animal into the trailer. "I don't need him right now, and he'll eat better at your place anyway."

After Joel had delivered the bull to his pasture on the mountainside above Fort Davis, he drove into town, looking for Chris Lacy's pickup. He spotted it outside Bob Dillard's Union Trading Company. Lacy, Dillard, and Cotton Elliott, one of the 06 cowboys, were loitering in the parking lot between the store and the Limpia Hotel, killing time and talking about the rain. "Anytime you see bees close to the hive, it's gonna rain," Elliott told the others. "I drove by a hive that sounded like a machine gun. I think it'll rain every day in July and August." Chris didn't comment on the possibility of more rain, but as he and Elliott were loading a lawn mower into one of the pickups, he shook his head and looked at the machine as if it was cargo from a spaceship. "We haven't needed this in a few years," he admitted.

"You want me to buy a thousand head of light calves while you're gone on vacation?" Joel asked the boss of the 06.

Chris thought about it a moment. That old pessimism was creeping back into his eyes. "Better wait," he said. "See if it ever rains again."

Folks in Fort Davis didn't need invitations to remind them that this was the weekend of Claytie and Desta's big party. It was August 17, and there wasn't a vacant motel room within miles of the Alpine–Marfa–Fort Davis triangle. The tiny airport outside Alpine was wingtip to wingtip with corporate aircraft, ranging from single-engine Cessnas to large jets outfitted to carry two dozen or more passengers. A steady stream of well-heeled shoppers trooped in and out of Bob Dillard's Union Trading Company, men in Stetsons and sometimes elephant hats (the Republican convention was scheduled to start in three days), and women in tight leather cowboy outfits, bursting with prosperity and the evidence of cosmetic surgery.

Fort Davis was accustomed to tourists. This was the highest town in Texas and one of the most scenic; geology students, dude ranch fanciers, and explorers of the unbeaten path visited regularly and were always made welcome. There wasn't much of what you call action in Fort Davis — no movies, no nightclubs, no public bars. People liked it that way. The town's only doctor had died, and the only drugstore didn't sell drugs, though it advertised "the best fountain Cokes in Texas." The Union Trading Company, located in an old stone building that dated back to 1906, was a Fort Davis landmark and a sort of hangout for locals, who sometimes gathered there after business hours to drink beer and gossip. All the gossip this Friday concerned Clayton Williams.

"He's done some good things," acknowledged a cowboy, hunkered down beside a keg of nails. "He got that operation for Ramon." That was true, admitted Bob Dillard, who ran newspapers in Alpine and Marfa as well as running the Union Trading Company. Williams had helped pay for an operation to repair the damaged knees of Ramon Hartnett, an old cowboy who operated the chuck wagon for the o6 and cooked for various other ranchers, including Williams. He had also donated $100 to the sonic boom fund, a campaign to pressure the Air Force to abandon its practice of holding dogfight maneuvers over the Davis Mountains. "Some of the others gave a thousand," Dillard said dryly.

The Williams Brangus Production Sale, as the auction was called on the engraved invitation, didn't start until 1 P.M. that Saturday, but by mid-morning the twelve miles of dirt road running from the highway to ranch headquarters were clogged with buses, campers, and other vehicles.

A tank truck nosed along the road, sprinkling precious water to hold down the dust. Every mile or so there was an oasis — elaborately constructed Hollywood facades with cute names like Margaritaville, Fort ClayDesta, and Claytie's Chicken Ranch — where neatly groomed young hosts in western costumes dispensed beverages and tough-looking, heavily armed, off-duty lawmen checked credentials. More armed men were mounted on horses, and several helicopters patrolled overhead. Closer to ranch headquarters guests could hear the music of a Dixieland band and smell the smoke from various cook fires.

Clayton's party had the pizzazz of a high-dollar county fair. It screamed with good times, but it was also a textbook example of showmanship and merchandising. Three flatbed trucks loaded with alfalfa hay, Klein grass, pipe, and drilling mud were displayed near the wide front lawn. Plastic drinking cups advertised Clayton's gas pipeline company, Clajon. A sign near the circus tent where the auction would take place proclaimed, "We Believe in God, Aggies and Brangus Cattle." Clayton was every bit as dogmatic and outspoken about the Brangus as Mr. Kokernot was about the Hereford.

His maroon pants stuffed in his maroon and white boots, Clayton had surrounded himself with a group of prospective buyers who were inspecting the pens of cattle near the auction tent. He was a little nervous that I was attending his party. I understood. His guests were rich, important people: If the wife of, say, a bank president got smashed and fell in the swimming pool—as had happened at previous parties—she would as soon not have it blabbed about in *Texas Monthly*. But nothing that interesting happened at this particular party. "Don't worry," I assured Clayton. "If anybody gets drunk and falls in the swimming pool, it'll probably be me." Truth was, I'd fallen asleep at parties far wilder than this one.

It's not easy to explain the dynamics or economic strategy of a cattle auction at which apparently intelligent people pay a huge sum of money for a single animal. When I visited his ranch earlier, Williams talked in detail about raising commercial cattle for slaughter—"the discipline of the 65¢ fat," he called it. This sideshow had nothing to do with that discipline. "This is a separate world," he explained. "I guess you would say the people here are reaching for the top—it's like trying to win the Kentucky Derby—and yet there is a tie to the real world." The cattle auctioned here were very special, prizewinning animals, certain to command top dollar as breeders. It was something like buying the stud rights to Secretariat. Clayton Williams was making the profits today, but on some future day the buyer might look forward to his own profits—so long as there was someone else willing to buy. One old-line rancher called this practice "brother-in-lawing."

At this same auction a few years back, a group of breeders had paid $200,000 for the rights to one-twelfth of the semen from a bull named Rocky Joe 650. That fixed the animal's value at $2.4 million. They didn't actually buy (or even get possession of) the bull. Williams, who was also part of the group, maintained possession of Rocky Joe 650, as well as an interest in the semen. Once a week a specialist in such matters got to masturbate Rocky Joe 650. The semen was stored in straws, or ampules, that were frozen in liquid nitrogen until it was time to artificially inseminate some lucky cow. Each ejaculation supplied between 60 and 250 ampules of sperm, and thus a bull that under natural conditions might service forty or fifty cows a year had the potential to service thousands.

Artificial insemination had been a recognized breeding technique for thirty years, but Williams was a trendsetter in the newer technique of embryo transfer. That was where the so-called supercows, the daughters of General MacArthur and other top-line bulls, came into play. If the eggs of a supercow were transplanted into common recipient cows, each supercow was able to produce twenty to forty calves each year. Calves born of common recipient cows had the genes of both the supercow and the top-line bull. Only one bull was available at this auction—his name was Bob of Brinks, and a one-tenth share of his semen rights sold for $300,000, making him even more valuable than Rocky Joe 650. The cows, sold by lots, were themselves the results of embryo transfers. Some were recipients due to calve in a few months (they sold for an average of $39,000), others were pairs of bred cows with heifer calves (they sold for an average of $71,000), and still others were unbred cows (average price $30,000). Most expensive of all were the flushes (eggs) of supercows, whose average price was $137,000.

Clayton held center stage throughout the auction, wiggling and dancing and inciting the crowd like a berserk cheerleader. With the Aggie War Hymn blaring from the speakers, Clayton's voice occasionally drowned out that of the auctioneer. "Larry, you son of a gun, you stole my heifer! You got performance built in. Look at the stretch and length of that female." There were a lot of "Gig 'em Aggies!" and jokes about "what good-looking wives Brangus breeders have," and at one point Clayton even took the microphone and sang a verse of "The Eyes of Texas." He stood on the auctioneer's table and waved his arms and implored the crowd to buy, buy, buy—he has been known to actually get down on the arena floor and paw dirt. When the auction ended, Clayton announced that the sales had totaled $2.73 million, then led the crowd in the singing of "God Bless America."

As the partygoers began to move out of the tent and up the meadow where the food was being served, roadies for the two star entertainers, Janie Fricke and George Strait, assembled equipment and tested the sound. The Dixieland band started up again, and a group of men in kilts marched down a hill, playing bagpipes. Claytie led Desta and other members of his family to the stage, said a prayer, did another chorus of "God Bless America," and announced that there would be fireworks as soon as it was dark, followed by dancing and singing until daybreak, at which time breakfast would be served. From the top of Polk's Peak, Old Glory flapped in the hot August breeze. Then there was a thunderous roar as a formation of corporate jets zoomed directly overhead and vanished over the tops of the mountains, saluting this august gathering of cattlemen and their be-jeweled ladies. "Stick around," Clayton shouted. "We're just starting to party!"

Thunderheads had been building all afternoon, and the squall hit camp just after supper. At first the rain was light, then it came harder, then the wind hit full force, driving the rain in parallel sheets. Then it started hail-ing. The cowboys gathered under the corrugated tin shed and began dig-ging trenches, and Ramon Hartnett did his best to cover the bed of coals that was his cook fire. A bolt of lightning narrowly missed the shed. Ty Holland, one of the full-time 06 cowboys, put on a yellow slicker and ran toward the corrals, where a night horse, frightened and near panic, was tied beside a metal fence. Halfway through the month of October, it had rained almost every night. Nevertheless, it was business as usual at the 06's annual fall roundup.

When the squall had passed, the cowboys examined the tepees, which were their individual shelters. All the tepees had weathered the storm, but some had leaked, and a few of the cowboys would spend the night in soggy bedrolls. That prospect didn't seem to bother anyone. The cowboys got back to their twilight routine, cracking bullwhips, practicing roping, pitching horseshoes. When it was too dark to pitch horseshoes, some of them played cards and others gathered by the cook fire, drinking coffee and swapping stories. Obra Denton, who had cowboyed all over the West for the past forty years, remembered spending a winter alone in the high country of northern Arizona. His only shelter had been two pieces of tin and a strip of canvas. "I thought that was about the best life there was," Obra told his companions, who nodded agreement.

About half of the fifteen cowboys who had signed on for the 06 roundup were drifters. They followed the flow from Montana to Nevada to Arizona to Texas, wherever there was branding or gathering or any other cowboy work that needed doing. Most of them were younger than Obra, and some had college educations, but they were cut from the same cloth; they were all willing to sacrifice anything for this archaic, ritualis-tic way of life. Most had been married at some time, but cowboying took its toll on a marriage. Ron Goddard, a young cowboy from Montana, had been married when he worked at the o6 the past spring. He and his wife and another couple had built a wagon and put together a contract branding outfit, hiring out to dilettante ranchers who were willing to pay someone else to brand, castrate, dehorn, earmark, and vaccinate newborn calves. Now Goddard's marriage was on the rocks and he had no idea where he would go from here.

Goddard and three others were generally referred to as "the Montana cowboys," though only one of them, Bob Blackwell, was from Montana originally. They were as authentic as cowboys got. Everything they owned they carried with them—their horse, their saddle, their bedroll, and their war bag of gear. These were men who paid $400 for a pair of knee-length work boots and $40 for a pair of dress boots. These were men who thought heaven was life on horseback, but who would settle for $700 a month in a line camp forty miles from the nearest town. Some were tall and some were short, but they were uniformly lean, sported facial hair, and wore floppy black hats and vests under their ragged, dusty coats. When you looked at the Montana cowboys, standing together or individually, you thought of a "Wanted" poster.

This particular camp, called Number Nine, was the cowboys' favorite. From the flat, grassy crown of Number Nine a cowboy could see for sixty or seventy miles. It was "on top," high above the streams and trees and paved roads. Several o6 pickups, including the one hauling the chuck wagon, had made it up here before the most recent rain, but getting them down again would be a problem. Frightening displays of lightning split the sky over the mountains of the Big Bend to the south and the deserts of Fort Stockton to the east, but up here you could see the Milky Way as clearly as most people can see their ceiling.

Hard rain battered the camp again during the night. A wet, dark chill settled over the top country several hours before daylight, and a full moon flooded the sky with an eerie radiance. Instinctively, Ramon Hartnett stirred and struggling out of his bedroll, rubbing his sore back, pulling on his boot, limped off into the darkness in the direction of the chuck wagon. Coals from the previous evening still smoldered. Ramon added four large logs and warmed his old bones for a few minutes before starting the coffee. For a man with bad knees, Ramon moved about with considerable authority; cowboys who stood between Ramon and the fire were liable to feel a shovel of hot coals under their back pockets. Ramon had cowboyed for the o6 and other ranches for forty years and had been cooking now for twenty-five. People who knew him said he looked twenty years younger out here on the range. At home he could barely walk across the room, but out here he joked and clowned and sometimes jumped on a horse and tore off down a canyon.

Ramon woke his assistant, a Mexican boy who spoke no English. As the boy began preparing pancake batter and frying bacon, Ramon raked a piece of firewood across the corrugated tin sides of the shed and hollered at the top of his voice: "Chuck!" Tent flaps opened, and the cowboys began crawling out, boots first. It was going to be a long day, the day they moved the bulk of the herd from the top country down to the holding pens at headquarters.

Breakfast was pancakes, bacon, and eggs—and chili colorado, left over from last night's supper. Nobody ate better than the cowboys at the o6. They ate quickly, talking in soft voices about the day's drive and other cowboy things. They seldom used profanity, even among themselves, and when they joked about women the tone may have been sexist but it wasn't sexual—it was the sort of homespun humor you heard from comedians in the fifties, about women drivers and that sort of stuff. They were un-failingly polite, especially to strangers, and even the give and take among equals showed a respect rare among professionals. When breakfast was finished, Ramon leaned on the handle of his shovel and watched the cow-boys jingle their morning horses. It was still dark, but he could see the flicker of ropes in the remuda.

When the men had saddled and mounted, Chris Lacy divided them into four groups, each headed by an o6 regular. Diane Lacy and their two chil-dren rode with Chris. Having women at roundup went against the grain of tradition, and some of the cowboys no doubt resented the intrusion, but Chris had decided that that was how it would be done at the o6—and Chris was the boss. Besides, Diane could ride with the best of them. The groups fanned out in separate directions, making a wide circle through the canyons and draws, gathering cattle as they found them.

I rode with Ty Holland's crew, sticking close to Ron Goddard as we moved slowly through heavy brush, down rocky canyons, and across end-less meadows. Though we could see for miles in all directions, we didn't see a single cow for nearly two hours. Most of the time I couldn't even see Ty Holland or the other two cowboys in our group, but Goddard knew where they were. "It's important we don't get behind or ahead of them," he told me. "We could miss some cattle." We stopped for a time and sat astride our mounts, listening to the wind. We could see the remuda strung out on the other side of the canyon, moving across the top of the next ridge to a camp called Number Eight, where we would meet with the other groups around noon and saddle fresh horses before driving the herd down to headquarters. There the herd would rest for a few days and recover from the drive before being loaded into trucks and shipped.

Presently Goddard spotted another rider scrambling up a ravine of brush, chasing a group of seven or eight calves. He spurred his mount to head them off and turn them along the opposite side of the ridge, toward Number Eight. I followed him around the ridge, and we stopped again on the opposite side of the mountain, above a draw leading up another hill to our rendezvous point. Ty Holland rode up beside us. "We're going down and work that brush," he told me. "Stay here and watch for strays." I interpreted that to mean "Kindly stay the hell out of our way"—which I did.

For more than an hour I sat there, astride an exceptionally gentle horse named Preacher, studying the spectacular terrain. More than half of the o6's 220 square miles were on top, above the rimrock, and though we would ride for nearly eleven hours this day, we would see only a tiny fraction of it. Nobody, including Mr. Kokernot himself, had ever seen all of it. Barney Nelson told me that she and Joel celebrated Thanksgiving every year by taking their provisions by pack horse and riding "as far as we can," to a pasture they'd never seen before. Sitting alone up there, I got a sense of why they loved it so desperately and an insight into the meaning of a quote I'd underlined in one of Barney's newspaper articles: "I am glad I shall never be young without wild country to be young in. Of what avail are forty freedoms without a blank spot on the map."

We didn't stop for lunch. When the herd had come together at the Number Eight pens, the cowboys saddled fresh horses from the remuda and we started down with the herd. We dropped off into a canyon and topped out through a pass, then down another smaller canyon and up a hill. From the crest of the hill we could see the great valley of Number Seven and the dirt road that led to headquarters. Polk's Peak was off to our left. I could just make out Clayton Williams's flagpole, naked on the horizon.

The herd spread out now into a long oval, with a point man out front, eight riders at the flanks, and the others riding drag, picking up strays and laggards. The horses were almost as expert as the riders. When a slobbering, mud-caked old bull at the rear of the herd turned back uphill, my horse, Preacher, wheeled around, and before I knew what had happened I had caught the bull—or rather, my horse did—and directed him back to the main body of herd. I looked at Chris Lacy, hoping my grin wasn't as foolish as it felt.

"Let's take 'em all the way to Abilene!" I shouted.

"If you're sure there's a railroad," the o6 boss shouted back, grinning at my attempt at cowboy humor.

At the floor of the valley, near a tank, the cowboys circled the herd and held it while Chris and Diane Lacy and Joel Nelson cut out the steer calves and their mamas, separating them from the cows with heifer calves and the young calves that had been born since spring branding. The heifer calves would be returned to their home pastures to help rebuild the herd, as would the young calves and most of the mother cows. The mothers of steer calves would lead their children to the shipping pens, then most of them would also be turned back to pasture. That was part of the grisly cycle of ranching—the mamas literally leading their babies to slaughter—then, by some ancient homing instinct, finding their own way back to pasture where they would breed again. When the mother cows had gotten worn out, they too would go to slaughter, ending up, in the inglorious argot of the industry, as "cheaper cuts."

It was late afternoon before we headed back up top to Number Nine. The ride back to camp was six or seven miles, so we stopped at a tank to water the horses. Nobody had eaten or had a drink of water since before daylight. Cowboys never carry canteens, Diane Lacy had warned me. They think canteens are for sissies. When one cowboy dismounted, scraped away the green scum, and drank from the tank, another said, "Hey, H. A., there's a dead bird in that tank." H. A. replied that he was too thirsty to care. "It's a buzzard!" the other cowboy added. By the time we returned to camp, riding at full gallop, I had blisters on my hand from gripping the saddle horn, and I could barely walk. I calculated that I had ridden fifteen miles that day. Joel and the others had ridden at least twice that far every day for two weeks, and they still had two weeks to go. Ramon had supper ready—steak, fried potatoes, camp bread, and cherry cobbler. I ate and was in my bedroll before dark. Another squall hit camp that night, but I didn't hear a thing.

They broke camp the following morning. From Number Nine they moved to headquarters, to Number Five, to Cienga, back to headquarters, to Willow Springs, to Berrendo Flat, and finally back to headquarters again. By the end of October the last of the cattle had been shipped. Normally the o6 shipped between two thousand and three thousand cattle, but this year the total was barely more than a thousand. A company in Guymon, Oklahoma, which would fatten them for about a year, bought most of them for about 65¢ a pound. The ranch's gross income for the year would come to about $350,000.

In early November I visited Clayton Williams's roundup. Williams's crew consisted of eight regular cowboys, mostly from his other Texas ranches, and a handful of neighbors. They rounded up eighteen hundred cattle in four days and later shipped another ten thousand yearlings from pens. Williams didn't actually "ship" cattle in the traditional sense, meaning he didn't sell them. Instead, he transferred them to wheat fields, feedlots, and his irrigated farm in Fort Stockton. Later he sold them at auction. "I'm waiting for the market to adjust," he told me. "The 06 and most of the others are selling right now for 65¢ a pound. I can't tell you what I'll get, but it'll be about double what they're getting now."

I wondered how he could round up eighteen hundred cattle in four days when it took the 06 four weeks to gather about half that. Of course it was easier to gather cattle on the flats than it was in high country, but still the difference seemed enormous. "I can tell you in one word," he said. "Improvements." Because of the extensive cross-fencing, he had pens and corrals scattered all over the ranch. His pastures were pens, huge pens, which meant, among other things, that there wasn't much rounding up to do. You could ride across the 06 for hours without seeing a single cow, but on Williams's place cows were thick as flies. Williams and his crew worked on horseback; they could just as easily have used pickups or even motor-scooters. It was quicker, cheaper, and considerably more efficient than the elaborate ritual at the 06.

"Another thing," Clayton Williams said, unable to resist a parting shot at his neighbors. "I imagine all those TV cameras slowed down the 06 just a little bit." I told him I hadn't seen any TV cameras, even though I knew he was just indulging in a little hyperbole. Clayton snapped up his chaps and mounted. "I may be a poor cowboy," he said as he spurred his horse and galloped off, "but I'm one helluva cowman."

A Star Is Reborn
Kris Kristofferson

I left the airport parking lot on the island of Maui an hour ago, and I'm still a hard two-hour drive away from the small, remote village where Kris Kristofferson lives with his third wife, Lisa, and their five children. The excruciatingly narrow road winds along the lava cliffs of the coast, through rain forests and deep ravines where waterfalls create permanent clouds of mist and vines large enough to swallow Houston choke the trunks of giant trees. I'm making this journey to talk to Kris about life in the wake of his role as the evil sheriff in *Lone Star*, which I thought was the best movie of 1996 and the best movie about Texas since *Hud*. There is a generation who barely recognizes Kristofferson's name, and yet in the seventies Kris was arguably the best songwriter of the decade and a huge screen star as well. Incredibly, *Lone Star*, which rejuvenated his film career, was his forty-third movie.

I also want to ask Kris about all the recent talk that the Academy of Motion Picture Arts and Sciences might allow an Oscar to slip into the hands of a rogue who has devoted the past quarter century to ridiculing everything the academy holds dear. The odds against Kris's even being nominated are enormous. But how can the academy ignore one of the most amazing entertainment careers of our times? Kristofferson has done and seen everything, been everywhere and met everyone. He has known Barbra Streisand and Janis Joplin, worked under the direction of Sam Peckinpah and Martin Scorsese, toured with Jimi Hendrix and Bob Dylan, smoked dope with Dennis Hopper and Willie Nelson, broken bread with Daniel Ortega, lectured Oxford dons on the poetry of William Blake, and written the best love songs of anyone since Cole Porter. Kris has walked the gangplank of contemporary history, and the damn sharks ain't ate him yet.

A long driveway climbs through an orchard of macadamia nut trees to the ranch home that Kris and Lisa built five years ago when they decided to reside permanently on the island. I spot Kris out back, at age 60 still as lean as rawhide, attacking a jungle of tropical growth with a chain saw. "I've been clearing this crap for the last four weeks," he tells me, pointing out a lemon tree, a star fruit tree, an avocado tree, and several papayas that he discovered in the process. "When Willie heard what I was doing, he said, 'How domestic!' " I tell Kris that I bring greetings from a number of friends in Austin, his second home. He periodically visits the city to hang out with Willie, do *Austin City Limits*, or make a film. "Say hi right back to 'em," Kris tells me, his famous lake-bottom rasp soft and direct.

In the family room we stretch out on a sectional sofa, Kris in his trademark faded jeans and dark T-shirt. The house sits partway up the green velvet slopes of Haleakala, the volcano that gave birth to this island. To the rear, on the uphill side, we can see the volcano's crater through a wisp of clouds. Far below us, down a swath of green hillside, the North Pacific stretches to the sky. "Yesterday we spotted a whale," Kris informs me.

I ask Kristofferson if he ever gets island fever. "This is the best move of my life," he tells me. "Before this, the happiest place I ever knew was Brownsville, Texas, where I grew up. This is the closest thing to Brownsville, a place where kids can go to school barefoot, where people know when you get sick and tell on you when you're bad. People here accept us as though we're part of an extended family. Kids here call me Uncle."

I decide this is the perfect moment to spring my proposition. It seems clear to me, I tell Kristofferson, that he deserves at last an Oscar nomination for his role in *Lone Star*, writer-director John Sayles's magnificent strip-down of the cultures and history of a small town on the Texas-Mexico border. The movie opened to universally good reviews, but as an independent film by a notoriously maverick filmmaker, it was ignored by the Hollywood establishment and, hence, the general viewing public.

Kris thinks on this a while, his deep-set eyes invisible in the weathering of his face. Finally, the eyes flash and sweep across the room like the beam of a lighthouse, and he says, "I'd like to see John Sayles get the recognition he deserves; his message is on the side of the people. The fact that anyone is even talking about my being nominated is so good for my morale it almost doesn't matter if it happens."

Kris talks a lot about his family and shows me an entire wall covered with photographs. I can see how far he has come. There are pictures of his

father and of Lisa's father, several of Kris as a child, and of his eight chil-
dren from three marriages. He points first to his in-house kids: 13-year-old
Jesse, 12-year-old Jody, 9-year-old Johnny (as in Cash), 6-year-old Kelly,
and 2-year-old Blake (after the English poet). Blake isn't much older than
Kristofferson's first grandchild, who was born last June to his daughter
Casey—who was born in 1973 to Kris and his second wife, Rita Coolidge.
Two other children, Tracy, who's 34, and Kris Jr., who's 28, came from his
first marriage, to his high school sweetheart in San Mateo, California.

"Through the love of my children I'm learning to love adults too,"
he explains, laughing at himself as though he has stumbled across an unexpected truth. The notion of starting over after two failed marriages
was daunting. Following his devastatingly bitter divorce from Coolidge in
1979, Kris told an interviewer, "When you get tossed out on the street,
you think you don't have the energy to go through all the unpeeling of
layers again to find out who you're dealing with. . . . The next one will have
to be carrying notes from the pope." Nevertheless he has been married to
Lisa for fourteen years, and he tells me, "This has been the best part of
my life."

In one wing of the house he shows me his writing room, guarded by
a no-nonsense black-and-white cat named Tuxedo, one of a dozen or so
pets-in-residence. "I sense that it's time to get down to business, which
means writing," he says. Like all musicians, Kris used to love the road.
The road meant freedom. Now he's not so sure. The recurring themes
in Kristofferson's work and in his life are loneliness, redemption, home,
and the double-edged nature of freedom. They are expressed grandly in a
line from one of his songs, "The Pilgrim: Chapter 33": "Never knowing
if believing is a blessing or a curse, or if the going up is worth the coming
down . . ."

"You seem haunted by the idea of home," I tell him. "It crops up in a
lot of your songs—trying to find your way back home, judging how far
you've come from home. Home seems to be a metaphor for something,
happiness and contentment, or maybe the Holy Grail."

"Whatever it is," Kris says, "it must be something profound in my
makeup. When I left the Army, it was like I was running away from home.
This place feels like coming home."

Kristofferson has lived at least three lives, and I mean *lived* them. His
turning points have resembled train wrecks. He grew up in Brownsville,
the son of a career air force major general and the grandson of two career

military men. There was never any doubt growing up that Kris would be career military. "Kris's whole life has been those army white gloves fighting against his jeans," says a longtime family friend. "You're a general's son who likes Hank Williams, where are you?" Kristofferson's first song, written when he was eleven (just before the family moved to San Mateo), was a Williams knockoff called "I Hate Your Ugly Face."

People who knew Kris in school remember that there was a sadness about him, a kind of separation. He was brilliant and popular, an acolyte in the Episcopal Church, class president of his high school, and a Phi Beta Kappa at Pomona College in California, where he played football, boxed, and was a company commander in ROTC. And yet he seemed to be forever looking for a place with no name, a place he might never find.

After graduation he got a deferment from the Army to accept a prestigious Rhodes scholarship to Oxford University in England. At Oxford Kris wrote a novel, but it was rejected, and he was writing his dissertation on Blake when he decided to leave academic life. He married his high school sweetheart, Fran Beer, and entered the Army with his ROTC commission. He volunteered for every hard job the Army had — flight school, jump school, ranger school. He started drinking. Like everything he did, Kris drank hard. " 'The road of excess leads to the palace of wisdom,' Blake wrote," Kris tells me now, smiling at the contradiction at the heart of this perceived truth.

"Whatever that means," I say.

"Whatever it means," he agrees.

Kris was a helicopter pilot in Germany for three years before he volunteered for Vietnam. "I was looking for something that would put some meaning in my life, something that was real," he tells me. "I didn't know anything except what I read in *Stars and Stripes* or got through military channels. I believed we were fighting for freedom over there." Instead of sending him to Vietnam, the Army assigned him to West Point to teach English. That was 1965, and he was nearly thirty. But Captain Kristofferson's first life was about to be abducted by aliens.

Before reporting to West Point, he took a leave and visited a friend in Nashville, bringing along tapes of some songs he had written in Germany. Nashville was exciting, intoxicating, potentially lethal. "I was still in uniform the first time I met Johnny Cash," Kris tells me. "He was backstage at the Grand Ole Opry, dressed all in black and pilled up — electric, dangerous, and unpredictable. And, frankly, it looked very attractive to me!" Kris resigned his commission, moved his wife and two children to Nashville, and got a job at Columbia Records as a janitor. "I accepted that it was a leap of faith, leaving home to do what I loved," Kris says, "but I knew from the minute I started doing it that I was right."

Not surprisingly, his marriage collapsed a few years later. Heavily in debt and facing $500 a month in child support, Kris took a job flying helicopters to offshore oil rigs in the Gulf of Mexico. He commuted between Baton Rouge and Nashville, consumed more than ever with making it as a songwriter, but increasingly confused about reality. "A lot of my pilot buddies from the Army were coming back from Vietnam telling horror stories," he remembers. "Some really good career officers went over there believing in what our country was doing and came back sickened by what they saw—throwing people out of choppers, killing civilians. It wasn't like a sudden change of mind, but the more I read, the more the scales fell away from my eyes. It was disturbing for a kid who grew up in Brownsville believing that God was on our side and our country stood for justice and freedom."

Kristofferson's first recorded song was "Vietnam Blues," which made fun of antiwar protesters. After that his lyrics turned to the left. Having grown up believing in justice and freedom, he began demanding them. "Nashville was a real Rubicon in my life," Kris tells me. "Joseph Campbell talks of following your bliss; that's what I did when I went to Nashville." His heroes were Willie Nelson, Johnny Cash, and Roger Miller. As a janitor at Columbia, Kris managed to pass along tapes of his music to Cash, who threw them into a lake. Nevertheless, Cash encouraged Kris to keep writing.

Pills and booze were Nashville's drugs of choice. "I thought the function of an artist was to burn, not rust," Kris recalls. They stayed up for days and nights and weeks, Kris and pals like Mickey Newbury, writing songs and playing them for each other. Country musicians were considered trash by the Nashville business establishment, and songwriters were the lowest of the low. Music City in 1965 consisted of just two streets, Sixteenth and Seventeenth Avenues. "The people I knew thought songwriting was a serious and worthwhile business, and I agreed with them," he remembers. "I'll tell you, it was like Paris in the twenties."

One morning in 1967 Kristofferson landed a helicopter in Johnny Cash's backyard. "He came stumbling out with a beer in one hand and a tape in the other," Cash recalled last year during an interview for a BBC documentary on Kristofferson. One of the songs on the tape was "Sunday Morning Coming Down," which Cash performed on his television show. Cash and Kristofferson bonded into a sort of brotherhood of the damned. "Kris said I looked like a black snake," Cash remembered. "He looked in my face and saw I was dying and wondered why. Then he wrote me a song." The song was "To Beat the Devil," a story about a poet who meets the devil in a bar, drinks his beer, then steals his song. It's the kind of thing that William Blake might have written if he'd had Kristofferson's sense of humor.

The seventies were a golden age for songwriters, much like the thirties, when the Gershwins and Hoagy Carmichael emerged not merely as songwriters but as trendsetters and celebrities. Writers like Willie and Kris forever changed country music, elevated it to an art. Kristofferson didn't just write about love, he wrote about sex. "Take the ribbon from your hair / shake it loose and let it fall," from "Help Me Make It Through the Night," is out-and-out foreplay. "It was the first time anyone in Nashville had taken this direct approach to sex," Willie says. Record producer Don Was once observed that Kristofferson was the most intelligent person he'd ever met. "That kind of enhanced consciousness can be a psychic burden to the poor soul who has got to live with it twenty-four hours a day," Was said, "but it sure makes for some great music."

Kristofferson has always thought of himself as a songwriter, not an actor and certainly not a singer. "I sing like a bullfrog," he told Combine Music founder Fred Foster, who replied, "Yeah, but a bullfrog who communicates." Two songs in particular sealed Kristofferson's reputation as a writer and indirectly led to his screen career—"Me and Bobby McGee" and "Sunday Morning Coming Down." Dennis Hopper heard Kris's tape of "Bobby McGee" and invited him to Peru to play a bit part in and write some songs for the cocaine-induced epic *The Last Movie*. Similarly, director Sam Peckinpah went wild for "Sunday Morning Coming Down," which landed Kris the title role of Billy the Kid in one of Peckinpah's films.

Janis Joplin began using "Me and Bobby McGee" in concerts after learning the words from a mutual friend, Bobby Neuwirth—which in turn led to her much publicized affair with Kristofferson. Contrary to popular myth, the real Bobby McGee wasn't Joplin but a secretary named Bobby McKee who worked at Combine Music. Kris wrote the song on assignment for Fred Foster, who came up with the title. Flying a helicopter over the Gulf, Kris decided that it should be a road song and wrote: "Busted flat in Baton Rouge, heading for the train." Listening to the rhythm of the helicopter and remembering one of Mickey Newbury's songs, he wrote, "Bobby thumbed a diesel down, just before it rained . . ." Later he remembered the final scene of *La Strada*, Federico Fellini's magnificent road movie, when Anthony Quinn realizes that he has dumped the only woman he truly loves, and that became the inspiration for the line, "Somewhere near Salinas, I let her slip away."

Kris explains to me: "It was that double-edged nature of freedom, when the pain of the loss more than equals the pleasure of the gain."

Kristofferson's meeting with Joplin came at the end of a drug-inspired journey that started as a party at a New York penthouse in 1969. The merrymakers were a cast of characters emblematic of that psychedelic period: Odetta (an enormously gifted black folk singer), Ramblin' Jack Elliott, Mickey Newbury, Bobby Neuwirth, Michael J. Pollard, Kris, and others. "There was much tequila and coke," Kris remembers, "and in the middle of the night Neuwirth says to me, 'Hey, Range Rider'—he always called me Range Rider—'do you want to go to San Francisco to see Joan Baez?' And Odetta says, 'I want to go too!' So we head straight for the airport, the three of us, Ramblin' Jack playing us to the plane and Bobby telling everyone that we're Peter, Paul, and Mary, and Odetta's been to the islands."

Somehow, they never got to Baez's house but went instead to Mill Valley, where Joplin lived with her dog, Thurber. Joplin was a big star at the time, Kristofferson a mostly unknown songwriter: All they had in common was that she had done "Bobby McGee" in concert and people had loved it. Though not physically attractive, Joplin had a sexual aura that could drive men to uncommon acts. "I've got a present for you, baby," Neuwirth said, pushing Kristofferson into Joplin's arms. A month later, Kris was still there. Joplin had been doing heroin, but she stopped completely during her affair with Kris.

"I lived with her, slept with her, but it wasn't a love affair," he tells me. "I loved her like a friend. She was very soulful, a passionate person but very childlike to me, a little girl in dress-up clothes. She was an unhappy person. Even though she was fun to be around, she felt that the only thing that made her attractive to the world was her art, her talent, her stardom. And she was intelligent enough to know that it was temporary. She told me, 'Pretty soon you're gonna be gypsyin' down the road to be a star.'"

Kris tells me about his last night with Joplin. They started with drinks at Barney's in L.A., Janis in her famous feathered hat, the world at their feet. A kid came by the table to say how much he admired Janis, and she almost bit his head off. "That night in bed, I just held her all night long. We didn't even . . ." Kris's voice breaks and he looks away, toward the ocean. "I knew she was sad because she believed nobody loved her. She told me if things didn't get better, she would go back on heroin and off herself. I didn't believe her. I told her, 'How do you expect to ever meet anyone if you snap their heads off?'"

Kris was staying at Joan Baez's house in Carmel when news arrived that Joplin had died of a drug overdose. He believes her death was accidental. The night after she died, most of Joplin's friends gathered at the Landmark Hotel in Hollywood. On that occasion, Kris heard for the first time Joplin's version of "Bobby McGee." Twenty-six years later, he saw a tape of her singing it at Threadgill's in Austin. "To this day," he tells me, "whenever I sing that line 'Somewhere near Salinas,' I think of Janis."

In 1970 Kris landed his first gig in show business, opening for Linda Ronstadt at the Troubadour in Los Angeles. A smashing review in one of the L.A. papers brought Barbra Streisand to the Troubadour to check out the young songwriter. Unfortunately, Kris didn't show up. "I had been out with Hopper the night before, and I fell asleep in the parking lot," he recalls. "When I woke it was dark, and I was supposed to be onstage."

Streisand came back two nights later, though. When they met backstage, the chemistry was instant. After that, the gossip columns crackled with items about Kris and Barbra. The affair caused a sensation back in Nashville. "We're shitting in the tall cotton now, aren't we, son?" Cash told Kristofferson. Almost overnight, Kris's career was moving at warp speed. All the big names were recording his songs. He played Carnegie Hall and did a concert on the Isle of Wight with Jimi Hendrix, which turned out to be Hendrix's last show. Hollywood began to notice too.

Hollywood is not equipped to deal with a force of nature like Kristofferson, a man who thinks for himself, measures truth by his own reckoning, and talks back. At the 1980 Cannes Film Festival, which held the premiere of *Heaven's Gate*, a $36 million flop that nearly wrecked Kristofferson's film career, an executive of the studio that made the film warned, "Unless control is taken away from the creative people, our industry is headed for disaster." To which Kris responded, "Who do you give it to— the uncreative people?"

Cracks like that don't win points with the academy. Neither did Kristofferson's response to the asinine turf war between executives of CBS Records and Tri-Star Production Company over the filming of Bud Shrake's brilliant and original screenplay *Songwriter* in 1984. Abetted by producer Sydney Pollack's weak-kneed refusal to intercede, the moguls not only sabotaged an excellent movie but also scuttled an extraordinary soundtrack of songs by Kris and Willie. Kris celebrated this showbiz snit by writing songs about the executives, whom he dubbed for the ages: "Sydney the Snake," "Danny the Dildo," and "Wally the Wus."

Kris's first landmark role was playing Billy the Kid in Sam Peckinpah's 1973 classic western *Pat Garrett and Billy the Kid.* The legendary director was throwing knives into his office door the first time Kristofferson met him. Within minutes they were lifelong friends. "We liked the same things—Mexico, women, and booze," Kristofferson says. "Sam loved being surrounded by turmoil. He used it for energy. 'Fuck MGM! Let's go make a movie!' Someone once said that Sam looked like a man tracking an animal much larger than himself. That's a good description."

At Kristofferson's urging, Bob Dylan reluctantly accepted a part in the movie. Peckinpah had no idea who Dylan was—and when informed, the director protested that the studio had cast him for purely promotional reasons. "The first time we watched dailies," Kris remembers, "the projector was out of focus, so Sam walked up and urinated on the screen. I looked over at Dylan. He didn't say anything, but I knew what he was thinking: 'What the fuck have I gotten myself into!'

"There were times when Sam wasn't worth shooting, but he tried to make real films, and I loved him for it," Kris continues. When Peckinpah died in 1985, Kristofferson headed up a host of celebrities who honored him. Alan Rudolph recalls that Kris began by chewing out Hollywood for not fully appreciating Peckinpah. "It was a terrific statement about Peckinpah, about Hollywood, and about Kris's loyalty and convictions," Rudolph said.

Acting for Kristofferson is more a cause than a profession. He succeeds at it for the same reason he succeeds as a singer and a songwriter: because he knows his range and has true convictions. Radicalized by his experiences, Kris finds political nuances—even messages—in every role he accepts. Kris says that *Heaven's Gate* was an attempt to show the fatal flaw in our society: We care for money more than for people. In his mind *Lone Star* is a dark allegory of the American experience in which the three sheriffs represent three sides of history—the genocidal, the merely bigoted, and the racially semitolerant. "Now, if you billed it that way," he admits, "nobody would come and see it."

Many of the fans of *Lone Star,* myself included, believe that the film demonstrates that Kristofferson belongs in an elite class of strong, silent, honest actors like Gary Cooper, Robert Ryan, and Gregory Peck—the three actors, incidentally, whom he most admires. Kris is believable as the corrupt and murderous sheriff Charlie Wade because he has absorbed a larger measure of the character than meets the eye. Sayles had the good judgment to understand that Kristofferson, like Cooper, is an actor who nails his character through an internal process, that on-screen he does a lot without appearing to do anything. Alan Rudolph, who directed Kristofferson in *Songwriter* and 1985's *Trouble in Mind*, has observed, "As the camera got closer to him, the movie got better."

In 1974, Kristofferson appeared in Martin Scorsese's *Alice Doesn't Live Here Anymore*, but his film career got its biggest boost in 1976, when Streisand chose him to play the self-destructive superstar in *A Star Is Born*. Streisand played the unknown whose star rises as Kristofferson's fades and dies. Though Kris and Barbra were no longer an item—she was living at the time with Jon Peters, who coproduced the film with her—the chemistry was still there, sparking rumors of a renewed romance. There were also stories about how Streisand's arrogance and overbearing attitude inspired the crew to put human excrement in her makeup.

That's not exactly what happened, Kris tells me. "We had come back to finish a scene where the two of us were rolling in the mud, and Willie Perez, the wardrobe guy, had wet down some fuller's earth to look like mud. In the middle of the scene, Barbra stops and tells the director, Frank Pierson, 'This stuff smells like shit!' I smelled it and it did. Pierson says he doesn't want to talk about it, and we go on with the scene. I'll say this, Barbra took it a lot better than you'd think."

Kris is not anxious to speak poorly of Striesand, even now. "Barbra opened doors for me," he acknowledges. "She put me in a whole different category." After the film premiered, Streisand and Peters gave Kristofferson a silver case for his marijuana cigarettes, inscribed, prophetically: "A superstar is born—let it be an easy birth." Kristofferson's movie career skyrocketed.

Kristofferson was convincing as the booze-and-drug-addled superstar because during the entire course of filming he stayed stoned. "I was drinking two bottles of whiskey a day," Kris tells me. He had been riding the whiskey-pills-and-pot roller coaster hard and fast since his early days in Nashville, and now it was catching up with him. Watching his own body on the screen, Kris had a premonition of death. He saw his young daughter, Casey, standing alone without him. "The idea of Casey growing up without me was inconceivable," he remembers.

That's when Kristofferson's life took its third hard turn. He stopped drinking. He started running seven miles, swimming fifty laps, and working out on a rowing machine daily. He also reconnected with his spiritual life, not by joining a church but by making a private accommodation with God. This happened while Kristofferson was on tour in Europe. He learned that his daughter Tracy had been injured in a motorcycle wreck and was unconscious and probably paralyzed. A friend in Alcoholics Anonymous had told him, "If you don't believe in God, ask for something impossible." Flying home to California that night, Kris started making a deal with God. "Please don't let her be paralyzed," he remembers pleading. When he walked into Tracy's hospital room, she was in a coma, tubes running everywhere, the room dark. But his face brightens as he tells me, "A minute later, the doctor says, 'Look!' Her leg had moved. I'm thinking, 'Okay, I'm your boy!' "

Kristofferson's marriage to Coolidge began to fall apart in the late seventies, just as Kris started filming *Heaven's Gate*. Kristofferson always had problems avoiding women: Stand him on any street corner in the world and they will flock around him like magpies around a tree of ripe apricots. What pushed Coolidge over the edge, however, wasn't infidelity per se but the passionate love scenes between Kris and actress Sarah Miles in *The Sailor Who Fell from Grace with the Sea*. The final straw was when *Playboy* published the outtakes from the film.

Director Michael Cimino remembers how the divorce devastated Kris during the six-month filming of *Heaven's Gate*. He speaks of Kristofferson's "Lincoln-esque black moods" and says: "There were days when one could almost not talk to him. He was literally at the bottom of the well and one had to find a way to pull him back up to where he could even speak. . . . A lot of the agony and pain you see on the screen is quite real. It's something beyond acting."

The failure of *Heaven's Gate* symbolizes Kristofferson's star-crossed film career, always a step short of greatness. Cimino's next project was supposed to be a remake of *The Fountainhead* (1949), with Kristofferson playing Gary Cooper's part. "Nobody on this planet could have played Gary Cooper like I could," Kris tells me. But when *Heaven's Gate* went south, so did the new project. At the time, Kristofferson was among the ten most bankable stars in Hollywood, right up there with Robert Redford and Paul Newman. "After that," Kris tells me, "I couldn't get a job."

In recent years Kristofferson's music as well as his life has become increasingly politicized, not always to his advantage. Songs about Vietnam, Wounded Knee, Martin Luther King, Gandhi, and Christ, while noble and well intended, are hardly toe-tappers. Willie has hinted to friends that he dearly wishes that Kris would shut up and play "Me and Bobby McGee," but of course he can't say that to Kris. Both Willie and Kris play a lot of benefits for farmers, Native Americans, human-rights advocates, and environmental causes, but Willie does it with a minimum of lecturing.

Kristofferson's reputation as a writer and a performer has diminished to the point that his acting career now subsidizes his music. During the filming of *Lone Star*, a local production assistant was furious to discover that it wasn't the hunk Matthew McConaughey she was driving to the airport but some geezer named Kristofferson. Like his other albums this decade, his 1995 release, *A Moment of Forever*, sold poorly. This is unfortunate because it was produced by Don Was, one of the best in popular music, and contains some good love songs, great satire, and a wonderful tribute to Peckinpah, which opens:

> *I have been with the best that the bastards could muster*
> *From Danny the Dildo to Sydney the Snake*
> *And I feel like a working girl pausing to wonder*
> *Just how much screwin' the spirit can take.*

Kris admits that his passion for causes ebbs and flows. But he once said, "You've got to think of the consequences if nobody speaks up. What it really gets down to, though, is living with yourself. If you don't live by the principles you believe in, then you become this hollow person."

What finally radicalized Kristofferson was the public reaction to his 1986 television miniseries *Amerika*. He caught hell from both the right and the left. The film was a fantasy about a Soviet invasion of the United States, with Kris playing the anticommunist leader of the U.S. resistance. The original screenplay, which he rejected, pushed a right-wing agenda, painting the United Nations as a tool of the Soviets. Kris agreed to the role only after most of the negative references to the UN were taken out of the script.

This infuriated right-wingers, who accused him of sabotaging the project. Left-wingers were even more ruthless. "Don't think you can atone for *Amerika* just by marching with us," a woman at an antinuclear demonstration in Nevada told him. "They acted like I made a film for the Nazis," Kris says. The experience helped focus Kristofferson's political ideas. In the weeks that followed, he played a number of human-rights benefits and made several trips to Nicaragua. He got to know the country's president, Daniel Ortega, who invited Kris to sing at the anniversary of the revolution that put him in power.

On one of his trips to Nicaragua, Kristofferson was asked to visit Eugene Hasenfus, the Air America crewman whose plane was downed while flying supplies to the contras. Kris took the prisoner a copy of the book *Fire from the Mountain: The Making of a Sandinista*, then told him the story of Tracy's miraculous recovery and repeated the challenge of faith: "If you don't believe in God, ask for something impossible."

Kris tells me now, "All the time I'm telling Hasenfus this story, I keep thinking: Why am I doing this? I knew that the hard-liners intended to make an example of him, that he'd probably serve thirty years, so why am I building up his hopes? That night, Lisa and I fly home to Maui, and when I check my answering machine, I learn that Hasenfus has been released and is already back in this country." Kris smiles and adds, "I don't know if it bolstered his faith, but it sure as hell bolstered mine."

Kris walks me to the car, his three dogs nosing him for attention. We shake hands and I realize again how much I admire him. I once told Kris that I thought of him, Willie, and Billy Joe Shaver as the Byron, Shelley, and Keats of our time. "I can't argue with that," Kris replied. Driving back to the airport in Maui, I keep remembering how the notion of Kris's being considered for an Oscar was more important to me than it was to him. It would be nice, but it's nothing that he needs. When you've been Kris Kristofferson, what else is there?

The Real Deal Meets the Real Meal
Holyfield vs. Foreman

In early March, when Evander Holyfield began training to defend his title against George Foreman, visitors came to the gym in North Houston in trickles, sometimes in expensive cars that looked out of place in the neighborhood, especially in daylight. Some brought their own photographers. Most of them wore three-piece suits, shiny Italian-made shoes, and excessive jewelry, and when they posed with the heavyweight champion of the world, they smiled as though this were a birthday party. They huddled for a while in the back of the gym with Lou Duva, the stubby, pugnacious onetime Teamsters Union boss who controls Holyfield and thirteen other current or former world champions, and ten minutes later, they were gone. You didn't want to inquire into the nature of their conversation.

By the time Duva opened the double-door entrance of the Heights Boxing Gym each morning at ten o'clock, there were people waiting to do business, not all of it related to the championship fight in Atlantic City on April 19. The sweet science of boxing has always attracted more hornets than honeybees. Drummers and hustlers of every variety came around, paying their respects to Duva, shaking hands with the champ, slipping their cards into the coat pockets of reporters. Firefighters from a neighborhood station stopped by some mornings, and so did youngsters from a local boxing association. One morning the only spectators were a pair of ladies in generous makeup and Frederick's of Hollywood evening wear, their oversized shades suggesting that it had been a while since they had seen the sun.

Holyfield seldom arrived before ten-thirty or eleven, and there were days when he didn't arrive at all. While his handlers waited, they worked with other boxers in Duva's Main Events boxing stable. The best was Raoul Marquez, an 18-year-old Houston middleweight, a good bet to win an Olympic medal next year and maybe a world professional championship a few years after that. There were usually a few broken-down fighters hanging around the gym too, looking for a job or just a kind word. Al Evans, a tall, angular black man with a creased face and gentle eyes, came in with his 4-year-old son, DaVan, telling anyone who would listen that he was searching for a filmmaker to document his career "and show the way Jesus helped me." Evans's single claim to fame was that eight years ago, in an amateur fight, he knocked out Mike Tyson. Evans became such a familiar figure around the gym that Duva finally put him to work doing odd jobs.

Holyfield liked training in Houston—he had even bought a condominium here—partly because he had got it in his head that Houston's heat and humidity helped him round into shape, but also because he associated his hometown of Atlanta with losers. Another reason was that Holyfield's conditioning coach, Tim Hallmark, lived here. Holyfield and Hallmark went back to 1986, when Holyfield was training for one of the last fifteen-round title fights on record. When they changed the rules of boxing to set the maximum limit at twelve, the sweet science lost more than just three rounds.

The Heights Boxing Gym was near the intersection of Heights and Washington, so close to downtown that you could see the skyline. Forty or fifty years ago, this neighborhood was white, middle class, and residential, but the homes were long gone and in their place were endless blocks of used-car lots, auto repair shops, pawnshops, fast-food places, and black jazz clubs. The gym sat off the main drag, at the rear of Sam Segari's trendy restaurant and bar, and in back of a parking lot used by Rockefeller's, one of the city's livelier nightspots.

The gym was excessively modest, a white concrete-block structure just large enough to accommodate a ring, an exercise area, and a simple dressing room with no shower. Two heavy bags hung from chains, but there were no speed bags—this despite the fact that earlier in his career Holyfield was obsessed with them. As an 8-year-old at a boys' club in Atlanta, Holyfield began boxing not because he liked to hit people or mix it up but because he fell in love with the rat-tat-tat-bang of the light bag. A row of mirrors covered part of one wall, reflecting a platform for rope skipping and a bench for weight lifting or stretching. Except for those spare furnishings, the only equipment was what Holyfield's entourage brought each morning.

This was the biggest fight in Lou Duva's fifty years in the game, bigger even than the one last October when Holyfield lifted the championship from an overweight and undermotivated Buster Douglas. Duva said that he knew that his man would knock out Douglas because Douglas had quit in three of his previous four fights: His upset of Tyson was one of those aberrations that mainly served to remind the public that the sweet science is sustained by periodic mutations. Duva had grown up on the streets of New York's Little Italy and in Patterson, New Jersey. He got his start in boxing as a bucket carrier at the legendary Stillman's Gym—the University of Eighth Avenue, the great boxing writer A. J. Liebling called it. While other students of the game were studying the fighters, Duva studied the old-time managers, noting how they maneuvered to steal fights. He had been a trucker, a bail bondsman, a bounty hunter, a union boss, a club-fight manager, and eventually a millionaire—but the one thing that Duva had never done until now was own (as they used to say) a heavyweight championship. He who controls the heavyweight championship controls everything.

Holyfield was Lou Duva's starry crown. Risking it against a 42-year-old phenomenon like George Foreman was a way to ensure a payday of, let us say, $100 million when the Holyfield-Tyson fight was arranged maybe a year from now. That would have to wait, of course, until Holyfield beat Foreman . . . if he beat Foreman. Sure, Foreman was much older than Holyfield: By the time Foreman was 28, Holyfield's age, he had already retired. But he was also bigger, stronger, wiser, and meaner. No fighter in history ever punched harder. Getting hit by Foreman was like getting pumped full of novocaine. Jimmy Young, one of only two fighters ever to defeat Foreman, still remembered the jolt of a Foreman left hook fourteen years later. Foreman's reputation bothered Holyfield more than the champion liked to admit. When former light-heavyweight champion Jose Torres visited Holyfield's camp, he sensed that Holyfield was nervous and apprehensive. If Torres smelled fear, Duva must have smelled it too. During the third week of training, Duva ordered red-and-gold banners suspended from the rafters, reminding visitors—and Holyfield—that the fighter was the "undisputed" heavyweight champion of the world, that he was "the real deal," that "youth beats age."

No Rolls-Royce had ever been treated better than Duva treated his man Holyfield. The gruff, pint-size manager had assembled a team of specialists to watch over the champion from the time he awoke until he went to bed. At the head of the team was trainer George Benton, who had been Joe Frazier's cotrainer in the second Frazier-Foreman fight, but Holyfield also worked daily with his conditioning coach, Hallmark, and with an assistant trainer, a weight coach, and a ballet instructor. The champ's nutritional program was closely monitored, and special exercise equipment was designed to increase his punching power. Instead of traditional roadwork, he ran wind sprints, a method of rehearsing his body to work without oxygen, as it would be required to do at the finish of a hard round. Holyfield spent his mornings in the gym, his afternoons watching film and resting, and his evenings in a health spa in the Galleria area. His only diversion was a Thursday-night ritual in which Duva treated the entire team to an evening of Italian food and bowling.

Holyfield didn't look like a heavyweight; he looked like a Michelangelo sculpture. Every muscle group seemed to have been copied from *Gray's Anatomy*, and all that was missing was the name tags. Outside the ring, he was unfailingly courteous and polite, and he seldom missed an opportunity to credit God for his success. People thought of him as nice, maybe too nice to beat George Foreman. "People don't see me as a threat," he admitted. "They see a guy who makes sense when he talks and doesn't act crazy. I don't intimidate people with my presence like Foreman or Tyson. For me, boxing has always been more mental than physical." Only when he climbed into the ring did this sweet-tempered young man seem possessed. His ex-wife, Paulette, recalled that she had been terrified the first time she watched her husband fight, that she hyperventilated and broke out with hives. His relentless quest to become the heavyweight champion broke up their marriage—four children later—she claimed.

Paulette was primary among many problems that burned in Lou Duva's ample gut. One of the champ's greatest assets, Duva insisted, was his ability to handle stress, to focus on the priority of boxing and put personal problems aside. But toward the end of the second week of camp, on a day that Duva had promised reporters that his man would be sparring four rounds, Holyfield suddenly bolted, flying to Atlanta to take care of "personal problems." Paulette had bumped her divorce-settlement demands from $4 million to $20 million—coincidentally, the exact size of Holyfield's purse for the championship fight. Holyfield was back after a few days, apparently as focused as ever. But you had to wonder. Sam Lanford, a great lightweight in the early 1900s, used to say, "You can sweat out beer, and you can sweat out whiskey, but you can't sweat out women."

To get his man ready for the fight, Duva imported a series of Foreman look-alikes as sparring partners. They arrived at camp like logs at a sawmill, each six foot four, 250 pounds plus, each a never-was posturing as a has-been, most strong enough to give the champ a taste of the mugging and mauling he could expect one month later in Atlantic City. With a ghetto blaster at ringside playing what sounded like rock music from hell, Holyfield went progressively longer each day.

"Don't lose your cool," trainer George Benton yelled above the music. "That's what he wants you to do. Stay loose, stay loose . . . go with the flow." Benton wanted Holyfield to push or pull away from the bear hugs of the imitation Foremans, to counter with uppercuts and punishing left hooks to the body. Since Holyfield was quicker and more mobile than Foreman, the strategy was to stay in what Lou Duva called "the zone," far enough away to duck but close enough to counterpunch.

"Foreman is heavy-handed, what I call a club fighter," Benton said. "He never knocks a guy dead with a sharp blow; he clubs him to the floor. Evander's got to be flexible . . . stick and move, stab and move, in and out . . . make Foreman rush his punches, keep him busy, tire him out. Foreman was never known for his stamina, even when he was a young man."

An amiable gentleman in his fifties, Benton was sort of a boulevardier with a fondness for wool golf caps, gold jewelry, and forgiving women. Like other members of the team, he wore a Real Deal T-shirt while working. He reminded me of Jersey Joe Walcott, the quick-study eyes, shoulders defined by many hours in the ring but none in the weight room. Benton grew up in North Philadelphia, in a tough neighborhood a few blocks from Johnny Madison's Gym. Naturally, his mother forbade him to hang out with the rabble at the gym, and naturally, by the age of 10, he was working there as a towel boy. "When Madison sold the gym to Joe Rose," Benton remembered, "he sold me with it. Rose started training me at age 12 and trained me until I retired at 36." A ranking middleweight in the sixties, he beat three champions but never in a title fight. Benton's career ended in 1970 when a gunman, apparently mistaking him for someone else, put a bullet in his back. For the past fifteen years, Benton has trained for Duva.

One week before it was time to break camp and head to Atlantic City, Holyfield rounded into peak form by boxing twelve rounds with four different Foreman look-alikes. To contain the crowd, Duva stretched a rope between the front entrance and the ring, and positioned Al Evans to keep small boys from climbing underneath, an assignment that gave Evans and the boys much pleasure. The only people allowed in the exercise area behind the ring were reporters, a few men in three-piece suits and Italian-made shoes, and members of Houston's sports aristocracy, such as Dicky Meagle, the old Rice University all-American halfback.

Holyfield looked sharp. He had learned his lessons well. He stayed in the zone, dodging jabs and countering with fast, sure combinations to his opponent's head and body—four, five, and six hard shots in a flurry. The imitation Foremans mauled, wrestled, and tied him up, but Holyfield kept his cool. Hallmark shouted encouragement—"Real Deal!"—and checked Holyfield's pulse between each round. In the final two rounds, Holyfield's lean, contoured body was lathered with sweat and he was breathing hard, but he was still sticking and moving.

Afterward, Duva personally removed Holyfield's gloves and wraps, changed the boxer's sweat-drenched T-shirt, and toweled him down as gently as a mother. "He got a little tired there at the end," the manager acknowledged, "but remember, he was in there with four fresh guys. I don't think Foreman is dumb enough to train for twelve rounds."

Just when the sweet science appears to lie like a painted ship upon a painted ocean, a new hero . . . comes along like a Moran tug to pull it out of the doldrums.

A. J. Liebling wrote that sentence in 1962 about a brash young heavyweight named Cassius Clay, but it worked just as well in 1991 when applied to George Foreman. This was one of the great stories in the annals of boxing—Foreman's comeback. The appeal of the fight was international, universal, timeless. Try to remember the last time a heavyweight championship attracted this kind of interest. You had to go back to the days of Ali, Frazier, and Foreman. In 1973, when Foreman knocked out Frazier and won the heavyweight championship, people predicted that he would hold the crown for twenty years. Instead, he held it for slightly better than twenty months—until Ali, who had lost the title to Frazier, reclaimed it from Foreman in Zaire. Now Foreman had returned, two decades later, and the prophecy was on schedule.

People had laughed at the notion of a Foreman comeback, none more relentlessly than kingpin promoter Bob Arum, who predicted that no one would take the comeback seriously. Foreman fought in tank towns, against mediocre club boxers, for purses starting at a few thousand dollars. Averaging a fight every other month, Foreman fought himself back into shape. Gradually, the purses got larger, and so did the demands for his talents. After four years, he had won all twenty-four of his fights, twenty-three by knockouts. When Douglas beat Tyson, and Holyfield beat Douglas—and the doldrums sucked the wind out of boxing's sails—Arum reviewed the situation. Working a deal with Duva's Main Events organization, Arum made himself copromoter of the championship fight. He first offered Foreman $10 million. Not enough, said Foreman, who negotiated for himself. Arum bumped the offer to $12.5 million. Nobody had ever paid a challenger that kind of money before, but then George Foreman wasn't merely the challenger; he was the draw. "Foreman is the first fighter I've ever negotiated with directly who didn't overestimate his worth," Arum admitted.

In an era in which sporting events had become more complex than grand opera, Foreman was a one-man band. He was his own promoter, his own manager, his own trainer, even his own cut man—in a fight last July, George applied a butterfly patch to his own eye cut. "He'll barely let you help him unlace his gloves," said Mort Sharnik, Foreman's publicist. Unlike Holyfield, who would split his purse many ways, Foreman would keep all except what he paid his attendants and advisers.

Nobody mentioned Foreman's age anymore, except in awe. Reporters seemed fascinated by his weight—did he really return from the island of St. Lucia in January weighing just 240?—but that was no more than another rainy-day angle for the press. The only people truly concerned about Foreman's weight were those in Holyfield's camp, who wished George would lose thirty or forty pounds. When George told reporters that dieting interfered with his sense of contentment—that he tended to hallucinate when he ate too lightly, and that the franchise hamburger had changed his life—he wasn't necessarily trying to be funny. Kathy Duva, Lou's daughter-in-law, who was in charge of publicity for Main Events, told a member of Foreman's camp, "We're really glad that George is taking this fight seriously," illustrating how badly Holyfield's people misread the situation. Foreman had been as serious as rent right from the start. His motive for a comeback may have been charity—he wanted to build an indoor arena for his youth club in Houston, and he had done that, and a lot more, with his winnings—but beyond the altruism was his deep-seated conviction that God wanted him to be the heavyweight champion of the world again. "It is my destiny," he said. "It is in the stars."

Not since Muhammad Ali had there been a heavyweight with such charisma and mystique. In the soft light of his reincarnation, Foreman emerged as a philosopher, wit, and elder statesman, roles he very much enjoyed. In his spare time, this ninth-grade dropout read *War and Peace* and books on the Great Depression, the Holocaust, and the New Deal. George wrote his own dialogue, coining a repertoire of self-effacing quips and one-liners that made him the hit of talk shows. "People say I made my comeback fighting guys just off the respirator," he would growl, looking menacingly at the camera. "That's a lie! I didn't fight nobody hadn't been off the respirator at least eight days." Publicist Sharnik, borrowing a gesture from *The Great White Hope*, got Foreman to shake his fist the same way Jack Johnson had and call out defiantly, "Here I is!" Interview requests poured in from all over the world. "This fight transcends boxing, even sports," said Sharnik. That wasn't just hyperbole from an overwrought PR man. As an investigative reporter for *Sports Illustrated* and later the boxing coordinator for CBS Television, Sharnik had been around sports for thirty years.

Foreman had a compulsion to control his own environment and an aversion to sharing the spotlight. Sharnik wanted to invite Willie Nelson, Nolan Ryan, Ann Richards, and Bill Moyers to a "Texas Treasures" barbecue in Houston—the idea being to establish that Foreman belonged in such company—but George vetoed the idea. Nor in the weeks before the fight would he agree to appear on the same talk show as Holyfield. "Why should I?" he asked. "My task is to put him in the shadows." But as the moment drew closer when he would have to share the ring with Holyfield, Foreman became more pensive and introspective. At times like this, he always retreated to the sanctuary of his heavily wooded two-hundred-acre ranch near Marshall.

The small East Texas town of Marshall had a mystical pull on Foreman. This was his place of birth. Though his mother took her flock of children to Houston's Fifth Ward when George was a baby, he had returned as heavyweight champion of the world and tracked down his true father. One of the many things Foreman and Holyfield had in common was that they grew up dirt poor, the babies of large families raised by deeply religious, hardworking mothers; and years later, fame and fortune secure, both returned to their roots to face their biological fathers. Later, George preached at the old man's funeral, then he placed his Olympic medal and his championship belt in the Harrison County Historical Museum in Marshall and bought a ranch south of town. The ranch was a sort of memorial. It was also the place he went when he wanted to be left alone.

When Foreman first began his comeback two years ago, most sportwriters called him a clown and predicted that he would be a menace to himself and to the sport of boxing—as though anything short of an artillery burst of dead skunks could sully boxing. But by now most were convinced he was a worthy contender. Those who drifted into Foreman's camp for the first time were always a little surprised to see the ex-champion up close. Foreman didn't look like an old boxer. Old boxers have splattered noses and ears like dried fruit, and they walk on their heels, looking as though they are about to topple backward. But there was not a mark on George Foreman, nothing you could see. He was forty-two, but he could pass for mid-thirties. Watching Foreman move around the ring, you were reminded of a circus elephant. He was ponderous, yet graceful and finely balanced. His expression was one of determination. The rage of youth had smoothed out, though it hadn't entirely vanished. There was still something menacing about the man, something barely suppressed and potentially deadly. His shaved head was circumscribed by a narrow strip of terry cloth, and the sleeves of his silver warm-up suit bulged as though there were enormous boa constrictors in there lunching on live pigs. He wasn't as quick on his feet as he once was, but then fancy footwork was never Foreman's weapon. He still had that relentless, merciless knack of stalking an opponent, of cutting off the ring and forcing the other boxer to take six steps to his two. And his punches still rattled the eyeglasses of onlookers at ringside.

In the final weeks of training, few reporters actually saw Foreman. He had gone into isolation at his retreat in Marshall. Except when his wife and children were there, George lived alone in his four-bedroom brick ranch home, seldom venturing outside the chain-link fence that surrounded the property. The compound included a house for his mother, a bunkhouse, stables for his Tennessee walking horses, two stocked fishing ponds, and a new tan-colored corrugated-iron gym—a replica of his church in northeast Houston. The gym was spartan. It had no dressing facilities, no mirrors, and bare panel walls. Equipment was minimal: some weight machines and a heavy bag. George held the speed bag in contempt, but the heavy bag was a virtual addiction. Sometimes he pounded it for the equivalent of fifteen or eighteen rounds, and what you noticed on collision was that the bag moved but his body didn't, not a ripple.

The one and only break in the gym's spare monotony was a large American flag displayed across one side of the interior. The flag was George's personal symbol, and had been since the 1968 Olympics when he thumbed his nose at the Black Power movement by waving a small American flag from the victory platform in Mexico City. This demonstration had outraged millions of blacks, who saw Foreman as a traitor and puppet to the white man. Walking to the ring the night of their fabled heavyweight title fight in Zaire, the great Muhammad Ali had reminded himself that Foreman was "white America, Christianity, the flag, the white man, pork chops."

In an interview two years earlier at his boy's club gym in Houston,

Foreman had explained to me that his feeling for the flag was based on his deep belief that America had rescued him from the evil streets of Houston's Fifth Ward, where he would surely have ended up in prison or in an early grave, and given him a second chance in the Job Corps. That's where he had learned to box. "What I did in Mexico City," he told me, his eyes teary and a catch in his voice, "wasn't no demonstration. I was just happy and proud to be an American. When I looked at America I saw a compassionate society that didn't give up on its underclass."

The only person who saw Foreman regularly was an apprentice boxer and weight lifter named Bobby Cook, who worked out with him daily. Cook was Foreman's majordomo, on twenty-four-hour call: When Cook went into town, he wore a beeper and carried a cellular telephone. He had curly brown hair and looked something like Mel Gibson—Foreman called him "my golden boy." Cook appeared to be in his early thirties, though Foreman had advised Cook not to reveal his true age. Since he had only seven professional fights in four years, Cook didn't have a clue about how to train for a championship fight, which was precisely the reason Foreman liked having him around.

Foreman made up his training schedule as he went along. He got out of bed when he wanted to, somewhere between four in the morning and noon. Unless his wife or mother was in camp, George did the cooking for both himself and Bobby Cook. Spiced turkey legs was his specialty. After breakfast, depending on how he felt that day, he would chop down hardwood trees for two or three hours, work on the heavy bag, and maybe spar five or six rounds. Or maybe he would take a nap. Sometimes he would harness himself to a wagonload of firewood and jog across a pasture, his yearling colt trotting behind. Some days he wouldn't work at all.

Five sparring partners and a small number of "advisers" stayed in town, at two motels on either side of the intersection of Interstate 20 and Texas Highway 59. The only adviser Foreman even pretended to consult was the great light-heavyweight champion of the fifties, Archie Moore, a ring legend whose 234-fight career spanned nearly thirty years—1935 to 1962—and included the incredible feat of holding a world's title at age 49. They used to call Moore the Mongoose, a tribute to his ability to dodge incoming blows. "I could take a punch, but it is prudent to evade them," explained the Mongoose, who talked like a character in a Bullwinkle cartoon. "Constant punching can cause severe implications over time." Foreman claimed that Archie taught him "breathology, escapeology, and all them other ologies." Contradicting Archie Moore would have been as unthinkable as sassing his own mother, and yet Foreman was able to pay homage to the 77-year-old immortal without asking a lot of questions. Moore spent most of his time in town, hanging out at a pawnshop or imparting wisdom to visiting journalists. What George Foreman really listened to was his own body.

Most of Foreman's attendants were straw men, retained because of old loyalties or family ties. Ron Weathers, a burly, bearded former gambler and saloonkeeper from El Paso, was there because he had promoted most of Foreman's comeback fights, which meant that he booked arenas and made up the difference out of his own pocket when gate receipts failed to cover expenses. "Promoting is a sickness, just like gambling," Weathers told me. "After you've booked enough losers, you're praying for just one winner—just one—and then you'll quit." In payment for his good faith, Weathers had been given a small piece of the promotional rights of the championship fight.

Even in isolation, Foreman found time to watch or read everything the media said about him. Three weeks before the fight, for example, a report on the *CBS Evening News* called Foreman "old" and "bloated" and referred to him as a "cafeteria with arms." George got a chuckle out of that. But almost at the same time, an article in the *Houston Chronicle* said that Foreman had turned surly and was reverting to the Sonny Liston–like scowls and recalcitrant nature of his younger years. The story quoted Lou Duva at length, and one passage in particular outraged Foreman. Duva had said that he couldn't imagine what was going on at Foreman's camp and speculated that "maybe they don't have control . . . over there."

In the war of nerves that foreshadowed every championship match, Duva was a master. He was using the media to needle Foreman, and he was getting away with it. George sulked for several days. Then he invited the media representatives to the ranch, where he proceeded to tie one end of a bull rope to his two-ton pickup and fashion the other end into a makeshift harness, which he slipped over his shoulders. The rope burning into his flesh, Foreman towed the truck a quarter of a mile along a gravel road.

Later Sharnik said, "George is a little apprehensive now, but as soon as we get to Atlantic City, he'll be okay. He calls it 'cutting in.' He'll cut in— reach a short state of grace—and after that nothing will bother him."

The reason this fight was held in Atlantic City was Donald Trump, who had guaranteed the promoters an $11 million site fee to use Trump Plaza, then tried to weasel out. The only two cities in America that were still interested in hosting a heavyweight championship fight were Las Vegas and Atlantic City, a situation that didn't flatter the sweet science but one that was increasingly irrelevant. The enchilada grande for this event—and for all future events of this magnitude—was pay-per-view and closed-circuit television, which together eventually attracted an audience of 1.5 million homes and grossed $77 million. The rest was thin gravy: They could have held the fight in Donald Trump's hat, and nobody would have known the difference.

Atlantic City seemed as good a place as any to stage what was essentially a primordial event in which members of the lower class attempted to beat each other to death for the profit and amusement of the upper class. In the decade since Trump and men like him had arrived to build their casinos, the old seaside resort had been ground into dust. Beyond the neon hum and ostentatious glitter of casino row, along dark, rutted, debris-strewn streets that belonged in Beirut, Atlantic City was boarded up, bombed out, leveled. The Victorian homes, the rambling hotels with turrets, parapets, and profusions of balconies, the mom-and-pop groceries that offered credit, the neighborhood bars, theaters, parks, trees, birds, people . . . gone, all gone. The famous Boardwalk was now a back path for the casinos, a way to get from one dice table to another and still claim to have seen the ocean. As in times past, the Boardwalk's landward side was lined with hole-in-the-wall shops selling cheap jewelry, novelties, saltwater taffy, hot dogs, pizza, and fresh lemonade. Its intersections were identified still by Monopoly-board names like Park Place, St. James Place, and Connecticut Avenue, but people no longer came to fish or swim or luxuriate in the simple pleasures of life. In most cases they didn't even spend the night. They came by bus, day-trippers from New York or Philadelphia, wild-eyed to get to the slot machines. Atlantic City made Las Vegas look classy.

Both fighters and their entourages stayed at Trump Plaza, and so did almost everyone else connected with the fight. There was hardly a nook of the hotel that didn't offer a reminder that the "Battle of the Ages" was upon us. Posters of Foreman and Holyfield lined the plush corridors, alongside posters of such coming attractions as Eddie Fisher and Theodore Bikel. One of the hotel's ten eating places featured the George Foreman buffet. Gift shops sold posters, programs, caps, and shirts printed with photographs of Foreman and/or Holyfield. TV sets that were suspended from ceilings just outside the casino entrances played commercials continuously. There was Big George in a rocking chair, saying, "I'm just a baby boomer, but I'm gonna lower the boom on that baby Evander." When you telephoned the hotel and got put on hold, you heard the voice of Evander saying that George must be off his rocker. That was about as nasty as it got. This was a fight in which nobody even pretended to be mad at anyone else.

A ring was constructed in the Imperial Ballroom, just down the hall from the pressroom, and the fighters trained there daily—Holyfield in the morning and Foreman in the afternoon. All of Holyfield's sessions were open to the public, for an admission price of $3, but when Foreman trained in earnest, he admitted no one, not even the media. Big George wasn't trying to hide, just concentrate.

Other than the times when he was actually working, Foreman was almost unavoidable. Six days before the fight, he preached a sermon at Atlantic City's Shiloh Baptist Church. You saw him in the hallway or the lobby of the hotel, an unmistakable figure in a floppy red hat and red-tinged sunglasses, always surrounded by admirers. When he took his daily strolls with Archie Moore along the Boardwalk, crowds flocked like seagulls, and George stopped to answer questions and bump fists—his way of shaking hands. He would pop into the pressroom unannounced and stay for two or three hours, until the questions became redundant and even ridiculous. Q. Have you ever had a cut problem? A. Not since the Fifth Ward.

Even the cynics—and there were many among the press corps—got caught up in George's shtick and found themselves swapping favorite quotes. What was it George said about Holyfield's strength coach? He said he had a strength coach too—his wife. He said she put big chains around the refrigerator at night, and they were so strong that he couldn't break them. On the night of the weigh-in (Foreman pushed the scale to 257, nearly 50 pounds heavier than Holyfield), George was back in the pressroom, eating fruit salad and calculating how many cheeseburgers he would need to consume to get his weight up to the record 270, which was how much Primo Carnera weighed when he went fifteen rounds against Tommy Loughran in a title fight in 1934.

Holyfield, on the other hand, was seldom seen except when there was a press conference or a scheduled workout. It was the champion's nature to be retiring and understated. On rare occasions, Holyfield and his entourage would pass through the lobby, wearing the snappy blue-and-orange team jackets that Duva had selected for the fight, but people were not always sure which one was the champion. One might assume that Holyfield resented merely being a prop for Foreman's one-man show, but in fact, he seemed to enjoy it. "George is funny," Evander said. "That's his thing, and it's good for business."

"Holyfield's idea of a good time is wearing brown shoes with a tux," said Bert Sugar, the editor of *Boxing Illustrated*. Sugar had become the fight game's unofficial historian since the death of Nat Fleischer, and he probably gave more interviews than both fighters put together. A lanky Runyon-esque character in a floppy gray fedora, blue blazer, garish scarf, and silk trousers with a print of little fish, Sugar gestured with his trademark cigar when he wanted to make a point. Many cynics had this fight figured as a sham—a front-page story in the *Philadelphia Inquirer* on the day of the fight called it "one of the most charming con games ever played" —but Bert Sugar disagreed. "To say that Foreman has only a puncher's chance is the most classic understatement since a Crow scout told General Custer that there might be a little trouble along the banks of the Little Bighorn," Sugar told me.

In the five days leading up to the fight, more and more people were picking Foreman. There was no sports book in Atlantic City, but reports from Las Vegas said that most of the betting was on Foreman, who was getting three-to-one odds. Archie Moore, always the mystic, hinted that George had developed a technique to offset Holyfield's speed, though he wasn't at liberty to discuss it. "I can't divulge secrets that must not be known to wayfarers," said the Mongoose, who could usually be found sitting (and sometimes napping) on a chair just inside the pressroom door, a white knit hat warming his ancient gray head.

With Moore in his corner—and with the addition of Angelo Dundee, who arrived a week before the fight—Foreman had better than a century of ring experience at his call. Dundee was one of the storied figures of boxing. He had been in Muhammed Ali's corner the night that Ali bamboozled Foreman in Zaire, far and away the most humiliating experience in Foreman's career. George had always believed that someone drugged his drinking water that night, though he didn't blame Dundee. Angelo's presence here in Atlantic City was mostly symbolic and motivational, but he would be viewed as a counterweight to Lou Duva, whose fiery Italian temper had been known to intimidate referees and ring officials. "He's our capo," said Ron Weathers. At the rules meeting two nights before the fight, Dundee demonstrated the point, arguing successfully, over Duva's vitriolic objections, that the water for both corners must be supplied by the boxing commission.

On the day of the fight, Foreman had his usual fare: bacon and eggs for breakfast, roast chicken for lunch, prime rib for dinner. It is not recorded whether he had a late-evening snack—the fight didn't start until 11:15—but it would have been in keeping with his belief that food nourishes the soul as well as the body. Many old-time managers concurred. John L. Sullivan ate beefsteak or mutton chops three times a day when he was training. One of Jack London's most poignant stories told of a boxer who could not muster the strength for one final rally because his family butcher had refused credit for a bit of beef before the fight.

The crowd at a heavyweight championship fight may not be richer or more important than the crowd at any other major sporting event, but it acts like it. Trump and his blond bimbo, Marla Maples, preened at ringside and strutted along the corridor leading to the dressing rooms, at all times flanked by a squad of goons in dark suits. Jesse Jackson pumped his hands and waved. Pat Robertson made himself apparent—Pat Robertson!—is this a great country or what? The list of celebrities introduced by the ring announcer sounded like Academy awards night: Kevin Costner, Gene Hackman, Robert Duvall, Sylvester Stallone, Billy Crystal. The biggest hand of all was for Muhammad Ali, who gimped down the aisle with his coterie and joined Joe Frazier in the ring.

The casinos had bought blocks of $1,000 tickets for favored customers, and there were obviously many high rollers seated in the first fifteen or twenty rows. Though ticket prices scaled from $100 to $1,000, all the seats on the floor of the mammoth convention hall (capacity: 19,000) appeared to be the $1,000 variety, at least for tax purposes. The ratio of men to women, I'd guess, was five to one, but the women were, almost without exception, gorgeous, stunningly dressed, and attached to the arm of some guy who looked as if he swapped toxic-waste contracts for a living. It was the ultimate statement of woman-as-ornament.

The crowd was overwhelmingly pro-Foreman. There was thunderous applause as the challenger approached the ring, led by his handlers in their red-white-and-blue jackets with "USA" sewn on the sleeves. One of George's men carried an American flag. George's wide face was absolutely radiant under the hood of his terry cloth robe: This was the moment he had waited for, prayed for, dreamed of. More subdued was the reaction to Holyfield's entrance, but the champion appeared quietly confident. He knew what he had to do.

Looking back, it was Holyfield's fight all the way. Foreman had his moments, especially early, but Holyfield was always able to rally. Foreman stung Holyfield with a clubbing right near the end of the second round, bringing the crowd to its feet, but Holyfield answered in the third round, rocking Foreman with a left hook to the head and scoring freely at the bell.

Holyfield was fighting smart, holding to the plan that trainer George

Benton had laid out, sticking, stabbing, moving, staying close, forcing Foreman to swing wildly or, more often, cover his face and upper body with his massive arms and wait for the assault to subside. "When Foreman's hiding," Benton had said, "he ain't hitting." But Foreman kept coming, taking more than he was giving, yet always a threat to end it with one punch.

Foreman's last good opportunity came early in the seventh, when an overhand right sent Holyfield reeling backward. Holyfield tried to clinch, but Foreman pushed him away and continued the barrage. The champion somehow collected himself, retaliating with hooks to the head and jabs to the body. You had to admire Holyfield's moxie, the way he ignored the crowd, which was chanting George's name now, the way he maintained his concentration, putting together combinations in batches of six or seven. Late in the ninth round, Holyfield had Foreman against the ropes, but the bell saved the challenger, and George wobbled back to his corner, dazed but still defiant, shaking off Angelo Dundee's offer of a stool. Foreman never once sat down between rounds, even when he could barely stand.

Knowing that he was ahead on points, Holyfield fought defensively in the final three rounds. Even so, Foreman was never more than an uppercut away from regaining the title. By the twelfth and final round, both fighters were hurt and exhausted, and still they continued to attack until the last seven seconds of the fight, when Holyfield sort of pulled Foreman to his body and hugged him. "I love you, man," Foreman whispered in the champion's ear. Holyfield nodded. It no longer mattered what the cynics said. This had been a classic battle between two great warriors, one of them a little younger and a little quicker and a little more able than the other. This had been a display of courage and dignity and ringmanship rarely surpassed.

Fans lingered near ringside, thousands of them, standing on chairs or clogging the aisles, knowing that there was nothing more to see and yet feeling an urgency to pay their respects. Some had booed Holyfield, especially in the late rounds, but this was a time for atonement, for absolution. Some had given their hearts to Foreman, and this was a time to say that they would do it all over again. After a while, they filtered out of the convention hall onto the Boardwalk, ignoring the early morning chill, talking, reviewing, critiquing, basking in the afterglow. Kids ran among the crowd, wads of unauthorized Battle of the Ages T-shirts bulging beneath their coats, hawking the shirts for $10 each until the cops chased them away. The throngs crowded the casinos and packed the few eating and drinking places that were open after midnight. Somehow they needed to sustain the magic, even if it was only in the company of one another.

In the dressing room later, Holyfield said that he had hit Foreman with everything he brought and it still hadn't been enough. "He just kept coming," Holyfield said, shaking his head in admiration. George offered no excuses, no alibis. Though his face was swollen and his lip split, he was still able to joke. "I was winning," he said, "until Lou Duva snuck that mule in the ring." Foreman said he was going to fly home to Houston and preach Sunday morning at his own church. Maybe he would box again—obviously the money would be there—but his admirers hoped that he wouldn't. There was nothing more to prove. Let the quest end here. George Foreman had lost on the scorecards, unanimously. And yet, as George himself might have said, it had been a victory for . . . pork chops, cornbread, black-eyed peas, pumpkin pie, grannies and grandpas, the overweight, the underappreciated, the unobserved, old dogs and kitty cats, the world . . .

"Nothing to It"

The Life and Death of My Son Mark

I was flying blind. Nothing in my experience gave me a frame of reference for this journey. My son Mark was dying of acute leukemia and the two of us were racing across the western margins of the Chihuahuan Desert east of Van Horn, searching for the new top leaves of the creosote bush, which if brewed into a tea were considered a cure for the disease by some Mexican curanderos. I had learned this in a letter from a man named Leslie Thompson, who was doing twenty years on a drug charge in state prison. I have received hundreds of letters from people in prison, but they always wanted something. This guy just wanted to do me a favor. Mark and I both knew that it was the longest of long shots, but long shots were all we had.

The trip was in early March, about six weeks before Mark died. It was long and arduous, and it sapped what little strength he had left. The letter had explained that the two of us had to make the journey together, and leave a "gift of water" for the creosote plants. So we flew from Austin to Dallas to Midland, then drove 125 miles to an isolated place within sight of the Davis Mountains, two liter-size bottles of Evian in the seat between us. Mark slept almost all the way, racked with fever, chills, and nausea. I stopped in Odessa to buy him a blanket, and still he couldn't stop shaking. I stopped again in Pecos to get something to eat. All Mark wanted was a Coke and he didn't even drink that. I parked well off the highway, the early spring sun still high in the vast sky. We climbed a fence and began walking across a desertscape littered with creosote plants and not much else. After a few hundred feet Mark was too weak to keep going, so I helped him back to the car and went back alone.

I had collected three bags of leaves and was sprinkling the last of the Evian on a plant when I spotted two state troopers who had parked behind our car and were waiting for me where I'd crossed the fence. They seemed friendly but guarded as I approached.

"May we ask what you're doing out there?" one of them said politely.

I explained as well as I was able. They looked at Mark, wrapped in his blanket and asleep in the front seat. "Okay," one said. "But be careful."

We spent the night in a Midland motel, the kid so sick that I wondered if he'd make it through the night. I was awake until 2 A.M., talking long-distance to friends and family, trying to figure out our next move. I was so intensely trying to deal with moment-to-moment reality that there was no time to be scared.

Mark was diagnosed in July 1996 at a cancer clinic in Atlanta, the city where he grew up after his mother and I divorced, and where he had returned after his own divorce in early 1994. He had undergone chemotherapy, six intensive doses of a powerful toxin that destroys cancer cells— and good cells as well. Cancer victims often die from chemotherapy or from organ failure brought on by chemotherapy. I suspect that one day we'll look back on this wretched drug the way we look back with revulsion at frontal lobotomies. But chemotherapy was the only treatment available for Mark's type of leukemia. It wouldn't cure him, but it could possibly put the cancer into remission long enough for doctors to perform a bone marrow transplant.

We had searched without success for a bone marrow donor for nine months. Unfortunately, no one in our family was a match, and neither were any of the 2.6 million people on the National Bone Marrow Registry. For Caucasians, one unrelated person in 20,000 (on average) will be a match for a given patient; for minorities, the figure is one in a million. One doctor speculated that finding a match for Mark was so difficult because there are traces of Native American blood in our family, but he was just guessing. Anecdotal evidence suggests that the genetic tissue typing done for bone marrow matching is a roll of the dice. In 1993, Ann Connally, the daughter-in-law of former governor John Connally, turned out to be the world's only perfect match for a 16-year-old Japanese girl, who is alive and doing well today because Mrs. Connally was tested and added to the National Registry in 1990.

In January and February of this year, our family and friends staged testing drives in Atlanta, Little Rock, and Austin, adding another fifteen hundred people to the National Registry. Cari Clark, who lives next door to Phyllis and me in Austin, turned out to be a perfect match for a man in

Sydney, Australia. And yet we still found no perfect match for Mark. We were desperate. Even as we slept, even as we prayed, the clock was ticking. After we ran a full-page ad in *Texas Monthly* pleading for help, people called from all over the country, volunteering to be tested, extending their support, and contributing money to the Leukemia Society of America. Roseland Wright, a sister of Austin writer Laurence Wright, telephoned from Lexington, Massachusetts, where she had rallied several tribes of Native Americans and personnel from two military bases to get tested. A friend in California who is a Buddhist monk sent a seed blessed by the Dali Lama with instructions on how Mark was to take it. The pilgrimmage to the desert was only one in a series of things we tried.

The worst day of my life—worse even than the day Mark died—started early the next morning when I drove Mark to Midland International Airport for a flight back to Atlanta. Until then I hadn't realized how far the disease had progressed. He was so weak that I doubt he could have walked unassisted to the gate. I helped him into a wheelchair and pushed him. He had eaten almost nothing for a week, so we stopped at the coffee bar; I bought him a Coke and a banana, and he was able to keep them down. For two days he had said almost nothing. A question that needed a response got a nod or head shake. Looking at him then, pale and weak as a newborn puppy, his life literally leaking away before my eyes, I remembered how much we had come through together, and how recently the future had seemed limitless. Less than a year before, we had worked out together at my gym in Austin, both of us fit and seemingly invincible. As recently as Christmas '96 he had looked reasonably strong and cheerful. We had celebrated Markie's fortieth birthday on February 11, in two large condominiums that I had rented on the beach in Galveston. Markie's ex-wife, Helen, brought their two children, Katy and Malcolm, from Little Rock. My daughter Lea flew in from Atlanta, and my other son, Shea, drove down from Houston. In all several dozen relatives and close friends gathered for the weekend, including Mark's current girlfriend, Susan Shaw. At one point Phyllis pointed out that three of Mark's former lovers were at the party. Markie and I sat on the balcony, enjoying the sun and the Gulf breeze, but unable to find much to say. The silence had become awkward and unnatural. We had shared so many good times, talking of our hopes and dreams and frustrations and solutions. I looked across the street at the ocean, grasping for something profoundly philosophical to say, but every time I formulated a thought and tried to put it into words, it came across as shallow and foolish. Maybe silence was the final way to communicate.

When it was time for him to board the plane, we hugged and kissed, knowing it might be our final good-bye. I was close to tears. Watching my son shuffle slowly down the ramp to his plane, his hairless head bowed in agony, his clothes hanging off his emasculated frame, a kid who had just turned forty but looked ninety, I kept thinking: Why him? Why not me? When a child dies, "Why?" is the last question to go away.

During our years together we said a lot of good-byes, Markie and I, but one in particular sticks in my mind. He must have been around ten— a bright, resourceful, resilient, uncommonly stubborn kid—and he was dogging me to take him along on a business trip to New York. I explained that I didn't have time to show him the sights, but he wanted to tag along, and I couldn't say no. Our first night in the Big Apple, in a hurry to make an appointment, I gave him $20 and a key to the apartment where we were staying, then dropped him off in Times Square. I remember asking him, "Will you be okay?" His cocksure reply was: "Sure, nothing to it!"

My cab hadn't gone half a block when the stupidity of what I'd done slapped me upside the head: I'd deposited my 10-year-old son in the geographical center of the evilest, most sinister square mile in America. I threw open the door and raced back into oncoming traffic, but by then he'd been swallowed up in the crowd. For the next few hours, I was nearly sick with fear, imagining what might have happened. But when I got back to the apartment there was Markie propped up in the king-size bed, a cat on his lap, eating a bowl of ice cream and watching a John Wayne movie. "Are you okay?" I asked, badly shaken. "Sure," he said, grinning at me as though we were coconspirators in a plot to overthrow the world. "Nothing to it!"

Because he grew up a thousand miles from where I lived, I saw him only a few times a year until he completed high school in May 1975. A week after that he moved to Austin to attend the University of Texas, and for the first year he slept in my large walk-in closet. I wasn't married at the time, so we hung out together, shopping, cooking, eating, listening to music, having adventures. My dad had passed on to me an appreciation for cooking and eating, and I handed it down to Mark. Before long he was cooking gourmet meals that took three days to prepare and five hours to eat.

Phyllis and I nicknamed him Maurice. Later, after he married Helen and moved into the professional world, Maurice's seated dinners became legendary in Dallas and Little Rock. Journalists and politicians (among them Bill and Hillary Clinton) jockied for invitations. For one of my birthdays he whipped up a five-course dinner that included rack of lamb, dove breasts wrapped in bacon and sauteed in wine sauce, roasted *ancho* peppers with salmon and goat cheese, and an unbelievable dome-shaped dessert with layers of crushed Heath bars, fudge cake, ice cream, and toasted butterscotch crust. Naturally, Maurice selected the appropriate wine for each course.

Sometimes we wrote songs, Markie strumming his guitar and me jotting down the words. We could compose an entire opera in an afternoon. When my friend Sue Sharlot graduated from UT Law School, we wrote a number for her graduation party called "All You Gotta Do Is Know the Law, Then Boogie Til You Puke!" Another all-time favorite was "Beat Me Like the Bitch I Am!" We wrote alternate lines, laughing so hard we could barely get the words out:

> *Reel and rod me*
> *Marquis de Sade me*
> *Makes me feel so fine*
> *But beat me like the bitch I am*
> *And tell the world you're mine!*

Two days after he died, I sang the words at a memorial service at the University Presbyterian Church, past caring if anyone might be offended.

We were never like father and son—more like brothers or best friends. He always called me by my nickname, Jap, never Dad or Daddy. He found it easier to express his love than I did, and in his effortless manner he taught me to express my love too. He also taught me to appreciate his favorite expression: Nothing to it. It was a manifesto of the indomitable spirit, an attitude that recognized no limit. I just naturally assumed Markie could do anything he set his mind to, and I guess he felt the same about me. Together, we thought of ourselves as unconquerable. And for many years we were.

In Greek, *leukemia* means "white blood." Mark had M-5 leukemia, a subcategory of adult acute myelogenous leukemia in which immature white blood cells called blasts take over the bone marrow and prevent it from making enough normal white and red cells and platelets. The blasts crowd out the mature white cells that fight infection, the red cells that carry oxygen, and the platelets that help blood to clot, spilling into the blood stream and infiltrating organs and glands until the process of life shuts down. M-5 is particularly nasty and extremely resistant to chemotherapy.

Scientists don't know what causes leukemia, only that there are different types that react differently to treatment: Children's leukemia can be cured, for instance, while adult leukemia is almost always fatal. Victims of chronic leukemia sometimes live for years because the blasts are more mature and progress more slowly, but eventually the progression of immature white cells quickens, and chronic leukemia explodes into acute leukemia.

Aubrey Thompson, a friend who has done leukemia research for twenty years at the University of Texas Medical Branch at Galveston, told me that Mark most likely had chronic leukemia for the last ten or even twenty years, even though no one had detected it. "What makes adult leukemia so extremely difficult is that the cancer cells come and go, hiding out most of the time," Aubrey explained. "You go along for years, having an occasional few bad days when you feel tired or run-down or flulike; then one day it explodes into acute leukemia. In children's leukemia, by contrast, the cancer cells are very active. They come out of hiding and grow rapidly, and therefore they are sensitive to certain drugs and can be wiped out."

A bone marrow transplant is the only way most adults can survive leukemia, but the process is long and dangerous, littered with formidable obstacles and treacherous ifs (if chemotherapy can force the cancer into temporary remission . . .). The transplant procedure is enormously expensive—it can cost up to $250,000—and it's highly risky: Between 40 and 60 percent of those who undergo a transplant survive, but many survivors of the bone marrow transplant later succumb to fatal complications from graft-versus-host disease.

Of course, to have a transplant you must have a matching donor, another treacherous if: One in four leukemia patients who need a transplant never find a donor. Part of the problem is that most people have never heard of the National Marrow Donor Program. Among all diseases, leukemia is the number-one killer of children—and it afflicts ten times as many adults as children—yet it is not high profile. In a nation of more than 267 million people, fewer than 3 million are on the registry, and fewer than 600,000 are minorities. Another problem is money. Because genetic tissue typing is so expensive, most people who are tested are asked to pay a fee, usually between $45 and $75 (since there are so few minorities on the registry, their tests are free). The cost aside, however, getting tested is really pretty easy. It takes only a couple of minutes: You fill out a short medical history and let a technician draw two small blood samples, which are sent to a national laborary to be analyzed for the antigens needed to make a match; the identity codes of the antigens are then recorded in the national registry's computer. If your antigens match a leukemia patient's, you'll be called in for more tests. Six out of six matching antigens are a "miracle match."

At any point, of course, a potential donor can back out. Shirley Laine, the bone marrow manager of the Central Texas Regional Blood and Tissue Center in Austin, told me the heartbreaking story of Victor Ojeda, a 9-year-old Austin boy who died after a woman who was a perfect match decided she didn't want to go through the ordeal of a transplant. It's not really that much of an ordeal, though. As a donor, you spend a day or two in a hospital, during which time a needle is injected in your hips and marrow is extracted from the upper back part of the pelvis. You'll have a sore butt for a week or two, but that's a small price for saving a life. (To find the bone and tissue center nearest you, call 1-800 MARROW-2.)

I know now that even if we had found a miracle match for Mark, a transplant would have been useless. All that horrible chemotherapy destroyed his immune system and did great damage to his organs, but never came close to stopping the cancer or putting it into remission. Mark's doctor, Daniel Dubovsky, compared cancer cells to cockroaches: "You might kill 95 percent of them," he told us, "but the remaining 5 percent emerge stronger and more resistant." Dubovsky encounters only one or two patients a year whose cancer is so virulent that it resists the strongest chemotherapy. Mark happened to be one. "He lived nine or ten months longer than a lot of people who do go into remission," Dubovsky said. "He had magnificent strength and energy."

Two and a half weeks after our journey to the Chihuahuan Desert, Dubovsky informed Mark that there was nothing more he could do. We were devastated. Markie said he'd like to go home.

Phyllis and I flew to Atlanta for the death watch, not sure how we would handle it but trusting that Markie would set the style. Getting reacquainted with his longtime group of pals, we realized he'd set the style years ago. In high school he had put together a combination rock band and chili cookoff team called the Chain Gang, and they were with him until the end, honoring his wish that nobody feel sorry for him or for themselves. Tom "Meat" Smith, one of Markie's oldest friends, sat at the foot of his bed and regaled us with stories about the Great Cartwright. It seems that the women of Atlanta were not quite unanimous in their undying devotion. Meat told us about one woman Mark jilted when he worked for Turner Broadcasting System. To this day, she is unable to speak his name without pausing to spit on the floor. Meat demonstrated, feigning a high-pitched voice: "Oh, you must be referring to Mark . . . *hock, spitooowee* . . . Cartwright." Sick as he was, Mark doubled over with laughter.

Also on hand was the latest and last of Mark's girlfriends, Susan Shaw. She was as tough and tenacious as they come. Almost single-handedly she had organized a drive that put five hundred new names on the bone marrow registry. She could have bailed out at any time—no one would have blamed her—but Susan wasn't the type to bail. The only time she lost it was the day Dubovsky told the family it was over. "It wasn't supposed to be that way," Susan said later, her eyes swollen and red from a day of crying. "I had imagined our twilight years, sitting on the porch watching our grandchildren. Suddenly I just went to pieces. I was bawling and shaking my fist at God saying, 'Why Mark? Why me?'" Late that afternoon, Susan got a phone call from the bone and tissue center in Atlanta, telling her that she was a match for a 55-year-old man in the Midwest. "God works in mysterious ways," she concluded.

What got us through those last few weeks was Markie's remarkable courage, the grace, dignity, and measured good humor with which he faced death, and his absolute refusal to complain that fate had dealt him from the bottom of the deck. He had resolved to put his affairs in order, and that's what he did. With another old friend, Sammy Rawlin, at his side, Markie dictated his will and made it known that when the end came he didn't want the paramedics to resuscitate him. He asked that his body be cremated and his ashes scattered in the Gulf of Mexico. (One exception: Some of the ashes would be handed over to the Chain Gang, whose members would select an appropriate urn—most likely a cowboy boot—and take them each year to the chili cookoff in Athens, Georgia.) He selected a Cajun friend, Gator Ordoyne, as his replacement in the Chain Gang. A year after Mark died, some of his ashes ended up in a small vial in the women's restroom at a Cajun restaurant that Gator opened in the Atlanta suburb of Dunwoody. I know Markie would have appreciated the gesture.

I asked him if he was scared. "No," he told me. "Strangely enough I'm not." He had been sick for so long that what he really wanted was just "a few good days." That became my prayer: "If you can't give us the miracle of sparing his life, Lord, then grant our fallback position: a few good days, then let him die quickly and without pain or fear."

My prayer was answered. Markie seemed to get better by the day, which is not unusual in terminal cases of leukemia. He got out of bed and spent several hours sitting in the sun, watching a titmouse build a nest in a tall Georgia pine. He was able to eat solid food and even hold down cups of the creosote tea. He went to a couple of movies with Susan, and the three of us spent an afternoon at the Atlanta Botanical Garden. We drove the rural backroads, where spectacular explosions of azaleas, redbuds, and dogwoods seemed to have blossomed specifically on Mark's behalf, and had dinner at his favorite Mexican restaurant.

The time had come for me to go home, we both agreed. "You've got to go sometime," Markie said, not unaware of the double meaning. My last night in Atlanta we had dinner at his favorite Thai restaurant, then Mark and Susan drove me back to my hotel. Standing there face to face in the parking lot was the hardest part. Neither of us wanted to drag it out. Mark kissed me and said he loved me. I said I loved him too. "I can't bring myself to say good-bye," I told him. "So until I see you again."

"Until I see you again," he told me back. I turned toward the hotel entrance, knowing it wouldn't be in this lifetime.

After that we talked daily by phone. Mark told me that he and Meat were driving to Augusta for the opening day of the Masters golf tournament. On Friday, April 11, he flew to Little Rock to visit his children, 9-year-old Katy and 7-year-old Malcolm. It was an act of sheer will and determination: His fever had returned, signaling that the brief reprieve was over. He somehow made it back to Atlanta on Sunday afternoon, and died early the next morning. His last words were to Susan. "I think this is it," he said softly, closing his eyes. "I'm packing 'em in."

Dealing with the "Why?" question is the ultimate test of faith. It took me a while to realize that God's not there to answer "Why?" questions, though He can help ease the other emotions that overtake a parent whose child dies: the guilt, the frustration, the anger. What should I have done? What *could* I have done? Phyllis told me that when her son Robert was dying of AIDS in 1994, she had an irresistible urge to hold him tightly, as though she might transfer her energy and her wellness to him. I felt the same urge.

Anger was the emotion that hit hardest and lasted longest. I was angry at his doctor and at the hospital for allowing him to waste away; there must have been something else they could have done. I hated the entire pharmaceutical industry for wallowing in profits while their researchers consistently failed to find cures. I even called my pal Aubrey Thompson to vent my anger. He assured me that researchers were doing the best they could.

I no longer waste time on guilt or anger. I miss Markie and think about him many times every day, not the way he was at the end but the way I knew him for forty years. I prefer to thank God for those forty years than wallow in regret. Mark hated negative energy. He didn't allow it in his life, and now that he's gone I'm not going to allow it in mine.

Willie at 65
Willie Nelson's at the
Peak of His Game

We're sitting alone in his bus, me and Willie, drinking coffee and sharing a smoke, two geezers talking about how it feels to approach age 65, commiserating about the predictable decline of kidneys, eyesight, knee joints, rotator cuffs, and sexual appetites. We agree that when dealing with life's vagaries—the hits, misses, insights, and sorrows—attitude is everything. "However you want things to be," Willie assures me, "create them in your own mind, and they'll be that way."

The miles are mapped on his face and crusted in his voice, which seems less melodic by daylight. Willie traveled all day yesterday, Thanksgiving Day, 1997, arriving in Las Vegas from the Bahamas just before show time. When he was in the Bahamas in 1978, I remind him, they threw him in jail for smoking pot and then banished him from the island for life. So they did, Willie recalls with a nod. He was so happy to be free of that damned jail he jumped off a curb and broke his foot. The following night, his foot in a cast, he celebrated again by firing up an Austin Torpedo on the roof of President Jimmy Carter's White House: "That was an incredible moment, sitting there watching all the lights. I wasn't aware until then that all roads led to the Capitol, that it was the center of the world." Also the safest spot in America to smoke a joint, he adds. Willie credits God and the hemp plant for much of his good fortune and openly advocates both at every opportunity. Without encouragement he begins to list the consumer items produced by the lowly plant—shirts, shorts, granola bars, paper products, motor fuel, not to mention extremely enlightening smoke. "Did you realize the first draft of our Constitution was written on hemp paper?" he marvels.

From the window of the bus we can see the afternoon players drifting through the front entrance of the Orleans Hotel and Casino. Though management has reserved a suite for Willie in the hotel, by long habit he sleeps aboard his bus, venturing out only to play golf or make it onstage in time for the first note of "Whiskey River," his traditional opening number. Willie says that inside his head is a network of communication outlets, that he has a mental tape recorder that starts with "Whiskey River" and lasts two and a half hours—the time needed to complete a concert. He also receives messages from angels and archangels and several bands of broadcast signals, some in languages unknown to the human race.

This bus, the Honeysuckle Rose, is Willie's home, office, and sanctuary, not only on the road but also at Willie World (his compound outside Austin that features a house, a recording studio, a golf course, and a western film set). The bus is the one place he truly feels comfortable. It's as well equipped as any hotel, with multiple TV sets, a state-of-the-art stereo and sound system, kitchen, toilets, showers, and beds. Willie's private compartment at the rear is as cozy and as densely packed as a Gypsy's knapsack. One of Willie's old aunts once confided to writer-producer Bill Wittliff, "That Willie, he can pack a trailer faster than anyone I ever saw." On his king-size bed lie three guitars, and surrounding it are Native American paintings, beaded necklaces, and breastplates; a giant American flag; photographs of his two youngest sons, Lukas and Micah (by his fourth and current wife, Annie); a jump rope; some dumbbells; and a speed bag anchored to a swivel above the door. Willie's elder sister, Bobbie Nelson, and his daughter Lana also travel on the Honeysuckle Rose. Members of the band and crew ride in two additional buses and a truck that make up Willie's relentless caravan.

"I don't like to be a hermit, but I'm better off staying out here by myself," Willie explains, taking a drag and passing the smoke across the table. "El Niño," a song from his new Christmas album, plays in the background. "Too many temptations. In the old days we'd stay in town after a gig and start drinking and chasing women, and some of the band would end up in jail or divorced. That's when I started leaving right after a gig, driving all night just to get out of town. If it wasn't for the bus and this weed, I'd be at the bar right now, doing serious harm to myself."

For a man who'll be eligible for Medicare on April 30, Willie appears fit, trim, content, and comfortably weathered, a man who has not only transcended his wounds and scars but also made them part of his act. In his unique American Gothic way, he appears semielegant, a country squire in an orange sweatshirt, jeans, and running shoes, his hair neatly braided, his eyes crackling with good humor. He looks ready to run with the hounds. Willie exercises daily, jogging, stretching, jumping rope. He can make the speed bag rattle like a snare drum. A few weeks earlier he went three rounds with former heavyweight Tex Cobb, and he is about to get his brown belt in tae kwon do. Onstage the previous night, without warning, Willie kicked a microphone off a stand higher than his head. This is a regular part of the show, and his audience roared its approval. How many geezers can high-kick like a majorette?

As we talk, Willie squeezes a rubber ball, releasing nervous energy. "I have so much energy that it gets to be a problem," he says. "I don't smoke weed to get high; I smoke it to take the edge off, to level out, so I'm not out there like a turkey sticking his head into everything." Though this natural energy is part of his creative process, it must obey the laws of physics: The action of whiskey, women, music, and life on the road eventually produces the reaction of self-destruction. Anyone who has spent time with Willie knows that he is as tightly wound as he is mellow. Bud Shrake, who helped Willie put together his autobiography, told me, "Willie has a violent temper. He gets so furious his eyes turn black, and he has to leave the room or kill somebody." In the book Willie tells about a twenty-minute bloody brawl in a parking lot in Phoenix after a concert—some irate husband swinging a Crescent wrench and Willie defending himself with a two-by-four. "Having a temper is like being an alcoholic," he says. "You always know it's there." He has learned to control his temper, or at least modify it. His mantra in the nineties is positive thinking. As he counsels in one his songs:

Remember the good times
They're smaller in number, and easier to recall.

Willie has battled his share of ailments—pneumonia four or five times; a collapsed lung that required surgery (he wrote the album *Tougher than Leather* in the hospital), followed by a relapse when he ripped out the stitches while on a movie set in Finland; chronic back pain that dates from stacking hay bales as a boy; the usual prostate and bladder problems—but an uncanny survival instinct has enabled him to weather the ravages of time. "I've never been healthier," he assures me. "I'm at the top of my game. I've got no domestic problems to speak of, nothing tearing me apart. I'm enjoying life more than ever: Now is the most important time, at least to me. If I start worrying about yesterday or tomorrow, I'll get cancer and die."

Watching from the theater wings at the Orleans Hotel, I realize again that Willie and his music are inseparable, that his songs are more than mere fingerprints of life, that they are a field of cosmic energy directing, shaping, and revealing everything he is or has been. Dressed in his stage "costume"—black T-shirt with sleeves and neck cut away, jeans, sneakers, a straw cowboy hat that he quickly exchanges for a headband—Willie is singing one of his legendary cheating songs, "Funny How Time Slips Away." His tone is generous but accusatory, reflecting the mixed emotions that he was feeling when he wrote it in the late fifties. Though I can't see her face from where I'm standing, I know that Willie is focusing on some knockout blond with large breasts seated in the fourth row, singing directly to her. It's a trick he uses to intensify his concentration onstage.

Willie was just 26 and in the middle of an incredibly hungry and productive period in his life when he wrote "Funny How Time Slips Away." He wrote it and two other equally memorable classics—"Crazy" and "Night Life"—in the same week, driving in the early morning hours from the Esquire Club on the east side of Houston, where he was playing six nights a week, to the apartment in Pasadena where he lived with his first wife, Martha Jewel Mathews, and their three kids, Lana, Susie, and Billy.

These were his pre-Nashville days, and he was as poor as a Sudanese cat. Living in Houston, Fort Worth, San Diego, California, and a lot of other places, Willie worked by day selling vacuum cleaners or encyclopedias door-to-door and played by night in honky-tonks. He worked as a deejay where he could. Whatever it took to survive, Willie did. He sold all the rights to "Night Life" (including claim of authorship) for a measly $150. "Night Life" is one of the greatest blues numbers of all time and has been recorded by everyone from B. B. King to Aretha Franklin, but Willie gave it away for the equivalent of a month's rent. He had to use the alias Hugh Nelson the first time he recorded it. He sold "Family Bible" for $50 and tried to sell "Mr. Record Man" for $10. Writers were like painters, Willie believed: An artist sells a creation as soon as it is finished so that he will have enough money to create again.

From his earliest years Willie knew that he was born to play music. Daddy and Mama Nelson, the grandparents who raised Bobbie and Willie after their parents divorced, taught singing and piano, filling their home in Abbott with music. Bobbie had the patience and the discipline to study music—her mastery of Beethoven, Mozart, and Bach is such that friends say she can play concert piano at any hall in the world—but with Willie it was all instinct. He started writing poetry when he was five and got his first guitar at age 6, a Stella ordered by his grandparents from a Sears catalog. Within a few weeks he had learned the three chords necessary to play country music—D, A, and G—and begun compiling his own songbook, called *Songs by Willie Nelson*. Daddy Nelson's death the following year had a profound effect on Willie. In his autobiography he wrote, "After Daddy Nelson died, I started writing cheating songs." Heartbreak and betrayal animated all of his early writings. Influenced by the voices and styles he heard on the radio—the songs of Bob Wills and Ernest Tubb and the voice of Frank Sinatra—Willie charted his destiny. Who could have predicted his amazing success or that he one day would be regarded by many, including me, as the greatest songwriter who ever lived?

"A lot of times when I'm driving alone," Willie tells me, "and my mind is open and receptive, it will pick up radio waves from somewhere in the universe and a song will start. A line, a phrase. You don't call up creativity; it's just there. Like the Bible says, 'Be still and know that I am.'"

"Do you pull over to the curb and make notes or what?"

"I never write it down until the whole thing is in my mind. If I forget a song, it wasn't worth remembering."

"But you must think about it."

"I don't like to think too much. It's better coming off the top of your head. Leon Russell had this idea of going into the studio with no songs, just turn on the machine and start writing and singing. You remember winging 'Main Squeeze Blues'?"

He's referring to my wedding night in 1976. Phyllis and I had been married earlier that evening in the back room of the Texas Chili Parlor and eventually found ourselves at Soap Creek Saloon, where Willie was playing. On an impulse, I hopped onstage with Willie and began improvising a song that I called "Main Squeeze Blues." I don't remember any of it except the title, but the audience seemed to think it was pretty good.

"I see what you mean," I admit. "When you're sailing high or when you're in a hard place worrying about the rent or food for the kids, something kicks in and words start gushing. But where do the melodies come from?"

Willie gives me the look you give a child who asks ridiculous questions. "I snatch them out of the air," he says patiently. "The air is full of melodies."

Willie's God-given ability to produce under pressure has delivered some of his best work. "Shotgun Willie," which turned out to be the title song of his first successful album, was written in a couple of desperate minutes in the bathroom of a New York hotel room, on the back of a sanitary napkin wrapper. The night before he was due in the studio to record *Yester-*

day's Wine, he popped some pills and wrote the final seven tunes, including "Me and Paul," celebrating his friendship with his longtime drummer Paul English.

Even in very personal moments, Willie can't help working on his music. Some years ago, when he was trying to find the words for a father-daughter talk with Susie, Willie asked her to drive him from Austin to Evergreen, Colorado, and along the way he delivered his lecture by writing "It's Not Supposed to Be That Way." Willie tells me: "She was young, trying to grow up, and it occurred to me that it was easier to sing it than say it. She's driving and I'm writing, singing, and picking, and finally it comes to me: 'Hey, I've got another fucking song half finished; all I need is a bridge and a steel turnaround!'" When the old well ran dry one time, Willie wrote a throwaway called, "I Can't Write Anymore," immediately followed by a beautiful ballad, "Be My Valentine," which celebrated the birth of his son Lukas, on Christmas Day 1988.

The music stopped exactly two years later, when Willie's eldest son, Billy, hanged himself. Of all the traumas in Willie's life—the screwings by record and movie producers, an early career crisis so desperate that he lay down on a snow-covered street in Nashville and waited for a car to run him over, his famous battle with the Internal Revenue Service—the only one that really rocked him was Billy's death. Willie has never talked about it or even acknowledged that it wasn't accidental. He knows that I also lost a son, so when I ask him how he dealt with Billy's tragedy, he thinks about the question for a long time, then says in a faraway voice, "Aw, you know, Jap,"—Willie never calls me anything except Jap, my nickname—"I just kept on. As it happened, we had a six-month gig in Branson, starting New Year's Eve. I had a legitimate reason to cancel all my dates and go bury myself from reality, which is what I felt like doing. But that old survival instinct cut in. So I went to Branson, cussed the place, and threw myself into my work."

As a young man, Willie made being broke and desperate into a profitable lifestyle, but he hasn't written much in recent years. Now that he is rich and famous, he tells me, "I don't have the leisure to write much anymore." Maybe that's true, I think. But it seems equally possible that at this stage of his life, Willie has said it all.

A̲ll of Willie's marriages have been wild and tempestuous, but none quite as crazy as his marriage to Martha. Both of them loved the nightlife and its vicious cycle of drinking, cheating, fighting, and making up. Once,

when Martha caught Willie fooling around, she tied him up with the children's jump rope and beat the hell out of him. Another time she broke a
whiskey bottle over his head. "Yeah, marriage to Martha was a running
battle," Willie confesses, recalling that in those days he always carried a
gun. "It was part of my uniform," he admits.

Willie's second marriage, to singer Shirley Collie, was more placid, at
least for a while. They were living in Nashville, though Music City wasn't
nearly ready for him. By universal agreement, a hillbilly song had just
three chords; Willie's songs had four or five. The formula for a country
lyric involved one catchy line, followed by shallow sentiments of heartbreak and betrayal, rhymed predictably. Nothing in Willie's songs was
predictable. His style was deceptively simple, relaxed, and conversational:
"Hello, walls. How'd things go for you today?" If the country music industry was threatened by such originality, country singers weren't. Faron
Young's cut of "Hello Walls" sold more than two million records. Patsy
Cline's version of "Crazy" eventually won an award as the most played
song on jukeboxes ever. Ray Price made "Night Life" his theme song. By
the mid-sixties everyone was recording Willie's songs, but no one was buying his records. Disillusioned, Willie bought a small farm outside Nashville and determined to be a gentleman farmer-songwriter. He smoked a
pipe, wore overalls, raised weaner pigs with fellow musician Johnny Bush,
and gained thirty pounds on Shirley's good country cooking. By 1968,
however, he was on the road again and life was becoming a living hell.
"Shirley was boozing as bad as I was," Willie says in his book, "and we
were all swallowing enough pills to choke Johnny Cash . . ."

The marriage ended when Shirley opened a bill from the maternity
ward of a Houston hospital, itemizing the cost of a baby daughter born
to Willie Nelson and one Connie Koepke. A year before, the knockout
blond in the fourth row at a club in Cut 'n' Shoot happened to be that same
Connie Koepke. She became wife number three, even before his divorce
from wife number two was finalized.

Willie's marriage to Connie lasted seventeen years, far and away his
personal best, but the strain of the road again took its toll. This time,
actually, it was a road movie—*Honeysuckle Rose*—whose theme song, "On
the Road Again," Willie had written in flight on the back of an airline
barf bag shortly after signing to do the movie. In the flick, Willie's character, a musician, has an affair with Amy Irving's character. At the same
time, Willie had a highly publicized romance with the actress. Marriage
to Connie flamed out during the filming. "Anything you want to tell me

about Amy Irving?" I ask him on the bus. "She was something else," Willie replies, then after a long pause adds, "and I'd do it again."

Willie met his current wife, Annie, on the set of the movie *Stagecoach*, where she was working as a makeup artist. "They say we marry what we need," Willie tells me. "Kris [Kristofferson] married a lawyer, and I married a makeup girl." They have been married for nearly ten years, a term that roughly corresponds to Willie's average time with one wife.

"Marriage gets easier as you get older," Willie admits. "There are still a lot of temptations out there. Mother Nature has a way of checking our appetites, but the girls still look good. If I stayed around [in a hotel or bar], the same thing would probably happen again."

The advent of the Armadillo World Headquarters in 1972 was a revelation for all of us—especially Willie, who had just moved back to Texas from Nashville and was more or less retired from the national music scene. "We had been trying to travel all over the world with a seven-piece band and compete with the others," he remembers, "but it just wasn't working. I knew I could make a living playing honky-tonks in Texas." Serendipity, in the form of a hippie hitchhiker, led Willie and the band to the soon-to-be-legendary Armadillo, a onetime National Guard armory in Austin that entrepreneur Eddie Wilson had transformed into a dance hall. This was the start of a wonderfully weird convergence of hippies and rednecks that would change music history.

I first met Willie on August 12, 1972, a few hours before his first gig at the Armadillo. Both of us were in our late thirties and relatively new to psychedelics and long hair. A couple of friends and I were in the small office that the Armadillo had set aside for Mad Dog, Inc., a shadowy organization that Bud Shrake and I had founded at roughly that same time. Artist Jim Franklin was decorating a wall of the Mad Dog office with a portrait of a crazed Abe Lincoln when we spotted Willie and the band across the hall. I didn't recognize him at first. I had been a fan since 1966, when Don Meredith handed me a copy of Willie's album that was recorded live at Panther Hall: Listening to it over and over that night was one of the most profound experiences of my life. The album cover pictured a straight-looking country singer with short hair and a bad suit. He clutched a guitar, but from his looks it could have easily been a pipe wrench.

The Willie that I saw that day at the Armadillo looked much different from his Panther Hall album cover. His hair fell almost to his shoulders, and though he was still clean-shaven and passably middle class, he was obviously undergoing a metamorphosis. "I saw a lot of people with long hair that day," Willie recalls. "People in jeans, T-shirts, sneakers, basically what I grew up wearing. I remember thinking: 'Fucking coats and ties! Let's get comfortable!'" The real eye-opener for me came that night. Who in his right mind could have predicted that the same audience that got turned on by B. B. King and Jerry Garcia would also go nuts for Willie Nelson? This Abbott cotton picker had merged blues, rock, and country into something altogether original and evocative.

Success came rapidly after that. His *Shotgun Willie* album sold more copies in Austin than most of his other albums had sold nationwide. The next album, *Phases and Stages*, sold even better. Willie decided to hold an annual picnic in the style of Woodstock. He appeared onstage at the first one, in 1973, in cutoffs, sandals, long hair, and a beard. Two years later he had a huge hit with "Blue Eyes Crying in the Rain." By 1978 his image and reputation were so established he convinced executives at CBS Records that his next album ought to be a collection of standards like "Stardust" and "Moonlight in Vermont." At first they thought he was crazy, but Willie pointed out that "my audience now is young, college age, and mid-20s. They'll think these are new songs." He was right. *Stardust* was a pivotal album for country music, opening up a whole new audience. "Willie has always been a prophet, slightly on the edge," Rick Blackburn, the president of CBS Records Nashville, said later.

The early seventies were also the formative years for Willie's other "family" — a motley and colorful crew of itinerant musicians, promoters, and roustabouts that Willie has collected along the way. Billy "B. C." Cooper chauffeured Willie around in a six-cylinder Mercedes before the first bus was purchased, and doubled as his bodyguard; he's one of the last of the original family. "I was just a old used-car salesman," B. C. told me recently at Willie World, where he now resides in peaceful retirement, "but Willie took a liking to me and told me to follow him, and I been following him ever since." Larry Gorham was a Hell's Angel in San Jose before Willie appointed him chief of security. Paul English was a Fort Worth pimp and burglar when Willie asked him to play drums in 1966. Mickey Raphael was a teenage nobody when he cornered Willie outside a Dallas recording studio and applied for a job as the band's harmonica player. "Follow us, kid," Willie instructed. Willie's judgment for new talent is instinctively good, and once discovered, they stay for life.

Backstage at the Orleans, I meet another of Willie's longtime mates,

Phil Grimes, now a Las Vegas developer and real estate executive. In the early seventies he was a freelance reporter for the Associated Press in Austin. "I went out to do a story on Willie," Phil tells me. "I got on the bus and it was three and a half weeks before I could find my way off." Looking around, it occurs to me that Willie probably has the last group of geriatric roadies in the business.

Saturday night in Las Vegas: Willie gives the Orleans Hotel audience two and a half hours to remember. He goes from cheating songs and blues to gospel numbers like "Amazing Grace" to a Sinatra-like cover of "Stardust" to a deeply moving rendition of his current philosophical favorite, "Still Is Still Moving to Me." By the end of the show fans have gone berserk, clapping, rocking, dancing in the aisles, calling his name. "We love you, Willie!" a female voice cries out. Willie has already tossed two headbands to his fans, and now he peels off his sweat-soaked black T-shirt and lobs it to a woman in the fourth row. The Orleans higher-ups are stunned by the reception. They had no idea how Willie would be received—they usually book acts like Phyllis Diller and Eddie Arnold—and immediately sign him for three dates in 1998, including another long Thanksgiving weekend. "It's not the three straight sellouts that impressed them," says Scooter Franks, Willie's traveling concessions manager. "What they care about is the drop—the money that people gamble after the show. We told 'em, 'Willie is like Sinatra: His people drink a lot of whiskey and they stay to gamble.'" Long after his roadies have cleared the stage and loaded the buses for the trip home to Austin, Willie is still signing autographs down front.

There is such a powerful presence about Willie that people sometimes believe he's a mystic or even a messenger from God, a misinterpretation that he hasn't always tried to correct. Billy Cooper almost convinced me that Willie has a magical ability to commune with snakes and birds and that he can, with a wave of the hand, convert negative energy to positive. Stage manager Poodie Locke tells of a ferocious gun battle in a parking garage in Birmingham, Alabama, after a concert, with cops squatting in doorjambs and civilians diving for cover. In the teeth of the chaos Willie calmly stepped down from the bus, wearing tennis shoes and cutoffs with two Colt .45 revolvers stuck in the waist, and inquired coolly: "Is there a problem?" In an instant, all guns were holstered and Willie was signing autographs. "He's got the kind of aura to him that just cools everything out," Poodie explains.

Willie believes that his life is a series of circles in which he is continually reincarnated, each version a little better than its predecessor. There is some theological support for this belief. Kimo Alo, one of the magician-priests, or Kahunas, who live on the island of Maui, where Willie has a vacation home, believes that Willie is "an Old King," reincarnated to draw the native races together. When I ask Willie about the Old King theory, he dismisses it—though I suspect he secretly thinks it's reasonable. In his autobiography he wrote, "Even as a child, I believed I was born for a purpose. I had never heard the words reincarnation or Karma, but I already believed them and I believed in the spirit world."

Raised as a staunch Methodist, Willie was taught that if he drank or smoked or went dancing, he was doomed to hellfire. He never bought this doctrine: Willie's God was always willing to give a guy another chance. An incident in the fifties, when he was teaching Sunday school at the Metropolitan Baptist Church in Fort Worth, reinforced this conviction. His preacher gave him an ultimatum—stop playing in beer joints or stop teaching Sunday school—and Willie quit the church for good, disillusioned with a policy that summarily condemned people like him. He went to the Fort Worth library and started reading books on religion. "Soon as I read about reincarnation," Willie wrote, "it struck me just the same as if God had sent me a lightning bolt—this was the truth, and I realized I had always known it." Willie had the good sense to see that it would take many more reincarnations for him to triumph over his lustful urges, but at least he knew he was on the right track. Today, Willie and family worship at the one-room church on Willie World's western film set, where *Red Headed Stranger* and a bunch of other movies were shot. Though the church is empty except for some benches and a portrait of Jesus hung by Lana and Bobbie, the music on a Sunday morning will stir the jaded soul.

Willie often jokes that he is "imperfect man," sent here as an example of how not to live your life. This was the theme of *Yesterday's Wine*, his most personal and spiritual album, and arguably his best. Written in the early seventies after a series of personal disasters, including a fire that burned his home in Nashville (Willie managed to save his marijuana stash from the ruins), the album follows a man from birth to death, ending with him watching his own funeral.

"Maybe I was imperfect man, writing my own obituary," Willie tells me during our conversation on the bus. Unexpectedly, he breaks into song:

There'll be a mixture of teardrops and flowers
Crying and talking for hours

And how wild that I was
And if I'd listened to them I wouldn't be there.

The album also includes a passage in which God explains to imperfect man that there is no explanation for the apparent random cruelty of life:

After all, you're just a man
And it's not for you to understand.

Two weeks before Christmas I drop by Bobbie Nelson's home on the sixth fairway at Pedernales Country Club in Willie World and am surprised to find Willie sitting at the kitchen counter, rolling numbers and listening to a blues album he was recording recently with Riley Osbourn and some other blues players. Bobbie is cooking breakfast—sausage, eggs, biscuits, and gravy. This was supposed to be a one-on-one interview with her, but it turns out to be something else. We sit for a while, sharing a smoke and listening to some great blues.

Pouring us more coffee, Bobbie asks Willie in her soft, sweet voice, "Remember where we first heard the blues?"

"Out in the cotton fields in Abbott," Willie says. "Somebody would start singing 'Swing low, sweet chariot' and somebody else would pick it up."

Bobbie has faintly romantic memories of the cotton fields, but not Willie. "By the time I was seven or eight," he says, "I was working the rows for a couple of dollars a day. My desire to escape manual labor started back there in the cotton fields."

A seven-foot grand and a smaller piano dominate the living room. Bobbie's first piano was a toy that she and Willie made out of a pasteboard box. The keyboard was drawn in crayons, and Bobbie sat under a peach tree in the backyard, practicing for hours. For years on long bus trips across the country, she propped a cardboard keyboard in her lap, shut out the world, and followed with her fingers as the works of Mozart or Bach played inside her head.

After a while, Lana stops by. She has brought Willie's Christmas present. He's leaving the following day for a couple of months in Maui with Annie and his boys. We all sit around the dining room table, passing heaping platters of biscuits. Bobbie and Lana are the two people closest and dearest to Willie, and they fuss over him like mama hens, tending to his slightest wish. Watching him in the nest of his true family, I realize that the private Willie is not much different from that little boy who grew up in Abbott. He knew that he was special, and so did everyone else.

"I married Bud Fletcher when I was sixteen," Bobbie says as she refills the gravy bowl. "Bud formed a band called the Texans, with me on piano and Willie on guitar and vocals. Willie was making $8 a night, which was very good money for a 13-year-old."

"The $40 to $50 a week we took home to Mama Nelson was a fortune back then," Willie says. "I'd hock my guitar every Monday for $20, and Bud would get it back out of hock on Friday so the Texans could hit another lick."

"Of course, Mama didn't like us playing beer joints."

Willie laughs, remembering. "She didn't even want me going on the road. Shadowland was five miles away—in West. But that was the road to her."

If Willie has learned anything in these sixty-five years, it's that Mama Nelson was right. When your life's the nightlife, all roads are pretty much the same.